EDUCATION AND IDENTITY

Arthur W. Chickering

EDUCATION
AND
IDENTITY

 Jossey-Bass Inc., Publishers
615 Montgomery Street • San Francisco • 1969

THE JOSSEY-BASS SERIES IN HIGHER EDUCATION

General Editors

JOSEPH AXELROD *and* MERVIN B. FREEDMAN

San Francisco State College

To
    my mother

PREFACE

$\mathbf{H}$igher education once aimed to produce men prepared to engage with the society of man. But as the changes of the last fifty years have occurred, higher education has altered its image of man. The focus has shifted from men to subjects, from persons to professionals. Consequently men themselves have become subjects—subjects to majors, to disciplines, to professions, to industries. Higher education and society are mired in frustration and conflict. These conditions will persist until men—not materials, nor systems, nor institutions—again become the focus of education and the focus of human concern.

Education and Identity suggests an alternative to higher education's increasing concentration on information and professional training. It elaborates a way already pointed, a direction already in the wind. It describes an approach to higher education relevant to the principal developmental concerns of students and relevant to our social condition. Robert White (1958) and Erik Erikson (1963) introduced us to "identity," and so doing sharply reminded us that there is more to development in college than acquiring information and developing intellectual competence. But "identity" is so abstract as to provide only a hazy guide for educational decisions, and its connotations have become so diverse that the term means very different things to different persons. In describing seven major dimensions of development that occur during the college years—competence, emotions, autonomy, identity, interpersonal relationships, purpose, integrity—I have attempted to move "identity" one step toward greater specificity and concreteness. I aimed to reach a level where connections could be made between these dimensions of student change and educational policies and practices. Some of these interrelationships are suggested for curriculum, teaching, and evaluation, residence hall arrangements, relationships with faculty and administration, relationships with peers, institutional size, and institutional objectives.

Mindful that five to seven variables are about the maximum that most of us can recall and use, I have synthesized accordingly. For my primary purpose is to increase the working knowledge brought to bear when decisions are made, not to push further the subtle insights of those already intimately involved with research and theory concerning student development in college. I would advance knowledge horizontally rather than vertically; I would spread it around rather than move it to deeper levels of complexity. Available knowledge and current practice stand far apart. They must come closer, and if they do educational effectiveness will thereby improve. Basically then, my aims have been to synthesize the research and theory that, to me, seem most significant for higher education and to generate a conceptual framework faithful to those findings—a framework sufficiently general to be relevant to a wide range of decisions and sufficiently simple to be held in mind for application as alternatives for action are considered—and to do so in a few, readable, words.

Clearly, my fundamental indebtedness in this work is to predecessors and contemporaries who have generated so much valuable research and theory concerning student development and college impacts upon it. I have called on many of them, and on some, extensively. It is my conviction that higher education will move ahead as their words are heard and understood. I hope some of the pet quotations I have cited will entice others to pursue or reexamine their works.

I have had some excellent teachers. Gertrude Driscoll, at Teachers College Columbia, first made clear to me the complexities of human development, and more important—by her own example—showed me what kindness, candor, and insight could be. More recent teachers have been Royce "Tim" Pitkin, George Beecher, Thomas Yakhub, Forest Davis, Wilfred Hamlin, Harold Boris—all colleagues during the *Experiment in College Curriculum Organization,* undertaken at Goddard College from 1959 to 1965 with the support of the Ford Foundation Fund for the Advancement of Education. The roots of the ideas presented here rest in the weekly faculty meetings, committee meetings, dinners, drinks, discussions, and data that filled those six years of research and teaching. But during that time I was instructed principally by younger teachers: Marge Lipko, Lee Mirkovic, Sue Caust, and other students with whom I shared classes, independent studies, counseling sessions; and student research assistants—Ada Silverstein, Frank Dorsky, Jill Mattuck, Mark Milbank, Carol Reiff, and others—who brought not only conscientious effort, but fine insights. My older associates simply helped me to understand better what these persons were saying. And, of course, I am indebted to all those students who sat through hours of tests, inventories, and questionnaires to provide the data for that work.

In 1965, the Project on Student Development (NIMH Grant MH 14780-04) began, a five-year study of institutional characteristics, student characteristics, attrition, and student development in thirteen small colleges, carried on under the aegis of the Committee on Research and Development of the Council for the Advancement of Small Colleges. And with this Project began unique instruction, still under way, by the presidents, institutional representatives, and faculties of the participating colleges, and by the rich data flowing from those institutions—data that drift high up office walls, obscuring windows, blocking doors. Laban Peachey and James McDowell, who spent sabbatical years with us, Dorothea Stockwell, and my less transient coworkers, Beverly Burns, William Hannah, Robert Mattuck, and Dennis Campagna, tip-toed gingerly with me through IBM-card Empire State Buildings. Thus by the computer were we transformed, no longer pencil, but paper pushers. Whatever order and sense exists in the preliminary findings reported, the credit is mainly theirs; but biased extrapolations and misinterpretations are mine.

The most important contributor to this effort has been my wife. By becoming auto-mechanic, carpenter, painter, plumber, electrician, and zookeeper, she relieved me of distractions so this work could be done. Her penetrating observations kept my feet on the ground, and by her constancy, kindness, kisses—and cooking—have I been sustained.

Some of the findings in this volume are based on my previously published articles. I wish to thank, for permission to use my copyrighted materials, the following publishers: *Educational Record, Improving College and University Teaching, Journal of the American College Health Association, Journal of Applied Behavioral Science, Journal of the Association of Deans and Administrators of Student Affairs, Journal of the National Association of Women Deans and Counselors, Liberal Education.* The portion of *Zima Junction* from *Yevtushenko Selected Poems* is quoted with permission from Penguin Books, Inc., and the Steig cartoon on page 178 is taken from *The Lonely Ones* with permission of the Meredith Press.

ARTHUR W. CHICKERING

Plainfield, Vermont
January 1969

CONTENTS

EDUCATION
AND
IDENTITY

INTRODUCTION

Adolescence is a fruit of the industrial revolution of the nineteenth century and the technological revolution of the twentieth. The increasing complexity of society, the increased number of jobs requiring specialized skills and training, and the extension of free public education through high school have created an adolescent period where none existed before.

Complexity continues to increase. So does the demand for skilled and specialized personnel. In 1953, 2,000,000 students enrolled for undergraduate and professional degrees; in 1963, the figure was 4,000,-000; by 1973, 7,000,000 are expected—about 46 per cent of the college-age population. Universal higher education is fast approaching. These new conditions are creating another developmental period, a period during which certain changes may be fostered and during which certain kinds of adjustment and development may predominate. Ex-

1

tending from age seventeen or eighteen into the middle or late twenties, this period is different from adolescence and different from adulthood and maturity. For many it will be the last opportunity for major change before the stability generated by more fixed social, interpersonal, and occupational roles and responsibilities.

Developmental changes do occur during this period. Numerous cross-sectional and longitudinal studies of college students indicate that changes occur in attitudes, interests, values, future plans and aspirations, openness to impulses and emotions, personal integration, and intellectual ability. Such changes have been found for diverse students in diverse institutions. Some of these changes are shared by those who do not attend college; but college does make a difference. In Trent and Medsker's (1968) study, for example, college students were more flexible, open-minded, tolerant, and objective than similarly bright nonattenders, and the scores of dropouts fell between the college graduates and the nonattenders. So a developmental period of young adulthood does seem to exist now, a period during which certain kinds of changes occur or strong potential for such change exists, a period during which certain kinds of experiences may have substantial impact. This period merits special attention because mounting evidence (Bugelski and Lester, 1940; Nelson, 1954; Newcomb *et al.*, 1967; Trent and Medsker, 1968) indicates that patterns established at this time tend to persist long into adulthood. And because so many young adults will move through this period in a college setting, it merits special attention so that institutions of higher education can better serve society and more effectively help young persons move productively from adolescence to adulthood.

To say that higher education is at the crossroads is to say the obvious—like telling the man with measles he itches. It's also inaccurate; a single intersection is too simple. The alternatives are many more than four and they are interconnected. The center of a web is a more apt metaphor, an interconnected system with numerous options in many directions. The web is apt in another sense. If the institution tries to move, and the web jiggles, the proprietor or his helpers swiftly run to wrap it up for safe keeping—and eventual death. But higher education must move.

One direction has been clearly and frequently described. A past president of the American Association for Higher Education has written, "Whether or not a student burns a draft card, participates in a civil rights march, engages in premarital or extramarital sexual activity, becomes pregnant, attends church, sleeps all day, or drinks all night is not really the concern of a collegiate institution as an educational institution. Colleges and universities are not churches, clinics, nor even parents. They are devices by which a limited number of skills, insights, and points of view are communicated to the young in the belief that possession of these somehow aids the individual to become a more skilled worker [Mayhew, 1968]."

This book suggests another direction. Its fundamental assumption is that colleges and universities will be educationally effective only if they reach students "where they live," only if they connect significantly with those concerns of central importance to their students. Civil rights, the draft, managing violence, conflict, interpersonal relationships, sexuality, and religious orientation, balancing short-run hedonism against restraint and self-discipline in the service of long-run satisfactions—these issues are of primary concern to the young adult. These are the topics of hot debate over coffee and beer, of quiet reflection, of unassigned papers and poems. These are the areas where learning and action are pursued vigorously and voluntarily, often against or in addition to the demands of the institution.

More important perhaps, if urgent and emerging national and international problems are to be met with the breadth of information, the complexity of thought, and the wisdom generated by diverse experiences, such areas must receive attention. In 1972, the next presidential election year, assuming no shift in legal requirements, the median age of voters will be twenty-six (Shoben, 1968). During the next twenty years it is the college graduate who will assume control of the industrial, political, educational, religious, and military organizations of this country. And as higher education becomes universal, college graduates will become the "grass roots support" for those leaders, the "people" they ultimately must serve. The college graduates will determine whether pluralism and democracy can meet these problems and survive. The society that results will depend upon the kind of persons they become. It is the prime responsibility of colleges and universities to help those persons. To do so requires more than preparing them to pass final exams and to score high on tests for graduate school admission, and it requires more than preparing them to become skilled workers.

It is true that more students attend college for occupational advancement and professional preparation than for any other single reason. It is true that activists and alienated together comprise less than 10 per cent of the college population. But it is also true that this visible minority, like the mountaintop island, is a peak of intensity and concern, supported at different levels and in different aspects by many others below the surface.

Professional preparation and educational programs that are relevant to social problems and that facilitate significant student development and professional preparation need not be mutually exclusive. William Heard Kilpatrick (1951) recognized the motive power in vocational interests and described how general education and personal expansion could be driven by it. Colleges that attract young adults with strong professional interests can capitalize on those motives. Professional preparation can be more than training students to use a common language, common skills, and common concepts. By modification of the processes and the experiences by which such preparation is achieved, significant vectors of student change can be amplified and accelerated, and students can place their future work in the context of life-styles and social issues that are important to them. But this acceleration cannot be achieved by turning a back to these central concerns and focusing more narrowly on training skilled workers. It requires meeting students where they are and establishing relevant programs that will take them where they want to go and where those who support and man the colleges want them to go.

Research addressing student development in college has increased dramatically during the last ten years. Jacob's (1957) survey, which found minimal impact of college on values, right or wrong, was a major stimulus. With Learned and Wood's (1938) early study and Newcomb's (1943) early research at Bennington shining like beacons from the past, and with the Vassar studies (Sanford *et al.*, 1957; Sanford, 1962; Sanford, 1966) as a contemporary benchmark, more and more investigators at more and more colleges are flooding students with questionnaires, personality inventories, and various measures of academic achievement and intellectual ability. These burgeoning efforts, almost without exception, have been exploratory. Few theories have been framed, few hypotheses tested. Thus, though much useful knowledge has been generated, it has remained in unintegrated form, a collection of significant items to be examined and interpreted by each investigator who would use it for his own research, by each teacher or administrator who would use it for making practical decisions. The need for some synthesis, for some systematic framework to order this growing field is acute. Newcomb and Feldman's (1968) recent summary is one response—a comprehensive presentation offering the major warranted generalizations. The formulation offered here is another response. It offers a point of view, based on relevant research and theory, in an effort to move research findings closer to application and action.

The primary aim is to be of use to those concerned with higher education, its present forms and future potentials—administrators, faculty members, students, parents, board members, and alumni. To this end the emphasis is on ideas and not on exhaustive documentation. Supporting evidence is presented, the general thrust of relevant research is described, and illustrative studies are mentioned, but the literature is not reviewed in detail. Case histories and comments from students put flesh and blood on abstractions.

To be useful to persons making decisions about educational policy and practice, about institutional organization, about teaching; to persons confronting students; to students confronting colleges; to parents and alumni concerned about both, a conceptual framework must be simple enough to be held in mind ready for application and comprehensive enough to be relevant. The problem is to achieve synthesis without oversimplification, and to accept the compromises required. Accepting these conditions and the attendant compromises, this book describes seven major vectors of student development and considers these vectors in relation to six major aspects of the college environment. The thesis is not that all students change along all seven vectors, nor that the environmental conditions operate with equal force for all students at all institutions, but that such changes do occur for some students and they can more frequently occur for others. Environmental conditions at some institutions do foster or inhibit such changes, and systematic modification can increase the frequency of valued development.

But persons other than behavioral scientists speak with relevance. In *Zima Junction,* Yevtushenko (1964) describes his own first steps toward adulthood:

> I scarcely had one single care in the world,
> my life, presenting no big obstacles,
> seemed to have few or simple complications—
> life solved itself without my contributions.
> I had no doubts about harmonious answers

which could and would be given to every question.
But suddenly this felt necessity
of answering these questions for myself.
So I shall go on where I started from,
sudden complexity, self-generated,
disturbed by which I started on this journey.

Into my native forest among those
long-trodden roads I took this complication
to take stock of that old simplicity,
—like bride and groom, a country matchmaking.
So there stood youth and there childhood together,
trying to look into each other's eyes
and each offending, but not equally.
Childhood spoke first, "Hullo then.
It's your fault if I hardly recognized you.
I thought you'd be quite different from this.
I'll tell you honestly, you worry me.
You're still in very heavy debt to me."
So youth asked if childhood would help,
and childhood smiled and promised it would help.
They said good-bye, and, walking attentively,
watching the passers-by and the houses,
I stepped happily, uneasily out
through Zima Junction, that important town [pp. 24–25].

These words evoke the feelings of the college freshman as he carries his new suit, floor lamp, tennis racket, and *Webster's Collegiate Dictionary* into the barren sterile cubicle that will be his room, as he meets other students in the registration line, and as he says "Sir" to his first faculty member. He is happiness and unease, tentativeness and courage.

What follows from this tentative and hopeful beginning? What changes occur as a student lives four years in the "climate" of his college, as he becomes part of that social system, as he encounters the strains, seductions, hypocrisies, opportunities, and dead spots of that setting? And what institutional conditions make a difference? What patterns of institutional organization and educational practice, what constellations of relationships provoke or inhibit change? At graduation four or five years later, what of consequence has been experienced, how has the young adult been positioned to step toward the future?

PART **I**

೭಄಄಄಄಄಄಄಄಄಄಄಄಄಄಄಄಄಄

*The major constel-
lations of development during adolescence and early adulthood have
been variously formulated as "growth trends," "developmental tasks,"
"stages of development," "needs and problem areas," or "student typologies." These different formulations accompany differences in point of
departure, in emphasis, and in approach, but they have in common
seven major areas: competence, emotions, autonomy, interpersonal relationships, purpose, identity, and integrity, each of which has its major
components. They are called* vectors of development *because each
seems to have direction and magnitude—even though the direction
may be expressed more appropriately by a spiral or by steps than by a
straight line.*

Achieving Competence

*Competence is a three-tined pitchfork. One tine is intellectual
competence; most educational institutions are devoted to fostering or*

THE YOUNG ADULT:
AN OVERVIEW

ſ*Sſ*Sſ*Sſ*Sſ*Sſ*Sſ*Sſ*Sſ*Sſ*Sſ*Sſ*Sſ*Sſ*Sſ*Sſ*Sſ*Sſ*S

*to forcing this kind of development. Another tine is physical and man-
ual skills; this kind of development is of concern to many noncollege
young persons, and, because of the prestige and recreational value of
athletic skills or because of the creative value of arts and crafts, to some
college students as well. The third tine is social and interpersonal competence; this kind of development is the one of greatest concern to the
young adult and one where significant development frequently occurs
without explicit support from family, employer, or college. But the
most important part of the pitchfork is the handle. Without a handle
you can't pitch much hay even if the tines are sound, and the handle
is the* sense *of competence, the confidence one has in his ability to cope
with what comes and to achieve successfully what he sets out to do.*

*White (1960) recently thrust the concept of competence into
the arenas of human motivation and personality development. He says:*

> I am referring to the adolescent equivalent of what Erikson calls
> a sense of industry. . . . No doubt I bring to this judgment an oc-

9

cupational bias different from that of a therapist. My professional life is spent among late adolescents whose sexual problems and social relations have for the most part not overwhelmed them. We talk together about their plans for study, their abilities and limitations, their struggles with materials to be learned and skills to be attained, their occupational leaning, career plans, and concerns about modern society as the scene of their future endeavors. We talk, in other words, mostly about their competence, and I do not believe that understanding is fostered by interpreting these concerns too much as displacement of instinctual drives, defense mechanisms, or interpersonal relations. They are "real" [p. 134].

Competence is pursued from early childhood and its importance continues through college. The development and demonstration of intellectual competence influences the professional and vocational alternatives later available. Interpersonal competence is also important; most tasks require cooperative effort, and effectiveness depends upon the ability to work productively with others. He who is crude in social relationships, who lacks poise, is handicapped. Within the family, such competencies can be neglected; when an independent life is launched, they cannot. Most important, the sense of competence upon completing college affects not only the assurance and vigor brought to adult tasks, but also affects other concurrent vectors of development.

Managing Emotions

Most reports about college students suggest that management of emotions is primarily a problem of self-control. But from inside the students there are added dimensions of equal significance. Sanford (1962) describes the typical freshman as authoritarian; "strong impulses are opposed by an alert, rigid, and punitive conscience. He exhibits," says Sanford, "stereotyped thinking, intolerance of ambiguity, punitive morality, submissiveness toward the powerful and dominance toward the weak, conventionality, anti-intellectualism, hostility toward people perceived to be different [p. 261]." Because of such repressive forces and automatic reactions, the student's first task is to become aware of feelings and to trust them more, to recognize that they provide information relevant to contemplated behavior or to decisions about future plans. Before emotional control can become effective, emotions have to be experienced, to be felt and perceived for what they are. Biological forces provoke sexual desire. Contact with a broadened life space provokes hostility toward parents and toward more generalized authority.

Until lust and hate are admitted as legitimate emotions, as legitimate as love and admiration, their motive power is not likely to be harnessed to productive ends. Further, problems of control are aggravated because such feelings as lust and hate may be expressed in unrecognized ways or with unexpected intensity, triggering unanticipated consequences.

There are basically two major impulses to manage: aggression and sex. Since childhood, the young adult has been trying to develop legitimate ways to express anger and hate. To achieve maturity still new modes must be developed in the face of fresh provocations and new conditions of living. He may not have to go so far as the college professor, who, when criticized by a colleague, feels like prying open his mouth and spitting down his throat, but instead says, "That's an interesting point—still, perhaps another explanation might be . . ." But the young adult does have to acquire new conventions and become sensitive to new subtleties. Sexual impulses are more insistent than before and require more widespread adjustments. Questions of interpersonal relationships, of value, and of identity are sharply raised and answers must be given. Pressures from parents and peers are great. Signals are often confusing or self-contradictory.

Increased awareness of aggressive and sexual impulses is only a beginning, not an ending. Integrating emotions with the stream of ongoing decisions and behavior requires tentative testing through direct actions or symbolic behavior, and reflection upon the consequences for oneself and for others. A larger range of feelings can thereby be fully experienced. New and more useful patterns of expression and control can be achieved. Genuine freedom of emotions can then exist because of the confidence that they won't run wild and because experience and observation have taught the likely consequences. Then, in time, management of emotions becomes not a matter of repression, but of time, place, and behavior, of learning what can be done with whom, when, and under what circumstances. Of course, increased awareness and developing more useful and effective modes of expression go along together; ideally, oscillation gives way to a spiral carrying the larger process of development.

Becoming Autonomous

Yevtushenko (1964) "stepped happily, uneasily out through Zima Junction, that important town [p. 25]." During the first weeks a college student steps with similar hesitancy. Soon he changes. He becomes independent; but it is the independence of a hog on ice. He is on slippery new territory and without familiar footholds; he responds with wild thrashing or bewildered and anxious immobility. Free of accustomed restraints or outside pressures, he exhibits random activity or rigid adherence to behaviors appropriate to former situations. The dominant impression is instability. There is conspicuous lack of coordination and little observable progress in any direction. Autonomy, the independence of maturity, is quite different. It is secure and stable; coping behaviors are well coordinated to personal and social ends. This kind of maturity requires both emotional and instrumental independence, and recognition of one's interdependencies.

To be emotionally independent is to be free of continual and pressing needs for reassurance, affection, or approval. It begins with disengagement from parents. Perhaps for the first time parents are seen for what they are, middle-aged persons neither omniscient nor omnipotent. The child's early faith in these strong and reliable guides cannot survive mounting evidences of their weakness and fallibility. Then come doubt, anxiety, disillusionment, anger. Reliance is transferred to peers, to nonparental adults, and to occupational and institutional reference groups. In time there is less need for such supports, and increased willingness to risk loss of friends, or approval, or status, to pursue a strong interest or to stand by important beliefs.

Instrumental independence has two major components: the ability to carry on activities and to cope with problems without seeking help, and the ability to be mobile in relation to one's needs or desires. Among college students, achievement of emotional independence may be hampered by limited opportunities to develop operational independence. In college, most "work" is academic: right answers are presumed to exist; prescribed ways to meet problems are spelled out; assistance can be sought if difficulties are encountered. These conditions, undergirded by financial dependence on parents, impede development of operational independence, complicate the development of emotional independence, and obscure the basic interdependencies existing between parent and offspring, old and young, teacher and student.

Recognition and acceptance of interdependence is the capstone of autonomy. One realizes that parents cannot be dispensed with except at the price of continuing pain for all; that he cannot be supported indefinitely without working for it; that he cannot receive the benefits of a social structure without contributing to it; that loving and being loved are necessarily complementary. Then as interdependence is recognized and accepted, boundaries of personal choice become more clear. One can become an effective agent for himself. He can carve a particular existence out of the larger physical, social, and historical context. Thus only with resolution of the ranges within which one can give and receive do problems of dependence, independence, and autonomy become more settled. But because changing conditions, skin-in and skin-out, make for changing tolerances, no final settlement can occur; autonomy must continually be recreated.

Establishing Identity

Development of identity depends in part upon the other vectors already mentioned: competence, emotions, and autonomy. But it is more than simply the aggregate of change in these other areas. White (1958) says:

> identity refers to the self or the person one feels oneself to be. . . . Gradually, the sense of identity becomes a fuller and richer establishment, compounded of bodily sensations, feelings, images of one's body, the sound of one's name, the continuity of one's memories, and an increasing number of social judgments delivered through the words and behavior of others [p. 332].

According to Erikson (1950), identity is "The accrued confidence that one's ability to maintain inner sameness and continuity is matched by the sameness and continuity of one's meaning for others [p. 135]."

Development of identity is like seeking one's "human rhythms," which Murphy (1958) illustrates by photic driving. If an individual submits himself to an instrument that emits flashes at intervals he may reveal his own breaking point, the point at which the rhythm induces a convulsion. If, for example, the number is sixteen, he may rapidly lose consciousness as this number is presented in the standard time interval. Seventeen and fifteen, however, are safe numbers for him. It is not until thirty-two or some other multiple of sixteen is reached that he breaks again. Like the piano wire that hums or like the glass that shatters, we all probably have our critical frequencies in a variety of areas. Development of identity is the process of discovering with what kinds of experience, at what levels of intensity and frequency, we resonate in satisfying, in safe, or in self-destructive fashion.

In addition to this inner sense and in addition to the change in the vectors already discussed, development of identity involves clarification of conceptions concerning physical needs, characteristics, and personal appearance, and clarification of sexual identification, of sex-appropriate roles and behavior. For older persons accustomed to relative stability in size and proportion, accustomed to wearing the same Sunday suit for five years, accustomed to a limited range of well-routinized motor coordination, the upset and disorientation caused by shifts in physique, environment, and culture are hard to imagine. To recapture a sense of such feelings, brush your teeth or wipe yourself with the wrong hand. The uncertainties, discomfort, and ambiguous results reflect in a small way the daily experiences of the adolescent and young adult.

College student concern with appearance is obvious. Many current styles distress some faculty members, deans, and presidents. Though gowns no longer prevail, town residents recognize students. Variation may be large or small, prevailing styles slovenly or impeccable, depending on the student culture and on college rules and regulations. But whatever the limitations or prescriptions, experimentation occurs; with clarification of identity, however, it diminishes. By graduation most of the early creative—or bizarre—variations are given up. A few retain an individualistic style; most have become comfortable within the normal range.

Sexual identification is closely related to experimentation with dress and appearance. It is interesting that experimentation with hair seems concentrated among men rather than women. Whoever wrote about Samson and Delilah knew his stuff; if preoccupation with hair is any sign, many college men are uncertain how much of the Samson there is about them. Finding out what it means to be a man or a woman and coming to terms with the limitations, the behaviors, and the usual roles absorbs much energy. For a few, the problem has special difficulties leading to homosexual relationships of varying explicitness, intensity, and duration. For all, clarification of sexual identification and development of appropriate and satisfying behaviors are central to the development of identity.

Once achieved, a solid sense of identity fosters change in other major vectors of development: the freeing of interpersonal relationships, the development of purpose, and the development of integrity.

Freeing Interpersonal Relationships

A sense of identity frees interpersonal relationships. As White (1958) observes, relationships become "less anxious, less defensive, less burdened by inappropriate past reactions, more friendly, more spontaneous, more warm, and more respectful [p. 343]." This aspect of development is different from interpersonal competence. That involved learning to manage oneself and others to accomplish tasks requiring joint effort; this involves developing tolerance for a wider range of persons. Tolerance *means not only to "put up with," but also not to be upset by dosages that earlier caused distress. Ideally, this tolerance develops not through increased resistance and immunization, but through increased capacity to respond to persons in their own right rather than as stereotypes or transference objects calling for particular conventions.*

In addition to increased tolerance, the quality of intimate relationships also shifts. For most adolescent couples, each is the pool and each the Narcissus. Satisfying relationships depend upon spatial proximity, so that each can nod to the other and in the reflection observe himself. As Erikson (1959) says:

> the youth who is not sure of his identity shies away from interpersonal intimacy; but the surer he becomes of himself, the more he seeks it in the form of friendship, combat, leadership, love and inspiration. There is a kind of adolescent attachment . . . which is often mistaken for mere sexual attachment or for love . . . such attachment is often devoted to an attempt at arriving at a definition of one's identity by talking things over endlessly, by confessing what one feels like and what the other seems like, and by discussing plans, wishes, and expectations [p. 95].

With the achievement of greater autonomy and a more firm sense of identity, such relationships shift toward greater trust, independence, and individuality. They are less symbiotic; the support provided is more simple and strong, more implicit, more taken for granted, more to be relied on. These friendships and loves survive the development of differences and episodes of disagreement. They persist through times of separation and noncommunication.

Clarifying Purposes

Many young adults are all dressed up and don't know where to go; they have energy but no destination. The dilemma is not just

*"Who am I?" but "Who am I going to be?"; not just "Where am I?"
but "Where am I going?" Development of purpose occurs as these
questions are answered with increasing clarity and conviction in three
domains: avocational and recreational interests, vocational plans and
aspirations, and general life-style considerations.*

White (1958) speaks of "deepening of interests." He says:

> interests are often of tremendous importance in the personal economy
> of happiness. The loss of opportunities to pursue them can sometimes
> be an irreparable catastrophe. . . . Under reasonably favorable cir-
> cumstances a person becomes increasingly capable of having his
> energies absorbed in the needs and properties of the objects with
> which he is working. . . . The trend we have in mind is away from
> a state in which interests are casual, quickly dropped, pursued only
> from motives that do not become identified with the advancement
> of the object. It is toward a state in which the sense of reward
> comes from doing something for its own sake [pp. 347–349].

*Kuhlen (1952), reviewing research on interests through the adolescent
period, reports findings congruent with White's observations; rate of
change in interests slowed down enough that tests given in the late
teens could predict adult interests.*

*Some of the increased stability and deepening of interests de-
rives from their relationships to vocational plans and aspirations, which
also are becoming more clear and firm. For boys, development of purpose receives its primary thrust from the clarification of such plans and
aspirations. For girls, the salience of vocational plans is either sharply
reduced by impending marriage or engagement, or is complicated by uncertainties regarding marriageability. Kuhlen (1952), after examining
research on the development of vocational plans, found vocational
planning and thinking to be most active during the middle teens. It
is worth noting that Kuhlen's book was published in 1952, so his observations are based on research reports prior to the increased interest
in higher education. The research of White and others with college
students suggests that the active vocational planning and thinking that
begins in high school continues in college. During these years alternatives are explored, but development does not necessarily depend
upon specifying a clear and explicit vocational choice or objective;
often it is simply discovery or confirmation of a general orientation,
leaving open a fairly wide range of future choices, but permitting
meaningful next steps.*

Research by Beardslee and O'Dowd (1962) demonstrates the interactions of vocational plans and general life-style considerations. From study of nondirective interviews they report:

students chose to talk primarily about the aspect of . . . occupations that may best be called their implications for style of life. They commented spontaneously on how a lawyer, doctor, or engineer and his family live rather than the character of his work. They described easily and naturally the community status associated with different occupational roles; the personality and quality of family relationships implied by each of several jobs were frequently mentioned. In general occupations were primarily seen as leading to different ways of life that varied considerably in attractiveness. . . . For most students the working hours in the occupational future were less real than the leisure hours. . . . In summary, an occupation is . . . the means by which they will attain a given mode of living, and only secondarily a set of skills and responsibilities [p. 598].

Development of purpose, then, requires formulating plans and priorities that integrate avocational and recreational interests, vocational plans, and life-style considerations. With such integration, life flows with direction and meaning.

Developing Integrity

Closely related to the development of purpose and identity is the development of integrity, the clarification of a personally valid set of beliefs that have some internal consistency and that provide at least a tentative guide for behavior. Such development involves three overlapping stages: the humanizing of values, the personalizing of values, and the development of congruence.

"Humanizing of values" is White's (1958) term to describe the shift from a literal belief in the absoluteness of rules to a more relative view, where connections are made between rules and the purposes they are meant to serve. Thus the rules for a ball game can change to accommodate limited numbers of players or other unusual conditions; rules concerning honesty, sex, or aggressive behavior can vary with circumstance and situation. This change has also been called "liberalization of the superego" or "enlightenment of conscience"—the process by which the rigid rules received unquestioned from parents are reformulated in the light of wider experience and made relevant to new conditions (Sanford, 1962, p. 278).

During an individual's childhood he internalizes his parents' values so that most behavior accords even when parents are absent. Contrary behavior produces either diffuse anxiety or specific fear of discovery and punishment. Most of the values are inexplicit and unconsciously held; the child can neither identify them nor explain their basis. Therefore they are little subject to conscious control or modification. With humanizing of values, much of this baggage comes to light. The contents are examined. Many items are discarded on brief inspection, sometimes with later regret. Some items are tried and found unsuitable. A few are set aside for the new wardrobe.

Personalizing of values occurs as the new wardrobe is assembled. Ultimately, the items selected are those required by the characteristics of the wearer, by the work he expects to do, by the situations he expects to encounter, and by the persons who are, and will be, important to him. In short, he selects to suit himself and to suit the conditions of his existence. In time the components of this wardrobe, in the words of Smith (1963),

> are actively embraced . . . and thus become constituents of self, part of what the person feels himself to be and to stand for. Characteristically their application involves more finely differentiated cognitive discriminations than is the case with superego values, and they can therefore be applied with more flexibility, appropriateness, and rationality. As one measures oneself and one's behavior against these standards, his self-esteem rises or falls. . . . Since they are integrated in the self rather than sealed off in infantile form, they are open to progressive modification and elaboration . . . they are sustained by the individual's active commitment to them as the values he chooses to live by [p. 339].

Personalizing of values, then, leads toward the development of congruence, the achievement of behavior consistent with the personalized values held. With this final stage, internal debate is minimized. Once the implications of a situation are understood and the consequences of alternatives seem clear, the response is highly determined; it is made with conviction, without debate or equivocation. Erikson (1963) puts it this way:

> Although aware of the relativity of all the various life styles which have given meaning to human striving, the possessor of integrity is ready to defend the dignity of his own life style against all

physical and economic threats. For he knows that an individual life is the accidental coincidence of but one life cycle with but one segment of history; and that for him all human integrity stands or falls with the one style of integrity of which he partakes [p. 232].

These, then, are the seven major developmental vectors for the young adult: achieving competence, managing emotions, becoming autonomous, establishing identity, freeing interpersonal relationships, clarifying purposes, and developing integrity. Each has its major components and more detailed study reveals further ramifications. This overview, however, suggests the major configurations. The following chapters consider in more detail research and theory relevant to each vector.

CHAPTER **1**

DEVELOPING COMPETENCE

𝄆𝄆𝄆𝄆𝄆𝄆𝄆𝄆𝄆𝄆𝄆𝄆𝄆𝄆𝄆𝄆

We likened competence to a three-tined pitchfork. Intellectual competence, physical and manual skills, and interpersonal competence are the tines, and sense of competence the handle. The pitchfork seemed appropriate because competence usually has to do with, and is signified by, productivity and achievement. The metaphor seemed appropriate also because we are concerned with the rather basic tools that preceded, and which for the most part do not depend upon, the technological developments that have increased our muscle and mobility, extended our vision, and sharpened our hearing. Finally, the pitchfork is fitting because all its parts are interrelated; when one is weak or absent its usefulness is diminished.

The aspects of competence are worth considering separately,

20

despite their interrelatedness, because each is fostered or inhibited by different sets of conditions and experiences. If a college would better foster interpersonal competence, its arena for effort and the relevant concepts to be considered will not be those most central to developing intellectual competence. The two may overlap. Actions that serve one may either conflict with or augment those that serve the other. And both may effect a third—sense of competence. But systematic and rationally based programs require attention to the components as separate elements of a larger whole.

Intellectual Competence

Intellectual competence has been studied more than any other aspect of development in college. The educational objectives most often mentioned concern the development of intellectual skills and the acquisition of information. Such development also appears to be the easiest to measure, though solid evidence of retention after graduation and persistence of skills still does not exist. But test-retest studies of change during college have found increasing scores on measures of general information, general intelligence, and critical thinking ability.

The Graduate Record Examinations (GRE) Area Tests provide measures of general information in social science, humanities, and natural science. Studies conducted by Educational Testing Service and others (Lannholm and Pitcher, 1956a, 1956b, 1959) have conclusively demonstrated progressive yearly increases as students move from entrance to graduation. Research on the Area Tests also indicates that mean scores of students whose majors lie within a particular area increase more than those whose major lies elsewhere. Score changes on advanced tests in chemistry, economics, and psychology showed that students who majored in each of these disciplines made significant gains during their junior and senior years. So, not surprisingly, study in a given area or discipline does lead, at least temporarily, to increased knowledge.

Other studies reveal variation from institution to institution in the amount of general knowledge gained and in the particular areas where greatest gain occurs. The years during which most gain occurs also vary. Finally, variation within a single institution occurs; for example, mean scores in natural science increased thirty-six points during the last two years for Goddard 1962 graduates, while mean scores for 1963 graduates showed no gain (Beecher *et al.*, 1966). Such inter- and intra-institutional variability is probably traceable to variation in curricular arrangements, in the faculty, in student interests and characteristics, and in the student culture, all of which lead students to study some areas and not others, to assimilate some kinds of information and not others.

In addition to the acquisition of information, improvement of mental ability also occurs. Studies during the past thirty years (Florence, 1947; Hartson, 1944; Livesay, 1939; McConnell, 1934; Nichols, 1964; Shuey, 1948; Silvey, 1951) reveal increasing scores in measured intelligence on tests such as the American Council on Education Psychological Examination for College Freshmen, the Ohio State Psychological Examination, and the GRE Aptitude Tests.

Nichols (1964), studying the effects of different colleges on aptitude, found verbal and quantitative scores on the GRE Aptitude Tests to be farther apart at graduation than at entrance. Some colleges provoked greater increases in verbal scores; others provoked increase in quantitative scores. He reasoned that colleges tend to concentrate students' energies in either verbal or quantitative channels, but not in both to an equal degree. Scores on the Verbal and Quantitative parts of the GRE Aptitude Test are farther apart at graduation than they were at entrance. He also found, however, that "The effect of the college was quite small relative to the effects of other variables. The very high correlations found between Scholastic Aptitude Test and GRE scores . . . indicate that even in a very restricted group of high ability students, about half of the variance in GRE performance is attributable to differences in initial ability of the students. The major field of study also had an effect on GRE scores about twice as great as that of the colleges [p. 53]." These findings are congruent with those concerning the acquisition of information. The kinds of study undertaken, in conjunction with the particular initial ability level, primarily determine the kinds of mental abilities which most increase.

Studies by Bayley (1956, 1957), and Bayley and Oden (1955) further document variation in development with variation in ability. Higher scoring persons at any age, in comparison with their lower scoring peers, not only increase faster in measured ability but also are farther from their level of maximum ability. Thus the greatest development in mental ability during college is to be expected from those who are most highly developed at entrance—a clear example of the relationship between personality differences at entrance and development in college.

The development of critical thinking ability also has been studied. The first major work was done by Dressel and Mayhew (1954) in evaluating general education programs. They report,

> In general it was found that students gained in ability to think critically in social science over a period of a year, although the size of these gains varied widely, depending on the institutions that students attended. Attempts to teach critical thinking in social science by making minor changes in particular courses did not appear to result in greater growth than was found in courses not making overt attempts to teach this skill. Attempts to relate growth in critical thinking ability to course organization or to specific teachers suggested that both of these were highly important, although the research could not identify specific factors that seemed to operate [p. 66].

More recently Dressel and Lehmann (1965), in a study of changes from freshman to senior year, reported that in nearly all instances there was a significant improvement in critical thinking ability [p. 253]. In addition they found that most change took place during the first two years, that changes in critical thinking ability were greatest in the freshman year [p. 264].

A recent study by Lehmann and Ikenberry (1959) indicates the interrelationships between the development of critical thinking and other personality characteristics. Testing students at the beginning and end of the freshman year they found increase in critical thinking scores accompanied by less stereotyped and more emergent values. While it is logical that these three variables interact, further research is necessary to indicate the patterns of causality and connectedness.

In a recent study of Goddard students (Beecher et al., 1966) it was hypothesized that scores would increase on the Graduate Record Examinations (GRE) Area Tests in Social Science, Humanities, and Natural Science; on the Sequential Tests of Educational Progress (STEP) in Reading and Writing; on the tests of Critical Thinking, Critical Thinking in Social Science, and Science Reasoning and Understanding; and on the Quantitative, Linguistic and Total scales of the American Council on Education Psychological Examination for College Freshmen (ACE). Our findings supported these hypotheses.

The data are generally congruent with the results of the other studies mentioned above. For most measures, increases are larger during the first two years than during the last two. There is, however, an exception to this generalization; STEP Writing scores, and Reading scores for one group, increase more during the last two years. This difference suggests that the timing for the development of different kinds of intellectual competence may vary.

For the typical Goddard student, much work during the last two years is done in independent studies where he pursues topics of his own choosing according to plans he develops. This curricular arrangement has three consequences: (1) students work in more sharply defined areas than in the general courses of the first two years, (2) they carry much more responsibility for interpreting and integrating their own reading because they are more on their own and see the instructor less frequently, and (3) they do more writing, both to order their own thoughts and to present them to the instructor. It makes sense, then, that the acquisition of general information and the development of critical thinking abilities occur primarily during the first two years in the context of general courses and small-group discussion, while skills in reading comprehension and in writing occur more during the last two in response to the requirements of independent study. The significant point—still a hypothesis—is that development of intellectual competence varies with the particular requirements and conditions set for students. If this hypothesis is valid, further study should reveal explicit ways to develop skills heretofore left to chance or to hazy and global aspects of curriculum or college environment.

Research so far has left untouched some of the most important aspects of intellectual competence that may be fostered in college. Development of the ability to identify problems and to define them in clear and workable terms, of the ability to synthesize and integrate information from diverse sources for a particular purpose, of the ability to invent answers or hypotheses rather than simply to search for and find them, of the ability to operate creatively within existing conditions and to establish and maintain conditions that enable continued creativity—all merit careful attention. And the ability to be orally articulate, and to listen, while perhaps more simple and obvious, are no less important.

The interaction between the development of intellectual competence and other vectors of change has been studied even less. Although there have been studies of relationships between personality characteristics and various indices of achievement, satisfaction, and success in college (Davie, 1958; Rust, 1958; Neugeboren, 1958), and studies to discover the characteristics that distinguish dropouts from others, except for the Lehmann and Ikenberry research mentioned above, I find no studies where development or change, intellectual or otherwise, has been a variable related to other aspects of change. The comments of a Puerto Rican boy who came to Goddard from Harlem suggest some interrelationships worth pursuit:

> I was fortunate enough in my first year to become aware of two basic inadequacies in my personality which led me to attempt to discover solutions. These were my ability to communicate verbally and in writing, and my development of abstract thought. It had never been necessary for me to stress either of these basic skills and therefore I was rather deficient in both.
>
> I began to solve my speaking problem with the help of Joe. All I had expected from the Voice and Phonetics class was improvement in my speech. The class not only gave me this improvement but also many other things. It helped me in my general manner and appearance, which is very important as one is often judged by manner and appearance in our present society. I was surprised to learn during the term that when one attempts to improve his voice he improves himself in many other ways at the same time. In general I would say that I gained something from that study that my society has been attempting to destroy, knowledge of my own speech errors and the power to correct them, and a new view of myself and the possibility that I could change.
>
> In order to bring my writing ability up to at least the high school level, I took a fourth course (in addition to the normally required three) with Steve which was an independent in spelling and sentence construction.
>
> Two courses in the first year, both with Tom, helped me to improve my ability to think more clearly. I was fascinated by the ability of my mind and by discussion which I was able to join and contribute to positively. I used these newly discovered abilities to participate in community affairs. It became almost impossible to keep me quiet at a community meeting. I felt very much as if I had accumulated some super powers and wanted the entire world to know about those powers. One major object was missing in this newly discovered power, and that was knowledge of my subject matter.
>
> My second year was very active. I had become interested in community affairs and was a member, as kitchen manager, of the

work program committee. This active participation in the affairs of the community gave me a chance to use my creativity in real situations. My classes, which began as three separate units, finally ended as a three-part independent study with the sociological, physiological, and psychological investigation of drug addiction as its major concern. I learned what independent study really meant from that study and I also discovered that my major interest was in sociology and began to develop this interest by taking courses in that field. In my fourth semester my interest in sociology became magnified when my paper was accepted to be read at the Eastern Sociological Society meeting.

Most important during the third year was the fact that I became a better listener. I discovered that listening can be just as fruitful as being an active discussant. I learned to investigate as much as possible before I write or speak on a subject. When I have completed my investigation I've learned to inject my own opinion. I read much more for my papers than I had done before. When I begin to write now, I write in several forms, and then choose the form which best integrates my thoughts.

These comments from a student who came to college with some deficiencies suggest the large waves created by increased intellectual competence. The ability to modify his own speech led to clarification of identity and augmented feelings of autonomy and self-direction. The ability to think more clearly, to handle abstractions, and to contribute positively to group discussion, fostered a sharp increase in his sense of competence; it enabled more vigorous participation in community affairs and assumption of responsibilities likely to foster further change. Once development of these competencies was well under way, gaps in knowledge could be recognized and creative steps taken. Purposes became more clear and plans for future professional activities could be made. For this student, increased intellectual competence functioned as a release. He was freed to move on several fronts at once.

There is still little theory about relationships between intellectual development and other aspects of change. E. M. Bower's (1966) recent article is perhaps the first real attempt to make such connections. He says,

The adjustment of an individual in the school (and later in society) can be conceptualized as a function of his competence to use referents or representations of objects and events. Such referents or representations are systematized in words, language, mathematics, and other symbol systems. Symbols are learned by individuals as a function of "experiencing" objects, events, and relationships. To convert an event or a happening into an experience (something learned) its essence must be ingested, processed and assimilated via symbolic vehicles such as words or mathematical formula [p. 109]. . . . The sparking between an event or object and its eventual incorporation within self through ego processes is a function of the symbolic posts to which the event or object can be tied. An event which cannot be tied securely to a symbol has limited educational utility. An object which has no representational correlate cannot be conceptualized or held in the mind. Our basic tool for this sparking between objects and symbol has been the written and spoken word. Indeed, language is our royal road to defining not only what surrounds us in the environment but what we are as an organism [p. 112].

Thus development, "ego development," depends partially on the ability to symbolize abstractly the events and objects of one's experience. And conversely, for the young person whose experiences are primarily verbal or otherwise symbolic, firsthand encounters with concrete materials and objects also are required if symbols are to be recognized as merely inexact representatives of objects and events, rather than as the objects or events in themselves. From such a standpoint, increasing intellectual competence assumes significance for other dimensions of development.

Physical and Manual Competence

Many college students invest substantial time in athletic and artistic activities to develop a variety of physical and manual skills. For a few, such skills and their augmentation may become a vocation; for more, they may become an avocation around which much of life is organized; for many, they become a source of occasional satisfaction or status. Yet even though this is so, and even though athletic programs are a major expense in many college budgets, I find no study of the development of physical or manual skills nor any study of the developmental consequences of participation in such activities in the literature of higher education. Perhaps it is so obvious to both learner and observer when one learns to hit balls of varying size, to handle body contact, to ski down a mountain, or to create in clay, wood, metal, paint, or stone, that systematic observation seems superfluous. But consequently, the contribution of these elements to student development remains unclear.

Some research, however, suggests the potentials are great. P.

A. Bower (1940), studying adolescent boys, found that popularity was unrelated to intelligence, height, home ratings, or school achievement, but significantly related to strength and to physical ability. He observed that the relationships occurred not merely because adolescents place a high premium on athletic proficiency, but also because strength and other aspects of physical ability are closely joined to such favorable traits as activity, aggressiveness, and leadership (p. 117). And consider these anecdotes from research by Ryan (1958a, 1958b) on good and poor competitors:

> A poor competitor of great natural talent was entered in two field events. The first effort of his first event went extremely well. Almost before he could prevent it, he had achieved by far the best performance of his career. He appeared pained and anxious. His remaining trials were incredibly poor, but, of course, the first mark stood as his performance. When the time arrived for his second event, he was not to be found. Later, it was found that he had left the athletic area in a panic. He could offer no explanation for his absence.
>
> A pole vaulter routinely cleared 12'6" in competition. Just as routinely he failed to clear the next height of 13 feet. His teammates noted that he usually had more than six inches of clearance at 12'6" and therefore reasoned that his inability to make 13 feet was "only mental." Thus they conspired to "help him." When his back was toward the take-off, they raised the bar from 12'6" to 13 feet. Unaware of the bar's true height, the vaulter made a successful attempt.
>
> A vaulter's first clearance of 13 feet is something of a milestone and traditionally calls for a minor celebration. Thus, as the athlete landed in the pit and the bar remained aloft, his teammates rushed toward him with cries of congratulations. When he realized his accomplishment, he was stunned. He left the area and never again vaulted [pp. 131, 132].

To understand better the differences among good and poor competitors, Ryan sent questionnaires to track coaches throughout the nation. The poor competitor turned out to be unhappier, more constricted, and more poorly adjusted. He had difficulty expressing his aggression and his inability to compete in athletics seemed to be a specific instance of that difficulty. In contrast, the good competitor was more conflict-free, less constricted, and better adjusted; he expressed aggression more freely [pp. 119, 120].

In the athletic events studied by Ryan, as in most, achievement must occur under predetermined conditions that usually include the presence of the other competitors and measurement of some kind. Only under such conditions is achievement recognized and recorded. Thus overt and publicly recorded achievement, which involves overcoming others in their presence, is the key element of the competitive situation. The behavior of the poor competitor therefore may reflect both a differential ability to accept achievement and to assert oneself over others. And to the extent that self-assertion is perceived as aggression, the poor competitor also reflects a differential capacity to express aggression.

These findings suggest that experiences encountered in athletics provoke reactions sharply relevant to the development of competence and sense of competence, and to the development of increased awareness of emotions and increased ability to manage them productively.

Athletics offers a context in which concrete, unequivocal, and public performance provides clear evidence of achievement and of developmental progress. Thus it is an arena where competence or the lack of it must be faced squarely, and therefore one's attitudes toward his own abilities and potentials are starkly revealed. It is therefore also an arena in which sense of competence may be significantly fostered.

Athletics also can foster increased awareness of emotions and increased ability to manage them. Pleasures purely sensual and esthetic derive from smooth, forceful, well-coordinated muscular activity. He who has carved a turn on skis or hit a long straight drive with a baseball bat or golf club knows well the feelings. In athletics, the open and direct expression of feelings that elsewhere must be properly muted or denied is legitimate. Rage and delight are expected reactions; their expression in voice, gesture, and action part of the game. Angers and frustrations from other encounters can also be unloaded. I know a tennis-playing dean. Often when he bashes his cannonball serve he shouts the name of a student. Those serves usually don't go in, but they have plenty of zip. Someone also said that football season was the only time a man could walk down the street with a blond on one arm and a blanket on the other without causing raised eyebrows.

Ryan's findings indicate how difficult and anxiety-provoking expression of aggression can be for some persons, and learning to manage aggression is a developmental task required for movement from adolescence to adulthood. The full experience and expression of emotions that athletics provokes and legitimizes may relax restraint enough to permit productive carry-over to other arenas. Hair let down in one situation may be loosened more readily in another.

Encounters with wood, stone, clay, or paint, and the development of skills necessary for their management, offer potentials similar to those of athletics. Like the unequivocal achievements on the field, tangible and visible creations offer clear evidence of achievement and progress. And the creative process requires similar confrontation of emotions, enables similar legitimate expression of feelings. Watch the child of an angry mother try to draw a friendly woman. Warm smiles become toothy grimaces or fanged snarls; soft hands become crooked claws; casual posture becomes a fixed stance. Observe the campus art of familiar students and see the same process working, perhaps more subtly.

Experiences to develop skills in arts and crafts also interact with intellectual competence and the development of identity. Many students, the "alienated," the "disassociated," and the "preprofessionals," bring to college a high level of verbal facility. They handle abstractions well and can pursue discussion of abstractions close to the edge of infinity. Yet these same students have limited experience with solid materials. They cannot look at a piece of machinery and grasp its logic, cannot use tools or convert raw materials into some kind of product, cannot handle their own bodies with ease, cannot manage tasks requiring either large-muscle coordination or small-muscle dexterity. Consequently, the abstractions handled with such facility are little grounded in tangible realities; their meanings are hazy and limited. Experiences of designing, modeling, and building, of learning the requirements, limitations, and possibilities inherent in different materials, may not only enrich understanding of abstractions, but also be transferred productively to more abstract concepts. A girl, for example, was explaining a paper by Ross Mooney:

> Mooney says that being creative is knowing how one operates oneself, and how to set up conditions which enable one to be creative. It is also knowing how to fit into existing conditions in order to operate creatively with them. And I have seen that in ceramics quite a bit. When you have had enough experience with clay and have tried a variety of ways, you kind of know how you work with it. You also know what your present position is and what the alternatives are which are possible. The more you work the more alternatives you see and the more you find out about your own position.

Thus Mooney's abstractions concerning creativity were enriched and "brought home" by the girl's experience with clay. Once these concepts are attached to such an integrated system of concrete experience they will be retained as working knowledge.

Thus development of physical and manual skills can foster development in other areas by permitting objects and events to be tied to symbols through action. When ideas are implemented in specific acts, when abstractions are translated into tangible and visible products, when goals are realized through concrete behaviors, then an integrated system results. Conceptualization, perception, and implementation join to constitute a larger whole. As E. M. Bower (1966) observes,

> It is . . . important for schools to provide real events, objects, and relationships to which symbols can be tied. "Democracy" or "freedom," as words, are meaningless and their use dangerous unless a child learns them in a context of doing and thinking. This is especially true of symbols with high level abstract meaning. Such symbols, unless tied down by first-hand experiences, are like boats in a storm, to be tossed this way or that, depending on the wind or current. . . .
>
> If objects are not bound into symbols by action, they tend to remain unintegrated and fragmented. Bergson suggested that, in some men, perceiving and acting are separate entities. When such persons look at a thing "they see it for itself not for themselves." These are people who are born with or have developed a detachment from life. This is a reminder of the Swiss gentleman who, when given a choice between going to paradise or going to a lecture about paradise, chose the latter [pp. 121, 131, 132].

In most colleges, intellectual activities are restricted to manipulation of abstractions and symbols. In most colleges, awareness of feelings and expression of them in thought or action are to be tempered in the service of propriety or simple self-interest. In most colleges, learning is more passive than active. In such colleges, the development of increased physical and manual skills through participation in athletic and artistic activities should enable change in other areas of equal or greater significance.

Interpersonal Competence

White (1963) observes:

> Every interaction with another person can be said to have an aspect of competence. Acts directed toward another are intended

consciously, or unconsciously, to have an effect of some kind, and the extent to which they produce this effect can be taken as the measure of competence. When interactions are casual, when we are merely "passing the time of day," the element of competence may be minimal, although even in such cases we are surprised if we produce no effect at all, not even an acknowledging grunt. When matters of importance are at stake, the aspect of competence is bound to be larger. If we are seeking help or offering it, trying to evoke love or giving it, warding off aggression or expressing it, resisting influence by others or trying to exert influence, the effectiveness of our behavior is a point of vital concern [p. 73].

A student's comments illustrate White's point. At the end of her first semester she said:

I started out with the tendency to monopolize the discussion, to be dogmatic about my ideas, and mainly interested in what I was contributing. I became aware of this—through seeing it myself and having it pointed out to me—and tried to fit myself in as a part of the whole.

At the end of her fourth semester she said:

In the beginning of this semester my whole life seemed to center around the Public Affairs Council of which I am chairman. I spent almost all my time trying to run the committee and arrange the affairs. I got in what I can term a "twitch"—being constantly upset. After talking my problems out and getting more experience in administering, I was able to calm down and things proceeded more smoothly. Toward the end of the semester, when all my undone work piled up, I didn't carry out all my PAC duties. The committee didn't fall apart, but I didn't do all I could. I learned a lot about organizing and working with people and feel confident things will go better next semester. . . .

When it became apparent to me that the majority of the group was not really working and seemed to be relatively uninterested in the class (Literature of Social Relations), I became discouraged and tried to figure out how to change this. At the same time, I realized that for me to do so much of the leading and initiating didn't help the group develop its own leadership responsibilities. Thinking it would be more help to the class and good practice for me, I attempted to play a following and resource role, rather than a leadership one. Thus I dropped my attempts to reform the working habits of the group. I became aware, as I stopped fighting the class, that there was some kind of group feeling and purpose that didn't coincide with mine. I then accepted what the group seemed to be moving toward and acted accordingly. It was hard not to play leader, and often I became too excited to restrain myself, but during the times I was a follower, I also became aware of the different ways that people do operate.

And at the end of the fifth semester she said:

I carried out my duties as Public Affairs Committee chairman in much easier manner than last semester. I learned how to work with people more successfully and was able to be a successful administrator.

These excerpts from a four-year record reveal some of the requirements for the development of interpersonal competence. She recognized that as part of a cooperative effort one must listen as well as talk, follow as well as lead, understand the concerns and motives of others, vary one's role in response to the requirements of varying conditions, avoid excessive imposition of one's own viewpoint. She recognized that the job of chairman required decisions concerning use of time and the development of some system of organization; it required also sensitivity to group processes and to individuals. Those comments support White's (1963) proposition that sense of interpersonal competence develops through effort and its efficacy in human interactions [p. 91]. In class and as a committee chairman she could see clearly the effects of modifying her own behavior. Consequently her competence and sense of competence could increase.

Sense of Competence

White (1963) describes sense of competence thus:

The competence of a living organism means its fitness or ability to carry on those transactions with the environment which result in its maintaining itself, growing, and flourishing. . . . To describe it neurologically, competence is an achieved state of affairs in the nervous system which makes effective action possible; . . . The subjective side of this can be called sense of competence. . . . In clinical work, sense of competence has been widely recognized in negative forms: feelings of helplessness, inhibition of initiative, the inferiority complex. The positive side has perhaps been poisoned for many of us by that hastily conceived dream-figure of perfect mental health who has attained invulnerable self-confidence and serene self-esteem—obviously a conceited fool. . . . Our best insight comes from the ordinary phenomenon of confidence, which is an aspect of virtually every act [p. 74].

Of course, one's sense of competence bears some relationship to the reality of one's competencies. A genuine and sound sense of security depends on the ability to solve, or otherwise cope with, life's problems; on the ability to maintain equilibrium in the "shifting sands of time." Thus development of intellectual, social, and physical skills is important. Yet the productivity and effectiveness achieved with a given level of intellectual, interpersonal, or physical ability varies greatly with the feelings about, and orientations toward, the levels of competence attained.

College students are much engaged with identifying and testing their competencies. In her study of Sarah Lawrence girls, Murphy (1960) observes, "Many students expressed an awareness of increased confidence in themselves and in their abilities; the increase in mastery of new intellectual skills and the multitudes of other skills for which college experience offers an opportunity, gives certain students new perception of what is possible for themselves." These words recall the releasing effect our Puerto Rican student felt when he acquired the ability to modify his speech, when his "superior powers" were revealed as they developed in the context of academic study and class discussions. Murphy goes on to say:

> The emancipation from parental direction and from the close supervision of preparatory school gives the opportunity to test oneself in independent intellectual and social activities, makes it possible to believe that one has "done it oneself," and to trust one's abilities to a degree that some students did not find possible as long as they were functioning under the supervision and support of parents and teachers [pp. 99–100].

This increased trust in one's abilities makes for more open and energetic action in the service of learning and development. There is greater readiness to take risks and greater willingness to persist at difficult tasks because success seems more likely. A second-year girl reports, for example:

> I have changed a great deal. I can connect ideas more easily now and I have just realized that I have a fine mind and can have good ideas of my own. I am much more able to stick with a prob-

lem for a longer period of time now and thereby develop ideas. I am progressively finding it easier to communicate both orally and in writing. I also have a lot more to say these days.

And an exchange with a second-year boy went as follows:

> I feel that from now on I won't be nearly as hesitant to talk in class just from my change in feelings. In fact I will probably be a pest in some classes because the way I feel now if I've got something to say I guess I'll just say it. If it takes two hours out of three hours they will just have to put up with me if they can.

The instructor commented, "It sounds like you are trying to get a little revenge." The student answered: "Not that, but it makes me feel good that I feel I'll be able to. I really do. It means so much to have more self-confidence. I don't think I have too much, just a lot compared with what I had."

Table 1

SENSE OF COMPETENCE
CHANGING FREQUENCIES FOR "WORRIES"

	Percent Responding			
Item	2nd Sem.	4th Sem.	6th Sem.	8th Sem.
Inability to read fast enough	34	38	30	20
Difficulty with college work	23	13	17	5
Feeling inadequate	44	35	30	35
Faculty overrating your ability	25	16	30	35
Unfavorable instructor reports	8	13	5	0
Unfair instructor reports	4	8	12	5
Being swamped with academic work	28	43	38	37

Data available from research at Goddard College (Beecher *et al.*, 1966) illustrate some specifics of this kind of change. A random sample of students each spring completed a questionnaire that asked them to indicate their major worries. The "worries" listed in Table 1 were judged relevant to sense of competence and it was hypothesized that they would be mentioned less frequently as students proceeded through college. On three of seven items, "Inability to read fast enough," "Difficulty with college work," and "Feeling inadequate," frequencies dropped substantially for both sexes. The item "Faculty overrating your ability" dropped for women but not for men, and "Unfavorable instructor reports" increased during the second year, prior to admission to the Senior Division, and then dropped during the last two. The lack of increase during the semester prior to graduation suggests that sense of competence has increased sufficiently that instructor reports and completion of college are no longer sources of anxiety. These data support the assumption that the changes suggested by comments of individual students occur more widely.

Variation in sense of competence has implications for other aspects of development. Perhaps most directly influenced is the development of competence itself. Ryan's (1958) poor competitors probably rate substantially lower than their "good" counterparts on sense of competence. He observes:

> Many of the poor competitors routinely berate themselves after each practice effort. Almost before completion of the trial they hang their heads in guilty fashion and bitterly reprimand themselves. One gets the impression that they are trying to forestall criticism, particularly from the coach. . . . In addition to the verbal pattern of self-condemnation, the poor competitor has curious methods of presenting an "argument." He may, at times, begin a defense of some technique or procedure he has embraced and the coach has opposed. The arguments are at first presented almost boldly, then tentatively. Finally, even with the most sympathetic listening on the part of the coach the argument is withdrawn. He reaches the conclusion that his point of view is "really rather silly after all" [p. 130].

Ryan (1958) also found the behavior of good and poor competitors to be sharply different. The good competitor may be hampered by trying too hard or by impetuous and uncontrolled effort; the poor competitor makes only feeble effort. The inability to accept achievement and to express aggression works in subtle and unconscious fashion. The poor competitor

> will sometimes negate an otherwise adequate performance by an apparently unnecessary action. The thrower will foul a good effort by falling or stepping out of the circle when from the standpoint

of body mechanics it appears that he can easily remain in. . . .
The vaulter or high jumper who has apparently cleared the bar
with a good effort will often, unnecessarily it seems, brush off the
bar with his hand. This pattern of behavior is in dramatic contrast
to that of the good competitor who will, in the face of a foul, fight
for body balance, or who will squirm to keep every inch of his body
clear of the cross bar [p. 126].

Thus, although sense of competence does depend somewhat on
how competent one is, it also influences performance and the extent to
which development of competence is vigorously, persistently, and fruitfully pursued.

Increasing sense of competence also has implications for the
development of autonomy. Achieving emotional independence is difficult without a sense that one can effect one's human environment,
that one is competent in interpersonal relationships. Achieving instrumental independence is difficult without a sense that one has the intellectual and physical capacity to cope with life's problems. And it is
difficult to recognize the interdependence of one's existence without a
sense that one can give as well as receive.

Argyris (1965) recently described three factors relevant to increasing interpersonal competence. These factors probably operate with
respect to the development of intellectual and physical competence,
and to sense of competence, as well. He says:

> human competence tends to increase (1) as one's awareness of rel-
> evant factors increases (relevant factors are those that have effect),
> (2) as the problems are solved in such a way that they remain
> solved, (3) with a minimal deterioration of the problem-solving
> process. . . . If these three criteria are to be met the individual
> will have to strive to verbalize his awareness of factors; to be able
> to *own up* to them; to accept responsibility for them. In addition,
> he will have to strive to be *open* constantly to new factors. Some-
> times the openness will have to go beyond the limits of his present
> capacity to be receptive. The individual will need to *experiment* or
> take risks with his self-esteem in order to enlarge his awareness of
> the relevant factors.

Experience with college students supports the proposition that
increased competence accompanies increasing readiness to take responsibility, increasing openness, and increasing willingness to take risks
with one's self-esteem. An exchange between a girl working on her

Senior Study and her advisor illustrates these three elements in operation.

GIRL: I want to come up with a structure that really does seem to have some better reason for being than just because it was convenient, that expresses some universal truths. I want to make it meaningful. I want it to be a big red balloon up there floating away and everybody can see. I imagine every senior student wants to do this same thing. Do you have any suggestions or words of encouragement?

INSTRUCTOR: If you really succeed in floating a big red balloon the main thing it will draw is rocks.

GIRL: Rocks? Why?

INSTRUCTOR: Well, small boys will throw stones at it.

GIRL: Oh. So you're warning me to watch out for all the little needles directed in pointy criticism of my glorious creation.

INSTRUCTOR: Well, that's part of the business of investing yourself in a red balloon.

GIRL: At the risk of having it burst.

INSTRUCTOR: Yes.

GIRL: Yes, and as this goes on it is going to get more and more tense because I will have to commit myself to certain ideas and the more I commit myself the deeper the needles will go. . . . It's kind of like an exercise in faith to see if you can do it. Can I perform and create this thing? And do I have faith in myself that I'll do it? If you don't have faith you miss out on any significant achievement. . . . Because achievement is a thing of the mind and having faith in oneself is really saying I have faith in my work and in my own ability to judge it satisfactory.

INSTRUCTOR: Are you saying now that whatever you do, you will think it is good?

GIRL: No, because that's saying you've thought everything out in advance and I don't think that's necessarily the case. It means, in a sense, that I would be accepting whatever the results might be and if it didn't work out too well, as in the case of most Senior Studies, if the paper did not come out as gloriously as I thought it would, if my big red balloon did pop and instead I just had one or two little ones that weren't half as spectacular, it means still having faith in myself and saying, "O.K., I lost the red balloon but I accept these little ones," and going on from there.

On such a basis does development of competence continue—intellectual competence, physical and manual competence, and interpersonal competence, each sustained and fostered by a realistic and growing sense of competence.

CHAPTER 2

MANAGING
EMOTIONS

꙳꙳꙳꙳꙳꙳꙳꙳꙳꙳꙳꙳꙳꙳꙳꙳꙳꙳꙳꙳

"One might say that the psychic achievement of early childhood lies in the mastery of the body, that of the latency period in mastery of the environment, and that of adolescence in mastery of the emotions [Blos, 1961, p. 174]." *Mastery* implies that managing emotions is principally a matter of command and control. But that is inaccurate, or at least misleading. Developing control is only part of the task.

A primary lesson of childhood and adolescence, rooted in our Puritan and Protestant heritage, implicitly and explicitly drilled in diverse contexts, is "Don't trust your feelings!" Resist the importunings of emotion. Delay gratification. Save today—and forty-five years more—for a happy retirement. Stoicism and unremitting self-discipline are sure roads to status and success. These traditional orientations are yielding to increased acceptance of greater gratification in the present—and current concern for nuclear war gives added impetus to this change. As social problems outdistance solutions, despite applications of science and technology, the valid contributions of intuition and emotion to decisions and actions are increasingly recognized. Adam said to Eve, as they left the Garden of Eden, "We are in a period of transition." Like them, we may be leaving a relative Eden for a more difficult existence, but we won't pursue that issue here. The point is that many young adults coming out of Puritan, Protestant, white, achievement-oriented middle-class culture do not take into conscious consideration emotions and impulses relevant to managing time and energy in the present and relevant to future plans—or if they do, they feel guilty or weak-willed.

Mastery of emotions is not completed by the end of high school. Aggression and sex are still wild horses to befriend, to tame, and to harness. First steps toward independence and autonomy reveal shackles and barriers not recognized or felt before. Unreasoning parents, arbitrary authorities, impersonal institutions, inflexible rules, frustrate strongly felt inclinations. Most of them don't yield easily, temper tantrums or sulking often aggravate, not alleviate. New persons of different backgrounds, tastes, habits, and values are encountered and must be lived with. Slugging it out may clear the air, but the differences remain, with the irritation, upset, and anxiety they provoke. So new ways of managing rage and hostility must be developed.

Sexual maturity is reached. Increased freedom from supervision and from the constraints of home and community put control more squarely in each person's lap. Freedman (1967), on the basis of his own research and others' findings, asserts that except for about 25 per cent of the men, most entering freshmen are relatively inexperienced sexually. He says, "The majority of women and a substantial portion of the men express rather conservative views about sexual matters at the time of college entrance, tending to disapprove of premarital intercourse [p. 105]." These views seldom go long unchallenged. Courses in literature, psychology, anthropology, and philosophy make discussions of morality and sexual behavior intellectually legitimate. Collegiate subcultures, interpersonal relationships, and dormitory bull sessions raise more direct questions and generate more forceful pressures.

Thus many forces work to foster increased recognition of lust and hate, of desire and anger, of contempt and admiration. The first task for many young adults, therefore, is to loosen repressions from earlier years and to notice recurrent patterns of incident and reaction. For only after such feelings are accepted as legitimate human emotions, and only after habitual responses—acquired from parents and community and practiced through childhood and adolescence—are identified, can self-control be achieved. And that is the complementary task —developing flexible controls congruent with the self one is and is becoming. According to Sanford (1962), there is a sharp increase in the ratio of ego to impulse after adolescence.

> The maximum crisis of adolescence is over and the controlling mechanisms are again in the ascendancy. But the controls developed for inhibiting impulse are still unseasoned and uncertain; they are likely to operate in a rigid manner. . . . The achievement of flexible control, an arrangement in which there is genuine freedom of impulses because there is little danger of their getting out of hand, still lies ahead . . . [p. 260].

Not the controls inherited unwittingly from parents. Not the controls called for by peers or by the dominant culture. But controls constructed for oneself, self-control that is truly one's own. As controls are reconstructed they become linked to personal purposes, attitudes, and values, to significant future plans and aspirations. So linked they become increasingly an integral part of the total structure from which they gain strength and to which they contribute. Of course increased awareness and increasing integration and self-control go together. That we call these tasks "first" and "second" should not suggest that there are two separate leaps, but rather a reciprocal process by which development moves ahead.

Increasing Awareness

Comments from a second-year student called Jim reveal some beginnings:

> I guess I began to realize that I wasn't really understanding how I felt about a lot of things. I realized that I had been ignoring this a long time. But realizing that you don't know what you are feeling, and changing it are two different things. You can't change when you are threatened by anything substantial. You can't relax enough to stop thinking objectively and sort of interpret and feel, sort of pay attention to yourself and interpret. Looking back there has been a gradual process of knowing what was going on and feeling things around more. It feels sort of strange to me. I sort of found I was seeing a lot more things. Just sort of seeping in.

When I was little, I was constantly getting told I should do that and shouldn't do this, more than other kids I think. I remember walking out of a store one time and turning to my mother and saying, "What did I do wrong that time?" I think I got so I tried to behave on an objective level. I tried to decide objectively what correct behavior was 'cause I couldn't really feel the reasons or feel the demands after awhile. And that has continued on one level or another all the way up to college. But now, I really am beginning to know what I feel and to act on it cautiously, and at the same time trying to be open to what is going on. Not using the caution to block anything, but just out of a little bit of fear, never having really tried out actions that seem to originate in my feelings, that were justified by my feelings. Things have not gone far enough to know whether it's working, whether the actions that go with my feelings are effective, or satisfying. I don't think it's gone far enough to be able to make any conclusions. But it has gone to a level where I know what it is and I'm not just living by knowledge, where I'm really somewhat freed of knowledge.

Most studies of college students have found change in the direction of increased awareness of emotions and increased freedom of expression in words or behavior. Webster, Freedman, and Heist (1962) reported that at both Bennington and Vassar "the older students are more developed, more mature, more free to express impulses than the younger students [p. 830]." At Harvard, King (1967) found freshman-to-senior increases on a "need-determined assertiveness scale," which contained such items as: " 'No values can be eternal; the only real values are those which meet the demands of the given moment'; 'Let us eat, drink, and be merry, for tomorrow we die'; 'Life is something to be enjoyed to the full, sensuously enjoyed with relish and enthusiasm' [p. 21]." And Newcomb and Feldman (1968), reporting their comprehensive review of research on change and stability during the college years, say that "college students tend to become somewhat more impulsive and somewhat less self-controlled, orderly and conscientious [p. 36]."

Six professionals associated with the Project on Student Development were given copies of the Omnibus Personality Inventory scale descriptions and asked to assign to each vector of development whichever scale was judged relevant to change in that area. The Impulse Expression scale is described as follows: "This scale assesses a general readiness to express impulses and to seek gratification either in conscious thought or in overt action. The high scorers value sensations, have an active imagination, and their thinking is often dominated by feelings and fantasies [Center for the Study of Higher Education, 1964, p. 5]." Not surprisingly, all six persons independently judged this scale as relevant to Managing Emotions, and it was hypothesized that scores would increase. Test-retest data for the first two years yielded the following results: Of the twenty-three possible cases (Men and Women for nine colleges, Business Administration and Engineering majors at Rocket, men only at Classic, and women only at Sacred and Bootstrap), seventeen changed in the hypothesized direction and eight reached statistical significance. In all six remaining cases scores were identical at entrance and after two years, and five of these six cases were men. At only one college, Simon, did scores for both men and women not change. The increasing scores occur even though students at the different colleges enter at very different points on the scale; institutional means span more than two standard deviations.

Four-year data on the Impulse Expression scale for two groups of Goddard College graduates raised an interesting question (Beecher et al., 1966). Mean scores did not increase for these two groups of students. In fact, for the 1964 graduates, mean scores were lower at graduation than at entrance. Sanford (Sanford, Webster, and Freedman, 1957) said, "there are those who seem primarily to need awakening, broadening, opening to experiences; and, on the other hand, those who seem primarily to need self-discipline or organization, or integration [p. 1]." The high entering scores for the Goddard students suggested that they were of the second kind, already awakened and open to experience. For them the principal developmental task was to achieve increased self-control, increased integration of emotions and other elements or personality. And the data also suggested that the college environment was one where such development might proceed.

Examination of the changing response frequencies for particular items makes more explicit some of the changes reflected by increasing scale scores in this area. The researchers at the Center for Research and Development in Higher Education (Berkeley) selected a list of items that were judged to reflect increases in impulse expression and flexibility, and examined the changing frequencies. Table 2 presents the resulting figures for some of these items for eight colleges studied by the Center and for Goddard.

It is worth noting that even though the frequencies for the Goddard freshmen are, on all items but one, higher than those for the sen-

Table 2

RESPONSE PERCENTAGES FOR ITEMS SHOWING INCREASE
IN IMPULSE EXPRESSION AND FLEXIBILITY

Item and Direction of Response		Fresh-man	Senior	Differ-ence
In illegitimate pregnancies abortion is in many cases the most reasonable alternative. (T)	Goddard	50	78	28
	Eight Colleges*	26	50	24
Human passions cause most of the evil in the world. (F)	Goddard	62	77	15
	Eight Colleges*	34	54	20
I prefer people who are never profane. (F)	Goddard	78	93	15
	Eight Colleges*	51	71	20
Many of my friends would probably be considered unconventional by other people. (T)	Goddard	66	81	15
	Eight Colleges*	30	43	13
I would disapprove of anyone's drinking to the point of intoxication at a party. (F)	Goddard	73	88	15
	Eight Colleges*	34	59	25
Good rules of etiquette are very important. (F)	Goddard	59	73	14
	Eight Colleges*	23	44	21
No man of character would ask his fiancée to have sexual intercourse with him before marriage. (F)	Goddard	77	85	8
	Eight Colleges*	38	72	34
For most questions there is just one right answer, once a person is able to get all the facts. (F)	Goddard	73	83	10
	Eight Colleges*	68	88	20
I like to have a place for everything and everything in its place. (F)	Goddard	45	52	7
	Eight Colleges*	28	42	14

* Eight colleges data received in personal communication from Paul Heist.

iors at the eight colleges pooled, the frequencies are still higher for Goddard students at graduation. So even when students enter relatively free, relatively more aware of their own feelings and impulses, change may still occur in particular areas.

We must recognize that such changes, at the general level at which they have been assessed, can reflect two quite different patterns of expression, two quite different personalities. For one person, increasing scores may reflect better achievement of flexible control. They may reflect increased ability to manage emotions symbolically and to gratify impulses vicariously, increased perception of underlying complexities and realities, and increased ability to obtain direct gratification through intelligently moderated behavior. Another person simply may have traded an overactive superego or a punitive and super-conscientious conscience for rampant impulsiveness. He may still be driven. A different driver is in control but self-control has not increased.

We should recognize also that actual behavior is usually more restrained and conservative than responses to questionnaires and personality inventories. And it is undoubtedly more pallid than dormitory discussions and personal accounts to peers suggest. Being the first to describe the party weekend or the vacation adventures is relatively easy, and if one has had a good time the gap between reality and report need not be great. But being fifth or eighth is difficult. For often each must top the former, and exaggeration serves the purpose. After one summer vacation I myself became a stock car racer—and thenceforward my driving times to Boston, New York, and Washington became incredibly short. Unfortunately, as far as I could tell at the time, these tales were not incredible to my peers. Nor were their tales incredible to me then, though now I recognize that some were patently impossible. In time the pressures to escalate behavior in accord with reports have effect—drive faster, get drunker, brawl more, exploit women—whatever your bag, crawl into it deeper to prove you really did it before. Thus do information exchange, peer pressures, and behavior interact for mutual escalation. But the basic point for now is that reporting often exaggerates behavior, and judgments of change on the basis of verbal responses should be tempered accordingly.

Differences in the quality of impulse expression and the capacity for managing emotions, and in personality dynamics and their concurrent characteristics, influence the way a student uses college, the kinds of experiences he has, and the kinds of change that occur. The

differential ability to manage aggression, which distinguished Ryan's
(1958) good and poor competitors, is a forceful example. Heath's
(1965) study of mature and immature Haverford students reveals more
widespread ramifications. He says:

> The immature youth has a greater sense of being bound up and
> limited by his own problems; he does not feel himself to be inwardly
> free or master of his talents and his will. The arena in which his
> developmental problems are being fought is an internal one, rather
> than in the more objective external world in which mastery or
> achievement is more readily recognized and rewarded. . . . If
> asked, the immature youth would not quarrel with the assessment
> that he was a disturbed and ineffective person. He too described
> himself as erratic, bottled-up, impulsively irresponsible, introversive,
> and nonsocial. . . . [He] was less reality oriented and had less cog-
> nitive resistance to the interfering consequences of aroused affect
> and drive. His control over strong internal disruption forces was
> erratic and tenuous and little energy was available for effective
> communication and adaptation [p. 170].

Thus Heath's findings document what most sensitive teachers
have observed. When management of emotions is impaired, learning is
hampered and achievement falls short of potential. And these conditions prevail until a higher level of integration is achieved.

Increasing Integration

As Jim's comments suggested, integration of emotions involves,
first, recognition that emotions can serve as a basis for action and decision, can often be a trustworthy guide and source of information
about what is best for oneself. But increased awareness is not all that
is necessary; it must be followed by action that produces perceivable
results. Only by tentative testing through action or symbolic behavior
can integration occur. Then in time flexible control may be achieved.
Genuine freedom of emotions can exist because there is confidence that
they won't get out of hand, and because there has developed a more
clear and realistic sense of the consequences when various expressions
occur in various situations. A second-year girl said:

> It's been hard to bring out that I'm being hurt by something
> or how I feel. I have been able to do it sometimes in relations with
> other students. There have been a few times this semester where in
> the dining room during a meal, it hasn't been justified, but I've

started feeling very much like I was being judged by everybody in the group in a very negative way and that everything I was doing was wrong, everything I said was wrong, and that everybody was just sort of attacking me. It was all exaggerated in my mind sort of, but I've been able now when this starts to happen to say how I feel and to say to somebody, "I feel you're unjustly attacking me. It's making me feel very upset," and by doing this it's made me feel so much better to be able to say it instead of just keeping it all to myself and really feeling terrible afterwards. I really feel glad I've been able to do it a few times. It just happened the other day too. Recognizing my feelings at the time as being my feelings and not trying to push them away and be bothered by them later on, but maybe sort of bring them out in the open at the time and see what's causing them and why I'm feeling that way and as a result I feel much better.

Another girl, when she entered, was already quite open to her own feelings. Her comments illustrate her increasing understanding of their effect on her behavior and the ways she developed to manage feelings more constructively. At the end of the first semester she says:

I am dissatisfied with all I am. This inner dissatisfaction has direct effects on my relationships with others. When I am at relative ease with myself I am easy on others; when my inner displeasure runs rampant, I unconsciously inflict this on others. However, I have become increasingly aware of my effects on others and I try not to be painful. Just in my normal living with others I have gained understanding of what things annoy others, what their needs are and what I am capable of doing.

At the end of her second semester she says:

Through a situation of strain with one class member I found out a lot about relating to people. Our hostility was enough to disrupt the class but by talking with this person and trying to understand and then compromise over our differences, we both gained insight into our behavior and were able to modify our actions.

By the end of her first semester in her senior year, she can say:

The whole semester was filled with "action." Things happening to me and things I made happen—crisis after crisis and oddly enough I didn't give up. As a matter of fact I rather enjoyed struggling with the problems, whether emotional or philosophic. I feel up to fighting; I have much more control. Life is possible and I am a good thing.

Close to graduation, in reviewing her four-year experience, she says:

I still have definite patterns of moods; despair and good spirits fol-low each other regularly. My personal relationships follow similar cycles. I still have doubts and dissatisfaction with myself. Yet, to a large degree, I am better able to cope with these patterns. . . . My moods are more in control. I still get depressed but don't allow my-self to "stay down" for long periods of time. I have found, much to my amazement, that I can stir myself out of a funk to come through when another person needs me.

These excerpts suggest that she became increasingly at home with feelings of which she was quite aware at entrance. At the same time, she was able to work for their long-range modification, and able to discover ways of expressing them, ways of working with them, and ways of working under conditions that provoked one or another kind of response.

All six judges associated with the Project on Student Develop-ment allocated to Managing Emotions two other Omnibus Personality Inventory scales that are relevant to increasing integration—Personal Integration, and Anxiety Level. These two scales are described as fol-lows:

Personal Integration—The high scorer admits to few atti-tudes and behaviors that characterize anxious, disturbed or socially alienated persons. Low scorers, on the other hand, may intentionally avoid others and often express hostility and aggressions. They also indicate feelings of loneliness, rejection, and isolation.

Anxiety Level—High scorers deny that they have feelings or symptoms of anxiety and do not admit to being nervous or worried. Low scorers are generally tense and high-strung and often experi-ence some difficulty adjusting in their social environment [Center for the Study of Higher Education, 1965].

It was hypothesized that scores on both these scales would increase; results for the thirteen Project colleges follow:

On Personal Integration, nineteen out of twenty-three cases— four of which reached statistical significance—scored higher after two years; two changed in direction contrary to the hypothesis (one of the two was significant); and for two cases scores remained the same at both testings. Only at W. J. B., whose students scored highest at entrance, did no increase occur; scores for women dropped significantly, and mean scores for men were identical. On Anxiety Level, sixteen cases changed in the hypothesized direction, of which three reached statistical significance; five changed contrary to the hypothesized direction, with one significant case; and two cases remained the same. The single case of significant contrary change on Anxiety Level also occurred at W. J. B., where again entering students scored highest.

W. J. B. students scored lowest among the Project college entrants on Impulse Expression and both men and women reflected significant increase. This college may represent a case at the opposite pole from Goddard. For W. J. B. students, "awakening" is the principal developmental task and it is occurring, accompanied by decreasing integration. The increasing scores on the Repression-Suppression scale for two groups of Goddard graduates—1964 and 1965—supported our hunch that increasing integration was the major aspect of Managing Emotions to which these students devoted themselves. On this scale, high scorers tend to be "prudent, cautious persons who are likely to inhibit behavior that appears unconventional or socially undesirable [Center for the Study of Higher Education, 1964, p. 6]." These Goddard students don't become high scorers, but they do achieve an average level of integration as reflected by this measure. Table 3 gives some of the items from this scale on which greatest change in response frequencies occurred. At Project colleges with less extreme scores than W. J. B. or the 1964 and 1965 Goddard graduates, increasing freedom of impulse expression is accompanied by increasing integration and reduced anxiety, exemplifying a reciprocal process through which development proceeds.

Emotions arising from sexual impulses offer the most pressing challenge to flexible self-control, the greatest provocation for either totalistic repression and asceticism or totalistic concentration on pursuit and gratification. Successful integration—where sexual behavior becomes a vehicle for expressing complex feelings of affection, nurturance and respect, and for satisfying a similarly complex network in ourselves—is probably most difficult to achieve in this area. But its achievement does make a clear difference. Freedman (1967) reports, and it fits college students I have known, that seniors who seem to have achieved the best sexual adjustment, who have a generous capacity for warmth, intimacy, and bodily enjoyment, and who can control their

Table 3

RESPONSE PERCENTAGES
FOR ITEMS REFLECTING INCREASED REPRESSION-SUPPRESSION
(Goddard Graduates)

Item and Direction of Response	Entrance	*Eighth Semester*	*Difference*
I sometimes wake up to find myself thinking about some impractical or irrelevant problem. (F)	33	59	26
I think I feel more intensely than most people do. (F)	45	64	19
I frequently find myself worrying about something. (F)	33	52	19
Sometimes an unimportant thought will run through my mind and bother me for days. (F)	31	50	19
I have sometimes felt that difficulties were piling up so high that I could not overcome them. (F)	33	48	15
I have had periods of days, weeks, or months when I couldn't take care of things because I couldn't "get going." (F)	33	48	15
I get excited very easily. (F)	40	48	8

behavior, usually have not been sexually precocious. In contrast, girls who began to have sexual intercourse quite regularly early in secondary school often lack basic integrity and self-respect. They appear uncertain of their sexual identity and cannot sustain intimate relationships with men for a long period. Men who share that pattern are often insensitive and shallow, and in their efforts to impress other men with their prowess suggest underlying uncertainty concerning their own masculinity. Both men and women seem to have become fairly fixed; intellectual and personal development have pretty much tapered off. Those who have achieved better integration, on the other hand, reflect a more slow and gradual unfolding and give the impression that development will continue to further levels of complexity and integration.

The neurology and biology of emotion have received considerable research attention recently, made possible by new techniques for implanting electrodes in various areas of the brain, thereby enabling direct stimulation that bypasses the peripheral sensory mechanisms normally employed. In turn, it has become possible to examine more precisely the relationships between the central nervous system (the brain and spinal column) and the peripheral nervous system (the outlying receptors and effectors)', and to examine interactions among receptors, afferent neurons (which conduct toward the central nervous system and from lower to higher centers within it), and efferent neurons (which conduct from higher to lower centers within the central nervous system and away from it to the effectors)'. R. G. Heath (1964), for example, implanted electrodes in the limbic system and arranged equipment so that a patient could stimulate himself by pressing a button. Stimulation in one area led to reports of good, happy feelings and pleasant memories. Pressing a button to stimulate a different area led to distress and unhappy thoughts. Happiness could be regained simply by pressing the other button.

Pribram (1967), reviewing neurological research, reports findings consistent with our position concerning the reciprocal relationships between increasing awareness and increasing integration:

> One road open to the organism in his recourse to variety in control is to act on his environment. As I have indicated elsewhere (Pribram, 1963) whenever a homeostatic system becomes stabilized, new sensitivities develop and new techniques, new programs, are adduced to handle these new sensitivities.
>
> But action is not the only way in which an organism can achieve variety in control. The possibility exists that he may . . . make internal adjustments with his neurological systems, adjustments that will lead to reequilibration without recourse to action. . . .
>
> There is now good neurophysiological evidence that such internal adjustments are possible and commonplace. A large number of experiments have been done to show that the organism's input channels and even the sensory receptors themselves are subject to efferent control by the central nervous system. . . . The results of these experiments suggest that the organism has at least two ways in which he can internally adjust his uncertainty, neither of which entails action. One way is to increase the rate at which he handles information, the other is to decrease that rate. One mechanism "opens" the organism to input, the other restricts input. Internal

adjustment can thus be attempted either through closer coupling with the external environment or by minimizing the external and placing reliance on internal configurations. . . . Another way of stating this is to say that control may be manifested in one of two dispositions or attitudes: a participatory attitude which facilitates the rate of information processing; or a preparatory attitude which diminishes uncertainty by allowing the organism to repair to previous, acceptable states of organization.

In short, the specificities of emotion, as viewed here, are the result of a process called, in engineering, the "Law of Requisite Variety." The capacity of an organism to regulate, to control, can at best equal its capacity to process information. In biological systems the converse also holds; the capacity of an organism whose channels are also capable of storage through the mechanism of habituation, to process information can at best equal its capacity to maintain control. A greater information processing demand on such a channel with storage characteristics can lead to greater uncertainty; as already noted, this can be biologically disruptive. Only by building up variety of control through habituation can the organism keep pace with the increasing complexity to which it becomes sensitive—the increase in interests aroused—whenever stability is achieved. Thus a reciprocal neurological mechanism is needed.

The orienting-habituation studies provide evidence that such a reciprocal mechanism actually operates to alter almost simultaneously the organism's information handling capacity and his capacity for taking measures of self-control [pp. 834, 835].

These comments suggest the following dynamics. Control fosters openness to new information and the ability to process it, leading to increasingly complex varieties of control and levels of sensitivity. Development proceeds. Noncontrol restricts input and hampers the ability to process it, and previous patterns based on internal configurations already established are employed. Higher levels of sensitivity and more flexible patterns of control are not fostered. Development stalls.

Is there here an echo of Freud's primary and secondary processes? It almost sounds like it. The primary process calls attention to what is needed, and it indicates a rough direction but can do no more. To achieve satisfaction action is necessary, and productive action requires that gratification be delayed, that tolerance of tension be developed. As this capacity increases, with increased experience through diverse conditions, and with memory—or storage—finer discriminations become possible, increasingly complex repertoires develop, and more varied alternatives for satisfaction become available. Judgment improves, alternatives are more wisely chosen. Thus are cognitive processes increasingly sharpened and thus are higher levels of differentiation and integration achieved.

But this reciprocal relationship between increasing awareness and increasing control does not imply "playing it cool." It does not imply "playing games" or dampening passion and commitment. The cool character has himself well insulated. Wary and cautious, his life is privatized. Goings on inside the head or gut become the focus. Comparing sixty-year-olds with forty-year-olds, Neugarten (1964) says:

> Preoccupation with the inner life becomes greater; emotional cathexes toward persons and objects in the outer world seem to decrease; the readiness to attribute activity and affect to persons in the environment is reduced; there is a movement away from outer-world to inner-world orientation. There is constriction in the ability to integrate wide ranges of stimuli, and in the willingness to deal with complicated and challenging situations. Certain types of rational thought processes, although they remain important, become separated from affective processes in motivating social behavior [p. 189].

We do not propose that college students manage their emotions as sixty-year-olds do. On the contrary, the task is to develop increasing capacity for passion and commitment accompanied by increasing capacity to implement passion and commitment through intelligent behavior. Increasing ugliness, conflict, and exploitation must be met with increasing love, respect, and courage, as well as with science, technology, and the best fruits of reason. Increased awareness of emotions and increased ability to manage them effectively are, therefore, developmental tasks central to social concerns as well as to full and rich individual development.

CHAPTER 3

DEVELOPING AUTONOMY

Excerpts from evaluations written by a Goddard girl I'll call June illustrate movement toward autonomy. Reflecting on her first semester she says:

> I have learned a lot about other people and myself. . . . I have gained in self-confidence. I am more self-responsible. I do not have to rely on other people to do my thinking. I have learned to live and work with people of my own age in a community situation. I have more self-respect. I do not allow people to take advantage of me. I am more outspoken. I have learned to take the initiative, to be independent.

She already sounds qualified for her degree. But by her second semester perspective creeps in. She says:

In last semester's evaluation I said that I had become more self-confident, self-responsible, outspoken, that I had learned to take initiative and that I had gained in self-respect. I have learned that these are all quite relative and that there will continue to be constant growth for me in these areas throughout my stay at Goddard. I have discovered that I have my own set of morals more or less the same but apart from my parents. I have done some thinking about them and I have attempted to be more consistent in living by them.

I have discovered that I *can* write papers and write them well. I no longer have a fear of writing and I found that this has cut down tremendously my procrastination. I am doing more and more reading as time goes on and have found that I am being more and more critical of what I read. I have learned to distinguish fact from theory, and not to depend on the printed word as always being the "truth" or "right."

This work term I worked with an outstanding teacher. I was allowed to be myself. I was never told what I should or shouldn't do or say. Through this experience I gained some hope. Maybe I could teach. If I could work as this teacher did there would be nothing I would enjoy more. But this was a Co-op nursery. I still have my doubts about working with the public school system.

The focus after her third semester shifts from study and the work term to interpersonal relationships and community responsibilities. She says:

My growth socially has come with increased self-confidence. Because I would not allow people to step on me their respect for me grew, and with it my respect for myself. I was elected president of my house, and as such, representative to House Council. I learned a great deal from this experience of organization, responsibility, and human relations. Since this was the first of this kind of experience for me I felt I left much to be desired. But, all considered, I think I made a good beginning. As secretary of House Council I kept the records and reported to Community Meetings. This also was a new experience and added further to my responsibilities as a community member. I don't mind saying that I was terrified of it all—although less so toward the end of the semester.

By the end of the fifth semester her ideas about the future have become more sharply defined. She has developed a concrete purpose that orients her study. She says:

At the beginning of the semester I started planning for a

study work term in Mexico. To make this possible I found I would have to earn at least $200 before the end of the semester. I spent an average of 12 hours a week working on various off-campus jobs, doing such things as washing windows, cooking, washing and ironing clothes, and washing and waxing floors. I didn't achieve my specific goal of $200 but I did earn enough so that by borrowing the rest I need through a bank, I will be able to go.

With this added responsibility I found I had to very carefully schedule my time as a student and member of the Goddard community. I attended recreation events and most community meetings as my schedule would permit.

I find this semester that I have become much less dependent upon my family and those around me at Goddard for moral and financial support. I think that this has had a lot to do with the fact that I lived and worked away from home during the summer and the realization that I could handle most situations on my own. The experience during the summer and my work experience this semester have helped me become a more self-confident and self-sufficient person.

During this fifth semester she undertook two independent studies in preparation for her winter months in Mexico, a study of Mexican history and culture, and study of the Spanish language. In evaluating the first she says:

Through dealing with the problems I faced in this study and the helpful criticism of my instructor, I became aware of the following things which I feel are necessary to further study in this area: (1) how to apply basic research methods and techniques, (2) the importance of having a purpose, (3) where to find resources and how to use them, and (4) what to include in a research paper and how to organize the necessary material. This study made evident to me a need to gain greater understanding of economics and the Spanish language before I can adequately continue research in this area.

Of her study of Spanish she says:

There were two aspects to this study: (1) the question of how one goes about learning a foreign language in general, and (2) my experiment in learning Spanish. Through reading and practice in the lab I have gained knowledge of what is involved in the aural-oral approach to learning a foreign language. I know the importance of having a purpose, (in my case a planned trip to Mexico and work with the Peace Corps), of regular practice, of repetition and hearing oneself speak for corrective purposes, and of having a native speaker to imitate. I learned that the way to learn a foreign language is to use it, that language learning is habit formation. I also learned that in speaking a foreign language one must exercise facial muscles never before used in speaking one's native language. This is one of the reasons that practice is so important.

She spent January and February living in Mexico City and studying at the University. Upon returning she reports:

Through this experience I found out more about myself, my potentials and limitations. . . . I think I could confidently manage the initial getting established in another country with knowing little or none of the language should I have the opportunity again. . . . I have gained considerably in self-confidence and self-direction.

Her comments at the end of the first semester of her senior year are:

All semester I felt the effects of what seemed more and more to be an unpredictable future. I could no longer feel secure with the knowledge that I would be returning to school in September. I had, until the middle of this semester, assumed that I would be joining the Peace Corps when I graduated. But I found myself questioning the value of the Peace Corps in aiding underdeveloped countries and consequently its value to me. I felt disillusioned when I lost faith in an instructor for whom I had great respect. Having reached the age of twenty-one my added civic responsibilities weighed heavily upon me at the death of President Kennedy. I became involved in a relationship with a friend to whom I have since become engaged. This engagement came only after considerable revision of my once "live happily ever after" ideas about love and marriage. My work and thinking this semester has been affected as never before by an awareness of the unpredictable. An awareness that demanded the security of direction from within myself rather than the kind of security derived from a dependence for direction on the people and institutions with which I am associated. It is difficult to believe the semester is over for I feel as if I have only just begun.

What does this history suggest about the development of autonomy? First, there seem to be three major components: (1) the development of emotional independence, (2) the development of instrumental independence, and (3) the recognition of interdependence.

To be emotionally independent is to be free from continual and pressing needs for reassurance, affection, or approval. The first step toward emotional independence is, of course, disengagement from the parents. June alludes to this in her comment about developing her own set of morals more or less the same as, but apart from, her parents. Probably her comment captures the usual pattern more accurately than some current stereotypes about the radical student-parent differences in values. But June's case illustrates two other important aspects of emotional independence: reduced dependence upon peers, and reduced dependence upon institutional forms. Her increased resistance to being "taken advantage of" and "stepped on" reflects her increased ability to risk loss of approval and affection. Her willingness to venture off alone to Mexico and to develop and carry through her own plans for preparation, including raising the necessary funds, reflects her increasing willingness to move beyond the usual institutional patterns and supports, and reflects her increasing openness to the range of alternatives available to her.

Instrumental independence has two major components: the ability to carry on activities and to cope with problems without seeking help, and the ability to be mobile in relation to one's own needs and desires. June reflects an increasing ability to cope for herself. She learns better to distinguish fact from theory and becomes less dependent on the printed word for answers. From independent studies she has learned that she can recognize gaps when they exist, and that she can acquire for herself the knowledge needed for what she wants to do. After her trip she believes that she could travel to another country and settle in without great difficulty.

Development of emotional independence is hampered by limited instrumental independence. Note that when June earned sufficient funds for her trip she also felt less dependent upon her family and Goddard for *both* moral and financial support. The development of autonomy may not be more fully completed in many college settings, not because conditions impede development of emotional independence, but because there is limited chance to develop, to demonstrate to oneself, the ability to cope with significant tasks alone—in short, because of limited opportunities for developing instrumental independence.

Development of autonomy culminates with recognition of one's interdependencies. June's final comments suggest this has begun for her. She feels increased civic responsibilities as she comes of age. She hesitates to enter the Peace Corps because she questions its effectiveness. She recognizes that marriage is no rose garden. She is concerned about the uncertainties of the future but at the same time notes increased security in self-direction. She sees herself at a beginning rather than an ending.

For June, then, autonomy involves emotional and instrumental independence and the recognition and acceptance of interdependence.

Emotional Independence

The road to emotional independence begins with disengagement from the parents, proceeds through reliance on peers, and ends with personal autonomy. Gardner (1959) describes the process:

> to the young child his very security is predicated on the "all knowingness" and the "all powerfulness" of his mother and father. Such powers have been his strengths, his reliable guides, and his protection in respect to his own impulses and the actions of others. But faith and reliance on such alleged omniscience and omnipotence of parental figures cannot be maintained in the unconscious concepts of the child, in the face of evidence repeated through the child's many experiences within and beyond the home that such is not the case; thus the anxiety of insecurity besets him. As a first step he tries . . . to place other people . . . in the same role as the parent, as the supreme counselor. . . . This device is doomed because . . . whatever knowingness or "power" adolescents are to achieve in order to become adult must be impersonalized and must reside within themselves—as a part of their self-concept and not as the concept of another, and as self-directed, not other-directed choices and controls. I need not emphasize the episodic . . . sometimes disastrous devaluation of parents that takes place because of this necessary step in growth [pp. 870–871].

Disengagement from parents, the development of self-direction, formerly was called *adolescent rebellion;* now the term is *alienation.* Of course it never was the case that all adolescents were rebellious and now not all are alienated. Both terms oversimplify and exaggerate; they only suit the most visible minority. Yet the shift in terms does reflect a shifting stance of adolescent toward adult. Rebellion is for breaking shackles, for eliminating active threats to existence or development. A mother's two-year-old fell into the water. "Help! Help!" she called. "Save him! My son the doctor!" If such a son escapes drowning at two he may still be fighting for air at twenty. Rebellion may be the only out. When daughters and sons more frequently followed parents' footsteps and were more constrained to do so, a vigorous leap was often required to escape an unwanted existence. But now, in adolescent eyes if not in fact, rapid change makes the world of parents obsolete. Constraints are few. The possibility of becoming like the parents seems so remote no threat is posed. So one moves away; simply, quietly. As Keniston (1965) has observed, "many a youth is so distant from his parents, in generational terms if not in affection, that he can afford to 'understand' them, and often to show a touching sympathy for their hesitant effort to guide and advise him [p. 205].

Disengagement and devaluation can be mutual. Some parents have little use for the child who has become a young adult. As Bettelheim (1963) points out, most adults want to have children and enjoy bringing them up. But little pleasure derives from the young adult who aims to move away and build a different life elsewhere, a life permitting infrequent correspondence and sporadic visits. Emotional support in old age seems unlikely and economic support is available elsewhere. In days past, when work was more one's own and demanded greater personal investment, the younger generation was needed to carry it forward. Now, when most people work for others, when yesterday's jobs are gone and today's will be superseded tomorrow, there is no such need. Under such conditions adolescent devaluation of parents may be reciprocated, for during these years parental needs are little fed and hopes for the future seem slim.

But such mutual devaluation need not be permanent. Freedman (1962), studying Vassar undergraduates and alumni, found that early rebellious independence, skepticism, and condemnation were replaced by more realistic evaluation and increased understanding and warmth. Perhaps Mark Twain provided the first self-report on this change. "My father was the stupidest person in the world when I was eighteen," he said, "but when I was twenty-three I was amazed at how much he had learned in five years."

The following comments from a sophomore, called here Dan, are illustrative:

> My family was very close but before I was always really afraid to voice opinions, to feel you know, to show any true feelings that I had about things because I felt there was something wrong

with it, for saying I don't want to do this or that. But now I feel that much more sure of myself that I think when I go home if a situation arises I can present myself in a fashion that will show them I am somebody who has given a lot of thought to things and does give a lot of thought to things, and that I have my own things I want and that I want to try. I can still be part of their things, more or less. I could go and work for my father if I wanted to now and still not have to worry about being stuck for the rest of my life. Because I know more about what I want and by being more sure of myself I don't have to worry about being stuck. And I think I respect them much more for what they want and what they have done. We don't have that much money but my father in a way, I don't know how he did it, but still he brought up his children that if they want anything it is just possible to get it. Another thing, he can associate with people that don't have any education and great people too. He is the kind of person who can go and work with the Town Manager and on Secondary Advisory Boards for schools and also talk and work with the hard working people, to improve the Fire Department or something like that.

Concurrent with these shifting parental relationships are shifting responses to authority and to institutions. Early rebelliousness gradually loses its all-or-none character. It becomes more particular as reason gains voice over emotion. Ultimately, for most students, as relationships of interdependence and mutuality of regard with parents take root, so also ways to work constructively within institutional forms and limitations are discovered.

These shifting relationships with parents and authority are supported by complementary shifts with peers. With couples of the same sex or of different sexes, during the period of rebellious independence, a satisfying relationship depends on being close enough so that each can cling to the other, and replace the support of parents and authority, which is crumbling under the onslaught of increased perspective and suffering active demolition to make space for structures more personally valid. Then, as more firm independence from parents is established, as it becomes possible to appreciate the good about one's parents as well as the bad, then relationships with intimates become less symbiotic. Mutual support becomes more simple and strong, more implicit, more taken for granted.

A similar shift occurs in the relationships between the individual and his reference groups. Dan, who spoke of his new perspective on his parents, at about the same time said:

When I was in high school I used to worry about being accepted. There are so many kids who, you know, are socially prominent and part of everything, had all the girl friends and this and that. Now I go home and meet them and I feel we both started out on the same level but they just stayed there. Because I can sit down now. Before I was unsure of myself. I had to go to the coffee shop twice a night so that I could get to see people and feel a part of things. If I didn't see somebody for a week I'd wonder, "Are you still my friend?" and "How secure am I in my position at Goddard?" Then all of a sudden I can go into my room and I can stay there and study until 1:00 every night and not worry about it, and I am just much more secure in my position.

Relationships with sympathetic teachers and other adults provide support and foster perspective during this period of disengagement. Dan reports, for example:

During the work term I had a terrific experience. I lived with a Unitarian minister and his family and they were such fabulous people. This guy wasn't afraid to tell me that he thought I was really just looking at things the wrong way, you know, he'd tell me and he wouldn't pull any punches. He'd say, "Do you want me to be honest with you or do you want me to just kid you? I'll sit down and I'll tell you where I think that you have missed the boat." It was so great you know. It hurt for a while, you know, but this guy was really giving me a lot of insight into a lot of things. The relationship they had within their family was a wonderful thing to watch. A very very warm, very close family and they just didn't seem to have many of the fears and inhibitions that I felt when I was their age and that I feel now for no good reason.

Here the force of a frank and admiring relationship with a nonparent adult is revealed, as is the force of living with another family. In this context, comments and advice from the adult could be heard and considered, well supported by the full experience of the persons, congruent with their words.

The frequent preference for spending vacations at the homes of college friends rather than their own is worth noting. And it is instructive to hear both the visitor and the host talk about the vacation, to see how differently a single family may be experienced. Once, a visitor returned glowing, much as Dan above, while the host returned disillusioned and angry. At a tea party his mother had accepted compliments about, and taken credit for, some cookies she had not made. The mother's dishonesty and smallness shocked her son. Yet his guest found the family warm and high-principled.

Test-retest data from personality inventories support case history evidence concerning the development of emotional independence. At Goddard College, several OPI scales were found to distinguish from their peers students nominated as high on independence by the faculty (Chickering, 1964b). Four of these discriminating scales—Social Maturity, Theoretical Orientation, Liberalism, and Originality—were judged relevant to the development of emotional independence; it was hypothesized that scores on the measures would increase. Two other scales, Autonomy and Non-authoritarianism, were not included in the comparative studies, but were included in the final analyses; it was hypothesized that scores on these measures would also increase. After these hypotheses had been set, data from eight other colleges became available. Following are the findings for the 1964 and 1965 Goddard graduates and for the eight colleges.

On Social Maturity and Autonomy, significant change occurred for the eight colleges and for both groups of Goddard graduates. Goddard graduates also changed in the hypothesized direction on Liberalism and Originality, and one group reached statistical significance. No change occurred on Non-authoritarianism. On Theoretical Orientation, no change occurred for the eight colleges; for Goddard students, significant change occurred, counter to the hypothesized direction. These findings support a picture of increasing emotional independence. The mixed results on Theoretical Orientation suggested that increasing emotional independence is not necessarily accompanied by a more logical, critical, or objective approach to problems, or by increasing interest in science. It is also worth noting that on both Social Maturity and Autonomy, Goddard students scored higher at entrance than students of the eight colleges did at graduation, yet scores still increased. Development apparently continues during these years even when students enter further along than most of their peers. The data also indicate that most change occurs during the first two years, a pattern found in other research with these measures and repeated elsewhere in the Goddard data.

Table 4 presents response percentages for Goddard students for a few items from each scale that changed in the hypothesized direction. These are items where the shift in response frequency was high,

Table 4

RESPONSE PERCENTAGES, OPI ITEMS FOR GODDARD FROM SOCIAL MATURITY, AUTONOMY, LIBERALISM, AND ORIGINALITY

Item and Direction of Response	Entrance	Eighth Semester	Differ- ence
Social Maturity			
No weakness or difficulty can hold us back if we have enough will power. (F)	29	83	44
I believe we are made much better by the trials and hardships of life. (F)	10	40	30
I would rather remain free from commitment to others than risk serious disappointment or failure later. (F)	58	77	19
When it comes to differences in opinion in religion, we should be careful not to compromise with those who believe differently than we do. (F)	66	81	15
Autonomy			
In the final analysis parents generally turn out to be right about things. (F)	31	69	38
Every wage earner should be required to save a certain part of his income each month so that he will be able to support himself and family in later years. (F)	52	83	31
It is better never to expect too much; in that way you are rarely disappointed. (F)	50	71	21
More than anything else, it is good hard work that makes life worthwhile. (F)	62	81	19

Table 4—Cont.

RESPONSE PERCENTAGES, OPI ITEMS FOR GODDARD FROM
SOCIAL MATURITY, AUTONOMY, LIBERALISM, AND ORIGINALITY

Item and Direction of Response	Entrance	Eighth Semester	Differ- ence
Liberalism			
I believe it is the responsibility of intelligent leadership to maintain the established order of things. (F)	62	78	16
It doesn't bother me when things are uncertain or unpredictable. (T)	40	62	22
Originality			
I am apt to pass up something I want to do when others feel that it isn't worth doing. (F)	58	77	19
I frequently ask people for advice. (F)	40	58	18
These days I find it hard not to give up hope of amounting to something. (F)	55	69	14
Perfect balance is the essence of all good composition. (F)	69	81	12
I am easily embarrassed. (F)	50	59	9

and which therefore contributed substantially to the changes in scale scores.

A more detailed study of twenty-two items judged to reflect increases in independence was carried out on the eight colleges data. Table 5 gives the results. The items are arranged according to the magnitude of change. Heading the list are items on relationships with generalized authority: school, home town, forefathers, established leadership, and thought. Then come items concerning parents and religious beliefs and practices.

The analysis also revealed that for each of the eight institutions, statistically significant change occurred in the direction of increased independence on practically all items for both men and women. Differences from college to college were greater than differences between sexes within the same institution. Thus men and women at a particular kind of institution are more like each other, in this aspect of development, than they are like persons of the same sex at a different college.

Table 5

RESPONSE PERCENTAGES, OPI ITEMS
RELEVANT TO DEVELOPMENT OF INDEPENDENCE*

Item	First Year	Fourth Year	Differ-ence
I generally attend the meetings of school or college organizations. (F)	25	62	37
Every person ought to be a booster for his own home town. (F)	50	80	30
I am active on the committees of school organizations. (F)	45	73	28
We should respect the work of our forefathers and not think that we know better than they did. (F)	41	67	26
I believe it is a responsibility of intelligent leadership to maintain the established order of things. (F)	39	65	26
I question the accuracy of statements made in my textbooks or reference books. (T)	42	66	24
It's a pretty callous person who does not feel love and gratitude toward his parents. (F)	29	53	24
Every person should have complete faith in a supernatural power whose decisions he obeys without question. (F)	60	83	23

* Pooled data on eight colleges from former Center for the Study of Higher Education, Berkeley, California (N = 1,269).

Table 5—Cont.

RESPONSE PERCENTAGES, OPI ITEMS

RELEVANT TO DEVELOPMENT OF INDEPENDENCE*

Item	First Year	Fourth Year	Difference
The prophets of the Old Testament predicted the events that are happening today. (F)	57	80	23
I should like to belong to several clubs or lodges. (F)	52	74	22
I have been quite independent and free from family rule. (T)	45	67	22
It is essential for learning or effective work that our teachers and leaders outline in detail what is to be done and how to do it. (F)	61	82	21
I go to church or temple almost every week. (F)	40	60	20
No normal, decent person would ever think of hurting a close friend or relative. (F)	38	57	19
God hears our prayers. (F)	23	42	19
I pray several times a week. (F)	41	58	17
One of my aims is to accomplish something that would make my mother proud of me. (F)	34	51	17
In the final analysis parents generally turn out to be right about things. (F)	17	34	17
We cannot know for sure whether or not there is a God. (T)	41	57	16

* Pooled data on eight colleges from former Center for the Study of Higher Education, Berkeley, California (N = 1,269).

Table 5—Cont.

RESPONSE PERCENTAGES, OPI ITEMS
RELEVANT TO DEVELOPMENT OF INDEPENDENCE*

Item	First Year	Fourth Year	Differ-ence
I am apt to pass up something I want to do when others feel that it isn't worth doing. (F)	44	58	13
Families owe it to the city to keep their sidewalks cleared in the winter and their lawns mowed in the summer. (F)	15	28	13
I want to be an important person in the community. (F)	43	52	9

* Pooled data on eight colleges from former Center for the Study of Higher Education, Berkeley, California (N = 1,269).

The Goddard studies also used the Stern Activities Index. Three scales are most relevant to the development of emotional independence: Abasement, reflecting self-depreciation and devaluation; Deference, reflecting sycophantic submission to the opinions and preferences of others perceived as superior; Succorance, reflecting dependence on others for love, assistance, and protection. On Abasement and Deference, significant change occurred for both groups of graduates; on Succorance, change for the '64 graduates reached significance, but change for '65 graduates, though in the appropriate direction, did not.

Another set of studies (Beecher et al., 1966; Chickering, 1967) carried out at Goddard College examined particular sets of behaviors reflected in student and instructor reports to see whether change occurred during the college years. Thus these studies translated general dimensions of development into more concrete terms. Because Goddard uses a system of written self-evaluations and instructor comments rather than examinations and grades, and because the nonresident work term, the on-campus work program, community participation, and extracurricular activities, as well as academic study, are subject to evaluation, student records are rich in material suitable for analysis. For the 1964 graduates, each semester's records were rated on several questions for each of six general dimensions of development. The dimension most relevant to the development of emotional independence was called *Venturing.* The venturing student was defined as open to experience, willing to confront questions and problems, to discover new possibilities, to disagree, and to initiate things for himself. Student records were rated on a scale from zero to ten for five questions:

1. How much does the student speak up in class? How ready is he to express his own ideas and join the battle? Does he brood and maintain a stoic silence or does he externalize his feelings and ideas?

2. How easily does he communicate with the instructor? How free is he to disagree?

3. To what extent does he engage in study or other activities to tackle perceived weaknesses or liabilities?

4. How frequently does he speak of lack of self-confidence, of fears that restrict his activities? (Reverse scoring)

5. To what extent does he seek out new, challenging, or unusual work term or summer experiences? To what extent is the work term used to engage in new experiences or to test new skills or attitudes?

It was hypothesized that average ratings on these five questions would increase over the four-year period. The results are portrayed in Figure 1 and indicate, consistent with the test-retest results for the OPI, that most change occurs during the first two years.

The dip at the third semester is puzzling. Perhaps there is some reason why caution and conservatism operate sharply at this time. It may be that the third semester is a period of recovery or quiescence after the difficult adjustments of the first year. Perhaps the student wants to hold things constant and safe for a while in order to consolidate some of the new positions achieved. He may be content to remain free from new challenges and from experiences that might create new disequilibrium.

Some findings for the Teacher Acceptance and Educational Acceptance scales of the Survey of Study Habits and Attitudes (Beecher *et al.,* 1966) call attention to another aspect of the development of emotional independence. During the first two years scores rise; during the last two they fall. This pattern follows the changes in students' identification with sympathetic adults who provide support and comfort during the period of disengagement from parents. Many of us who, as teachers, administrators, counselors, and family friends, have experienced close relationships with freshmen and sophomores have found ourselves on a pedestal. But as these idolaters move toward more

FIGURE 1

Venturing

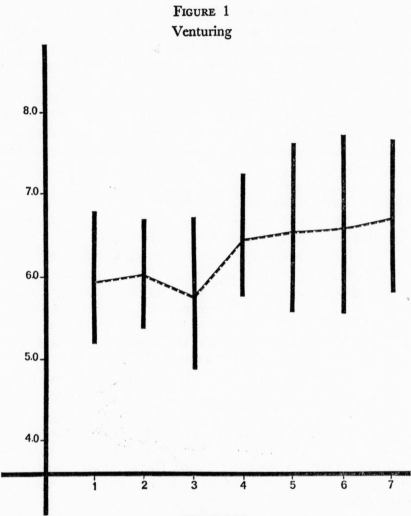

SEMESTERS

Vertical lines indicate range of ratings within which 2/3 of the students fall.
Horizontal line connects mean ratings for twenty students.
Difference in means for first and fourth semesters likely to occur less than five
times in one hundred on the basis of chance.

realistic perception of their parents, as they can grant parents more,
so also do they perceive us more realistically. We find ourselves less
frequently flattered, more frequently portrayed in stark and revealing
terms. Their disposition to tackle problems rationally and critically may
be temporarily elevated, fostered by an unjustified or inaccurate per-

ception that teachers or administrators operate that way. As we are perceived more clearly in situations where prejudice and emotion rather than reason govern behavior, then disillusionment may occur and the students' intellectual orientation shifts or declines.

So much for emotional independence. The fit between theory and data is fairly close; the evidence that such development occurs is reasonably solid.

Instrumental Independence

As Dan's comments about his shifting relationships with parents and peers indicated, emotional independence and instrumental independence are linked and mutually facilitating. As he felt increasing self-assurance with his parents, he could work at home and elsewhere without fear of being stuck. As he no longer needed continual assurance of his acceptability, he could work longer and concentrate more intently. But disengagement from the parents and achievement of emotional independence is often hampered by lack of opportunities to develop instrumental independence. Most colleges offer only academic problems, to be met with academic discussions, to achieve theoretical, but never practical or concrete, results. Prescribed ways of meeting the problems are spelled out; assistance is to be sought if difficulty arises. Extended financial dependence on the parents compounds this state of affairs. Even marriage during college no longer necessarily implies self-support; parents often continue support through college and into graduate school. These conditions impede development of instrumental independence and confuse and complicate the development of emotional independence.

Instrumental independence has two major components: (1) the ability to carry out activities on one's own and to be self-sufficient, and (2) the ability to leave one place and get to another if one wishes.

The Goddard study of Resourcefulness and Organization is relevant to the first component. The resourceful and organized student was defined as practical and able to work out intermediate steps to a goal, as knowing when he needs help and how to get it; he is efficient and knows how to make good use of available resources. Faculty members used four questions for rating students on this variable. They were:

1. How freely does the student make use of a wide range of resources for his own learning?

2. How well does he make plans, follow through on them, or modify them consciously and judiciously and then carry through?

3. How well does he discover or develop new ways of going at matters of concern to him? Of circumventing or overcoming obstacles that appear?

4. To what extent is he able to handle a variety of responsibilities and sustain good effort and performance in relation to all? How well is he able to avoid being overwhelmed or snowed under at the end of the semester or at other times when several obligations seem to coincide?

It was hypothesized that average ratings for these questions would increase.

Despite the rather large standard deviations, the differences between the first and fourth semesters and the first and seventh semesters are well beyond that which might occur by chance. Again most change occurs in the first two years; during that period there is steady growth, which tapers off during the last two years.

The other major component of instrumental independence is mobility; the ability to leave one place and get to another, to leave a bad situation and arrive safely at a better one. Erikson (1963) talks of "Wander-schaft," of youth's "craving for locomotion . . . expressed in a general 'being on the go,' 'tearing after something,' or in running around [p. 11]." Comments from a graduate illustrate the point:

> I spent the summers of my sophomore and junior years in France. The first summer I worked for the Unitarian Service Committee and the second I attended the University of Dijon. My work with the service committee in the foothills of the Pyrenees did not prohibit me from going to Biarritz to gamble on weekends, and in six sojourns I won about $500 with a system for roulette. We had ten days to travel at the end of the summer and after about six I wound up in the casinos of Nice. The first night I won and the second I lost everything but my train ticket to Rotterdam and my boat ticket to Hoboken. Black came up fifteen times in a row and I ran out of capital. But I worked off my hotel bill, shared the nuts and cheese of some Italian peasants on the train to the boat, and hitch-hiked from Hoboken to the loving wallets of my fraternity brothers at college.
>
> Through these experiences I found I was happy and healthy, and indeed I enjoyed the challenges involved. And most important, I realized that with few beginning resources I could go to Hong

FIGURE 2
Resourcefulness and Organization

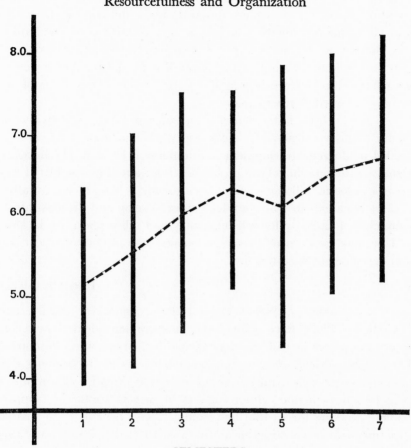

SEMESTERS

Vertical lines indicate range of ratings within which 2/3 of the students fall.
Horizontal line connects mean ratings for twenty students.
Difference in means for first and fourth semesters likely to occur less than one
time in one hundred on the basis of chance.

Kong if I wished. And that was the way I thought of it at the time.
I guess Hong Kong carried connotations of magic, romance, and
far away places. Somehow that realization carried great force and
I can still visualize my dress and my room as it struck me.

Much of the aimless and spontaneous travel, the carelessness
about advance planning and arrangements for eating and sleeping, are
part of testing and developing the capacity to move freely about. I re-

member a psychiatrist commenting about a girl who blithely set off from his office to return to college without much sense of how she was going to get there or what she would do if she did not get there very fast. He wondered whether this was a sign of disturbance; perhaps it was. But it is not uncharacteristic of many college students; perhaps it is in the service of this important aspect of independence. In any event the relationship between feeling able to move and other aspects of autonomy are worth further exploration.

So much for instrumental independence. When an individual is unable to carry out activities alone and when unable to go or come as needed or desired, development of autonomy is limited. The development of autonomy in college probably is not more fully completed, not because emotional disengagement from parents is hampered, but rather because situations in which students must develop and demonstrate to themselves a capacity for self-sufficiency and self-support are lacking, and because freedom of movement in response to needs for learning and development is curtailed.

Interdependence

As Yahkub (1960), Vispo (1966), Fairbairn (1952), and Whitehorn (1962) have pointed out, "mature dependence," or recognition and acceptance of interdependence, is the capstone of autonomy. For college students this mature dependence means recognizing that one cannot dispense with his parents except at the price of continuing pain for all; that one cannot comfortably accept continuing support without working for it; that one cannot receive benefits from a social structure without contributing to that structure; that loving and being loved are necessarily complementary. As interdependencies are recognized, boundaries of personal choice become more clear. Then can one become an agent for oneself; he can carve a particular existence out of the larger physical, social, and historical context. Thus only with the clarification and resolution of the ranges within which one can give and can receive do problems of dependence and independence become reasonably settled.

Of course, no final settlement can be reached because changing conditions make for changing tolerances. Work may become so demanding that no energy remains for other purposes. A failure may shatter self-esteem so that the warm support of others is required for healing. Or life may be so rich and rewarding that love can expand and large amounts of energy are freed for other than direct self-service.

Student comments suggest that for many this kind of change is occurring. Recall June's comments concerning her feelings of increased civic responsibility as she came of age, and Dan's comments reflecting increasing acceptance and respect for his family. Another girl reports:

> I found a new, stimulating challenge before me in the form of a new government and in the greater amount of independence granted to the student body. I took an active interest in writing our house plan, as I feel these small houses are an excellent opportunity for all of us to work constructively toward the particular goals we choose to set up for ourselves. I honestly believe that it is up to each of us to perform consistently as conscientious, concerned members of a community that is ours for the making; if we fail to assume our responsibilities then we have no right to demand the privileges of self-government. By doing my share I naturally expected others to do theirs and consequently I saw how very much of an interdependent community we are, for if a few links gave way the whole chain collapsed. The cries for self-rule from people who may not realize the extent to which they are committing themselves through their very demands fascinate me and I am most anxious to actively follow the course of our new government.

Another student put it more simply:

> The community meeting here at Goddard is a good thing and I enjoy going to them and taking an active part in them. I think they should always be continued and for those who object to it because as they say it is a waste of time, I say, don't go, but don't question the rules the community makes.

Interdependence was another of the six variables in the Goddard studies of student records. The interdependent student was defined as nonpunitive, nonhostile, attuned to the whole and aware of his own resonances with it and his own responsibilities to it. The questions used for rating were more explicit:

1. Is the student ready and able to work with others on community affairs such as recreation events, community government, house business, and so on?

2. Does the student pull together with others well on the work program? To what extent is he conscious of his role in a broader work program context, when such a relationship exists?

3. Does he seem to be aware of the relationship between his own behavior and community welfare in general?

4. Is the student tolerant of differences in behavior or in point of view on the part of other students or faculty members?

It was hypothesized that average ratings for these questions would increase.

Figure 3 indicates that change is not spectacular. It is interest-

FIGURE 3

Interdependence

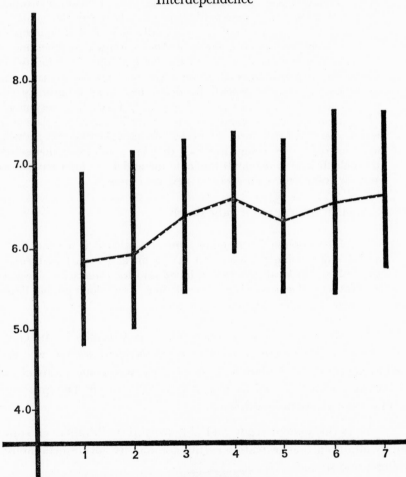

SEMESTERS

Vertical lines indicate range of ratings within which 2/3 of the students fall. Horizontal line connects mean ratings for twenty students.

Difference in means for first and fourth semesters likely to occur less than three times in one hundred on the basis of chance.

ing to note that the sharpest change occurs during the third semester, and that fourth semester ratings are about as high as those for the seventh. These data are consistent with other observations that participation in extracurricular and community activities increases rather sharply during the second year and then levels off.

The development of autonomy can be summarized as follows. Change occurs along three major vectors, emotional independence, instrumental independence, and recognition and acceptance of interdependencies. Development of emotional independence begins with disengagement from the parents, and rebelliousness in relation to them, to other adult authorities, and to established institutions. During this period, relationships with peers and sympathetic adults provide transitory emotional support. Maturity in this vector comes when relationships of reciprocal respect and helpfulness are developed with parents and peers such that the strengths and weaknesses of self and others are recognized and mutually satisfying relationships are sustained through vagaries of distance and disagreement.

Development of instrumental independence occurs as the confidence and capacity to carry out most of life's activities by oneself is strengthened and as one becomes able to leave one place and go to another when it is worthwhile to do so.

These two vectors are complementary and change in one is limited without change in the other. Both gradually culminate in identification of significant interdependencies, and with gradual definition of one's limits for giving and for receiving in the various areas required.

CHAPTER 4

ESTABLISHING IDENTITY

$\text{\textasciitilde}$

At one level of generalization, all the developmental vectors could be classified under the general heading "identity formation." Clarification and stabilization of identity certainly involves the areas of competence, emotions, and autonomy, along with interpersonal relationships, purpose, and integrity. Indeed Erikson (1959) mentions or implies all these in a single article:

> It is important to understand [adolescent] intolerance as the necessary defense against a sense of identity diffusion, which is unavoidable at a time of life when the body changes its proportions radically, when genital maturity floods body and imagination with all manner of drives, when intimacy with the other sex approaches, . . . and when life lies before one with a variety of conflicting possibilities and choices. . . . It is difficult to be tolerant if deep

down you are not quite sure that you are a man (or a woman), that you will ever grow together again and be attractive, that you will be able to master your drives, that you really know who you are, that you know what you want to be, that you know what you look like to others, and that you will know how to make the right decisions without, once for all, committing yourself to the wrong friend, sexual partner, leader, career. . . . Psychologically speaking, a gradually accruing ego identity is the only safeguard against the *anarchy of drives* as well as the *autocracy of conscience.* . . . An increasing sense of identity, on the other hand, is experienced preconsciously as a sense of psychological well-being. Its most obvious concomitants are a feeling of being at home in one's own body, a sense of "knowing where one is going," and an inner assuredness of anticipated recognition from those who count. Such a sense of identity, however, is never gained nor maintained once and for all. Like a "good conscience," it is constantly lost and regained, although more lasting and economical methods of maintenance and restoration are evolved and fortified in late adolescence [pp. 83–91, 118].

Correlates of well-established identity found by others document its interaction with other, more particular dimensions of change. S. R. Heath (1959) discovered a group of "reasonable adventurers" at Princeton—men who had in common "integrative ego functioning." The distinguishing characteristics of these men were: (1) future orientation, (2) intrinsic interest or involvement in liberal arts subjects, (3) close friendships with peers, (4) self-objectification and a capacity to create lively challenges that have little to do with status seeking or security operations, (5) values and convictions based primarily on personal experiences, (6) tolerance for ambiguity, (7) wide-ranging curiosity, and (8) a lively but benign sense of humor. And D. Heath (1965), at Haverford, found that "stability of self-organization" was directly related to academic achievement, strength of motivation, productive imaginations, openness to disturbing information, and social interest.

One could, therefore, simply talk about "identity crises" and development of identity as the single major task for young adults. But that is no small umbrella; it covers a multitude of diverse events and activities. Such inclusiveness makes it difficult to use when concrete decisions must be made concerning curriculum, housing arrangements, student-faculty relationships, and other matters of educational policy and practice. And it is similarly difficult for individuals who must identify concrete actions and formulate specific plans to cope with problems and to serve their own development. So the other six vectors were carved out for more discrete treatment.

With identity thus broken down, what remains for this chapter on identity itself? The primary element remaining is that solid sense of self that assumes form as the developmental tasks for competence, emotions, and autonomy are undertaken with some success, and which, as it becomes more firm, provides a framework for interpersonal relationships, purposes, and integrity. It is "the inner capital accrued from all those experiences [Erikson, 1959, p. 89]"—it is the self, the person one feels oneself to be. It is that "fuller, richer establishment, compounded of bodily sensations, feelings, images of one's body, the sound of one's name, the continuity of one's memories, and an increasing number of social judgements delivered through the words and behavior of others [White, 1958, p. 332]."

Developing this inner feeling is like learning to drive. First, signals and signs must be learned and behaviors must be mastered. Despite intense concentration much goes unobserved and mistakes are made. Progress occurs in fits and starts, with much wandering from one side of the road to the other. But with time and practice change occurs. Driver and vehicle become acquainted. Peculiar requirements for starting and operating become understood, customary noises assure soundness and unusual ones prompt informed action. The ways of the road become familiar, the driver learns his own limits and those imposed by varied conditions. In time, snow, heavy traffic, and mechanical failures are met with ease and assurance. Driving becomes a pleasure, not a chore, and other things can be attended to while doing it.

The following series of comments communicate a sense of such change. On her college application one girl said:

> To me the most important thing in the world is understanding. I would like to have an understanding of myself, of other people, and of the whys and hows of this world.

She reports, after her first semester:

> The change has been a classic denial of all that is and the search for what I really am. I am looking for what I really believe in, to find my values, and realities.

Of the second semester, commenting on a course, she says:

The area of study was adolescence from which I gained a greater understanding of myself and those my age; from the discussion I was put more at ease concerning the sexual act, able to relate more realistically in the part it will play in my life, as well as gaining knowledge about the physical parts and functions and contraception; family and marriage; and femininity. I began a great deal of thinking about myself and my role in society.

The fifth semester seemed to be the most difficult, although it ends on a hopeful note. She says:

I was very depressed and unfeeling during the first part of the semester. I functioned "explicitly" but "implicitly" I wanted to leave school because I wasn't doing much work and couldn't find direction. This is the same as before—every other semester—but suddenly I was very tired of the same crap. I wondered idly if I should "lose the semester" just for the heck of it. I couldn't see returning to Goddard to spend another semester in this way. . . . I'm sure a paradox is seen. I struggle. Unsure. My high holy standards—of course unmeetable—are my bain. OK, they'll come down. Just slightly, but enough so that I can sometime meet them. I am tired of being told that I do well without being satisfied myself. I've passed by on other people's satisfaction. . . . I care about the community, I care about people, I care about classes, yet I am very tired of struggling with myself. Of course, there won't be an easy resolution, yet I think it can come.

The hopeful note was not misplaced, for by the end of the next semester some kind of substantial shift apparently has occurred:

This semester represented a new phase in my life. Actually, this "new phase" began at the end of the last semester and developed over the work term. The newness is a basic happiness and self-acceptance. I still have many problems but they are not so much turned inward.

By the end of her four years she can say:

As for doubts and dissatisfaction with myself—it is interesting that my general evaluations for the first and seventh semester were very similar. I was asking the same questions—who am I and why am I —and saying that I hadn't done as well as I could have. By my last semester, however, I was a bit more sophisticated and not so destructive in my questioning. When the answers aren't obvious, I don't stop functioning or accepting myself. I guess I never let my-

self get too "lost." I am still dissatisfied with myself but not in a way
to make my life miserable. I have learned to ease my impossibly
high standards and to find some measure of satisfaction with my
accomplishment. . . . It is impossible to know now all the ways
that I am a different person or how they occurred. It is enough to
say that Goddard has enabled me to live, change, and learn. The
friends, enemies, teachers, classes, community activities, work terms,
and pine forests have all helped me become what I am today.
Hooray.

For this girl, positive feelings about herself and her performance have not come easily; her struggles with herself made driving an
unsatisfying chore. At graduation dissatisfaction persists, but in a climate of greater confidence and higher self-regard so that on balance
the future can be approached with more of a bang than a whimper.
This confidence and optimism is a fruit of perceptible progress in other
vectors of development as well—of the development of competence
and autonomy, of freer interpersonal relationships and better management of emotions, of increased clarity and strength of purpose. But
binding and supporting all of these is her increased respect for and
acceptance of the kind of person she is and the kind she is becoming.

Two principal components of this increasing sense of self are
conceptions concerning body and appearance, and clarification of sexual identification. The surge of sexual impulses and the development
of mature sex organs, changing bodily contours, bigger muscles and
greater strength, combined with unavoidable comparisons in locker
rooms and residences, all focus attention on the body. Appearance becomes a matter for conscious concern and decision. Some, with diets,
exercises, and careful dress, aim to enhance strong points and to modify, compensate for, or at least disguise weak ones. Others, on principle, will not rest self-esteem on surface appearance. It should rest on
more fundamental attributes of person and behavior; by those they
should be judged. "If I can't get an interview in my open shirt and
sandals, then I wouldn't want to work for that company anyway." "If
a man won't hire me because I have a beard, then he's not the kind
of person I want to be associated with." "If an agency is more interested in how I look than in what I can do or how I perform, they can't
be much good." "If prospective donors or students' parents are put off
by our appearance, then we're better off without their money or their
children." Certainly such statements sometimes ring with bravado and

defensiveness, and sometimes basic feelings of unattractiveness and worthlessness underlie the rationale. But more often high levels of competence, sensitivity, and autonomy accompany such a stance. Probably, however, slavish styling to others' tastes and conscious adoption of styles outside the accustomed patterns both signify a still uncertain identity. For while sense of self is unclear, presentation of self remains an issue. With clarity and confidence, dress can comfortably reflect varied balancing of personal preferences, the desires of others, and situational expectations.

Issues of sexual identification intimately interact with concerns for bodily appearance and self-presentation. Discovering what it means to be a man or to be a woman, coming to terms with some of the behaviors and roles required, and developing a position consistent with one's own peculiar blend of masculinity and femininity is an absorbing and complex task. Can I be both halfback and painter, wrestler and poet? Can I be sufficiently submissive? Or dominant, strong, and tough? Interests must be reappraised, career plans reexamined. Perspective on fundamental feelings and responses—culturally defined as feminine or masculine though parts of both reside in each of us—must be achieved. Reviewing the research of masculinity and femininity, Newcomb and Feldman (1968) say:

> most of the differences in scale scores in this area show that male seniors have somewhat less conventionally masculine interests and attitudes than do male freshmen; and, although the results are not as consistent, in the majority of the studies female seniors have somewhat less feminine interests and attitudes than do female freshmen—again in the conventional sense [p. 37].

These findings support the notion that the stereotypes of masculinity and femininity that students bring to college, in terms of which they have viewed themselves, do yield to more complex views—that both men and women are able to recognize and accept more fully the blend most suitable to their particular interests and nature.

The following episode suggests the emotional load and impact of this area, both for the pranksters and the others. A boy is talking:

> About two weeks ago when those Northpoint men were up here and they had the scuffle, I was with Mary and we were just walking along by the library and about fourteen of them walked by us. She said, "Do you want to do something to frighten them a little bit," and

I said, "I suppose so." We changed clothes and I wore her dress
and she wore my slacks and shirt that I had on at the time and
then we went out to try to find them. We finally found them in
a dormitory lounge and we just walked in and sat down very calmly
right in the middle of them. They were there by themselves, just
standing around. They were very upset. And then an instructor
went by and he made a few comments and he asked me for a date
and all this, and I accepted, and they were very upset. They left
and just didn't know what to make out of it. Then we changed
again and after that a few people were making comments around
the community. Up until then I wouldn't have been able to do that.
I wouldn't have even thought of doing that because I would have
been so afraid of any criticism. Now their criticism didn't bother
me because to me it was just very innocent and I knew my motives
and it was just something to throw a shock into those people and
I didn't care what people around here would say because I knew
what my reasons were.

These comments reveal not only the students' awareness of, and
accurate assessment of, the shock value of such behavior, but the hint
of overmuch protesting also suggests lingering uncertainties for the reporter himself.

For some students problems of sexual identification are not easily resolved. As any college dean or faculty member who has known
many students closely will testify, and as evidenced by records from
college counseling services and by the studies of Kinsey (1953) and
others, neither homosexual experimentation nor homosexual relationships of varying intensity and longevity are rare. Such relationships occur much more frequently for men than for women. Often intimate
friendships involving sexual relationships will be sustained for some
time with both another man and a woman, and on occasion all three
can be close friends or part of a larger friendship group. The concurrent homosexual and heterosexual relationships may be more or less
explicitly recognized. I don't mean to imply that strain and concern
are absent. On the contrary. The situation is usually difficult for all.
But frequently there are tolerance, understanding, and attempts to help
the bisexual person work toward some dominant orientation. Many
such persons successfully progress toward consistent heterosexuality and
later marry without difficulty. The danger is premature assumption that
a homosexual affair signifies lasting homosexuality. Particularly where
relationships with the opposite sex are difficult and anxiety provoking,
such an experience and such an assumption may reduce still further

the frequency of heterosexual contact and the possibilities for finding satisfaction in such relationships. Thus the unwarranted assumption sets in motion events which eventually make it valid.

A study of change in Personal Stability and Integration, (Chickering, 1967), carried out by the Goddard College faculty, suggests the pattern that development of identity may take during the college years. According to the definition developed by the faculty, students high on this dimension knew the kind of person they wanted to be and had a sense of balance and perspective. They tended to see things whole and with a well-ordered set of values. They had sorted out what was important to them and were aware of their own strengths and weaknesses. They were relatively at ease about problems concerning academic work, future vocation, marriage, and family life. Not that such problems do not still exist, or that they necessarily have resolved them, but their level of anxiety and concern about such things is relatively low and their comfort and confidence in their present state with regard to such matters is relatively high. A faculty team used three questions as a basis for rating students' records each semester: (1) What is the student's level of reliability and responsibility on work program in relation to other responsibilities undertaken? (2) What level of personal stability and integration is reflected by students' comments in relation to self, or self-development? and (3) How comfortable is the student about the kind of person he is, or about the kind of person he was during the semester? How comfortable is he about his own past behavior?

Figure 4 gives the results from the pooled ratings of all 1964 graduates for each semester, for all three questions. The picture shows substantial and fairly regular change. It is interesting that the first semester ratings for this area are considerably lower than ratings for the other areas examined in the faculty studies. Thus observations that the first semester presents a constellation of upsetting problems, that considerable "culture shock" is experienced by the entering student, are supported by these data. It is also interesting that in addition to the sharp rise from the first to the second semester there is another acceleration in the seventh semester. This suggests that perhaps the transition from college to the adult world has already begun, that with the imminence of the Senior Study, and with graduation approaching, a step is taken toward a higher level of personal organization and integration.

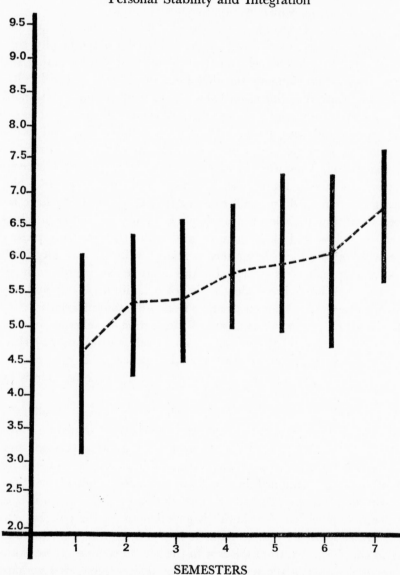

FIGURE 4

Personal Stability and Integration

SEMESTERS

Vertical lines indicate range of ratings within which 2/3 of the students fall. Horizontal line connects mean ratings for twenty students.

Difference in means for first and second semesters likely to occur less than ten times in one hundred on the basis of chance; between sixth and seventh semesters, about fifteen times in one hundred.

Two OPI (1963) scales, Schizoid Functioning (SF) and Lack of Anxiety (LA) seemed relevant to the development of identity and it was hypothesized that scores on the first would fall and scores on the second rise. The SF scale is designed to reflect feelings of isolation, loneliness, rejection, and hostility; also, identity confusion, daydreaming, disorientation, restlessness or loss of control, and obsessional or delusional processes. On the LA scale, low scorers are either neurotic or anxious, or else chronic complainers. The data for Goddard students and for students at eight colleges studied by the Center for the Study of Higher Education indicate that substantial change in the hypothesized direction occurred for both groups on the SF scale. These findings are consistent with Newcomb and Feldman's (1968) review of research which indicated that studies using the SF scale consistently found seniors scoring lower than freshmen, with almost all the differences statistically significant. Thus, they say, "seniors are less likely to have, or to admit having, attitudes that generally characterize socially alienated persons [p. 39]."

On the LA scale the change, while in the hypothesized direction, was less and reached statistical significance for only one group of Goddard students. Table 6 presents some of the items from these two scales for which response frequencies changed most.

Although no hypotheses were generated for them, four scales of the Stern Activities Index (1958) seem relevant to the development of identity: Reflectiveness, introspective preoccupation with private psychological, spiritual, esthetic, or metaphysical experience; Narcissism, preoccupation with self; Exhibitionism, self-display and attention seeking; Aggression, overt or covert hostility toward others. For 1964 and 1965 Goddard graduates, the test-retest findings for these scales show that on the first three change occurs in the expected direction for both groups. On the Aggression scale, scores are somewhat higher during the fourth semester, and then return to the level at entrance during the eighth semester. Thus these data also are congruent with a picture of increasing clarity of conceptions concerning self and an increasing sense of what one means to others and what one is perceived to be by them.

Topics of conversation and "worries," as they reflect dominant areas of concern at a given time, can also, through their changing frequencies, suggest increased ease and clarity for various particulars relevant to identity formation. For the items presented in Tables 7 and

Table 6

OPI Items Reflecting Substantial Change for Goddard

Scale, Item, and Direction of Response	Percent Responding		
	Entrance	Eighth Semester	Differ- ence
Schizoid Functioning			
Often I wonder who I really am or what I should really be like. (T)	77	40	−37
My way of doing things is apt to be misunderstood by others. (T)	78	43	−35
I have little or no idea what I will be like a few years from now. (T)	69	40	−29
I sometimes wake up to find myself thinking about some impractical or ir- relevant problem. (T)	66	40	−26
I often find myself listen- ing without hearing. (T)	78	52	−26
I often count things that are not important. (T)	58	33	−25
I usually feel that I am drifting along in life with no particular role to play. (T)	43	19	−24
Sometimes an unimpor- tant thought will run through my mind and bother me for days. (T)	69	50	−19
I have had bad periods of days, weeks, or months when I couldn't take care of things because I couldn't "get going." (T)	66	52	−14

I often get the feeling that I am not part of the group I associate with

Table 6—Cont.

OPI Items Reflecting Substantial Change for Goddard

Scale, Item, and Direction of Response	Percent Responding		
	Entrance	Eighth Semester	Difference
and that I could separate from it with little discomfort or hardship. (T)	55	43	−12
Lack of Anxiety			
I frequently find myself worrying about something. (F)	33	52	19
I am not unusually self-conscious. (T)	40	59	19
I have sometimes felt that difficulties were piling up so high that I could not overcome them. (F)	33	45	12
Life is a strain for me much of the time. (F)	73	77	4

8, decreasing frequencies from first to eighth semester were predicted. Of the eighteen items in both tables fifteen change in the hypothesized direction. On seven, the first five "worries" and the first two topics, change was substantial. Six of these—"Being depressed," "Not knowing where you stand on social or political issues," "Not getting enough fun out of life," "Not being good looking," "Not knowing what to think of yourself," and "Your psychological problems"—are quite nonspecific and reflect a general sense of greater self-esteem and comfort. The different patterns for "Sex" as a topic of conversation and "Sexual Problems" as a worry are thought provoking. The patterns are strikingly similar during the first three years, both reflecting a sharp drop after the first year and much smaller decrements for the third. But then worry about sexual problems doubles in frequency for the fourth year, even though frequency of conversations drops again. What's going on? Do "sexual problems" for the senior come up again because questions of marriage and engagement are more frequently involved? Are "conversations" then only with the prospective mate or a close friend rather than more frequent general bull sessions? Or are worries more frequently mentioned because resolutions suitable for the college scene need reexamining with impending graduation and new conditions for living, but kept more private than in earlier years? We cannot tell. But both the practical and theoretical questions raised justify further investigation.

Table 7

GODDARD COLLEGE
CHANGING FREQUENCIES OF TOPICS OF CONVERSATION

| | Percent Responding | | | |
| | 2nd | 4th | 6th | 8th |
Item	Sem.	Sem.	Sem.	Sem.
Your psychological problems	26	13	5	2
Sex	23	15	14	7
Philosophy	12	12	12	15
Personal Values	36	25	27	31
Problems of society	25	20	16	20
Other students' psychological problems	12	8	21	10

Erikson (1962) observes that development of identity reaches a turning point

> in that period of the life cycle when each youth must forge for himself some central perspective and direction, some working unity, out of the effective remnants of his childhood and the hopes of his anticipated adulthood; he must detect some meaningful resemblance between what he has come to see in himself and what his sharpened awareness tells him others judge and expect him to be [p. 14].

What creates this turning point and enables it to be used productively? Three basic conditions appear to foster the development of identity: relative freedom from anxiety and pressure, varied direct experience and roles, and meaningful achievement (Erikson, 1950; Sanford, 1966). We are familiar with the anxiety and pressures that characterize many college environments and Barger (1963) has charted their ebb and flow. We see, in response to the competitive

Table 8

GODDARD COLLEGE
CHANGING FREQUENCIES FOR "WORRIES"

Item	Percent Responding			
	2nd Sem.	4th Sem.	6th Sem.	8th Sem.
Being depressed	61	45	25	35
Not knowing where you stand on social or political issues	23	18	16	12
Not getting enough fun out of life	23	12	5	12
Not being good looking	19	8	7	7
Not knowing what to think about yourself	34	31	25	26
Eating too much	26	30	27	20
Not being an officer on campus	4	2	0	0
Concern over your family's social standing because of other students' snobbishness	4	2	0	0
Lack of rules at college	10	7	7	7
Religious problems	10	10	7	7
Sexual problems	26	18	16	31
Lack of privacy	32	38	33	39

pressures, premature settling on one style of life, a single frame of reference, as the focal point for self-organization and self-esteem, as the core of one's being. We see the grinds, the jocks, the party boys, the hippies, the activists—and depending upon our values and perspective, we are dismayed or delighted. And the emphasis on vocational and professional training at many institutions legitimizes another kind of premature fixation which may hamper the development of identity. Because when training for a particular role takes precedence over diverse experiences in varied settings, the self-testing through which competencies and satisfactions are clarified cannot occur. Meaningful achievement can counterbalance totalistic adoption of a particular role. But meaningfulness is difficult to determine. Parsons (1965) observes:

Ours is a society in which the nature of its values cannot have a single clear-cut societal goal which can be dramatically symbolized. The individual is relegated to contributions which are relatively specialized, and it is not always easy to see their bearing on the larger whole. Furthermore, the general erosion of traditional culture and symbols, which is inseparable from a scientific age, makes inadequate many of the old formulae once used to give meaning and legitimation to our values and achievements [p. 120].

Unfortunately, students testify to the meaninglessness of much college work. The recent conference on student stress which impelled the notion of relevance onto the educational scene is only one of many pieces of evidence (Shoben, 1966). The basic point is that in twentieth-century American society, in contrast to earlier times and more homogeneous cultures, identity is no longer simply "given." No longer do young persons experience a unified and internally consistent framework of beliefs, behavior, and adult roles that can be assimilated almost automatically through the pores, that has been built in since early childhood. Now, conflicting values, diverse behaviors, and mutually exclusive models combine to offer multiple alternatives from which a particular identity must be constructed, and then reconstructed again in the light of new opportunities or new frustrations. Once the principal task of education was "socialization" and the problem of individuals was to learn the attitudes, actions, and skills necessary for a satisfying and productive fit with "society." The symphony had a clearly stated theme and rhythm. The traditional instruments, their numbers and positions were settled. To contribute, one had merely to choose one of the standard instruments, learn to play it, and practice the part. In twentieth-century society, where change is the only sure thing, not socialization but identity formation becomes the central and continuing task of education. And as Keniston (1965) observes, "The more incompatible the components from which the sense of identity must be built and the more uncertain the future for which one attempts to achieve identity, the more difficult the task becomes [p. 211]." Institutions of higher education, soon to be encountered by most young adults, can help, if they will.

CHAPTER 5

FREEING INTERPERSONAL RELATIONSHIPS

*F*reeing of interpersonal re-
lationships is a phrase used by White (1958) to describe one of his
four major "growth trends" for young adults. It is not easy to see persons as they are, to respond to them as individuals instead of as representatives of some stereotype, or of some other individual we have
known in the past. Nor is it easy to respond with warm, open, and
respectful friendliness, instead of with anxiety, defensiveness, or arti-
ficiality. Describing this trend of change, White says:

> Social interaction becomes more free not only from neurotic trends
> but also from the impulsive inconsiderateness and egocentricity of
> youth. The person learns not to be so immersed in his own be-
> havior, so intent on the impression he is making or the point he is

93

trying to put across, that he fails to perceive the people around him. He becomes increasingly able to interact, responding in a way that is related to their responses. As he moves in this direction he develops a greater range and flexibility of responses. . . . The person moves in the direction of increased capacity to live in real relationship with people immediately around him [p. 343].

Such growth involves two discriminable aspects: (1) increased tolerance and respect for those of different backgrounds, habits, values, and appearance, and (2) a shift in the quality of relationships with intimates and close friends. By increased tolerance we mean not simply an improved capacity for teeth gritting and tongue biting in the face of those who differ, nor the development of callouses and screening devices that shield us from, or obscure, the values and behaviors of others that might threaten our own sheltered and carefully protected structure. Instead we refer to an increasing openness and acceptance of diversity, which allows our own sensitivities to expand and which increases the range of alternatives for satisfying exchanges and for close and lasting friendships.

The shift in relationships with close friends is away from dependence toward an interdependence that creates a larger space around each person and makes possible more wide-ranging freedom of movement and behavior. It is characterized by greater trust and greater stability. When this change has occurred, close feelings persist despite sharp disagreements. They are quickly resumed at the same level after periods of long separation or noncommunication.

Increased Tolerance

The following comments put some flesh on the bony abstractions. One girl said:

Through my classes—first by fighting, then by beginning to accept— I began to see that people are truly different from me. Especially classes like Rural Economic Development and Community Lab and my senior study [Poverty in Vermont] have given me an understanding of what people are like who live differently from me.

And from a different starting point, a Vermont girl said:

In *Individual and Society,* through the study of more fundamentally simple cultures than our own, I feel that I have become better able to see our society much more objectively. The reasons behind so many of our social situations have become clearer and it is somewhat easier to see how we must appear in the eyes of other nations.

Murphy (1960), reporting her study of Sarah Lawrence girls, says:

> many students are aware of changes in their relationships with others, both with adults and with members of both sexes of their own age. Tolerance of parents and other adults with different attitudes and emphases in their approach to life increases. . . . The family-centered, ethno-centric, and in other ways narrow approach to people gets loosened up in many instances through the interaction of college work with wide experiences so that a number of students speak of a greater appreciation of people from other social classes, other religious groups, other racial groups, people with values different from their own. They also speak of greater appreciation of the problems, difficulties, and limitations of the lives of others [pp. 101, 102].

There is another kind of tolerance not often mentioned. That is tolerance for persons who exhibit unusual idiosyncrasies or who may be suffering from transient or more lasting emotional disturbance. Szasz (1967) has called attention to the recent history of rejection of the mentally ill and to the growth of the "myth of mental illness." Whether or not one agrees with Szasz, it is a useful thing for students to increase their understanding and perspective concerning deviant persons. The following exchange between an instructor and student is illustrative:

> GIRL: I don't know if the administration knows about her or why they allow her to stay here if she is seriously disturbed. But she is not functioning too well from what I observe.
>
> INSTRUCTOR: What do you observe?
>
> GIRL: Well, I have her in one of my classes. She will come and maybe for an hour in the beginning [of a three-hour class] she will sit and watch and if she says something it takes her about five minutes to get up a sentence and her voice is very weak. Most of the time people can't hear her anyway. At least she tries. She gets upset very easily. If there is any kind of disturbance or discussion with tension involved in it within the class, she will get up and leave, sometimes she'll run out of class and once the instructor had to go out and see what was wrong. And I was noticing her around the community and she very often walks around and, you know, the look on her face is as though she was cracking up, right then and there. Or sitting in the dining hall, sitting staring into

space. Like she sat with us at breakfast one morning and she just
sat for about two minutes with the salt shaker in her hand, just
holding it, looking at just nothing. I got really scared. You know,
I mean, a person like that I don't know, what good is it doing her
to be here?

INSTRUCTOR: Are you afraid she would do something to you?

GIRL: No, not me. I just wonder what is wrong. Does she
have some kind of mental condition? And I'm, well, torn between
two things. I feel as though I should help her in some way. I feel
it is very hard to get through to her and then also I feel a burden.
I don't know why the administration has allowed her to stay here
when she is a burden, I think, to the community in that people
have to watch over her you know. I'm first torn between feeling
responsibility to help her and at the same time feeling that it isn't—
not really wanting to do it and I don't.

INSTRUCTOR: You don't want to? Why?

GIRL: I just don't want to take the time.

INSTRUCTOR: That's a good reason. One of the best I guess—
I think one reason she has continued here is that it is hard to think
of a better place for her to be. And if you can think of a better
place then it is hard to help her move into that place in a way that
is constructive for her. I think you are right in observing that she
is having difficulty functioning here and that she has things to deal
with that make it difficult for her to operate. I think, first, the
general feeling is that from her point of view, there is about as much
potential for her own development here as there is anywhere else
and that the college should enable her continued presence long
enough so that she has substantial opportunities to test the possibilities
for her that reside here. Second, the view would be that her con-
tinuation should be enabled as long as there really isn't a drastic
drain on the community, as long as her presence doesn't severely
hamper other students. I agree that it is, well, a burden in the
sense that it is a kind of presence that other people would rather
not have to deal with or respond to, just as other kinds of persons
are a burden in quite a different way. Persons who may be much
more disruptive, for example. At the same time, her presence is a
kind of education for other people, and I would encourage most
anyone to try to get to know her.

GIRL: You would, is that what you said?

INSTRUCTOR: Yes. Because I think she is a very good and
interesting person to know and because this is a kind of person you
don't run into very often and is therefore worthwhile knowing.
Further, I think the more persons she has friendly relationships with
the better for her. At the same time I think your feelings of ambiva-
lence are to some extent justified, and that it is accurate to recognize
that when you involve yourself with a person who has problems

some sacrifice may result. Just as when you make friends with someone who is broke. If she doesn't have any money and you do, then
that may create certain kinds of pressures on you, so you are
entering a certain kind of relationship that has some forces attached
to it. You said you were scared. I don't know if you really meant
scared, but I don't think there is any danger of her hurting anybody.

GIRL: No, I don't think that there is that. I was afraid for
her.

The point is that people differ, not only with respect to religious, racial, ethnic, national, and social class backgrounds, but also in
many other more individualistic ways. The more a student can gain
perspective concerning idiosyncratic deviancies, as well as more widely
shared differences resulting from more general conditions, the more
freely will she be able to encounter others, and the wider the range of
satisfying relationships open to her.

The general shift toward increasing tolerance and understanding appears to be quite widespread during the high school and college
years. A study of traits admired in people illustrates one aspect of this
shift. On a list of admired characteristics, boys and girls at grade eight
ranked broadmindedness last after brave, reliable, quick, cooperative,
and funny, but college seniors ranked broadmindedness first (Pressey
and Robinson, 1944). Research at Vassar (Webster, Freedman, and
Heist, 1962) found that seniors, in comparison with freshmen, were
more flexible and impunitive. And study of items selected to reflect
increased impunitiveness found changes in the expected direction for
both male and female students at eight colleges studied by the Center
for Research and Development in Higher Education. The changes in
frequency of response to some of these items are presented in Table
9 along with combined figures for the 1964 and 1965 graduates of
Goddard College. Even Jacob (1957), in the report that provided
much impetus for research concerning student change in college,
found that, "Social harmony with an *easy tolerance of diversity* per-
vades the student environment [p. 2]."

There seems to be little doubt that tolerance does increase
among college students. Plant's (1958) research provides perspective,
however, because he found similar change among students who did
not attend college. On test-retest data for students who were admitted
to San Jose State College, and for their equally qualified peers who
were not admitted because of space limitations, he found increasing

Table 9

RESPONSE PERCENTAGES FOR ITEMS
INCREASED IMPUNITIVENESS

Item and Direction of Response		*Entrance*	*Eighth Semester*	*Difference*
A large number of people are guilty of bad sexual conduct. (F)	Goddard	45	85	40
	Eight Colleges	31	48	17
Most of our social problems could be solved if we could somehow get rid of the un-moral, crooked, and feeble-minded people. (F)	Goddard	78	98	20
	Eight Colleges	87	96	7
The surest way to a peaceful world is to improve people's morals. (F)	Goddard	66	78	12
	Eight Colleges	62	75	13
What youth needs most is strict discipline, rugged determination, and the will to work and fight for family and country. (F)	Goddard	78	88	10
	Eight Colleges	41	66	25
Young people sometimes get rebellious ideas, but as they grow up they ought to get over them and settle down. (F)	Goddard	71	77	6
	Eight Colleges	62	71	9

liberalism and decreasing dogmatism and ethnocentrism. Plant did find that amount of change increased with length of college attendance, so that students who completed four years changed more than those completing only two, and that students completing two years changed more than their peers who did not attend at all. So although such changes apparently do occur among all young persons, college attendance seems to amplify or accelerate them.

In addition to increased tolerance, increased ease in relationships with peers and adults also develops. And for the few students who experience difficulty in this area, who have long felt themselves left out, isolated, friendless, change of this kind is important. The following excerpts communicate, if only by their succinct understatement, some sense of what it meant to one girl. They also suggest the interrelationship between increasing tolerance and increasing ease. At the end of her first semester she said:

> Socially I have made my greatest change. From a sullen taciturn recluse I've managed to become more friendly and talkative and to enjoy doing it. There is a fairly good-sized group on this campus that suits my temperament beautifully and for the first time in about ten years, I'm enjoying company of my own kind. This I consider to be quite valuable. . . . Besides this I learned a considerable bit about the peoples of the world and in such a way that, while recognizing their differences, I felt an underlying unity to the world, a different perspective which makes me think a bit kinder of it than before.

This increased sense of her own potentialities and the concurrent release of energy are illustrated by comments about her second and third semesters:

> Socially I feel settled down to a point where I can actually enjoy being with people (albeit I have spent more time working than before). . . . I feel considerably better adjusted to the college situation than I had before. I can now charge ahead and work without wasting overmuch time on the fine Goddard art of self-imposed misery.

In the fourth semester she was, for the first time, able to develop a limited but fruitful relationship with her faculty counselor, able to think about herself in more long-range terms, and able to value more highly her own development. She reports:

> I found the very few counseling sessions I had very valuable. I am beginning to take an interest in my goals after graduation. This gives me a feeling of purpose I have never really had before. The work I do is more planned and has more meaning. I also intend to work on some of my weak points which never "mattered" before.

The next comments, in a touching way, reveal her desire to be a contributing member of the community, concurrent with an inability to become more intensively involved. She says:

> Generally, I don't find it necessary to rely on the communtiy as a source of entertainment, much less expression. Close friendships are one thing, the community quite another. One small service that I did tend to this semester was satisfying, the daily tending of the flags.

Goddard College flies both a United States and a United Nations flag. This solitary act at the opening and closing of each day may have alleviated momentarily the experiences of the intervening hours, during which the distance from herself to both the local and world communities seemed far.

Another student reflects the problems encountered and the kinds of development that more typically occur. In the first semester of her third year, she comments:

> I learned something about myself when working in a small independent group for Alan's class. I found that I pushed other members to do the work—not always being pleasant. I guess I've found out a great deal about how people operate. I've seen how my standards get in the way of seeing another person's problems and needs. I know again that I can't shape people to be the way I should like to see them. I've allowed myself to get quite close to a few individuals and have begun to sort out what it means to be a friend and a girl friend.

A year later she says:

> I find that all I can do is be friendly, understanding, and encouraging. I can't solve other people's problems for them. I have become aware of the power in the three aforementioned traits in making other people's living just a little easier.

Another third-year girl says:

> Each semester I discover new people at Goddard and I have finally really admitted to myself how often one ignores or dislikes another person merely to protect oneself. Certainly I can get along with a great variety of people, and I think I am becoming increasingly tolerant of others. Not merely putting up with them, but accepting them for what they are, and looking at them in a far less destructive way than in the past.

Sanford (1966) mentions the self-doubts of the entering student with regard to interpersonal relationships, doubts which include relationships with members both of the same sex and of the opposite sex. The comments of the different students quoted above reflect those doubts and illustrate the gains that can occur.

Some empirical evidence is also available. In the context of the Goddard Experiment in College Curriculum Organization (Beecher et al., 1966) it was hypothesized that change in this area would be reflected by decreasing scores on the Social Introversion scale of the OPI. The findings for two groups of Goddard graduates as well as for students at the eight colleges studied by the Center for the Study of Higher Education reveal no substantial change. On the Social Introversion scale "high scorers withdraw from social contacts and responsibilities. They display little interest in people or in being with them. The social extroverts (low scorers), on the other hand, seek social contacts and gain satisfaction from them [OPI, 1964, p. 6]." At first it seemed surprising that scores did not drop with increased freedom in interpersonal relationships. Elsewhere, however, it is indicated that this measure "reflects more a style of relating to people than an expression of avoidance of people [OPI, 1964, p. 20]" and that the measure was "one of two introversion-extroversion dimensions" taken from earlier work by others. Thus it may be that increased ease in personal relationships occurs without change in "style of relating," or without movement toward increased extroversion. Table 10, which presents some items where shifts occur for Goddard students, illustrates this point.

For these same students, the scores on the Affiliation and Dominance scales of the Stern Activities Index (Stern, 1958) dropped. The Affiliation scale reflects close, friendly, reciprocal associations with others, but most of the items concern participation in group activities: going to the beach with a crowd, belonging to a social club, leading an active social life, going to parties where one is to mix with the whole crowd, going on vacation to a place where there are lots of people. Thus this measure reflects what many persons would call extroversion. The Dominance scale reflects assertive or manipulative control over others; persuading a group to do something my way, directing other people's work, influencing or controlling the action of others.

As the earlier comments from students suggest, freeing of interpersonal relationships does involve a diminished need to dominate, to override others with one's own ideas, to coerce or manipulate others

Table 10

SOCIAL INTROVERSION
OPI ITEMS FOR GODDARD

Item and Direction of Response	Entrance	Gradua-tion	Differ-ence
I usually enjoy parties. (F)	14	43	29
I generally attend the meetings of school or college organizations. (F)	40	62	22
I prefer social functions to which only a small group of intimate friends are invited. (T)	71	78	7
I am active on the committees of school organizations. (F)	62	69	7

to become something alien to themselves. And as interpersonal relationships become easier the need to participate in group activities may well decline in favor of spending more time with a few good friends. High Affiliation or low Social Introversion scores, on the other hand, may be associated with a period during which interpersonal relationships are not secure and when the group, therefore, provides the major context for interpersonal contact. Indeed, the relatively greater importance of the group during early adolescence is consonant with the proposition that during later adolescence and early adulthood, increased maturity of interpersonal relationships involves increased "introversion," at least as that tendency is reflected by less need to be a "joiner" and by less need for association with more than a few close friends.

"Worries" are also relevant to this aspect of change and it was hypothesized that those listed in Table 11 would be mentioned less frequently as the four years progressed. The small but consistent changes suggest that the hypotheses are supported.

These varied data concerning relationships with peers and "worries" are consistent with findings from the *Fundamental Interpersonal Relations Orientations* instrument used in research at Harvard (King, 1967). This test deals with interpersonal needs for "inclusion, affection, and control," each of which has two aspects, "expressed" and "wanted." Thus "expressed affection" is a need to give love and

Table 11

Changing Frequencies for "Worries"

Item	2nd Sem.	4th Sem.	6th Sem.	8th Sem.
	Percent Responding			
Conflict with roommate	25	23	23	15
Your relation to a friend at college	48	46	41	43
Disagreement between you and other students on social or political issues	15	18	14	10
Not being popular on campus	10	10	9	5
Difficult human relationships with a friend	40	31	45	39
Loneliness	47	38	48	48

affection to others, "wanted affection" the need to receive it. From freshman to senior year scores increased at a "high level of statistical significance [p. 22]."

Increased ease in relationships with adults also develops. As one girl reports during her third year:

> Professors unknown to me before were introduced as people, not as faculty members, and this has helped me to see that they too may have shortcomings. I have become acquainted with people who work at the college. Thus, I have been able to widen my world from that of "students only" to people in general, working, making a living, and finding meaning in their existence.

For other students, relationships with adults are more loaded, and therefore meaningful contact can have added significance. One student, for example, said:

> I also have a tendency often to, especially with adults or teachers, to look for cues for my behavior from them and so I'm ultrasensitive to anything they might say. Instead of criticism of my ideas I often take it as criticism of myself and so I'm very much afraid to say things because of this sort of fear. Where with B. P. [an instructor] I feel very much as though he accepts anything I say.

And that if he would criticize it I know that it's just my ideas and that I don't have to feel that he's threatening my self at all. I know I should be able to do this with others. I know it intellectually, but to do it is another thing. But I think the fact that I am aware of it more means that I'll be able to consciously work on it.

Of course, ease in relationships with adults not only allows academic learning to proceed more fruitfully and efficiently; it also fosters emotional independence from parents and more flexible relationships with authority. Further, through closer association with respected persons working at things that might become the focus of one's own future endeavors, the development of identity and purpose is assisted.

Shift in Intimacy

Erikson (1950) says:

What I have in mind is that late adolescent need for a kind of fusion with the essence of other people. The youth who is not sure of his identity shies away from interpersonal intimacy; but the surer he becomes of himself, the more he seeks it in the forms of friendship, combat, leadership, love, and inspiration [p. 114].

Such fusion is sought with persons of the same sex as well as with those of the opposite sex. External manifestations may not be so obvious as for heterosexual couples where overt physical expression is more culturally acceptable, and where "being in touch" as continually as possible seems to be required. In some cases it is almost as though the reality of one's own existence was in question, as though the sense of that reality diminished as one was "out of touch." Yet, though the tactual component may be less significant in relationships between intimates of the same sex, the level of symbiosis is often similar. Time schedules are tightly interlocked so that each knows where the other is, what is being done, and what the situation will be in the immediate future. Schedules are arranged to permit maximum association. Goods are shared to foster joint welfare. Assistance is freely given and loyalty is high.

Yet the time perspective usually is quite short. Plans are tight for the next twelve to twenty-four hours, perhaps, but beyond that commitments are often left indefinite unless the end of the semester or other considerations make the question unavoidable. It is as though there was tacit recognition that one or the other member might, on short notice, wish to "move out," to widen the scope of his own free movement, to loosen the ties that bind.

Physical expression of feelings accompanies intimate heterosexual relationships, but variation in behavior is great. Some couples hold hands and kiss, and manage that limit outside the context of engagement and marriage without great difficulty. For most, kisses and caresses sufficiently complement mutual exploration of self and the other, implemented through continual conversation and closely shared experiences. For a few, close relationships must be accompanied by sexual intercourse. But usually such physical expression is limited to serious relationships where long-term commitment is assumed. The point is that while identity is only tentatively established, intimate relationships primarily serve self-discovery and self-definition. Physical intimacies and sexual relationships are one domain for further exploration and self-definition—but they are only a part of the larger tasks and are secondary to it. Few are promiscuous, be they men or women, and for those that are development of identity and freeing of interpersonal relationships seem stalled.

During the later college years, this pattern shifts. Although the interpersonal ties are stronger—again with persons of both sexes—they are considerably loosened and less binding. Couples don't have to walk with arms around each other or even hold hands. Public necking— that vehicle for personal declaration of attractiveness and likeability, and mutually supportive commitments and assurances—is no longer required. Physical intimacy plays its important part. But again, for most students, the context is one of respect, commitment, and love. Sexual intercourse in the absence of such feelings is infrequent. Freedman's (1967) cogent observations are to the point:

> Most educated women are not inclined to surrender the equality of station and outlook they have won. And it is this sense of equality that serves, among women, as a very strong barrier to sex relations in the absence of love. The chances are that a woman who gives of herself in such a relationship has a rather low opinion of herself. She may feel inferior because she is of lower class status than the man; she may feel that she has nothing to give a man of higher social station except her body [p. 120].

At this stage vacations can be spent apart and the relationships sustained. Differences of opinion can develop and be maintained without upsetting the relationship or challenging the integrity of the partner.

These shifts in the character of intimate relationships probably have major importance for marital success, and for establishing productive working relationships and friendships during adulthood. Marriage is risky when relationships involve high dependency, when they are primarily serving self-exploration and self-definition, when identity, autonomy, and purposes are still very loosely established. For when further development and stabilization occur in one or more of these areas, significant incompatibilities may emerge which create lasting strain or discomfort. On the other hand, chances for a rich and rewarding marriage should be considerably improved after this shift in intimacy has occurred, and when marriage is between two autonomous persons, whose sense of who they are and what they want to become is sharper, whose interests have become more stabilized, and whose conceptions concerning future life-style and vocation have become more clear and strong.

CHAPTER 6

DEVELOPING
PURPOSE

𝄞𝄢𝄞𝄢𝄞𝄢𝄞𝄢𝄞𝄢𝄞𝄢𝄞𝄢𝄞𝄢𝄞𝄢𝄞𝄢𝄞𝄢𝄞𝄢

Lewis Carroll observed that no good fish goes anywhere without a porpoise, and many personality theorists agree. Adler emphasized the role of fictional goals (Ansbacher and Ansbacher, 1956). Erikson (1964)' says, "Purpose, then, is the courage to envisage and pursue valued goals uninhibited by the defeat of infantile fantasies, by guilt, and by the foiling fear of punishment [p. 122]." Allport (1961) asserts, "The core of the identity problem for the adolescent is the selection of an occupation or other life goal. The future, he knows, must follow a *plan,* and in this respect his sense of selfhood takes on a dimension entirely lacking in childhood . . . long range purposes and distant goals add a new dimension to the sense of selfhood [p. 126]." And later (p. 391) he observes that it is the pursuit of major goals that "configurates a life."

Miller, Galanter, and Pribram (1960) have elaborated in detail how plans and purposes guide behavior. They point out that knowledge, action, and evaluation are essentially connected; knowledge guides action and action is rooted in evaluation, for without comparative values deliberate action is pointless. They ask, "Does a plan supply the pattern for that essential connection of knowledge, evaluation, and action [p. 61]?" The rest of their book answers yes. Murphy (1960) found this dynamic at Sarah Lawrence College. She says:

> Some students express surprise and pleasure at their new ability to work thoroughly and intensively in an area that seems important to their purposes and for the sake of greater thoroughness at the points where thoroughness is most needed, and to deal with other materials more casually. This flexibility is most satisfying where it occurs in connection with increasing clarity about one's goals, plans, vocational aims, interests, and educational purposes. Some students reflect a change from thinking about educational values in absolutistic terms to a way of thinking which is more relevant to the meaning of each piece of work in terms of their own purposes [p. 100].

Development of purpose requires formulating plans for action and a set of priorities that integrate three major elements: (1) avocational and recreational interests, (2) pursuit of vocation, and (3) life-style issues including concerns for marriage and family. Increasing integration gives shape to experience, meaning to existence, and releases energy for coordinated action.

Avocational and Recreational Interests

Stabilization and deepening of interests probably results from three concurrent forces. First, there is increased emphasis on what Kuhlen (1952) terms "sex-social interests." He reports that increased interest in these areas is accompanied by decreased participation in other activities that lack sex-social meanings [p. 212]. This trend, which begins in high school or even earlier, reaches full force during college. To have a date is not to do something else. Going steady means less time for activities formerly of interest; stamp collecting may just have to go. Even with maximum good will, venturesomeness, flexibility, and capacity for self-development, whenever two persons spend substantial time together some interests of each will receive less attention. Thus, pursuing one of the opposite sex means not pursuing other interests. True, new interests may emerge as a result of the friendship, but because both must find some satisfaction from them the net effect is reduced diversity. And as the relationship persists there is increased stability of those interests which both share and find most satisfying.

Clarification of vocational plans and aspirations exerts a second force for stability. When the choice has real meaning increased time is spent on study and other exploratory or preparatory activities. As commitment increases role considerations begin to be felt. Somehow those activities that were so enjoyable when one was a young and carefree college student are not appealing now that graduation is near and one is practically a young business executive or professional, or wife and mother. Student memberships in professional associations and student attendance at professional meetings attest to this shifting identification.

Indeed it is not surprising that students with the most diverse, rich, and meaningful interests often seem to have difficulty settling on future plans, seem to have difficulty developing clear purposes that provide motive powers. For it is difficult to recognize, and more difficult to accept, that every affirmation is 90 per cent renunciation, that every choice to do one thing is a choice not to do ten others. It is hard to give up becoming an expert skier, an accomplished musician, and a successful entrepreneur, in order to pursue a profession. It is hard to give up reading contemporary literature, dabbling with mobiles, lying in the sun, building with wood, gambling. All interests provide satisfaction and stimulation; who wants to surrender them for the abstract, hazy, and unexperienced rewards that may reside down some vocational path. Small wonder many secure, able, and creative students put off such decisions and spend prodigious ingenuity and energy keeping as many balls in the air as possible.

Vocational Plans and Aspirations

For boys, development of purpose primarily involves clarification of vocational plans and aspirations. For girls, the importance of future vocational plans is reduced by impending marriage or engagement, or is complicated by ambiguity and uncertainty in that area. For both boys and girls, however, the presence or absence of vocational goals or clear plans for the future appears to influence how time is spent and what is gained from college.

Excerpts from the record of a student called Alan illustrate

relationships among personal interests and background, developing vocational plans and aspirations, and college study. On his admission
application, Alan indicated that his chief interests lay in the out-of-
doors, in forestry, wild life management, hunting, boating. His first
year courses were Individual and Society, Modern Literature, Contemporary Africa, Small Community Life, and two semesters of Visual
Arts.

During his second year, courses were Contemporary America,
Introductory Psychology, Man and Nature, Literature of Social Relations, Field Botany, and Water. Reviewing this year, he says:

> My studies proved to be beneficial in that I furthered my in-
> tellectual growth in subject matter and also in discovering my pri-
> mary field of interest. The relationship between my courses and this
> interest correlated well, which enabled me to acquire an enthusiasm
> for my work that I have never experienced quite as fully. I always
> possessed an interest in the field of conservation and this semester
> offered me a strong indication that I should continue with it. I
> sensed a definite level of achievement with my work.

Toward the end of that year he applied for admission to the
Senior Division at Goddard College and wrote, in part, as follows:

> My experience at Goddard in the junior division has been
> somewhat rewarding. I say "somewhat" not in a derogatory sense,
> but rather in the sense that the task I have undertaken is not yet
> complete.
> I began these past two years not knowing exactly in what
> direction I was heading, but I knew that one of my primary aims
> in coming to this college was to find out where my real interest
> lay. I undertook an investigation of a variety of subjects, which I
> feel has proved to be beneficial, in that it has not only broadened
> my experience, but has also enabled me to grasp and develop a
> partially hidden interest and ability.
> Thus, in the last year or year and one-half, I have concen-
> trated my efforts in the field of conservation; specifically, conser-
> vation of forests, wildlife, and water. I consider these three re-
> sources to be interrelated and of equal importance. There have been
> examples of overwhelming mismanagement of natural resources in
> the past. Problems of resource management continue to be of para-
> mount importance. These resources certainly supply the vital means
> for outdoor recreation. As the population grew, natural resources
> experienced great changes in demand. They are essential for the
> survival of mankind, and play an important part in the economy of

this nation and the world. These are some reasons why the subject is an important one, and it is important to me because I feel that I may be useful by obtaining an increased knowledge in the field of conservation so that I may be able and better qualified to help improve the conditions that the lack of understanding in this field has caused.

To continue my study in the senior division will be of the utmost importance to me, for I wish to expand upon the basic knowledge of conservation that I have now. I will be using such resource aids as the following in my work: The County Forester and other forest and state personnel, Hawk's Hill Demonstration Woodlot in East Barnard, Vermont, the Soil Conservation Service, the Fish and Game Department, and the Water Resources Board. Most likely I will incorporate the use of certain areas on Goddard property for my study also. I expect that much of my study will be on an independent basis, but I also expect to engage in some group studies. To a certain extent, this will depend on the selection of group studies offered. Of course, the majority of my work will deal with the sciences, however, I will not limit myself to that. I think that it will be necessary for me to diversify my efforts somewhat, devoting a portion of my time to other areas.

Alan was admitted to the Senior Division and during the third year studied Economics of Labor, Game Management, World of Animals, Studies in Literature, Soils and Resource Planning, and Ecology. Of this work he says:

I feel that my accomplishments academically were good, and that I worked harder, and longer, and more independently than I have previously. In dealing with the field of conservation I find these studies eminently important for understanding, or for working in the field. I hope to learn more as my work in conservation progresses.

During his last year he took courses in Natural Resource Policies, Dance, and Anthropology, and his Senior Study, to which he devoted his last semester, was entitled *Conservation as a Way of Life*. Of this work he said:

I feel that this has been one of my best semesters both socially and academically. I feel that I met most all of my commitments to the college and to myself quite successfully. I had no roommate this semester, which I think was a definite advantage for me. I spent more time "at the desk" than I have in the past, and was able to do more reading.

In looking back over the four years at the end of his last semester, he says:

> There have been significant changes in my life since I first
> arrived on campus. I felt that perhaps I was better equipped for
> college life than many were at first, but I also realized that I had
> much to learn in the way of living with others and developing my
> personal and academic responsibilities. Goddard gave me the
> leeway to make many decisions. I made them—some good; some not
> so good, but on the whole I think that I made the right ones for
> myself. I had no particular field of study in mind, at first, so it
> seemed to me that I should pursue a program of a general and
> broad nature. After all, I had come to a liberal arts college. I did
> this, in fact, by registering in a wide variety of courses. I enjoyed
> this kind of program, for I touched on many unfamiliar subjects
> that I was able to gain an interest in. When the time came for
> senior division applications, I had to do some serious thinking as
> to what I thought I should do with my college education; what
> I should make of it, and what it would lead to. Being in Vermont,
> being from a farm and country background, and always possessing
> an interest in nature and the natural environment—all were
> significant factors in my decision to concentrate my academic efforts
> during the last two years in the study of conservation. Of course, I
> did not limit my study to conservation alone; but I did take a
> number of courses in conservation and resource management. I am
> well-satisfied to have "majored" in this area. I am not nor could
> I be considered a well-rounded conservationist at this time. Never-
> theless, it has been a start.
>
> I have been in and out of community government during
> the past four years. I spent a year or more on the former Executive
> Committee as Fire Commissioner and have been a house president.
> At one time, I attended community meetings regularly, but later
> found that I was losing interest in much of the ways of community
> government.
>
> Generally speaking, I feel that my performance and con-
> tributions to Goddard have been good. I have worked hard on
> work program and, in some cases, accomplished a worthy amount.
> For the most part, I have attempted to be a strong and helpful in-
> fluence in community life and house life, and so on, and responsible
> and reliable in all areas. I am pleased with my academic endeavors,
> but I have learned as much about "living" as anything else at
> Goddard. I am more familiar with the Vermont hillsides, Vermont
> government, and Vermont way of life than I am with my home-
> town state. I have developed a liking and concern for Vermont and
> hope to be able to spend more time here; hopefully on my own
> land. I have no regrets or recriminations about my four years at

Goddard. I feel fortunate and happy that my time has been well-spent and that I have been able to develop my mind and character so that I can now move on.

These comments reveal much about the clarification of vocational plans and aspirations. First, when such plans have meaning, they serve to carry forward interests, values, and a way of life that has been rewarding in the past—in Alan's case, his enjoyment of the outdoors, his concern to be a socially responsible person, and the general satisfactions he derives from a rural existence. Second, when plans become more clearly formulated, learning becomes organized in relation to them. Greater time and energy are invested in such activities, sometimes at the expense of other significant interests, among which, for Alan, were the position of Fire Commissioner and his participation in community government. Third, the importance of study not directly or only tangentially related to future professional plans is recognized more clearly. Thus Alan could take courses in literature, dance, and anthropology.

Spohn's (1960) study at Sarah Lawrence supports the implications of Alan's record. Spohn found that students who show no interest in some kind of work after college do not, on the whole, become deeply enough involved in their college work to seek or find some clear direction for it; their personal interests and inclinations may remain lively, but they are not strong or deep. When students were rated on the intellectual level of their work, flexibility, and objectivity, those with no vocational interest scored lowest [pp. 139, 140].

The reasons for choosing courses or areas of study also reflect clarification of vocational plans. At the end of each year a sample of Goddard students was asked to indicate, on a list of thirteen alternatives, the three most important reasons for their choice of each course or independent study. It was hypothesized that with progress through college, "Discussion with your counselor," "Special interest in the subject," and "Subject necessary for professional plans" would increase in importance, and "Snap course," "Description sounded good," "Light reading course," "Couldn't get into courses I wanted," "Gave me a good schedule," and "No definite reasons" would decrease. Table 12 presents the findings and indicates general support for the hypotheses. "Advice from other students," "Advice from your family," and "Special talent in the area," also decrease in importance. Thus reasons for choosing courses reflect increasing clarity of purpose.

Table 12

FACTORS INFLUENCING CHOICE OF STUDIES

Option	Hypoth-esized Direc-tion	2nd Sem.	4th Sem.	6th Sem.	Average
Advice from other students	(Down)	.51	.36	.19	.30
Discussion with your counselor	(Up)	1.41	1.08	2.39	1.53
Advice from your family	(Down)	.21	1.15	.00	.17
Special interest in the subject	(Up)	6.42	6.20	7.12	6.14
Special talent in the area		1.00	.83	.66	.93
Subject necessary for professional plans	(Up)	1.56	2.84	2.86	2.23
"Snap" course	(Down)	.15	.05	.00	.06
Teacher has good reputation		1.50	1.90	1.66	1.46
Description sounded good	(Down)	1.66	1.46	.79	1.32
Needed a light read-ing course or non-reading course	(Down)	.30	.08	.05	.13
Couldn't get into courses I wanted	(Down)	.36	.23	.02	.17
Gave me a good schedule	(Down)	.10	.15	.14	.12
No definite reasons	(Down)	.51	.18	.25	.28

The differences in average scores for all three years indicate those reasons that carry most weight; "Special interest in the subject" far outranks the others. Then come professional plans, special talent, good-sounding description, and teacher reputation. In the general scheme of things, considerations of schedule, course difficulty, advice from family and the amount of reading required did not carry much weight.

Some of the "Worry" items also are relevant to the development of purpose. It was hypothesized that "Not knowing what to do with your life," "Not wanting to work up to capacity," "Not enough leisure," and "Being bored" would be mentioned as worrisome less frequently as the student progressed. Table 13 presents these findings,

Table 13

DEVELOPMENT OF PURPOSE
CHANGING FREQUENCIES FOR "WORRIES"

	Percent Responding			
Item	2nd Sem.	4th Sem.	6th Sem.	8th Sem.
Not knowing what to do with your life	8	5	9	2
Not wanting to work up to capacity	12	8	21	10
Not enough leisure	4	18	14	10
Being bored	26	26	16	17

and on three of the four items the hypotheses are supported, although the low frequencies and small differences require cautious interpretation.

In 1963, faculty members at Goddard College were given a list of randomly selected students and asked to rate them on "development of purpose." The ratings were then correlated with inventory scale scores to discover where significant relationships might exist. Seven scales of the Stern Activities Index significantly correlated with ratings on purposefulness. Adaptiveness, the readiness to accept advice and criticism, Conjunctivity, behaving in organized fashion, and Pragmatism, interest in practical concrete achievement, were positively associated with purposefulness. Fantasied Achievement, daydreams of success and narcissistic aspirations for personal distinction and power, Impulsiveness, impulsive, spontaneous, impetuous unreflected behavior, Change, unroutinized changeable behavior, and Understanding, detached intellectualization or abstraction as an end in itself, were negatively associated with ratings on purposefulness.

On the basis of this exploratory study it was hypothesized that if development of purpose occurred during the four-year period, scale scores would increase or decrease according to the relationships described above. The test-retest data for two groups of graduates showed that for four of the scales—Adaptiveness, Conjunctivity, Fantasied Achievement, and Understanding—the change in the hypothesized direction was great enough to reach statistical significance for one or both groups. On Change and Impulsiveness, the amount of change was not significant. On Pragmatism, for one group, significant change occurred in the direction opposite to that expected. The items on the Pragmatism scale involve such activities as typing, knitting, radio and car repair, managing business affairs or a fund drive and do-it-yourself type activities, gardening, and so on. Although in the exploratory research students rated as more purposeful more frequently liked these activities, apparently change in purpose is not accompanied by increasing interest in such things. Generally, however, the Stern Activities Index data support the proposition that purposes do increase in strength and clarity during the college years, and that this change influences the way a student makes use of the institution.

Additional relevant findings come from the Goddard faculty studies (Beecher *et al.,* 1966; Chickering, 1967) of Goal-Directedness and Full Involvement, Motivation and Persistence. A goal-directed student was defined as one who had conscious and fairly well-defined goals meaningful to himself, who has developed an ability to see the relationships between his purposes and other aspects of his life, and whose study has increased in focus and depth through its relationship to his goals. Eight questions to make this definition more specific were used as a basis for rating student records, which comprise student self-evaluations and instructor comments. They were:

1. Does the student plan his program with reference to a clear goal or purpose?

2. Are courses or independent studies evaluated in terms of their helpfulness or contribution to a larger purpose?

3. Are objectives for study explicitly related to more general plans or purposes?

4. Is there recognition of gaps in knowledge or skills in relation to purpose?

5. Are efforts made or plans formulated to deal with gaps or weaknesses?

6. Are there general expressions of feeling lost, at loose ends, without any purpose or direction? (Reverse scoring)

7. Do plans for the Nonresident Work Term reflect concern for some general plan or purpose?

8. How solid does the final commitment seem?

Averaging the ratings on these eight questions, from two independent raters, yielded a score for each semester for each student. The results shown in Figure 5 reveal increasing Goal-Directedness. It is worth noting that the sharpest increase occurs in the fourth semester, the semester during which application is made to the Senior Division. The Senior Division application requires clearer specification of what one is going to do in the future and is probably responsible for the increase reflected for that period.

The faculty also said that the "purposeful student" is well motivated and working for his own satisfaction. He has the energy and determination to keep at a job. The purposeful student is willing to tackle routine or difficult jobs congruent with his purposes and is resistant to obstacles. He continues in spite of mistakes or difficulties. He can sustain effort in the face of distractions and seeks out, in addition to academic work, extra activities that relate to his goal. This variable was called Full Involvement, Motivation, and Persistence. The questions used for rating student records were:

1. In general, how well motivated, persistent, and fully involved was this student?

2. What was the general level of effort reflected in preparation for classes, work on papers, and in relation to other kinds of responsibilities?

3. How consistent, steady, and regular was the student's output?

4. How great was the student's interest, enthusiasm, and intensity of involvement with his work?

5. How good was his attendance in relation to the general expectations and the nature of the class?

6. What was his level of participation as compared to that which seems to be usual or satisfying for him?

Figure 6 shows that change does occur over the four-year period. Ratings drop during the fifth semester, after admission to the Senior Division, but recovery is strong during the sixth and seventh semesters.

FIGURE 5
Goal Directedness

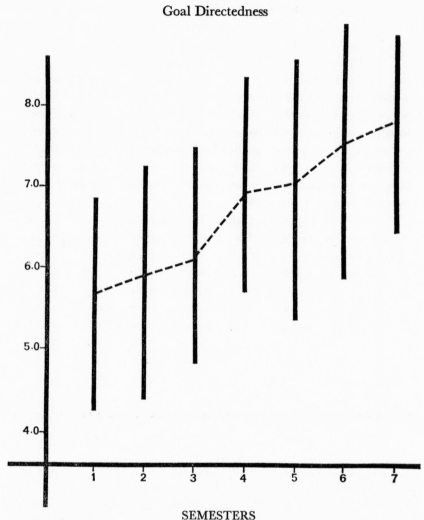

SEMESTERS

Vertical lines indicate range of ratings within which 2/3 of the students fall.
Horizontal line connects mean ratings for twenty students.
Difference in means for third and fourth semesters likely to occur less than five
times in one hundred on the basis of chance; difference in means for first and
seventh semesters likely to occur less than one time in one hundred.

The evidence from these various sources supports consistently
what most persons working with college students observe. Vocational
plans and aspirations become increasingly clear during college. Purposes important to the student become increasingly strong. This in-

FIGURE 6

Full Involvement, Motivation, and Persistence

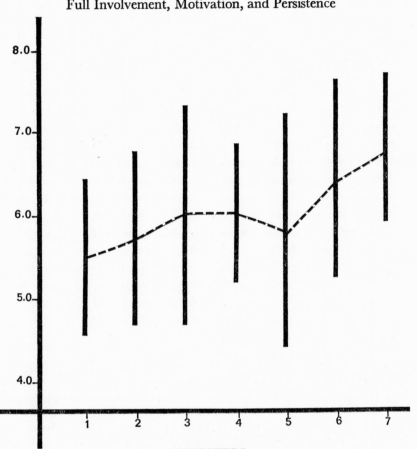

SEMESTERS

Vertical lines indicate range of ratings within which 2/3 of the students fall.
Horizontal line connects mean ratings of twenty students.

Difference in means for first and fourth semesters likely to occur less than ten
times in one hundred on the basis of chance; between fourth and seventh
semesters less than one time in one hundred.

creasing strength and clarity influences the areas of study selected and
the reasons for their choice, the amount of energy given to study and
other preparatory activities, and the nature of the student's engagement with other aspects of his college experience.

Of course it is relative clarity of plans, relative clarity of direction to be pursued, that makes a difference. Purposes need not be
highly specific nor must commitment be absolute. Sufficient clarity of

direction must exist to permit identification of appropriate present behaviors and next steps, but often a general orientation that leaves open a wide range of future choices is enough to provide substantial motivation and well-integrated activity.

Style of Life

Considerations of life-style and family also enter the equation. As intimate relationships with members of the opposite sex increasingly involve the question of marriage and as education and vocational experimentation draws to a close, clarification of long-range goals, intermediate steps, and immediate minimal requirements becomes more urgent. It is difficult to construct a plan that balances life-style considerations, vocational aspirations, and avocational interests. Many compromises must be borne if any plan is to be adopted.

One response to this difficult task is the development of subcultures where indecision and noncommitment are shared values. Robert Frost pondered the possibilities of the road untaken, but he did so while progressing down the other. For some students, the main thing is to avoid the fork; if a fork is encountered, as it must be, then one comes to a standstill. Reuel Denney (1965), observing one such subculture, says:

> their aim was part-time work for a part-time life with a part-time ego. In Venice, California, the new Bohemian seems at times to prefer the job that constitutes at once the shallowest commitment of one's self and the broadest satire on the rat race. (Some of them, report their jobs as those of deodorant testers.) This retreat from the job market seems to have been dramatized partly in clothes: the sandals and bare feet would scare a plant-safety man out of his head. Even certain aspects of clothing that were originally tinged by industrial utility (for example, the minimally tailored trousers favored first by the cowboy and later by industries wary of loose clothing) have become so attenuated that they suggest the hose that once went with the breeches in the times of Henry VIII. Surely no young man tottering about with a Henry VIII profile, with short coat hung over shoulders as if it were a flaring cape and legs as thin and irresolute as green noodles, can be expected to lift a tool [pp. 171, 172].

The "Beats," the "disaffiliates," the "alienated" (seen by some as evidence that immorality and irresponsibility are rife among contemporary youth, and by others as evidence that perceptive criticism of contemporary society may persist for yet another generation), though highly visible, represent a small fraction of the total college population. There are others, equally sensitive to injustice and hypocrisy, who formulate a direction and orientation and can proceed. Goddard seniors during their last semester were asked, "When you think about what really matters in your own life, what are your wishes and hopes for the future? In other words, if you imagine your future in the best possible light, what would your life look like then if you are to be happy?" The responses below illustrate typical formulations, first by two boys:

> Most importantly, I would like to live forever in good health. I can do without disease and death. Since that's not possible I suppose I'll be satisfied with being a doctor to the situation and all its unpleasantness. I can't imagine myself happy about life. However, I am happy about making the most of the situation —if I were a college president who concentrated on helping people—rather than building systems without respect for complexity— and if I were able to publish everything I wished to I imagine I would be about as happy as I could get on this planet.

> My planned career as a minister is not just a vocation, but a way of life. My goal is a sense of satisfaction from accomplishing that which I feel is important in life. Certainly, an adequate income would help me to enjoy life, for I don't think that living in poverty would be fun or worthwhile. But I can't be satisfied with myself unless I do everything that I can to insure a better world.

And by two girls:

> 1. To do something of value—value will have to be measured in terms of its impact—positive—on other people's lives.
> 2. Have a satisfactory sex and love life.
> 3. Raise children who were able to make satisfactory lives for themselves.
> 4. Have enough money to do some traveling and be able to withdraw from society—once in a while—to something like sailing or a house in Vermont or a similar rural area.
> 5. Be able to write good poetry.

> Primarily I think of a peaceful life pervasively calm and involving a reasonable sense of emotional strength and well-being. It is from this basis that my most creative and meaningful experiences can result. These experiences include primarily worth-

while, tender, and warm contact with other humans—contact
that encompasses as much as possible of myself and another. Enrichment of that contact relies on strong interests and broad interests which I must develop in myself. Ideally, then, they would
be developed. I see these not only as genuine concern with society
and the affairs of society; but also genuine concern with creative
womanly activities: sewing, cooking, raising children (assuming I
marry—which is also included in my ideal "happy" picture). I'm
sure that I will always want to be involved with fairly active and
progressive pursuits. For instance, as a housewife, I would also see
myself involved in various community functions like a Committee
on Mental Health; volunteer work in a hospital; school boards, and
PTA's, etc. Furthermore, I shall continue in my basically psychological orientation to living which largely defines the kinds of steps
I'll take toward involvements of one form or another. I hope to lead
a full life wherein I've learned to enjoy much—even the tiny things
which the uncreative mind dismisses as insignificant—and to thereby
live a life not pervaded by boredom through basic dullness and
routine, but excitement through sensitivity and awareness.

Students like these, perceptive of the need for social change and
concerned about social problems, have been able to achieve increased
integration of interests, of vocational plans and aspirations, and of
general concerns regarding marriage, family, and future life-style. Thus
they can proceed with some sense of direction and some sense that an
existence of their own can be carved out of or constructed within the
larger social matrix—an existence both satisfying to themselves and of
worth to that larger context.

CHAPTER 7

DEVELOPING
INTEGRITY

ιϜ·ϜϜ·ϜϜ·ϜϜ·ϜϜ·ϜϜ·ϜϜ·ϜϜ·ϜϜ·ϜϜ·ϜϜ·ϜϜΊ

Development of integrity is closely related to establishing identity and clarifying purposes. A personally valid set of beliefs and values that have internal consistency and that provide at least a tentative guide to behavior, affect, and are affected by, conceptions of the kind of person one is and would become, and by dominant interests, occupational plans, and life-style considerations. For values point the way and self-respect rises or falls as we follow or stray from that path. Values are the standard by which behavior is evaluated. As Smith (1964) says:

> Personal values pertain to the desirable, the preferable, rather than to the merely desired or preferred; the realm of "ought" rather than that of "is" or "want." . . . The cue words are "right" or

123

"wrong," "better" or "worse." All these words carry for us the connotation that standards apart from personal whim are being applied . . . [pp. 332, 334].

The development of integrity, therefore, involves the development of standards by which one appraises himself and in terms of which self-esteem varies as a consequence of the appraisal. This definition gives a central place not only to the content of values but to the way they are held and to their salience with regard to behavior and self-appraisal.

Barron's (1963) research makes it clear that the content of values and the way they are held may be two very different things. He discovered four different patterns, which he labeled *Fundamentalist Belief, Enlightened Belief, Fundamentalist Disbelief,* and *Enlightened Disbelief.* Fundamentalist Believers and Fundamentalist Disbelievers had in common low ratings on flexibility and adaptability, even though the particular beliefs they held were dramatically opposed. Barron concludes:

> Fundamentalism in either direction thus appears to be associated with rigidity and lack of ability to adapt. . . . Thus the person who expresses extreme and angry disbelief with the claims of religion appears essentially rigid, prejudiced, and poor at evaluating ideas [p. 152].

These comments recall similarities between "authoritarians" and "anti-authoritarians" found by Stern (1962). When compared to "rationals," both groups were more rigid and dogmatic in their views, unable to moderate their position in the light of extenuating circumstances, and closed to evidence of information contrary to their beliefs.

Most research on the values of college students has focused on content, however, rather than on the way values are held or on their salience. In general, such studies indicate a shift toward increased liberalism. In a survey of past research, Webster, Freedman, and Heist (1962) reported that change occurred in the direction of greater liberalism and sophistication in social, political, and religious attitudes. Newcomb and Feldman (1968)', in their recent comprehensive review, say, "Declining 'authoritarianism,' dogmatism and prejudice, together with decreasingly conservative attitudes toward public issues . . . are particularly prominent forms of change [p. 298]."

And the evidence further indicates that these changes persist. In 1936, Nelson (1954) tested freshmen through seniors with a "Conservative-Liberal" questionnaire, and followed them up again in 1950. He found that student attitudes had persisted during the fourteen years. In a more recent twenty-five-year follow-up, Newcomb, Koenig, Flacks, and Warwick (1967) found that the sociopolitical attitudes held by Bennington graduates in 1938 generally were still evidenced in 1963.

Most discussion of changes in values carry the implicit assumption that "change" means replacing one value with another—capitalism is replaced by socialism, a theologically based religious orientation is replaced by a humanistically based one, prejudice is replaced by respect and support. But the evidence is that such dramatic changes seldom occur. The more typical pattern is that modification of the values brought to college is gradual and limited.

Findings from the Project on Student Development are illustrative. Two Omnibus Personality Inventory scales were judged relevant to the development of integrity and it was hypothesized that scores would increase: (1) Altruism "the high scorer is an affiliative person and trusting in his relations with others. He exhibits concern for the feelings and welfare of people he meets. Low scorers tend to be much less concerned about the welfare of others and often view people from an impersonal, distant perspective"; and (2) Religious Orientation, "high scorers are skeptical of conventional religious beliefs and practices and tend to reject most of them, especially those that are orthodox or fundamentalistic in nature. Persons scoring near or above the mean are manifesting a liberal view of religious beliefs and low scorers tend to be conservative in general and rejecting of other viewpoints (Center for the Study of Higher Education, 1965)." The test-retest data, covering the first two years of college, indicate that Religious Orientation scores increased in twenty-one of twenty-three cases (although there were thirteen colleges, three of them had only male or female students, giving us twenty-three groups rather than twenty-six) but in only four instances was the increase of sufficient magnitude to reach statistical significance. Altruism scores, on the other hand, increased in ten cases—one significant—and decreased in eleven, with two cases having identical scores. Seven Project colleges are closely identified with varying religious orientations, and some of these are strongly conservative. Some of the other Project colleges have strong value orienta-

tions that are humanistically based. Yet whether Altruism scores increase or decrease bears no apparent relationship to these institutional
differences. And the same is true for the consistent increases in Religious
Orientation scores—two of the significant cases occur at church-related
colleges, and the other two at an institution with no clear value framework.

    These findings are consistent with the two general points made
above. First, the content of belief can shift—toward increased liberalism—without concomitant shift in the salience of the values held, as
evidenced by behavior or other attitudes—concern for the feelings and
welfare of others. And second, change involves limited movement from
where one is, not dramatic conversion; our data show that the men at
W. J. B., for example, changed Religious Orientation scores from 36
to 37, one and one-half standard deviations below the mean, and the
men at Kildew, from 61 to 62, a standard deviation above the mean.
Such findings are neither surprising nor undesirable. As Dressel (1965)
points out:

> The student who enters college at the age of seventeen or eighteen
> has had many home, community, and school experiences which are
> potent in molding his value patterns. If values as a basis for judge-
> ment and behavior have any significance whatsoever, it should
> hardly be expected that a limited amount of educational experience
> will bring about changes in value pattern. This is particularly true
> if one recognizes that diverse value patterns exist among and within
> colleges. It is possible for a college student to seek out those per-
> sons and experiences which reinforce his own value pattern rather
> than provoke examinations of it. In any case, marked changes
> within limited periods of time in an individual may be indicative of
> shallowness, which may simply mean that, in later months or years
> when exposed to different experiences with different underlying
> values, the individual will take on, chameleon-like, the value pat-
> terns of his new environment. A reasonable conclusion is that value
> patterns of college students need not, in every case, be thought of
> as requiring change, and indeed that marked changes in short
> periods of time must be regarded as having doubtful validity
> [p. 65].

    Thus the content of values and the patterns of their interrela-
tionships may not change dramatically during college. But there may
be other changes of greater significance. The bases on which values
rest, the ways in which they are held, and the force with which they

operate in daily life, may be of more importance—within limits—than the particular values held. In a democratic society with many different cultures, where cultural pluralism is itself a value, and where every man has a right to his own convictions and to their expression as long as others are not damaged, the most significant contribution a college can make is to increase the role of values in the lives of its students rather than to modify the content.

Movement toward integrity, toward increased congruence between behavior and values—whatever their content may be—involves three sequential, but overlapping, stages: (1) humanizing values, (2) personalizing values, and (3) developing congruence.

Humanizing Values

Humanizing of values is White's (1958) term; describing it he calls attention to Piaget's (1932) work, which "demonstrated a trend from a literal belief in rules, almost as if they had an independent physical existence, to an attitude or relativity, in which precepts were perceived in relation to the social purposes they were designed to serve. . . . [p. 353]." Sanford (1962) calls this change the "liberalization of the superego" or the "enlightenment of conscience [p. 278]." Adolescents, young adults, and many adults yearn for universally agreed upon, universally adhered to, and thus unchallengeable, standards for behavior. Barron's liberal and conservative fundamentalists, Stern's authoritarians and anti-authoritarians, and many persons we all know, demonstrate that totalistic acceptance of a formula appeals to many. As Havens' (1964) research suggests, a more flexible enlightened conscience or humanized value system is difficult to achieve and to sustain. He found that juniors and seniors, when compared to freshmen and sophomores, experienced deeper conflicts between reasoned agnosticism and faith, experienced more unsatisfied longing for faith, and were more inconsistent in behavior and belief.

But as social change occurs, and as the rate of change increases, humanizing of values becomes ever more important. For example, when most persons assumed adult roles and became self-supporting by age eighteen or twenty, when techniques of contraception were only partially effective, when each person was more intimately and extensively connected to friends, relatives, and local community, then sexual abstinence outside of marriage was desirable. But when the age for assuming adult roles and self-support is delayed, often into the

mid-twenties, as techniques for contraception improve, as society becomes more dehumanized and as more relationships become deper-
sonalized, conceptions concerning sexual relationships, marriage, and
family may shift in reaction, to produce more humane, respectful, and
satisfying conditions, more informal and flexible alternatives. Or when
provisions for one's future welfare are minimal then thrift and limited
expenditure for present gratification makes sense. But when the future
looks secure and when provisions for future welfare seem adequate,
then short-run hedonism may become more valid than delayed gratification. When production of goods is expensive in terms of man-hours,
then care of materials is important and "putting things away" to protect them from damage or deterioration is justified. But when technological improvements and assembly-line procedures cut man-hour costs
sharply, then it may be cheaper to let things lie, throw them away,
and buy another, than to invest much effort in "taking care of your
things." Thus the values of an earlier generation must suffer modification, must be reconstructed by today's young adult, in order that his
own welfare and that of society be maximized in response to changing
conditions.

For many college students, humanizing of values is like urban
development. Old structures are torn down, blown apart, or otherwise
demolished—and the demolition frequently is carried out at the same
high level of indiscriminate fervor and ponderous momentum that
recently has destroyed many fine and sound buildings of former times.
Misery and misgivings are the lot of nearby inhabitants and distant
admirers. But dig he must, and for some college students, blasting is
the only way to prepare the ground for new structures better able to
carry the increased traffic and new modes of existence.

Ideally such reconstruction—such humanizing of values—occurs through objective analyses of existing conditions and through
sound estimation of the consequences of given alternatives. In reality,
of course, conditions never can be described with complete accuracy
and data are often insufficient for sound predictions. And human beings have limited ability to be completely objective about either. That's
why "value differences" exist. For as conditions and consequences become clear and objectivity becomes high, these "value differences"
diminish because the indicated behaviors are unarguable. Fifty years
ago there were sharp differences concerning the value of social security

and positions taken derived from more general value differences. In-creased information about the conditions of the elderly and increased insight concerning the consequences of practices then in existence grad-ually resolved the differences. Consequently, whether or not to have social security is no longer a "question of values." Recent extension of social security and government-supported medical care for the aged and poor was debated not in terms of value differences but in terms of administrative questions concerning efficiency and quality of service. In a longer perspective, to illustrate a converse shift, Athenians de-spised work and those who did it, and that attitude still persists for most of us. Work is opposed to play, to be put up with because it makes other activities possible. But for a few it is an activity to be valued highly, and some predict it will soon become a privilege. To work or not to work, and whether social planning should provide for it, may become a "question of values." The point is that the very ex-istence of value differences implies a high degree of uncertainty con-cerning the relevant conditions and the consequences of alternative policies or practices. And the difficulties generated by high uncertainty are compounded by low levels of objectivity. For strong differences provoke anger, and insecurity provokes anxiety.

Yet in principle, if values are to serve the human condition, thoughtful interpretation of objective evidence should supplement per-sonal intuition and faith. Thus when a person analyzes conditions as best he can, when he makes the best prediction he can about the af-fects of alternative actions, and when he protects himself as much as possible from the influence of his own biases and when these processes are tempered by, and temper, fundamental metaphysical assumptions and commitments, he has generated the soundest basis he can for his own position.

For many young adults, humanizing values and developing congruence and integrity, are essentially problems of religious belief and conviction. The faith of their fathers is called into question. Pre-cepts and dogma, which were solid anchors, begin to slip. What is God? Is there an ultimate power or an ultimate reality? Who—or what—was Christ? What does the Bible mean when it speaks of life after death, of Heaven and Hell? Is man basically evil, born in sin and needing salvation—or is he basically good, but spoiled by an im-perfect society?

Underwood (1966), Director of the Danforth Foundation's Campus Ministries Project, has conceptualized the problem clearly from this frame of reference:

> The students on our campuses eagerly inform themselves about the latest advances in techniques for the control of natural environment and of persons in large-scale organizations. They have few illusions about the pervasive importance which technology will play in their leisure and in their work. But they cannot gather this highly rationalistic and specialized world into their passionate drive for personal integrity and identity in the modern world.
>
> If this is the situation, then exploitation in the colleges and universities of what is valuable and alien to human beings in the technological world may be a pressing occasion.
>
> The first thing that can be noted about the day-to-day life of people who work within technological organizations is that they must master a necessary knowledge and skill to operate the machine and use its products, whether it be a computer, a typewriter, or a lathe. Second, the technological organization cannot produce a good to serve a great number of people without a rational division of labor or specialization. Third, the people who possess these specializations must work together, must integrate their talents and skills in the achievement of the final result. . . . And finally, it should be noted that the person in his unique individuality is not necessary for the achievement of this service. Neither is a distinctive language arising out of his subjective being, nor are intimate encounters in which one spills out the troubles and problems of his life conspicuously present in the relations of men and women in the technical organization itself. All of us know these characteristics of collective life, for they have penetrated every corner of existence, education as well as industry.
>
> Now when we turn with these features of the technological world in mind to the religious interpretations of what is meaningful and worthwhile in life, it is not hard to see the sources of suspicion in our students that their personal integrity and identity are threatened. Pietistic, evangelical faith puts a special premium on spontaneous, heart-felt acts of charity and love; it dwells on home and family as the place where Christianity received its fullest expression. Existentialist theological literature of Kierkegaard, Martin Buber, and a whole host of campus favorites identifies love with the relationships of personal intimacy between two individuals, with authentic personal "encounters and dialogue," with sensitivity to others and affirmation of their value as persons whether one agrees with them or not. Solid, affectionate relationships, established independently of agreement on particular norms or competent suc-

cessful performance of a particular function in the society are viewed as the most valuable and worthy contexts of human life. In the realities of the I-Thou world there are no objects, no things standing in external space to hinder authentic meetings of persons seeking to know one another in depth through a relationship of genuine love.

The theological literature is not the only intellectual source of this alienation from the technological world. The Weberian tradition of social sciences also perceives a vast, uncontrollable press of modern society toward increasing functional rationality and depersonalization of life and increased separation of the individual from control over corporate enterprise. The implication is that these developments crush sensitivity and reduce the areas of significant free choice. The pervasive acceptance by faculty and administration . . . made students mere appendages to "the clattering process of bureaucratic machinery."

The prevailing pictures of technical and technological society as devoid of meaning and integrity and of Christianity as a religion alien to the world of mass production and service must be challenged.

It is simply not the case that specialized work and manipulating and controlling of environment through technology dehumanize people and destroy their capacity for intimacy and affection. The contrary is closer to the truth. The deepest and richest human experiences more often occur, not in relations of private intimacy, but when human beings share in some creative corporate enterprise, when they combine a number of special skills and talents and meet real social needs. The collective technology of modern culture provides the necessary and worthwhile services and goods for human life today in most of the world and makes possible an ever-widening range of personal choice and freedom. Participation in the work and volunteer activities of university department, companies, bureaus, and professions is the way by which most people today extend their influence on matters that deeply concern them. If the student wills to live for others, his capacity for patient, critical work in the particular collectivities of our time will best fulfill these hopes. Most of the specialization for which students now prepare requires all the imagination, human sensitivity, self-discipline, and objective knowledge they can muster.

A further ground for rejecting the gospel of personalistic love comes from the Scriptural account of Christ's own understanding of the love of God and man. For the New Testament, love of neighbor involves a genuine effort and readiness to serve others in the most effective way and with all the appropriate resources. There is no evidence in the parable of the Good Samaritan that he sought an eyeball-to-eyeball, authentic conversation-in-depth in order to

help the man fallen among thieves. Love, for Christ, is a relationship of concern for the other, an absorption in finding out what
is really happening to people in a situation and then giving of the
best one has, one's technical skill, political influence, artistic talent
. . . to heal the sick, feed the hungry, inform the fearful [pp. 55,
57, 58].

Perhaps Underwood's assertion that deep and rich human experiences are to be found in the context of creative corporate enter-
prises, that they occur when one's particular skills and talents are
joined with others' to meet a social need, is unjustified. But even if
Underwood's view is erroneous, he has rendered great service by putting the issue squarely in contemporary terms. And the evidence available to date suggests that many college students are grappling with it.

The Danforth Foundation's Campus Ministries Project is a
comprehensive, multidisciplinary study of contemporary religious beliefs, their likely directions of change, and of the role of the church,
the university, and social policy in the development of religious belief
and relevant behavior. Preliminary reports by Underwood (1968) and
his associates document student concern to develop a viable religious
world view that can be held with integrity. Students are seeking, in
this new religion, a transcendent foundation that accepts science and
technology as legitimate ways of knowing and as contributors to social
good, but which also recognizes that reality is not thereby exhausted,
that these are not the sole bases on which social development rests, but
that other ways of knowing, through God, through revelation, intuition, and self-awareness, have similar legitimacy. This view affirms a
theistic position while admitting ambiguity and doubt. It sees ethical
action and concern for others as the crucial test of serious faith. It
believes that although man is a mixture of good and evil, he is capable
of action to serve the needs of others. This new religion, therefore, has
become a quest for a transcendent meaning that gives shape to experience, purpose to existence, and moral energy to action.

Some evidence of the seeking and of its success comes from a
San Francisco Bay Area survey carried out in the context of the Campus Ministries Project. Underwood (1968), reporting the findings, suggests that the war between the "romantic-existential theological advo-
cates" and the "fanatical defenders of scientific and technological
reason" is outdated. Most students know that rational faculties and
scientific methods have their place but at the same time recognize their

limitations. Only 10 per cent, for example, agreed with the statement "There is nothing which science cannot eventually comprehend." D. Heath's (1968) findings are similar. He reports that the principal effect Haverford College had on men's religious lives was "to develop a meaningful ethical humanism divorced from formal religious doctrines," and 54 per cent of the alumni indicated that their Haverford experience either initiated or strengthened their interest in religious and ethical issues.

Preliminary findings from the Project on Student Development also suggest that such changes are under way. All students entering the thirteen Project colleges in September, 1965, were asked, "To what degree do you feel religious faith has been an influence in your life . . . ?" When asked the same question again at the end of their sophomore year, in twenty-four of twenty-five cases (men and women separately for eleven colleges, business administration and engineering students separately for one, and women only for one) students indicated greater influence than at entrance. So religious faith seems to become more important, not less. But do the beliefs change? And are the changes congruent with the more complex and comprehensive view posited by Underwood and his associates? Table 14 gives test-retest data for seven colleges with strong church ties and for six with limited or nominal affiliation, or no church ties at all, for three other items to which these same students responded. The differences in the two sets of Fall '65 figures indicate the difference in beliefs held by entering freshmen, and as the descriptions of the Project colleges given in Chapter Eight will suggest, some of the single institutions reflect opposing patterns much more sharply. The general point, however, is that frequencies for both groups increase most sharply for moderate responses that recognize both science and religion ("Religion and science are completely compatible if properly understood"), that recognize fundamental values along with the need for their flexible application ("There are fundamental value principles in human life but they must be interpreted in different ways to meet different situations"), and that reflect personal and individualized religious belief. These shifts toward moderate responses rather than toward one extreme or another, suggest that students are trying to formulate belief systems where scientific knowing is legitimate, and where at the same time faith, God, and metaphysical assumptions have a place. And they also suggest that values are becoming more humanized.

Table 14

PROJECT ON STUDENT DEVELOPMENT
SHIFTING RELIGIOUS BELIEFS*

Item	Church		Non-Church	
	Fall '65	Spr. '67	Fall '65	Spr. '67
Which of the following best expresses your view on the relation between religion and science?				
Religion and science cannot be reconciled, and we must trust science.	0	2	8	5
There are some areas of agreement between religion and science, but where there is conflict we must trust science.	2	1	21	20
Religion and science are completely compatible if properly understood.	47	60	54	65
There are some areas of agreement between religion and science, but wherever there is conflict we must trust religion.	49	34	12	9
Religion and science cannot be reconciled, and we must trust religion.	2	3	5	2
Which of the following best expresses your feelings about human values?				
There are absolute human values which are not simply man-made but which exist whether man acknowledges them or not.	53	53	33	17
There are fundamental value principles in human life but they must be interpreted in different ways to meet different situations.	18	35	40	53

* Figures are percents averaged for 264 students across seven church colleges and for 216 students across six non-church colleges. Institutional n's ranged from 12–79.

Table 14—Cont.

PROJECT ON STUDENT DEVELOPMENT
SHIFTING RELIGIOUS BELIEFS*

	Church		Non-Church	
Item	Fall '65	Spr. '67	Fall '65	Spr. '67
Values are totally man-made; they have no objective existence of their own.	5	1	13	18
I am uncertain about the status of human values.	24	10	14	11
Which of the following statements most nearly expresses your opinion of what you personally need to lead a good life?				
Some sincere working philosophy or code of ethics, not necessarily a religious belief.	2	11	36	32
Some religious belief, but it may be purely personal. Church membership contributes nothing.	2	7	6	13
Some individual religious belief. Church membership is minor importance.	10	16	5	10
An individual religious belief. Church membership helps but is not absolutely necessary.	42	44	28	25
An individual religious belief is not sufficient. You must also be a member of a church.	21	10	17	5
None of the above.	22	13	7	14

* Figures are percents averaged for 264 students across seven church colleges and for 216 students across six non-church colleges. Institutional n's ranged from 12–79.

At Goddard College (Beecher *et al.*, 1966), an attempt was made to observe more directly whether humanizing of values occurred. Nineteen items judged to reflect such changes were selected from the Omnibus Personality Inventory and the direction in which response frequencies would increase during college was predicted. Two criteria governed selection: (1) where direction of response would be influenced by whether one thought the indicated value or behavior depended upon relevant circumstances or conditions (For example, "It is a pretty callous person who does not feel love and gratitude toward his parents," "I am in favor of strict enforcement of all laws no matter what the consequences"), and (2) where direction of response would be influenced by increased willingness to suspend judgment, to deliberate, or to accept more qualified answers ("It is annoying to listen to a lecturer who seems unable to make up his mind about what he really believes," "I often act on the spur of the moment without stopping to think," "Our thinking would be a lot better if we would just forget about words like 'probably,' 'approximately,' and 'perhaps.' ")

Response frequencies for fifteen of the nineteen items shifted in the predicted direction, for two no shift occurred, and two changed contrary to predictions. Table 15 lists the items and frequencies in order of the magnitude of change in the predicted direction.

Taken together, the evidence from these diverse studies, undertaken from the framework of religion and religious beliefs and from the study of values and attitudes, reflects a shift away from automatic application of uncompromising beliefs, rooted either in religious tradition and doctrine or in pure scientific rationalism, toward a more comprehensive and complex system, applied flexibly according to changing circumstances.

Personalizing Values and Building Congruence

Humanizing creates a condition where values may be highly relative to variation in circumstance and situation—so relative that adequate guides are lacking, principles that enable decisions and behavior that seem right are absent. Considerable anxiety and tension often accompany this condition; consequently, work begins on some kind of internalized and more solid supporting structure, a framework of greater conviction and commitment. At first it helps only under certain conditions or particular circumstances—and even then it may be wobbly. But with time, testing, and redesigning, a broader and

Table 15

HUMANIZING OF VALUES
RESPONSE FREQUENCIES FOR GODDARD STUDENTS
ON SELECTED OPI ITEMS

Item and Hypothesized Direction of Response	*Percent Responding*		
	Entrance	*Eighth Semester*	*Difference*
A large number of people are guilty of bad sexual conduct. (F)	45	85	40
In illegitimate pregnancies abortion is in many cases the most reasonable alternative. (T)	50	78	28
Unquestioning obedience is not a virtue. (F)	0	17	17
I often act on the spur of the moment without stopping to think. (F)	33	48	15
It is annoying to listen to a lecturer who seems unable to make up his mind what he really believes. (F)	26	38	12
It is a pretty callous person who does not feel love and gratitude toward his parents. (F)	62	73	11
One of the most important things children should learn is when to disobey authorities. (T)	28	36	8
It is not the duty of a citizen to support his country right or wrong. (T)	55	63	8
I am in favor of strict enforcement of all laws no matter what the consequences. (F)	85	90	5
I am embarrassed by dirty stories. (F)	83	88	5
No normal decent person would ever think of hurting a close friend or relative. (F)	66	71	5

138

EDUCATION AND IDENTITY

Table 15—Cont.

HUMANIZING OF VALUES

RESPONSE FREQUENCIES FOR GODDARD STUDENTS ON SELECTED OPI ITEMS

Item and Hypothesized Direction of Response	Percent Responding		
	Entrance	Eighth Semester	Difference
Nothing in life is worth the sacrifice of losing contact with your family. (F)	73	77	4
Our thinking would be a lot better if we would just forget about words like "probably," "approximately," and "perhaps." (F)	14	17	3
Moral codes are relevant only when they fit the specific situations; if the situations differ, they are merely abstract irrelevancies. (T)	71	73	2
Sex crimes, such as rape and attacks on children, deserve more than mere imprisonment; such criminals ought to be publicly whipped or worse. (F)	90	93	3
At times I have been so entertained by the cleverness of a crook that I have hoped he would get by with it. (F)	28	28	0
Disobedience to the government is sometimes justified. (T)	93	93	0
In matters of religion it really does not matter what one believes. (F)	58	48	−10
I don't like to work on a problem unless there is the possibility of coming out with a clear-cut and unambiguous answer. (F)	78	77	−1

more stable platform is achieved on which one can more frequently rest. Gradually, beliefs become less tenuously held. They provide a more comprehensive basis for judgments about the actions, policies, and personality characteristics of others, and provide implicit and explicit criteria for one's own behaviors and choices.

This is the development of what Smith (1963) calls "self-requiredness." Values are "owned up to." They are accepted as part of oneself and as what one stands for. They are consciously held and can be articulated. And therefore, they also can be challenged and can be modified in the light of further experience, or new evidence from the experiences of others. It is like acquiring and maintaining a new wardrobe. Not only is it necessary to keep things clean and pressed, but worn and outmoded items must be replaced. Usually such replacement occurs piecemeal and does not tax the budget. But occasionally change in circumstance or personal characteristics may require extensive outfitting, accomplished at considerable cost and strain to personal economy.

In the Goddard research (Beecher *et al.*, 1966), twenty-three OPI items were judged relevant to this aspect of integrity and the direction of change was predicted for them. Items selected were those where direction of response would be influenced by (1) increased clarity of position ("I have frequently found myself, when alone, pondering such abstract problems as free will, evil, etc.," "I think I am no more strict about right or wrong than most people"), (2) increased recognition that behavior is expressive of values ("Almost nothing a person says about himself reveals very much about what he is really like," "I don't blame anyone for trying to grab all he can get in this world"), and (3) increased ability to recognize values as one's own and to act on them ("Conscience is another name for fear," "When someone talks against certain groups or nationalities I always speak up against such talk even though it makes me unpopular"). Of the twenty-three items selected, sixteen changed as predicted, two reflected no change, and five shifted in contrary direction. Table 16 lists them.

For Rogers (1961), congruence is the peak of personhood. The congruent person achieves an accurate "matching of experience, awareness, and communication [p. 339]." He is without facade. Where he stands is clear to others, and more importantly, clear to himself. Erikson's (1950) description of integrity is consistent with Rogers'. He says:

> It is the acceptance of one's one and only life cycle and of the people who have become significant to it as something that had to be and that, by necessity, permitted of no substitutions. It thus

Table 16

PERSONALIZATION OF VALUES
RESPONSE FREQUENCIES OF GODDARD STUDENTS
ON SELECTED OPI ITEMS

Item and Hypothesized Direction of Response	*Entrance*	*Eighth Semester*	*Difference*
I don't blame anyone for trying to get all he can get in this world. (F)	62	85	23
I usually feel that I am drifting along in life with no particular role to play. (F)	58	81	23
I think I am no more strict about right and wrong than most people. (F)	38	58	20
I often feel as though I had done something wicked or wrong. (F)	66	83	17
When it comes to differences of opinion in religion we should be careful not to compromise with those who believe differently than we do. (F)	66	81	15
I have frequently found myself, when alone, pondering such abstract problems as free will, evil, *etc.* (F)	31	45	14
Conscience is another name for fear. (F)	71	83	12
I like to discuss the values of life, such as what makes an act good or evil. (F)	19	28	9
When someone talks against certain groups or nationalities, I always speak up against such talk even though it makes me unpopular. (T)	45	52	7
I do not blame a person for taking advantage of someone who leaves himself open to it. (F)	78	85	7

Table 16—Cont.

PERSONALIZATION OF VALUES
RESPONSE FREQUENCIES OF GODDARD STUDENTS
ON SELECTED OPI ITEMS

Item and Hypothesized Direction of Response	*Entrance*	*Eighth Semester*	*Difference*
Almost nothing a person says about himself reveals very much about what he is really like. (F)	78	83	6
I hardly ever tell people what I think of them when they do something I dislike. (F)	54	59	4
I think nearly anyone would tell a lie to keep out of trouble. (F)	52	55	3
I do not always tell the truth. (F)	17	19	2
When prices are high you can't blame a person for getting all he can while the getting is good. (F)	64	66	2
It is hard for me to communicate my intermost thoughts. (F)	50	52	2
Maybe some minority groups do get rough treatment but it's no business of mine. (F)	90	90	0
I dislike women who disregard the usual social or moral conventions. (F)	85	85	0
If I could get into a movie without paying and be sure I was not seen, I would probably do it. (F)	64	46	−18
Never tell anyone the real reason you did something unless it is useful to do so. (F)	85	71	−14
I frequently find it necessary to stand for what I think is right. (T)	77	64	−13
The best philosophy is eat, drink and be merry for tomorrow we die. (F)	78	73	−5
It is difficult for me to take people seriously. (F)	93	90	−3

means a new, a different love of one's parents, free of the wish that
they should have been different, and an acceptance of the fact that
one's life is one's own responsibility. It is a sense of comradeship
with men and women of distant times and of different pursuits, who
have created orders and objects and sayings conveying human dig-
nity and love [p. 143].

Some persons may believe in honesty and openness but be unable to refrain from the use of "hidden agenda" or from suspecting
it in others. Some may believe in chastity but be unable to resist sexual
temptation. But as congruence is achieved such inconsistencies diminish. When fully realized, integrity is reflected in consistency of belief
and behavior, of word and deed. Internal argument is minimal. Once
the implications of a situation are understood and once the consequences of alternative actions seem clear, the response is highly determined. It is made with conviction, without debate or equivocation.

Achieving congruence is a lifelong task. Traumatic experiences
may sorely test or shatter long-standing convictions. Few have the
strength of Job. Faith, responding to doubt, must be renewed and re-
worked. Past behaviors that served us and others well become ineffec-
tive or damaging. Close friends who supported us when congruence
was difficult to maintain may die or leave us, relationships may de-
teriorate. New sources of strength must be discovered or developed,
in ourselves or others. In four years of college the young adult cannot
complete the process. But he can begin it, and by beginning stand better positioned to continue this fundamental human task.

PART **II**

*W*hat conditions make
a difference to student development? What arrangements enable stu-
dents to pursue the tasks through which change may occur? We hy-
pothesize that each college can accelerate or retard development in
each vector, and past research suggests six major sources of influence:
(1) clarity of objectives and internal consistency, (2) institutional
size, (3) curriculum, teaching, and evaluation, (4) residence hall ar-
rangements, (5) faculty and administration, and (6) friends, groups,
and student culture.

In this overview six general hypotheses are posed, one for each
area, accompanied by a glimpse of relevant evidence. For clarity and
succinctness the hypotheses are baldly stated. Qualifying expressions like
"under normal circumstances," "in general," "tend to," "probably,"—
those ubiquitous terms and circumlocutions by which educators and be-

144

CONDITIONS FOR IMPACT:
AN OVERVIEW

ᔑᔑᔑᔑᔑᔑᔑᔑᔑᔑᔑᔑᔑᔑᔑᔑᔑᔑᔑᔑᔑ

havioral scientists protect their rears and obscure their meanings—have been dropped. An exaggerated implication of conviction and dogmatism may result. Therefore, insert your own qualifying phrases and any of these hypotheses will move toward greater accuracy. Note also that hypothesis *has two principal definitions: "a tentative theory or supposition provisionally adopted to explain certain facts and to guide in the investigation of others," and "something assumed or conceded merely for the purpose of argument or action [Webster's, 1961]." In the context of this overview, both are appropriate. The balance between the first and second will shift with the reader and with the topic.*

Clarity and Consistency of Objectives

Hypothesis: *Impact increases as institutional objectives are clear and taken seriously, and as the diverse elements of the college and its program are internally consistent in the service of the objectives.*

Eddy (1959), reporting his study of college influence on student character, said, "The potential of environment is measurably increased by a feeling of community. And that feeling appears to begin where it should—in common understanding and acceptance of commonly shared goals [pp. 143–44]." Jacob's (1957) survey of research concerning the effect of college on attitudes and values found little influence except at a few institutions where a distinctive climate prevailed. At the time of Newcomb's (1943) study, Bennington in the late 1930's was dominated by a liberal social and political outlook. Students whose attitudes changed were those who most identified with this dominant orientation. And the follow-up study (Newcomb et al., 1967) of these same students twenty-five years later indicates that for most the change in attitudes has been sustained.

Of course it is not the simple statement of objectives that has an impact. Every college catalog contains such statements. But where objectives are taken seriously, institutional impact is strengthened three ways. First, policies, programs, and practices tend toward greater internal consistency. When faculty members manning ubiquitous committees make decisions in terms of commonly shared and explicit institutional objectives, then the various parts fit together with greater coherence and integration. The developmental impact of one element less frequently runs counter to another. Second, clear objectives help students make more explicit their own reasons for attending the college and their own purposes while there, and help them use time and energy more directly in the service of those objectives they value. Third, it is important to be explicit about objectives because they contain within them strong value commitments. No institution is without such commitments. Often they are absorbed unwittingly by students and are learned as matters not to be questioned. At some institutions, for example, the work-success ethic, rugged individualism, personal achievement, self-denial and future time orientation, or a Puritan morality, are among the dominant values assumed; at others, such emergent values as sociability, a relativistic moral attitude, conformity, or a hedonistic present time orientation are left unquestioned. Such unconscious learning seals off these matters from conscious control and modification. Enter rigidity and dogmatism. When objectives are explicit and when the attendant values are overtly expressed, they can become the object of examination, disagreement, and challenge. Then the learning that occurs makes for more conscious and flexible integration of these values with other components of personality and behavior.

As institutional objectives remain salient and are clearly expressed, a distinctive atmosphere develops. It develops not only out of the conscious effort of those who stay with the institution for some time—more importantly, it develops because prospective students and prospective faculty who resonate with the objectives and their modes of implementation, are accepted and remain. Through this process a community of shared values, which sustains its members and influences those who join, comes into being.

Institutional objectives are thus of primary importance. Not only do they influence the emphasis given to one vector relative to another—for one college competence is most important, for another integrity, for a third autonomy and purpose. But their clarity and the internal consistency with which they are implemented largely determines whether any substantial development will be fostered or whether the student, subject to opposing forces, remains fixed or changes only in response to other outside pressures.

Institutional Size

Hypothesis: *As redundancy increases, development of competence, identity, and integrity, and the freeing of interpersonal relationships decreases.*

When the number of persons for a given setting exceed the opportunities for active participation and satisfying experiences, Barker and Gump (1964) call that redundancy—*like when the best man joins the honeymooners. When persons are superfluous because of excessive numbers redundancy exists; if three runners end up on second base, two are redundant. Redundancy is one person driving from behind the wheel and another from the back seat, three persons to change the tire, or four to diagnose the engine failure. It's ten hunters per acre in Vermont, one thousand per golf course in the suburbs, ten thousand per Central Park in the city. And when redundancy occurs—when increasing numbers cause decreasing individual participation and satisfaction—then forces operating for personal development diminish.*

For as redundancy sets in, the activities and responsibilities of those who do participate become more specialized and those with marginal qualifications are more quickly and more completely left out.

A hierarchy of prestige and power develops, and evaluation shifts from an emphasis on the fit between abilities and the requirements of a job to an emphasis on how one person compares with another. Rules and standards for conduct become more formalized and rigid.

Under such conditions, the opportunities to cope with significant problems become more limited and challenges to existing skills and knowledge are encountered less frequently. Experience becomes less varied and self-testing more restricted. The range of different persons to be dealt with in contexts important to one's own life decreases, and situations provoking examination of values and consideration of the consequences of one's actions have to be faced less often. Thus, development of competence is more limited except when provided by special ability or special interest; the development of identity, the freeing of interpersonal relationships, and the development of integrity are fostered less than is the case when the ratio of persons to settings is smaller.

Institutional size, therefore, conceived in these terms, sharply affects institutional impact. For as the number of persons outstrips the opportunities for significant participation and satisfaction, the developmental potential of available settings is attenuated for all.

Curriculum, Teaching, and Evaluation

Hypothesis A: *When few electives are offered, when books and print are the sole objects of study, when teaching is by lecture, when evaluation is frequent and competitive, ability to memorize is fostered. Sense of competence, freeing of interpersonal relationships, and development of autonomy, identity, and purpose are not.*

Hypothesis B: *When choice and flexibility are offered, when direct experiences are called for, when teaching is by discussion, and when evaluation involves frequent communication concerning the substance of behavior and performance, the ability to analyze and synthesize is fostered, as are sense of competence, freeing of interpersonal relationships, and development of autonomy, identity, and purpose.*

These two hypotheses cover much ground. But curriculum, teaching practices, and evaluational procedures are so systematically linked that one element is difficult to disentangle from the other two. What is some of the evidence concerning the impact of various systems and their elements?

Intellectual competence does not just happen. It is the result of long learning. An untrained mind may be sufficient for trial-and-error behavior, but training is required if analytic, synthetic, and creative skills are to develop. Evidence indicates that different teaching practices produce different kinds of cognitive operations and therefore may foster different kinds of intellectual competence. The differential effects of lectures versus discussion classes in most settings is well documented. Lectures are superior for the transmission of information (Barnard, 1942), either quite specific in nature or integrated in a way not otherwise available, that does not run counter to beliefs already held. Discussion classes provoke more active thinking than lecture classes (Bloom, 1953), and several experiments have demonstrated that active learning is more efficient than passive (McGeoch and Irion, 1952). Group discussion provides experiences in integrating facts, formulating hypotheses, amassing relevant evidence, and evaluating conclusions. When information encounters intellectual or emotional resistance, discussion can reveal the source so it can be examined and dealt with. And group membership can contribute to changes in motivation and attitudes because it is often easier to effect change with a group than with a single individual (Lewin, 1952). Research concerning student-centered teaching is also relevant. In ten of eleven studies reviewed by McKeachie (1962), greater changes in ability to apply concepts, in attitudes, in motivation, or in group membership skills were found for discussion techniques emphasizing freer student participation than for discussion with greater instructor dominance.

Evaluational procedures also influence cognitive behavior. If grades are based on memorization of details, students will learn to memorize. If grades are based on integration of diverse materials and application of principles, students will try to develop such abilities. Meyer (1936) and Terry (1933) found that an upcoming essay exam leads to study emphasizing the organization and interrelationships of facts and principles while an upcoming multiple choice exam leads to memorization. Dressel (1958), at Michigan State, observes that the need to cover large masses of material leaves little time to reflect on the meaning, interrelationship, and applicability of the knowledge being gained. And even the able student often is reluctant to think for himself, partly because such efforts are time-consuming and difficult, but also because they apparently contribute little to better grades.

Sense of competence is also affected. Thistlethwaite (1962) found that curricular flexibility, controversial instruction, informality,

and warm student-faculty contacts characterized colleges "outstand-
ingly successful in encouraging undergraduates to get the doctorate in
humanistic fields [p. 313]." Davis (1964) found that intellectually
elite colleges significantly underproduced graduate students in science,
and blames the competitive grading practices, which restrict faculty
encouragement to those few A students at the top of the curve—even
though all the students may have high ability in science.

Variation in curriculum, teaching, and evaluation also has im-
plications for the development of emotional and instrumental inde-
pendence. When the curriculum specifies in detail what shall be stud-
ied, when teaching is essentially training students in the language,
thought, and behavior appropriate for a given profession or vocation,
when learning involves memorizing information and developing skills
called important by the teacher, and when grades and future success
depend upon conformity to and cooperation with this system, emo-
tional independence is unlikely to flourish. Instrumental independence
is fostered when one must cope with diverse tasks that have conse-
quence for oneself and when one must find and get to whatever one
needs. But most work prescribed in college is academic. Only a lim-
ited set of skills and competencies are taxed. Successful achievement
adds little to the coping abilities needed outside the classroom. And
when trips to the library and use of the card catalog fill the demands
for mobility, search, and discovery, instrumental independence is little
challenged.

According to Erikson (1950) and Sanford (1966), develop-
ment of identity is fostered by varied experiences and roles, meaning-
ful achievement, and relative freedom from anxiety and pressure. Few
colleges offer these conditions. Grading systems and detailed curricular
requirements work directly counter to the sampling and self-testing
through which self-definition proceeds. High academic pressures make
thinking for oneself risky. That all important index of worth, the GPA
(grade-point average), makes venturing into areas of weakness dan-
gerous. Meaningful work can counterbalance a narrow role. But most
college work is meaningless to most students. Observe student-taught
courses and programs of study in "free universities." Teacher behav-
ior, learning activities, student role, content, and evaluation, depart
markedly from the usual curriculum, lecture, and examination.

Interpersonal relationships also are affected. Competitive grad-
ing pits one person against another. Use of a grading curve means

that your good grade makes mine more unlikely. And the problem is amplified if we're both training for the same kind of work, both in the same department shooting for graduate fellowships, assistantships, and other significant goodies. It is not so much that close friendships are precluded, but that they have to carry such a burden. On the other hand, when the emphasis is on cooperative effort to complete complex tasks with excellence, then diversity of skill, perspective, and insight become valuable, and the orientation is toward sharing and toward knowing different persons and being able to work with them. Then more wide-ranging friendships and easy relationships become possible and valued. Clinging together in couples and cliques becomes less necessary.

Curriculum organization has particular import for the clarification of vocational plans and aspirations, a central component in clarifying purposes. In most colleges, curricular decisions are vocational choices. Indeed, the choice of college itself is a statement of general orientation. Choice of a major, however, is a more explicit commitment; required early, most students must make it with little relevant knowledge or experience. Once made, exploration of other alternatives is sharply curtailed. The boundaries of the disciplines are clearly marked. Few hours are left free. Most important, the choice is never again questioned by the institution. A department, lustily crying for more curricular pie and busily seeking students to strengthen its voice, will not ask recruits, new or old, whether their choice was wise, whether they should reconsider, whether some shift or modification would better serve developing interests or vocational aspirations. And if other circumstances—friends, incompetent teachers, increased awareness of where the choice really leads—should raise such questions, most systems exact substantial payment if change is made. Most students cannot generate the wherewithal—literal or figurative—to pay the price. Consequently they continue through graduate school and into future professions while wishing they were in a different line—or at least while suffering the nagging question whether an alternative existence might have suited them better.

Residence Hall Arrangements

Hypothesis: *Residence hall arrangements either foster or inhibit development of competence, purpose, integrity, and freeing interpersonal relationships, depending upon the diversity of backgrounds and attitudes among the residents, the opportunities for significant interchange, the existence of shared intellectual interests, and the degree to which the unit becomes a meaningful culture for its members.*

Development in residence hall settings stems from two major sources: close friendships and concomitant reference groups, and the general attitudes and values carried by the house as a cultural entity. Well-considered action can call on these forces to amplify several vectors of change. Students who live together learn together—when studies overlap sufficiently to permit it. Stephens College pioneered "living and learning centers," putting books, classes, and instructors' offices in dormitories and building academic and cultural programs in the residence context. Experimental units sprouting at Berkeley, Michigan State, and the University of Michigan take pains to establish residence units where their students can continue discussion of issues raised in class and where cooperative study is possible. Without such pains, in a large university there is little chance that a fellow member of Freshman English, Section 32, or History of Western Civilization, Section 10, or Advanced Calculus will be encountered outside of class. And in a small college such encounters as do more frequently occur will be sporadic and superficial if other settings do not provide a context for more sustained interaction. Thus judicious allocation of students to residences and curricular coordination can boost intellectual competence.

The direct and full encounters with roommates, hallmates, and housemates, when there is diversity of background and prejudice among them, create the context for increased tolerance and freedom in interpersonal relationships. Conflict, argument, and debate, as well as friendly sharing and exchange, occur. On occasion blows may be traded along with clothes. But through this process individual biases and idiosyncrasies are faced and those of others are revealed. In time perspective develops, mutual give-and-take is more readily granted and received.

Many words are spent on mutual interests, future plans and aspirations, and existential questions. What one's parents are, what they would have one be, and what I want to do—such questions are passed around, turned over, challenged, and supported. And thus are purposes clarified and strengthened. Persons differ, not only in religious, racial, ethnic, national, and class backgrounds, but in many in-

*dividual ways. But friends and acquaintances are usually selected from
among those most like ourselves. Thus are we insulated. Misconception
and prejudice continue uncorrected and untempered. Colleges
can influence residence hall membership to provide diverse relationships
that counterbalance the increasing homogeneity that follows
from complete self-selection.*

*A residence hall has most impact when it becomes an effective—and
affective—subculture, when it becomes a reference group
for its members. The values and behavioral norms of the group become
the background against which individual decisions about behavior,
values, and attitudes are taken. Under such conditions the
shared standards and rules for conduct are not viewed as arbitrary,
capricious, or functionless, nor are they felt to be unduly coercive, intrusive
or authoritarian. Of course, decisions are not made on a simple
one-to-one relationship with group standards. Through continuing interaction
alternatives are developed, tested, and modified, and thus
individuals assume their own positions and roles. Such conditions exert
powerful forces for the development of integrity. For discrepancies
between expressed beliefs and behavior will not go unchallenged, and
when one is known and observed through a year or more such discrepancies
as exist will out. All may be fooled for a while and some
may be fooled forever—but most, before long, will see us clearly for
what we are. And, given sufficient concern and a supporting atmosphere,
they will not keep their knowledge from us.*

Faculty and Administration

Hypothesis: *When student-faculty interaction is frequent and
friendly and when it occurs in diverse situations calling for varied roles,
development of intellectual competence, sense of competence, autonomy,
and purpose are fostered.*

*Wallace's (1966) research illustrates the impact of student-faculty
relationships on intellectual competence and sense of competence.
For all, and especially for high aptitude students, admiration of
faculty members was associated with higher GPA's and with spending
less time on dates. For the most apt students, admiration of faculty
also affected graduate school aspirations. These findings recall those
of Davis (1964), where faculty encouragement was a major influence
for going on to graduate school. Thistlethwaite (1959), on the basis*

of his research on many colleges, describes the teacher who stimulates graduate study:

> He does not see students only during office hours or by appointment; open displays of emotion are not likely to embarrass him; students need not wait to be called upon before speaking in class; in talking with students he frequently refers to his colleagues by their first names; students do not feel obligated to address him as "professor" or "doctor" [p. 189].

The first step in achieving autonomy is disengagement from the parents; when the first step is taken, support of nonparental adults and peers is sought. Idolization and idealization of warm, sensitive teachers and other adults follow. Thus accessible adults, open enough to be fully known, can have substantial impact whether they be cook, custodian, or college professor. With them the actions and reactions learned during childhood and habitual with parents or other authorities can be reexamined, alternative behaviors can be tested. New modes of relationship with persons in authority and with institutional expressions of authority can be developed. Movement from dependency or rebellious independence toward relationships of mutual respect and regard can occur. Areas of interdependency can be recognized. Space for an autonomous existence can be carved out of the larger context. By demonstrating varied life-styles and value orientations, such adults can also help foster development of purpose and integrity. In them, students can see more clearly the satisfactions and frustrations of varied vocations and avocations, of varied marriage and family relationships. Through conversation with them, students can clarify their own values and interests, their own notions of a satisfying existence.

Substantial evidence suggests the impact of student-faculty relationships on variables relevant to the development of Autonomy and Purpose and Integrity. Both Jacob (1957) and Eddy (1959) found "values" and "character development" influenced primarily by relationships with individual teachers who made clear their commitments. Wilson (1963), at Antioch, found that courses and teachers accounted for 41 per cent of new interests, tastes, and appreciations developed.

Of course, as Adelson (1962) points out, a teacher may also serve as an "anti-model," as a lodestar from which the student sails away as fast as he can, saying to himself, "Whatever he is, I will not be; whatever he is for, I will be against [p. 414]." Teachers who are such a force for repulsion also provoke development, and each of us must recognize that if we are a force at all, for some students the va-lence will be negative, not positive. But better that students encounter a substantial being than a calculating role player or an elusive shadow.

Student Culture

Hypothesis: *The student culture either amplifies or attenuates the impact of curriculum, teaching and evaluation, residence hall ar-rangements, and student-faculty relationships.*

The student culture defines the acceptable working agreements between student and institution. It sets the framework for attitudes and activities with which the student responds to the opportunities and frustrations, the freedom and constraints, the ideals and the disillusions, provided by the institution. The student culture interprets to the new-comer the range of deviancies tolerated and the likely consequences of stepping out of bounds. The culture may carry values and emphases of its own, distinct from or in opposition to, those of the institution; or it may go beyond the faculty and administration in endorsing and act-ing on values to which the institution ascribes. Thus student culture has substantial impact on student development.

Its impact on the development of intellectual competence is well documented. Hughes, Becker, and Geer (1962) describe the ways in which student culture in medical school influences not only how much work will be done but also which knowledge and skills will be given most attention and which will be neglected. Studies of fraterni-ties and sororities also reveal the strength of this force. Wallace (1966), for example, found that membership in Greek-letter societies imparted a powerful downward push to the orientation to achieve high grades. On the other hand, as Stern's studies (1962, 1964) have demon-strated, the student culture can also maintain a strong intellectual cli-mate where readings, writings, and artistic products are valued and shared, and where the principal focus and substance of student con-versations are ideas rather than the latest developments in heterosexual relationships, on the social front, or in athletics.

It is the student culture that principally defines the appropriate responses to institutional authority and the accepted modes of inter-action with faculty members. Thus it may facilitate or limit the de-velopment of autonomy. If friendship with a faculty member is seen as currying favor to receive higher grades, easy relationships where free exchange and mutuality of regard might grow are difficult to develop and sustain because the attendant jibes are too painful or the risks of rejection too great. When the culture maintains a conspiracy of silence and supports subversion of regulations, quiet deviation, and playing it cool, those confrontations with persons in authority and those challenges to outdated rules and regulations necessary for both individual and institutional growth do not occur. Or when the culture demands intransigent rebelliousness, which precludes listening, reflection, or compromise, then impasses develop that fix both students and institution in antidevelopmental positions.

Student culture similarly effects the development of identity and purpose. Identity is best developed by ranging freely through varied situations, testing one's reaction to them, by trying different roles with varying degrees of commitment and investment, and by receiving clear feedback uncontaminated by others' stereotypes and unclouded by one's own anxiety. But where status is accorded to only a limited set of roles, be they athlete or intellectual, activist or addict, party boy or preprofessional, and when the range of situations for approved activity is limited, then development of identity suffers. Premature and totalistic investment in a single alternative, or passive noninvestment, are frequent responses. Neither provides the wide range of resonances through which a satisfying and productive sense of self can be built, by which future plans and aspirations are clarified. As Wallace (1966) reports,

> The main criteria of friendship selection and the main influence of resulting friendships may not be on attitudes relevant to . . . life as a student, but rather on those . . . larger and often more burning problems of developing an orientation to life in general; problems of becoming an adult in an adult world; problems, in short, of life cycle . . . [p. 114].

When the culture accepts such friendships, and values the intimate exchanges that accompany them, identity and purpose can move ahead.

The impact of student culture on freeing interpersonal relationships needs little elaboration. Where the culture precludes, or assigns second-class citizenship to, students of particular background, particular talents, particular interests, values, or attitudes, then stereotypes are reinforced and opportunities to learn how to live and to work with such persons are limited. Therefore, the degree of openness and flexi-

bility that characterizes a particular student culture and the extent to which restrictive subcultures exist on a given campus are factors of special significance for freeing interpersonal relationships.

Thus student culture is a moderator variable, an amplifier tuned to highs or lows in different areas, a screen sifting out those too coarse or wrongly shaped. And it is also a force in its own right, carrying its own values, exerting its own pressures and rewards.

This overview, then, proposes that differences in institutional objectives and internal consistency, size, curriculum, teaching, and evaluation, residences, faculty and administration, friends and student culture, make a difference to student development. The following chapters examine each in more detail, and offer illustrative evidence.

CHAPTER 8

CLARITY AND CONSISTENCY
OF OBJECTIVES

At most colleges, process has taken over, leaving purpose to shift for itself. Objectives rarely surface when questions of policy and practice are raised. It is seldom asked whether the conditions for living and learning as they are encountered by the particular students who attend actually enable the desired development. Apparently the only person concerned about objectives is the catalog writer—he raises a question every two or three years when it's time for revision. Consciousness of purpose has been supplanted by deference to tradition and authority or uncritical acceptance of current practice. Innovation and experimentation—the shibboleths and panaceas of the 1960's—are often undertaken or borrowed with no apparent thought to institutional objectives.

At most institutions, administration, faculty, and students as well are caught in the machinery. The main thing is to keep it running smoothly. Squirt oil where it squeaks. If that doesn't work, replace the part or redesign it till it goes again. If something rubs the wrong way, don't ask whether the rubbing is conducive to valued development, eliminate the rub. Comfort becomes the prime criterion. For the administrator—a steady boat, a shiny image, solid financial security. For the professor—lectures that can become books and articles, minimal teaching and maximum time for professional advancement and personal interests, two office hours per week to keep individual students at a safe distance. For the student—free access twenty-four hours a day to drugs, drink, and the opposite sex, study what I want, when I want, as much, or as little as I want, hire whoever agrees, fire whoever doesn't. The examples may be exaggerated but the basic point is not—comfort does not always accompany significant development, institutional purposes are not always best realized when things go smoothly.

Clear and internally consistent objectives are the starting point for discussion and the criteria for decisions. Conditions and practices are properly modified when objectives are better served by the change. To operate without salient objectives is to sail without keel or rudder, subject to varied and conflicting forces of wind and current. Consider the institutions most plagued with problems of "power"—student power, faculty role, administrative prerogatives. Of those I know about, at none have institutional objectives been concretely described and at none have relationships between objectives and practice been clearly articulated. In such a vacuum reasoned analyses, rational decisions, and systematic evaluation cannot occur. So the basis on which questions of power and accountability might be settled is absent.

Several studies suggest that clear and consistent objectives make a difference to student development. Bennington College started in the late 1930's with a clearly spelled out orientation and philosophy, and with a program consciously designed to be consistent with it. A liberal sociopolitical viewpoint was pervasive. Daughters of Republicans, curiously enough, came to the college. Upon graduation many were, in today's jargon, activists; they held strong liberal beliefs and worked for them. Those who most identified with the dominant orientation of the college changed most. They enjoyed most prestige on campus, while those who maintained more conservative beliefs were less popular (Newcomb, 1943). These converted liberals more often than not married men who were similarly inclined, joined organizations congruent with these interests, and generally created, or moved into, conditions that sustained this orientation. So twenty-five years later their views were relatively unchanged (Newcomb *et al.,* 1967). The few institutions judged by Jacob (1967) to have influence on student values had their own prevailing atmosphere where teachers with strong value commitments were accessible to and sensitive to the students, and where value-laden personal experiences of students were integrated with the general educational program.

Clear and salient objectives make for internally consistent policies, programs, and practices. Such objectives reduce the frequency with which the developmental impact of one component runs counter to that of another. Thus, if development of purpose is an objective of major concern, curricular requirements, teaching styles, and evaluational procedures can be coordinated accordingly, and the resulting arrangements will differ from those where intellectual competence has higher priority. Clarity of objectives also helps faculty members operate as individuals in ways more congruent with each other. Most of us have little control over our routine behavior. Our manner of teaching, our ways of responding to students, and our allocations of time and energy, all are pretty well built in. To modify these in response to differing purposes and differing student needs and characteristics is enormously difficult. It requires a high degree of self-consciousness and unremitting efforts at self-correction. With clear institutional objectives, which can be kept in the forefront of our mind, such self-correction has a chance to operate and in time may enable modification of our own behavior. We may learn to work more effectively under certain conditions or with certain kinds of students. Research and demonstration programs with movies, video tapes, and sound tapes have revealed the potency of self-observation in helping teachers, therapists, and parents to see more clearly where their means run counter to their ends and have helped them to change accordingly. A video tape machine for every faculty member is a financial and psychological impossibility, but with clarity of objectives a frame of reference is provided, against which pictures captured or recalled without the aid of mechanical devices can be checked. As Heath (1968) pointed out in his study of Haverford:

> A community that has an ideal or vision has, in effect, expectations of what its members are to become. . . . When such expectations are consistently expressed in all structures and activities of the institution, then different communal experiences may mutually rein-

force one another. It is rare that a specific type of educational experience is very significant in a person's life, as our data so clearly show. Rather, it is the coherence, the consistency, the "atmosphere" of one's environment that makes its impact upon development.

Salient institutional objectives also keep alive for students their reasons for being in college, and at that particular college. They can then organize time and energy more consciously to reach those objectives they value. Thus institutional clarity and commitment generate similar clarity and commitment on the part of students, leading not only to increased efficiency but also to higher levels of motivation. Further, when institutional objectives are explicit and widely shared, students teach each other; thus whether the objective is development of analytic skills or development of identity, conversational content and patterns of relationship become organized to serve those ends most salient.

In time another factor begins to operate. Because the objectives are those of "the college" they can be perceived as somewhat outside of and beyond any particular student. One can thus become identified with them and become somewhat missionary; one's own self-interest is tied up with the realization of the college's objectives by oneself and by others. Under such conditions campus visitors young and old frequently may be exhorted to modify their own behavior and orientation to accord with the valued objective, and the virtues of the institution in fostering integrity, social concern, breadth of perspective, highly developed cognitive skills, or whatever the dominant objectives may be, are persuasively extolled.

When objectives have been taken seriously by faculty and students, they come to pervade various aspects of the institution, affecting parietal rules, academic and nonacademic expectations and requirements, student-faculty relationships, and admissions criteria. This then leads to a third phenomenon, self-selection by prospective students and faculty members, which adds momentum and provides for self-perpetuation. Thus, in time, a community of shared ideas and goals becomes a reality sustained by processes of self-selection, which operate with increasing force and subtlety. The evidence for subtle and sharp student self-selection when institutional objectives are clear and pervasive is abundant and unequivocal (Astin, 1964; Heist, 1965; Pace, 1962; Stern, 1964).

Because several of the thirteen colleges participating in the Project on Student Development have distinctive goals and climates, they well illustrate the intimate relationships among institutional objectives, college policies and practices, and the characteristics of students who apply and are admitted.* Members of each faculty and administration were given a College Goals Rating Sheet, which listed twenty-five characteristics of graduates, and asked to represent the objectives of their institution by indicating the two most desirable characteristics, the two least desirable, and then the five next most desirable and the five least so. Table 17 gives the objectives rated most and least desirable at each institution.

Four basic patterns emerge: Christ-Centered, Intellectual-Social, Personal-Social, Professional-Vocational. The Christ-Centered colleges are remarkably similar not only in the characteristics most desired, but in those least desired. Whenever an item has an explicit religious reference it is ranked high at W. J. B., Simon, Savior, and Divinity. Thus the five such items among the twenty-five choices are ranked highest. Friendly and Sacred are similar except that "Capable of effective judgment based on sound analysis of relevant information," and items concerning responsible citizenship without religious reference ranked high often enough to displace items mentioning Christ and God.

It should be noted that faculty and administrators at the Christ-Centered colleges may think that the intellectual, social, and professional-vocational dimensions of the other patterns are expressed within the five items they ranked highest. Indeed, how the graduate who is committed to Christ differs in behavior from the secular graduate who is strongly committed to a similar value system that has a humanistic basis remains unclear. The difference has real meaning for faculty and for many students, but clear communication of that difference to someone outside the community seems difficult to achieve.

Colleges not Christ-centered consistently rank as least desirable some of the items with religious referents, most commonly, "Committed to Christ" and "Guided by God's Will." These colleges share with the Christ-Centered frequent assignment of "Chooses friends carefully" and "Mixes easily but chooses friends carefully" to the least desirable category. Thus these two items did not contribute much to the discriminative power of the instrument.

* Unless otherwise noted, the material on the thirteen Project colleges presented on the following pages is from Chickering et al. (1968).

Table 17

PATTERNS OF INSTITUTIONAL OBJECTIVES EXPRESSED AS MOST
AND LEAST DESIRED CHARACTERISTICS OF GRADUATES

Pattern and College	Five Most Desired	Five Least Desired
Christ-Centered A		
W.J.B. Savior Simon Divinity	Educated in the liberal arts within the context of a Christian world view Committed to Christ Guided by God's Will Activated by Christian ideals in the various pursuits of life Dedicated to Christian service	Independent member of society Recognizes and accepts feelings as relevant to decision Chooses friends carefully Educated in the traditional liberal arts Mixes easily but chooses friends carefully
Christ-Centered B		
Friendly	Same as above except that "Dedicated to Christian service" gives way to "Capable of effective judgment based on sound analysis of relevant information."	
Sacred	Same as above except that "Guided by God's Will" gives way to "Capable of effective judgment. . . ." "Socially responsible and participating citizen," and "Constructive and creative member of interdependent society," also were ranked high.	
Intellectual-Social		
Elder	Capable of effective judgment based on sound analysis of relevant information Activated by the intellectual, cultural, moral, and spiritual values of our civilization Constructive and creative member of interdependent society Socially responsible and a participating citizen Educated in the liberal arts within the context of a Christian world view	Chooses friends carefully Committed to Christ Guided by God's Will Mixes easily but chooses friends carefully Independent member of society

Table 17—Cont.

PATTERNS OF INSTITUTIONAL OBJECTIVES EXPRESSED AS MOST
AND LEAST DESIRED CHARACTERISTICS OF GRADUATES

Pattern and College	*Five Most Desired*	*Five Least Desired*
Classic	Same as Elder except that "Socially responsible . . . ," and "Educated in the liberal arts . . . world view" are replaced by "Has understanding of self as an individual and as a member of society," and "Aware of the broad cultural foundations of our society"; and "Independent member of society" is replaced by "Dedicated to Christian service and leadership."	
Stonewall	Same as Elder except "Constructive and Creative member of interdependent society" is replaced by "Possesses skills and abilities for future vocation."	
Personal-Social		
Kildew	Has understanding of self as an individual and as a member of society Constructive and creative member of interdependent society Capable of effective judgment based on sound analysis of relevant information Able to recognize and develop own creative potentials Socially responsible and participating citizen	Committed to Christ Guided by God's Will Dedicated to Christian service Educated in the liberal arts within the context of a Christian world view Activated by Christian ideals in the various pursuits of life
Professional-Vocational		
Rocket	Prepared for future professional activities Possesses skills and abilities for future vocation Capable of effective judgment, etc. Socially responsible and participating citizen Constructive and creative member of interdependent society	Committed to Christ Guided by God's Will Dedicated to Christian service Educated . . . within the context of a Christian world view Chooses friends carefully

Table 17—Cont.

PATTERNS OF INSTITUTIONAL OBJECTIVES EXPRESSED AS MOST
AND LEAST DESIRED CHARACTERISTICS OF GRADUATES

Pattern and College	Five Most Desired	Five Least Desired
Bootstrap	Same as above except that "Aware of broad cultural foundations of our society" replaces "Constructive and creative member of interdependent society."	Independent member of society Educated in the traditional liberal arts Guided by God's Will Activated by personal value system relevant to own needs and social circumstances Chooses friends carefully

Elder, Classic, and Stonewall rank highest characteristics reflecting intellectual ability, breadth of information, and social responsibility. Classic replaces one item concerning social responsibility with one concerning increased self-understanding.

Kildew's desired characteristics are predominantly related to personal development and responsible citizenship, with one item reflecting development of intellectual competence. No items concerning information or breadth of knowledge are ranked among the top five. At Rocket and Bootstrap, the emphasis on professional and vocational preparation is reflected along with concern for intellectual competence. At Bootstrap, "Constructive and creative member of interdependent society" is displaced by "Aware of broad cultural foundations of our society."

The College and University Environment Scales (CUES) (Pace, 1962) were completed at each college by a random sample of one hundred students across all four classes, selected to assure sample representation proportionate to class size and sex distribution. Figures 7, 8, and 9 illustrate the results. The six most conservative church-related colleges generated very similar patterns, not unlike those described by Pace (1963) for similar institutions in his standardization sample. Three other institutions generated similar patterns, although Elder consistently scored higher than the other two. The pattern for

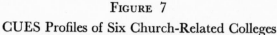

FIGURE 7

CUES Profiles of Six Church-Related Colleges

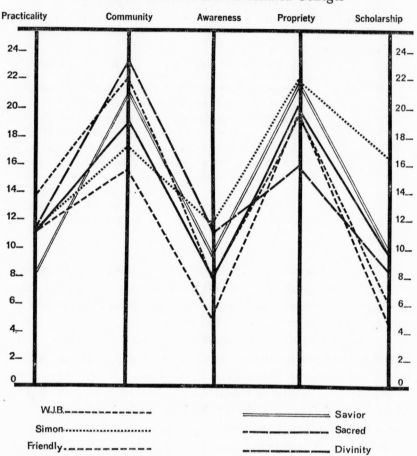

these three is something of a counterpoint to the first, with low scores on Practicality balanced by relatively high scores on Awareness. These are three of the four colleges where Intellectual-Social and Personal-Social objectives were primary. The four remaining are more varied. Three profiles are fairly similar, but Woodbine is a maverick. All four share the distinction of scoring lowest on Awareness and three of the four are lowest on Scholarship. Note that two of these, Rocket and Bootstrap, gave primary place to the Professional-Vocational objectives. At several Project colleges these scales were also completed by members of the faculty and administration. Their profiles, and the actual scores,

FIGURE 8

CUES Profiles of Three Colleges

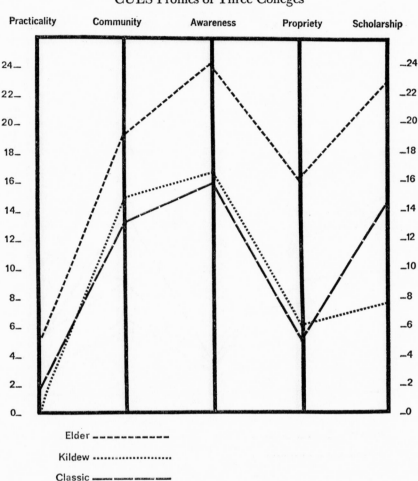

were very close to those generated by the students, except—not surprisingly—faculty members consistently rated their institutions higher on Scholarship.

To gather information about actual programs and practices associated with these differences, three-man teams traveled to each campus and talked to students, faculty, and administration; went to classes, chapels, assemblies, ball games; visited dormitories, snack bars, cafeterias. Table 18 indicates roughly the relative positions of the colleges in religious emphasis, regulations and supervision, student-

FIGURE 9

CUES Profiles of Four Colleges

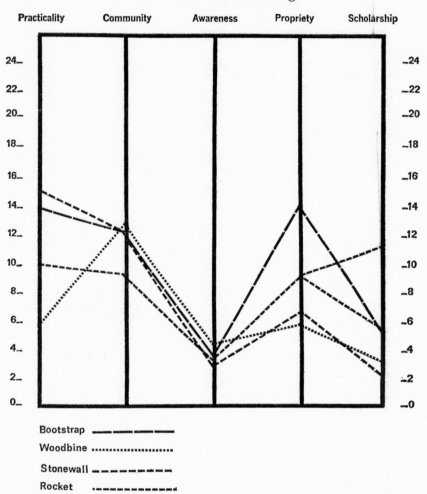

faculty relations and sense of community at the time of the visit in 1966. A few excerpts from the reports of visiting team members will illustrate the diversity behind our crude table. (It should be noted that some of these colleges are changing rather rapidly so that the picture taken then is already somewhat outdated.)

Simon, Savior, W. J. B., and Divinity all require daily chapel attendance and twelve to sixteen credit hours in religion, theology, and Bible studies. Faculty members must sign a statement indicating ad-

Table 18

RELATIVE POSITIONS FOR
RELIGIOUS ORIENTATION, REGULATION AND SUPERVISION,
STUDENT-FACULTY RELATIONSHIPS, AND SENSE OF COMMUNITY

Religious Orientation	*Regulation and Supervision*	*Stu.-Fac. Relations and Community*
Conservative, Strong Emphasis	*Numerous Regulations, Close Supervision*	*Distant, Formal, Weak Sense of Community*
Simon	Savior	Rocket
Savior	W.J.B.	
		Stonewall
W.J.B.	Simon	
Divinity		
	Divinity	Friendly
	Bootstrap	Sacred
Bootstrap		
		Savior
	Friendly	Woodbine
Sacred	Sacred	Elder
Friendly		
Stonewall		
		Simon
	Rocket	
Elder	Classic	Bootstrap
	Stonewall	Divinity
Woodbine	Woodbine	
	Elder	W.J.B.
Classic		
Rocket		
		Kildew
Kildew	Kildew	Classic
Liberal, No Emphasis	*Few Regulations, Limited Supervision*	*Close, Informal, Strong Sense of Community*

herence to a religious creed as a condition of employment. Prayer meetings are part of the week's routine. At Simon, for example, frequent prayer meetings among girls in the dorm are reported, "usually one big dorm prayer meeting per week, one small group (5–7) meeting per week, and one off-dorm prayer meeting per week." At Divinity, "Prayer meeting, held once a week, lasts about an hour, is student planned, organized and operated, and was attended by roughly seventy five students of both sexes. Hymn singing was followed by prayer and testimonials, then by more prayer to end the meeting. Attendance was voluntary and was taken seriously." About W. J. B., a team member reports, "The extent to which the religious convictions of the W. J. B. community permeate its life is revealed by the frequency of references to its theology and religious beliefs in conversations with students and faculty and by the practice of opening each class with prayer or readings from the Bible."

Friendly, Stonewall, and Elder occupy middle locations. At Stonewall, attendance is required at a "convocation period" three times a week, one of which is devoted to "worship services with sacred music and inspirational talks," and there is a Religious Emphasis Week "to focus the thoughts of the entire student body and faculty on the significance of religion and its contribution to the life of the individual." However, only four hours of "religious courses" are required for graduation. At Elder, the Meeting House with its Quiet Room open at all times for meditation and prayer, together with comments in the catalog and by members of administration, faculty, and students, make clear the religious orientation. Graduation requirements may be fulfilled by six hours of study in either philosophy or religion. At both Stonewall and Elder, while a significant portion of the faculty share the respective religious background, there is diversity of belief, and religious orientation is not a major criterion for employment.

At Kildew and Rocket, representing the "heathen" end of the continuum, there is no chapel on campus and no plan to have one. Nor is religious study a prerequisite to graduation. The literature of the institutions and the conversations of administrators, faculty, and students make no mention of religious philosophy or belief. At Kildew there is much talk about values, attitudes, morality, and socially responsible behavior, but the basis is humanistic not theological. Thus the colleges run the gamut from strong emphasis on religious belief and commitment in the context of conservative, fundamentalistic, or evangelical traditions through more moderate emphasis in the context of Catholic or more liberal religious views, to complete absence of religious or theological components as such.

Similar diversity exists in regulation and supervision of students and relative positions are similar. At Savior, W. J. B., and Simon regulations are numerous, supervision is close. Ten to twenty pages of the student handbooks spell out standards, expectations, and consequences of misbehavior on campus, off campus, and in the residence halls.

The most important of these regulations rest on the religious beliefs; thus Simon "Protests: engaging in activities on Sunday which are not in harmony with the spirit of the Lord's Day; attending theatres, movies, poolrooms or similar places of amusements; the use of playing cards; music and radio programs not in keeping with Christian principles; spending excessive time in games and other recreational pursuits."

Savior says, about dress:

For Men Students: for classes, sport clothes (slacks, sweaters, and sport jackets) are usually worn. Coats are expected for the evening dinner except during extremely hot weather. For recreation areas men may wear T-shirts and shorts. Shorts are not permitted for general campus wear. For Women Students: standards of modesty, femininity, good taste and neatness are expected of all. Women students are expected to avoid the excesses of modern fashions and tight-fitting apparel. Dresses and evening wear must have a minimum of capped sleeves. Sleeveless dresses, low necklines, open backs, and excessively short or tight skirts are not in keeping with the above principles. For classes, dresses, skirts and blouses are worn. Hose are expected for the evening dinner except during extremely hot weather.

Socializing between the sexes: "Couples spending an inordinate amount of time together on or off campus will be given counseling or discipline. Freshmen should refrain from socializing before 3:30 P.M. Monday through Friday."

W. J. B. spells out expected dining room behavior in detail. For example:

Please refrain from talking with those who are serving you. . . .
All requests, such as asking for another napkin, etc., are to be given

to the hostess, who will give them to the waitress serving that table. . . . Playing with dishes, flipping water with your spoon and tearing doilies are all childish traits, and may not be tolerated. . . . When you have completed the meal, place your knife and fork in the center of the plate, side by side with handles on the outer edge. Do not merely place them on the edge of the plate. . . . Please do not hang your arms over the back of the chair at any time during the meal. At no time should you lean on the table while eating. . . . Do not chew with your mouth open. . . . Hold your knife and fork in the proper manner. . . . Do not dunk.

Authorized persons supervise behavior: adults living in the dormitories, student assistants living on each dormitory floor, and Deans of Men and Women who in some cases also have student assistants. Consequences for misbehavior rest with the deans, although preestablished monetary fines or other punishments are associated with some infractions, and in severe cases action usually rests with a faculty committee. Student judiciary committees operate in a limited fashion.

Obviously, not all the rules and expectations are seen as equally important nor are infractions treated with equal severity. Many are more statements of expectation than strict regulations. They do, however, suggest two basic principles on which these colleges seem to operate: (1) that students should be told in writing just what they are to do and what they are not to do, that the more things are spelled out the better, that no area should go unmentioned, and (2) that extensive regulation and close supervision fosters the development of responsible behavior.

At Kildew, by contrast, the rules are few and fuzzy. According to one reporter there are four: "(1) No unmannerly drinking, this is not explicitly defined. (2) No drinking under 21. (3) Limitation on inter-dorm visitation. (4) Sign out at switchboard when leaving campus." The College Regulations indicate that during the fall semester, 1965, members of the opposite sex are permitted in the sleeping quarters of student residences from 4:00 to 10:00 P.M. on weekdays, and 2:00 to 10:00 P.M. on Sundays. Each house must be closed to members of the opposite sex one day each week, and within these limits each house may set its own hours. For dress, one sentence: "Appropriate standards of personal appearance are expected of community members at all times both on and off campus."

Neither faculty nor student assistants supervise residence halls.

Students are expected to manage their own affairs and all students are expected to assume responsibility for their fellow students and for the welfare of the community. Commenting about handling of offenders, a team member said:

> There is a social standards committee which is also a fact finding committee—ninety percent of their energy has to do with inter-dorm visitation violation (students in sleeping quarters of opposite sex outside prescribed hours). There is no enforcement machinery. When asked who they have to back up regulations, student answered: "We have the Dean, he knows everything, almost. Last year he asked a student to leave."

At Kildew, the operating principles and assumptions are clearly the opposite of those at W. J. B., Savior, and Simon; namely, (1) that expectations and standards of behavior should not be spelled out in writing, nor even barely hinted at, and (2) that conditions of minimal regulation and limited supervision by adults or other authorized personnel foster the development of responsible behavior.

The other Project colleges fall between these two poles. Divinity and Bootstrap, while basically similar to W. J. B., Savior, and Simon in arrangements for supervision and enforcement, leave more unsaid and allow greater freedom and self-determination. Classic, Stonewall, Woodbine, and Rocket have the typical array of rules concerning gambling, drinking, smoking, dormitory curfews, late permissions, signing out, automobile use, and so forth. Elder's rules and standards are not strikingly different, but there is a strong honor code, and considerable responsibility for implementation rests with the students.

It is worth noting that the issue of rules and student behavior seems to be most salient at both the colleges with numerous regulations and close supervision and at Kildew with conditions of great freedom. But there is a difference. In the first instance, much energy is spent on implementation and enforcement. At Kildew, on the other hand, most of the energy goes into discussing and debating the standards themselves, with relatively minor modifications sometimes resulting. At Elder, Stonewall, and Sacred, by contrast, the existing structure of regulations seems to be accepted without much fuss.

Judgments about student-faculty relationships and sense of community based on brief visits are risky. Yet there seem to be clear differences from college to college. One reporter says of Rocket:

The order of the day seemed to be a kind of standardized urban anonymity. Serious-faced young men . . . came and went singly, in pairs, or small groups, chatting pleasantly and easily in quiet tones. Beyond the immediate circle however, the other students were treated as strangers with the not unfriendly distance often accorded other people eating in a restaurant or traveling on a train. A number of faculty (at least 3) complained of the lethargy of the students, saying they seem to have no interests; they are commuters; their lives are lived away from the college. "They come to class, take notes, go away."

At Sacred and Savior, the dominant impression is formality, distance, and respect. Students and faculty are acquainted. Students feel positively about the faculty and are at ease with their teachers. But, with individual exceptions of course, banter, casual conversation, or other informal exchange is rarely observed.

At Bootstrap and Divinity the atmosphere is more relaxed. At Bootstrap, "One . . . senses a great deal of warmth and friendliness— a high regard by the faculty for students and the feeling among students that teachers are their friends." This warmth and friendliness seems stronger at W. J. B., and carries also a feeling of community or extended family: "One needs to be on campus only a short time to sense a strong community spirit characterized by warmth, concern for the college, and devotion to its religious principles. According to statements made by students . . . they place a high value on the friendliness of the faculty and their readiness to respond to personal requests for help, whether in studies or personal problems."

At Kildew and Classic, relationships of friendship and informality are relatively frequent and there is a strong sense of community. At Kildew students and faculty operate for the most part on a first name basis. Each student has a faculty counselor, usually of his own choice, and it is expected that individual conferences will be held every one or two weeks. In this context, as well as in the small classes, independent studies, and numerous joint student-faculty committees, close relationships of mutual regard develop. The sense of community is particularly strong at Classic. Few members of the community can define precisely what it means to be a Classic type, but in his heart everyone knows. As is the case at Kildew, and also at W. J. B. to a lesser extent, this sense of community derives primarily from a wide range of informal, inexplicit, and frequently unidentified agreements and understandings that are learned only through living as a member of the community.

The team reports also reflected differences in curriculum organization for some of the colleges. Ten conform quite closely to the standard undergraduate liberal arts curriculum. That is to say, the organization of course requirements, the content of courses, and the procedures for evaluation basically conform to those found in most college catalogs one might pick off the shelf at random. Distribution requirements assure that each student takes at least one or two courses in the humanities, natural sciences, and social sciences. Evaluation is through quizzes, midterms, finals, and papers. And the course content is fairly predictable.

Some colleges vary this standard theme. At colleges with strong church ties, Bible courses are required for up to sixteen hours of credit. Until recently, post-college employment opportunities for the graduates of Bootstrap, a predominantly Negro college, were limited to teaching and the ministry, and therefore their liberal arts program has developed within that context. At Bootstrap there is also experimentation with the freshman English courses, and with remedial work in reading and speech. Sacred has developed one interdisciplinary course bringing together history and the humanities, has another ready to begin soon, and is seeking support to extend this approach to other areas. At Divinity, team teaching in history is working well and being tested in other areas; opportunities for independent study have been opened up to senior students and may start to filter down to lower grade levels. The psychology department has developed an original sequence of courses and off-campus activities that allow close connections between on-campus learning, participation in a local mental hospital, and participation in research. Elder enables independent study for upper division students and offers interdepartmental courses and fields of concentration. Independent research supported by a $600 stipend is also possible for thirty students during the summer. Foreign programs and other off-campus study opportunities at centers in Washington and New York, at the Hoover Institute at Stanford, and at the Merrill Palmer Institute in Detroit are also available.

Three colleges differ sharply from the standard pattern. Rocket differs because it is primarily training students in either business or engineering. The general studies component is strong, and a distinct liberal arts unit is under way, but a student's program is determined clearly and in detail by whether he majors in business management or engineering. Thus Rocket differs primarily in the content of its curricula.

Classic and Kildew differ from the other Project colleges and from each other. Classic has a highly structured and tightly integrated curriculum, emphasizing skills in analysis, rhetoric, logic, and integration, and a comprehensive background of basic information. Classes are usually intense small-group discussions of limited reading materials frequently prepared in mimeographed form by the staff responsible for the particular course or sequence. Evaluation is by comprehensive examinations in humanities, natural sciences, and social sciences, and by integrative examinations in foreign language, history, and philosophy. Figure 10, taken from the Classic catalog, portrays the general pattern and reveals that somebody developed some kind of skill to a high degree. Notice that Nat. Sci. IV and Hum. III go down for a pass while Soc. Sci. II follows Math I in a fake line plunge over right guard.

Kildew's student-centered and highly flexible curriculum is in direct contrast to Classic. There are no required courses. Independent study is open to all students from the second year onward. Students are expected to undertake three studies each semester but may carry only two if the nature of the studies warrants it. Independent study may be pursued singly, or with one or more other students who share similar interests and who can agree on a plan of work for the semester satisfactory to themselves and to whatever teacher will work with them. Courses arise out of the interests of the students and the interests and capabilities of the teachers. Three days are usually given to registration, during which students confer with teachers and with counselors about courses and prospective independent studies. During the first three weeks of the semester, course changes can be made with ease and planning of independent studies may be carried forward.

The usual system of examinations and grades is replaced by a system of written self-evaluations and instructor comments and the last four or five days of each semester are given to final conferences with teachers and counselors about the work of the term. Figure 10 diagrams the classic student-centered curriculum.

The pictures of each college that emerge from the diverse views provided by the College Goals Rating Sheet, the College and University Environment Scales, and campus visits are highly consistent.

FIGURE 10

The Curriculum

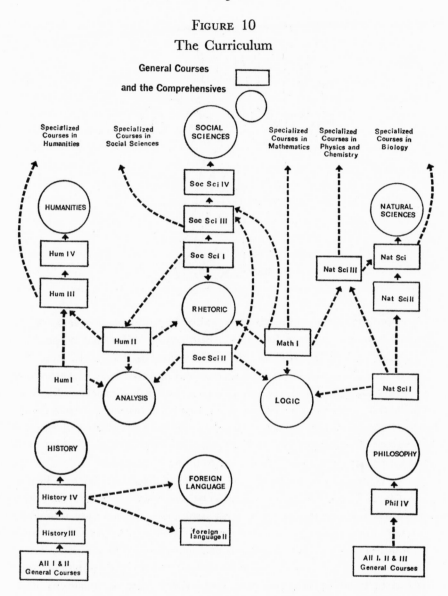

Institutional objectives, college programs and practices, and the characteristics of the institution, as perceived by students and faculty, all fit together like a neatly cut puzzle. Are the clear and consistent differences among these colleges accompanied by similarly distinct differences among the students who apply and are admitted?

All freshmen entering the thirteen Project colleges in September

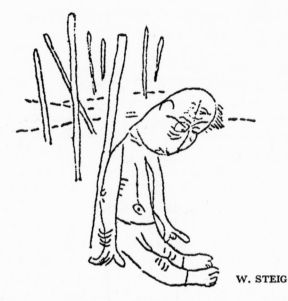

W. STEIG

1965 completed the Omnibus Personality Inventory and several other instruments during their first week. Substantial differences appeared, which are well illustrated by the OPI scores in Tables 19 and 20. When factor and scale scores are compared, three major patterns— which we labeled Practical Conservatives, Altruistic Conservatives, and Intellectual Altruists—account for ten of the institutions. The colleges that cluster together in these patterns are those that shared similar objectives, similar College and University Environment Scale patterns, and that looked similar to visiting team members.

Thus, Intellectual Altruists are the mode at Kildew, Classic, and Elder. These students show diverse interests in the arts and appreciation for literature, music, and dramatics. They enjoy reflective thought and academic activities; their thinking is relatively free from domination by objective conditions and generally accepted ideas. They are also interested in science and are generally logical, analytical, and critical in their approach to problems. They admit to sensitivity and emotionality.

These entering students are generally ready to express impulses and to seek gratification either in conscious thought or in overt action. They have an active imagination and value sensual reactions. They are experimentally oriented and fond of novel situations and ideas. Tolerant of ambiguities, they prefer to deal with diversity and complexity as opposed to simplicity and structure. They have concern for the feelings and welfare of others and are trusting in relationships with them. They are skeptical of conventional religious beliefs and practices and especially reject orthodoxy or fundamentalism.

The Practical Conservatives predominate at W. J. B., Savior, Sacred, and Stonewall. Their pattern is a counterpoint to the Intellectual Altruists; when Intellectual Altruists score low, Practical Conservatives score high, and vice versa. Thus Practical Conservatives are interested in practical applied activities and tend to value material possessions and concrete accomplishments. They are authoritarian and conservative, with nonintellectual interests and a preference for overt action. They tend to deny interest in esthetic matters and to evaluate ideas on the basis of their practical immediate application.

Compared with the Intellectual Altruists, they are less concerned about the welfare of others, more impersonal, and more distant. They have strong religious commitments and ascribe to conservative, evangelical, or fundamentalistic religious beliefs.

Like the Intellectual Altruists, the Altruistic Conservatives are concerned about others and trusting. Like the Practical Conservatives, they are wary of expressing impulses either in thought or action and are nonexperimental, preferring the known and tried over the novel. They also share a strong religious commitment and subscribe to conservative or evangelical beliefs. Their level of interest in things intellectual falls between the other two groups.

Thus, the Altruistic Conservative differs from the Practical Conservative primarily in his high level of social concern and sensitivity to the welfare of others, and he differs from the Intellectual Altruists primarily in his religious orientation, his hesitancy with regard to the expression of his own impulses, and his caution with the new or experimental.

These three major patterns account pretty well for the OPI characteristics that most sharply differentiate among entering students at ten of the thirteen Project colleges. Three colleges, Woodbine, Bootstrap, and Rocket, present unique configurations. Woodbine students stay close to the mean. Only once do they deviate more than one half standard deviation from the norms group and the small variations that do occur show no systematic relationship with any of the patterns so far observed. Bootstrap entrants combine a strong practical orientation with moderate levels of intellectual interest. This combination is ac-

Table 19

OMNIBUS PERSONALITY INVENTORY
INTELLECTUAL ORIENTATION*

	Practical Outlook (PO, Au-Reverse)	Intell.-Esthetic (Es, MF-reverse, TI)	Intell.- Scientific (TO, TI, MF)
Practical Conservatives			
W.J.B.			
Males	56	42	49
Females	56	51	42
Savior			
Males	58	46	49
Females	58	50	42
Sacred			
Males	58	44	48
Females	57	50	44
Stonewall			
Males	56	42	48
Females	58	51	42
Altruistic Conservatives			
Simon			
Males	55	47	48
Females	54	52	44
Divinity			
Males	52	46	49
Females	53	51	43
Friendly			
Males	54	44	48
Females	55	50	42
Intellectual Altruists			
Kildew			
Males	39	57	53
Females	37	61	51
Classic			
Males	39	59	50
Females	41	53	54
Elder			
Males	45	49	47
Females	44	55	54

* Figures are averages of mean standard scores for scales under each factor. N's for men, 39–526; for women 52–177. Standard deviations for Project colleges typically 7.0–9.0 on individual scales. For N = 100 and S.D. = 8, a mean difference of 9 is likely to occur by chance less than one time in a hundred.

Table 19—Cont.

OMNIBUS PERSONALITY INVENTORY
INTELLECTUAL ORIENTATION*

	Practical Outlook (PO, Au-Reverse)	Intell.-Esthetic (Es, MF-reverse, TI)	Intell.-Scientific (TO, TI, MF)
Nonaligned			
Bootstrap			
Males	59	49	49
Females	60	52	47
Woodbine			
Males	51	46	49
Females	51	52	43
Rocket			
Males	55	40	49

* Figures are averages of mean standard scores for scales under each factor. N's for men, 39–526; for women 52–177. Standard deviations for Project colleges typically 7.0–9.0 on individual scales. For $N = 100$ and S.D. $= 8$, a mean difference of 9 is likely to occur by chance less than one time in a hundred.

companied by low concern for the feelings and welfare of others. They are moderately conservative in religious orientation and hesitant about impulse expression and experimentation. Rocket entrants, all men aspiring to either business or engineering, reflect much stronger intellectual interest in science than in arts or humanities. At all other Project colleges, intellectual interests were fairly consistent across both areas, but at Rocket not so. Rocket students also have relatively little social concern or concern for the welfare of others and are close to the mean on impulse expression, innovation, and religious orientation.

Do entering students differ from campus to campus? Yes. Do similar institutions attract similar students? The evidence suggests they do; the institutional clusters for entering students resemble those reflected by the College Goals Rating Sheet, the campus visits, and CUES.

To test this matter more systematically, McDowell (1967a) studied relationships between the five CUES scales—Practicality, Community, Awareness, Propriety, Scholarship—and four OPI measures—Practical Outlook, Intellectual-Esthetic, Impulsive-Innovative, and Religious Orientation. The results showed that colleges scoring high on Practicality attract students high on Practical Outlook; those scoring

Table 20

OMNIBUS PERSONALITY INVENTORY
SOCIAL-RELIGIOUS ORIENTATION*

	Impulsive- Innovative (IE, Co)	Altruism (Am)	Religious Orientation (RO)
Practical Conservatives			
W.J.B.			
Males	47	47	38
Females	44	52	38
Savior			
Males	47	47	41
Females	42	52	39
Sacred			
Males	50	46	45
Females	45	52	42
Stonewall			
Males	52	42	50
Females	48	48	47
Altruistic Conservatives			
Simon			
Males	47	50	40
Females	44	54	39
Divinity			
Males	47	51	40
Females	42	56	38
Friendly			
Males	47	46	45
Females	42	55	43
Intellectual Altruists			
Kildew			
Males	64	50	61
Females	61	54	63
Classic			
Males	59	46	57
Females	59	55	60
Elder			
Males	53	51	54
Females	48	56	51

* Figures are averages of mean standard scores for scales under each factor. N's for men, 39–526; for women 52–177. Standard deviations for Project colleges typically 7.0–9.0 on individual scales. For N = 100 and S.D. = 8, a mean difference of 9 is likely to occur by chance less than one time in a hundred.

Table 20—Cont.

OMNIBUS PERSONALITY INVENTORY
SOCIAL-RELIGIOUS ORIENTATION*

	Impulsive-Innovative (IE, Co)	Altruism (Am)	Religious Orientation (RO)
Nonaligned			
Bootstrap			
Males	51	44	46
Females	46	46	44
Woodbine			
Males	54	45	56
Females	52	49	53
Rocket			
Males	51	42	50

* Figures are averages of mean standard scores for scales under each factor. N's for men, 39–526; for women 52–177. Standard deviations for Project colleges typically 7.0–9.0 on individual scales. For N = 100 and S.D. = 8, a mean difference of 9 is likely to occur by chance less than one time in a hundred.

high on Awareness attract students scoring high on measures of intellectual and esthetic interests; those scoring high on Propriety attract students of conservative religious orientation.

McDowell also studied relationships between CUES scores and freshmen orientations to college—Vocational, Academic, Collegiate, Nonconformist—which further document sharp self-selection. His findings, consistent with the others, indicate that students had quite accurate perceptions of the colleges and chose accordingly. Colleges with high Practicality scores were chosen by Vocationally oriented students, not by Nonconformists or those with Academic orientations, in contrast to colleges scoring high on Awareness, where there are more entrants with Nonconformist or Academic orientations.

The evidence clearly shows that most of these colleges have developed their own clear purposes and pervasive atmospheres, which shine brightly enough to allow students to distinguish accurately one from another. Most of these colleges admit a high proportion of those who apply, so self-selection is the principal force at work. And as this force operates through time, it creates a strong community of like-minded students whose characteristics fit well the objectives, programs, and practices of the college they choose.

The thirteen Project colleges contrast sharply with the Liberal Arts College at Syracuse University, for example, where the variability among the students found by Stern suggests several different student cultures within the larger "macrocosm" (Stern, 1962). While the Syracuse student can seek out that culture within the college most comfortable for him, the Project college student must drink at a more singular fountain or slake his thirst elsewhere. Thus those who find refreshment and who persist to graduation are likely to have more particular tastes. If not, given the strong and ubiquitous pressures, they probably either develop those tastes or leave.

In these ways the clarity of institutional objectives and the internal consistency with which they are implemented operate as a major influence on student development. The particular vectors of development affected, of course, will depend upon the particular emphasis of a given institution. For one college, competence is most important; for another, integrity; for a third, autonomy and purpose. But it is the clarity and consistency that determine whether development will be fostered, or whether, in their absence and diffuseness, the conflicting forces that follow will immobilize the student and leave him passive and noncommitted, swinging like a pendulum, permitting little progress from dead center and little gain over the momentum provided by the diverse and general social forces that operate outside the institution.

CHAPTER 9

INSTITUTIONAL
SIZE

❦❦❦❦❦❦❦❦❦❦❦❦❦❦❦

Institutional size interacts
with institutional objectives. It is no coincidence that colleges with
clear and salient objectives are most frequently small; if they have
grown larger now, they established their institutional clarity while enrollments were less than one thousand. For while small size is not a
sufficient condition for clarity of purpose, the evidence suggests it is
a necessary one. Although many small colleges are indistinguishable
from each other and from their university counterparts and have
failed to develop a coherent integration of purposes and practices, the
diversity of persons and diversity of functions that come to characterize
the "multiversity" make such development nearly impossible, even
when the undergraduate liberal arts college itself has considerable
autonomy and freedom of movement. In large university settings,

185

where small units have been developed, where institutional purposes have been made explicit, and where sufficient time has elapsed, as with Monteith at Wayne State and New College at Hofstra, distinctive atmospheres have developed. Furthermore, the dynamic of self-selection that sustains and reinforces those atmospheres seems to be gathering momentum.

But institutional size has implications for student development in its own right, beyond its implications for clarity of institutional objectives. Taylor (1964) postulated the law that "people tend to disappear when huddled together in large numbers." A corollary to that law is, when students are superfluous they don't develop much, or to put it more elegantly, development varies inversely with redundancy. The basic point is that the more a student is superfluous in a given situation, the less he is apt to be affected by it or to develop in the ways the setting is designed to foster.

What does *redundant* or *superfluous* mean? Redundancy is five persons for a game of bridge, or ten persons for a baseball team. It's three persons to carry a suitcase, or six to carry a trunk, or twelve to move a piano. It's twenty persons on a trout stream or two thousand on a beach. It's a class play that calls for twenty, in a class of eighty, or an athletic program with places for eighty in a school for eight hundred. To put it more generally, redundancy occurs when increases in the number of inhabitants of a setting lead to decreasing opportunities for participation and satisfaction for each individual. It occurs when manpower available exceeds the number necessary to do the job.

Some of the things that happen as the ratio of persons to settings changes are illustrated by my own experiences with baseball. I first grew up in a neighborhood where there were five other boys about my age and we all liked to play baseball. Fortunately for us there were three younger brothers and two younger sisters among these six families; in addition, there were two fathers and one mother who were energetic, if not athletic. Out of this assortment of talent we used to construct baseball games. This baseball setting had several salient characteristics:

We were all in action most of the time. Each usually had a lot of territory to cover, and it came your turn to hit often. Sometimes a teammate would have to come out on base and run for you so you could go to bat.

We seldom played the same position in two consecutive games, or even within the same game. Different persons pitched, caught, or played right field, depending upon who was available. If another player came home from a piano lesson, positions would shift to accommodate his particular capabilities. We evaluated persons on the basis of what things they could do and how well they could do them; assignments were made and accepted accordingly. We would press into service whoever was available and willing. Visiting peers and adults were vigorously enjoined to play. No small child was spared.

We played by rules never heard of in the majors, and seldom by the same ones twice. Where one could hit the ball, whether a team "caught for itself," which team covered home plate, these and other regulations were modified with impunity in order that our purposes were best met. Even within an inning the rules would change; the pitcher would have to move up halfway and pitch underhand to the younger brother, for example.

At age eleven I moved downtown. In this new neighborhood of about twenty-five boys, enough players were usually available "for a good game." This setting differed strikingly from the other:

In the field or at bat we stood or sat around a lot. Specialists developed. A few were good pitchers and did little else. One boy loved to catch and always did. First base and shortstop were usually nailed down. A hierarchy of leadership developed. The rules were standard.

Younger brothers and inept parents were never included and some peers with marginal skills were consistent spectators when "we had enough." And some were punished severely even when they were able to play. I can recall clearly the tension that developed as there were two places to be filled and four or five persons left. Not to be chosen was painful, but frequently to be chosen last was not much better.

After a while I entered a college along with about 300 others, and played some baseball there. These seemed to be the salient characteristics of the college baseball setting:

Competition was severe. Most persons didn't get to play at all and coaching was reserved for those already highly skilled. Evaluation was comparative and choices were made on the basis of fairly fine distinctions. A good hitter could always play. Exceptional skills in some other area sometimes could counterbalance mediocre hitting, but lack of that particular skill ruled one out.

Only infrequently did players move from one position to another, and each developed to a high degree the skills associated with his position. There were both a formal leadership hierarchy with a captain and co-captain, and an informal hierarchical structure of prestige and power.

Examination of the differences in these three situations, differences that result from the increased numbers of persons per setting, suggests several propositions. A cautious scientist would state them as hypotheses, but for the sake of clarity, they are stated baldly. As the number of persons increases in relation to a given task or setting six things occur: (1) A smaller proportion of the total inhabitants actively participate. (2) The activities and responsibilities of those who do participate become less varied and more specialized. (3) Persons with marginal ability are left out, deprived of changes to develop further the skills they lack. (4) Evaluation shifts from how well a person's abilities fit the requirements of a given position, to how good one person is compared to another; distinctions are made on an increasingly fine basis. (5) A hierarchy of prestige and power develops. (6) Rules and conduct considered appropriate become formalized and rigid.

These propositions seem to hold true for other situations in which the ratio between the number of persons and the number of settings changes. Most of them are documented by the work of Barker and his associates concerning both communities and high schools of varying size. Some of this research is reported in *Big School, Small School* (Barker and Gump, 1964), which is the source for the comments that follow. In these studies, community size varied from 169 to 101,155; school enrollment, from 35 to 2,287; settings, from 58 to 499; ratio of persons to settings, from .58 to 4.58; and the varieties of settings, from 28 to 43.

A setting has two major components: behavior, and objects with which behavior is transacted. The behavior and objects within a setting are organized in nonrandom fashion and the boundary of the setting is usually easily distinguished. The persons who inhabit a setting are to a considerable extent interchangeable; there may be a continuing stream of persons, but the setting remains fairly constant. A living room, for example, is a behavior setting. The behavior and objects within this setting are organized so that it is easily distinguished from the kitchen or the bedroom, and living room behavior across many different kinds of families is more similar than living room and kitchen behavior within the same family. Similarly, a college is a behavior setting. It differs from a living room in the number of subsettings it contains and it belongs to a different variety of settings, but both are places where behavior is patterned in recognizable ways and through which different persons move without effecting serious change.

Obviously there are different varieties of settings and the criteria for classification depend on the purposes to be served. An institution could be classified within a variety called *college,* or called *coeducational college,* or called *coeducational liberal arts college,* or within other varieties depending upon the purposes for classification.

As Table 21 indicates, Barker and Gump found that as schools increased in size, the number of persons increased much faster than either the number of settings or the varieties of settings. In the smallest school there were about two *settings* for each person while in the

Table 21[a]

SIZE, SETTINGS, AND STUDENTS

School	Community Population	School Enrollment	Settings	Students per Setting	Varieties of Settings
Otan	199	35	60	0.58	29
Dorset	169	45	58	0.78	28
Walker	450	83	96	0.86	31
Malden	507	92	78	1.18	33
Meadow[b]	—	113	94	1.20	32
Midwest	781	117	107	1.09	33
Vernon	1,150	151	98	1.54	29
Haven	2,907	221	154	1.44	36
Eakins[c]	551	339	139	2.44	34
Booth	3,004	438	218	2.01	39
University City	23,296	945	312	3.03	36
Shereton[c]	4,739	1,923	487	3.95	41
Capital City	101,155	2,287	499	4.58	43

[a] Adapted from Tables 4.1 and 4.3, pp. 42 and 49, Barker and Gump, 1964.
[b] Meadow was two miles from the nearest town; it served two towns.
[c] High school that served several communities in addition to the one in which it was located.

largest there were more than four *persons* for each setting. And while the largest school has only half again as many varieties of settings, it has sixty times as many students.

What are the consequences of these differences for the students? Here are some of the findings:

Students in small schools held an average of 3.5 responsible positions per student (members of play casts, officers of organizations, members of musical groups, members of athletic teams); students in large schools averaged .5 responsible positions per student. Put differently, on the average, in the large schools every other student held a single position; in the small, each student held two positions. Furthermore, students in small schools held twice as many different *kinds* of responsible positions as those in large.

Students in small schools received twice as many pressures to participate, or to meet the expectations of the school, as those in large; and academically marginal students in small schools received almost five times the pressures to participate as those in large.

Self-evaluations of students in small schools were based on the adequacy of their contributions and on their level of competence in relation to the job requirements; self-evaluations of students in large schools were based on comparison with others.

Students in large schools exceeded those in the small in satisfying experiences related to vicarious enjoyment of others' activities.

Students in small schools exceeded those in large schools in satisfying experiences related to the development of competence, to being challenged, and to engaging in important activities.

Students in small schools tended to achieve relatively limited development in a wide variety of areas while those in large tended to achieve greater development in more narrow or specialized areas.

The findings of others who have studied the effects of size in factories, in public agencies, in discussion groups and task groups, and in other school settings are generally consistent with those of Barker and Gump. All suggest a negative relationship between size, and individual participation, involvement, and satisfaction. The dynamics that underlie these findings were first postulated by Willems (1964), but he should not be held responsible for the comments that follow.

Behavior settings offer a variety of satisfactions and opportunities that individuals find attractive. When the number of persons is low there are more opportunities to participate per person; thus each experiences the attractions with greater force. In task-oriented settings, there are functions and purposes to be carried out that impose obligations on the participants. When manpower is low, each participant has to assume more responsibilities and each becomes the focus for more obligations. Under such conditions individuals perceive more clearly the importance of their own participation and of the participation of others. Thus, feelings of loyalty or responsibility are added to the initial intrinsic satisfactions that attracted the individuals in the first place.

In addition to these internal or personal forces, if the setting has importance as part of a larger context, external pressures will increase as manpower diminishes. There will be more invitations or demands, and the social rewards for contribution will increase. At the same time requirements for admission or for certain kinds of positions will become more liberal. Thus persons who usually might only be spectators will be pressed into service; reticent followers more often will find themselves in leadership roles. In this way, those who under circumstances of overpopulation might be seen as unsuitable or marginal, under conditions of limited manpower or underpopulation find themselves in demand.

Anyone who has been a member of a small town PTA has seen all these principles in operation, I'm sure. In our town, the last two presidents had lived in the community and in the state, for less than two years, and in Vermont, that's about as marginal as you can get. And it was difficult to find members who were not on at least one committee and who didn't help in other ways during the year.

What are some of the likely effects of institutional size, or more accurately, of redundancy, on student development? To the best of my knowledge, there has been no research that has attempted to study relationships between personal development and college size. It should be emphasized that the following comments about the effects of institutional size on student development rest solely on theory and personal observation and on no research findings of which I am aware. Thus, I can only hypothesize that redundancy has implications for the development of competence, the development of identity, the freeing of interpersonal relationships, and the development of integrity.

Under conditions of redundancy, less development of intellectual competence will occur. Because of fewer opportunities to deal with problems of significance, and because fewer challenges are encountered, intellectual skills and working knowledge will be less fully developed among most students. Some students who are particularly talented, or strongly motivated, or who catch the interest of a faculty member, or who capture a position on the college paper or debating team, for example, may develop to a high degree in a particular area. But for most students, development will be less than it would be if they were not so superfluous.

Similar effects occur for physical and manual skills. In college, these are developed primarily in the context of athletics and other extracurricular activities. But the larger the institution, the more rare the three-letter man. One may become a leader in student government or in the outing club, or become a folk-dance specialist or artist, but participation in several of these areas is impossible for most to manage.

The development of interpersonal competence is more limited also. Because of increased selectivity of participants there is less need to find ways of working with persons of diverse abilities and attitudes. Deviants are screened out and one doesn't have to discover productive ways of working with them.

Most important, because of fewer opportunities to hold positions of leadership and responsibility, and because of fewer opportunities for active mastery and successful coping with a wide range of tasks, sense of competence develops less fully, rests on a more limited basis, and operates in a more limited sphere.

The shift in the basis of self-evaluation may have even more significance for sense of competence than the limited opportunities for significant achievement have. As self-evaluation comes to be based primarily upon comparisons with others, it is difficult to see oneself as very competent. Those who are better in the areas to which one aspires are highly visible; there seem to be so many of them up there in front. Those less skilled then are quite invisible and their presence carries little force. Because by definition only a few can be on top, the rest struggle along, frequently using as much energy to cope with feelings of inadequacy as to cope with the tasks at hand. But when the emphasis is on who can do the job and who is willing to undertake it, and where esteem and respect derive from the successful completion of significant tasks rather than from relative standing, there is a more accessible and solid basis for learning where competencies lie and how far they extend.

In general, I would hypothesize that under conditions of redundancy, less development of competence occurs, except for a minority of talented individuals in whom special abilities and knowledge may develop to an unusually high degree.

The implications of redundancy for development of identity seem clear. If opportunities for active participation and involvement are limited, and particularly, if the variety of environments and activities are limited, then so are the opportunities for the kinds of self-discovery, or "resonance testing," through which a full and rich sense of identity may come about. If only rarely can one get behind a wheel —and if then one can drive only on a country lane, in sunshine, with an automatic transmission—then not much development occurs and one feels uncomfortable if other conditions must be faced. Of course, a similar result occurs if one drives only through snow and mud with smooth tires in a car without a heater.

The response to the combination of limited opportunities and competitive pressure is often observed. In high schools there is the too frequent settling on either beauty, brains, or athletic prowess as the center of one's self-esteem, as the core of one's being. In college it takes more particular forms: the beats, the grinds, the party boys, and others. However, when opportunities are many and varied and when competitive pressures are lessened, one can range more widely; one can relax his grip on those roles found satisfying. The increased range of vicarious experiences available to the person in the overpopulated setting may somewhat compensate for the decreased opportunities for more active participation, but they do not provide the experience of self-testing on which a sense of identity ultimately is built.

Under conditions of redundancy, freeing of interpersonal relationships is less likely to occur. In-groups and out-groups develop and assume greater force. Relationships become more hierarchical. Increased competition for entry into attractive settings may generate personal animosities. Those who are congruent with one's own peculiar ideas and behaviors are more numerous and thus those who are incongruent are more easily done without. As a consequence, stereotypes and biases carried to college from earlier years more frequently remain untested and the cooperative working contexts in which such attitudes might be examined and modified are not experienced. This narrowing of the range of contacts, which probably occurs with increasing overpopulation, may be primarily responsible for the large number of students who go through college relatively untouched. For it is basically the significant personal relationships that have an effect, whether they be with students or with faculty members. And when these relationships become highly self-selective, then it is less likely that change, liberalization, or enrichment will occur.

Redundancy also works against the development of integrity. Humanizing of values is fostered when one must make choices that influence the lives of others and where the effects of those choices are observable. The context may be a committee to consider parietal rules, or a dormitory meeting to deal with a problem of noise or stealing, or an honor system. Value choices reside wherever decisions must be made regarding the living conditions in the college community; in underpopulated settings the opportunity for each individual to confront problems and to think through alternatives occurs more frequently. Similarly, where there are few individuals, the impact on the whole of the behavior of each is significant and observable. A student working with a group of five or ten others, or living in a house of twenty or thirty, sees quickly and clearly the consequences of his choices for the lives of others.

Limited size carries particular force for the development of congruence. When the totality of a student's behavior is visible to many others with whom he goes to class and to parties, sits on committees and in general meetings, it is difficult to talk one kind of life and to live another. Thus the development of congruence is significantly related to institutional size and organization.

There is empirical evidence relevant to this. Bowers (1964) found that the proportion of schools with high levels of cheating increased with the size of the school. Bowers observes:

> at small schools, students tend to know most of their peers, whereas at large schools they get to know only a fraction of the student body. Therefore, the student at the large schools is apt to feel relatively anonymous vis-à-vis the student body as a whole. The larger schools may provide a setting that facilitates the formation of deviant subgroups in which cheating is approved or at least tolerated [p. 174].

There are other aspects of student development for which institutional size has implications, but those described are probably the ones most affected. The basic point is that as redundancy occurs, less development is fostered. Redundancy occurs when increase in the number of inhabitants leads to decreasing opportunities for participation and satisfaction for each individual, when manpower exceeds what is needed for the jobs to be done.

As redundancy sets in, the activities and responsibilities of those who do participate become more specialized and those with marginal qualifications are more quickly and more completely left out. A hierarchy of prestige and power develops and evaluation shifts from an emphasis on the fit between abilities and the requirements of a job, to an emphasis on how one person compares with another. Rules and standards for conduct become more formalized and rigid.

Under such conditions, the opportunities to cope with significant problems become more limited and challenges to existing skills and knowledge are encountered less frequently. Experience becomes less varied and self-testing more restricted. The range of different persons to be dealt with in contexts important to one's own life decreases, and situations provoking examination of values and consideration of the consequences of one's actions less often have to be faced. Thus, development of competence is more limited except when supported by special ability or special motivation; and the development of identity, the freeing of interpersonal relationships, and the development of a personal value system are fostered less under conditions of redundancy than they are when the ratio of students to settings is smaller.

Some institutions with very large enrollments are developing creative ways of increasing the number of settings and reducing the number of persons in each. And many colleges with small enrollments have not capitalized on their condition, and are rapidly increasing enrollments without concurrent increases in the number and variety of settings available to students. The basic point is that an institution should be large enough so that each student frequently must confront and operate within a variety of significant settings, but not so large that he becomes superfluous and disappears in the huddle.

CHAPTER 10

CURRICULUM, TEACHING, AND EVALUATION

$\int\!\!\int\!\!\int\!\!\int\!\!\int\!\!\int\!\!\int\!\!\int\!\!\int\!\!\int\!\!\int\!\!\int\!\!\int\!\!\int\!\!\int\!\!\int\!\!\int\!\!\int\!\!\int$

Curriculum arrangements, teaching practices, and evaluational procedures are systematically linked. To consider one element in isolation from the others is unwise; to modify one part without threatening the others is impossible. Those who attempt curricular change, new teaching practices, or grading reform, discover early that jiggling a part sends vibrations throughout the whole. These tremors of the web quickly call forth those who, almost as if by instinct, quickly entangle whoever flies against it. If not devoured or sucked dry, he is immobilized or given limited room for movement. It is probably because these three large areas are so closely intertwined that innovation and experimentation come hard; because beliefs and assumptions are intricately interlocked, change, when it does occur, is frequently dramatic or drastic, and made in response to strong inner or outer forces.

One could say that the function of college is transportation. It offers rapid transit from adolescence to adulthood, from dull or poorly paid jobs to more interesting or better paid ones, from slum to suburb, from lower to middle or upper class. Its function is to help the student get from where he is to where he wants to be, and to where those who man and support the college want him to be. Perhaps, therefore, a vehicular metaphor can describe economically the major curricular carriers currently in business.

Four Models

Granting that many diverse constellations of curriculum, teaching, and evaluation exist, and granting that new combinations and practices are annually generated here and there, four models characterize the major variations: the rocket, the Cadillac, the horse and buggy, and the junkyard.

The Rocket. The rocket curriculum aims to get you into orbit fast. The line is direct. The course is precisely precalculated. There is no stopping by woods on a snowy evening nor any dallying about the road untaken. The choice of routes is limited, and while some reorientation during flight is possible, basic change of direction is not, unless one is willing to leave the system entirely. The point of departure is clearly specified. It has been determined by others operating in concert, considering complex factors known to them but shared by few outside their specialties. Only those who can submit to and can master the rigorous, detailed, and extended training program get very far off the ground. Throughout training, dependence upon others is great. But in many ways it is greatest when in orbit; because once training is completed and you board and blast off, the stakes are high. You step outside only after careful preparation and then you are on a short tether. If the tether breaks you are lost. While you are in orbit, your environment is restricted. Problems arise primarily because of faulty parts within the system itself and not often because of external forces. Ultimately the rocket and the person become as one, a single symbiotic system with continuous exchange. And this man-machine system and the exchanges within it are monitored and modified by the larger supporting organization to which both components are linked.

The various vocational, technical, and professional forms of the

rocket curriculum are familiar. They exist primarily in large universities or well-endowed technical institutions because varied and expensive material resources and numerous highly trained trainers are
required. Thus they can be developed and maintained only under conditions of substantial size and support.

The rocket curriculum typically comprises a collection of numerous and diverse courses organized in sequences of increasing specialization. Like the roots of a maple as it ages, there develops an increasingly extensive network; the single root of twenty years ago now
leads to numerous offshoots. After a brief spell on the main stem, a
student selects one root and examines as many major ramifications as
possible. Usually he does this by taking five courses each semester for
eight four-month semesters. These courses are chosen within the framework of an intricate series of requisites and prerequisites.

The teacher functions in two major ways: he gives information
through lectures and reading assignments, and he fosters particular
skills and competencies by setting written problems or laboratory tasks.
The job of the student is to assimilate the information and to develop
the judgment and skill to apply it. Most teaching goes on in class-
rooms and other facilities designed especially for the purpose. It is
assumed that the most important learnings occur in these settings,
supplemented by the work assigned between classes. A single source,
the textbook, sometimes amplified by selected optional readings, is the
usual basis for outside work.

Most important, however, is the nature of the subject matter
and the stance of student and teacher in relation to it. Remember we
speak of undergraduate education, and whether it is engineering or
business administration, pre-med or pre-ed, basically, the teacher has
the answers and the student has not. The subject matter does not deal
with questions important to both teacher and student. For the teacher
the issues are usually settled; there is little basis for joint search and
little possibility for the teacher to be instructed or enriched by the student. Further, the subject matter itself, taught as an instrument for
occupational advancement, infrequently is used to raise questions of
value and meaning, and rarely touches problems of social or emotional
concern to the student. Thus neither the content nor the position of
student and teacher in relation to it is likely to provoke intercourse
beyond that required to check accuracy of understanding and recall.
When these conditions dominate, as they do in the rocket curriculum,

counterefforts in the name of general education or liberal arts carry little force. Inconsistent with the basic instrumentalist thrust, general courses or activities in the service of personal expansion or enrichment are viewed at best as useful hurdles quickly to be leapt for entry to that which is really important; and at worst as irrelevant and immaterial. The occasional teacher or student whose orientation would differ makes little headway against this tide.

As curricula and teaching vary, so must procedures for evaluation. In the rocket curriculum, courses are the sole object of evaluation and the primary pillar is the multiple-choice exam. Short answer questions may be used occasionally, but essay examinations are rare. Although there may be occasional quizzes, the major evaluational occasion is the final. Midterm examinations may provide another point of appraisal and, when used, they do "count," although the final carries most weight. The emphasis is on the product. The accompanying processes of thought and learning receive scant attention. In those courses that involve laboratory work or other performance situations, evaluation tends to be more continuous, with weekly work graded and compiled for its contribution to the total judgment. Feedback is almost entirely limited to a single number or letter grade produced by complex computations from the various numbers supplied from these sources. Usually the grades for a given course must conform to some prearranged distribution so that the proportions of A's and F's, B's and D's, are restricted.

So much for the rocket curriculum. Its principal aim is vocational or professional preparation; its teaching aims primarily to give students the language, the concepts, and the skills common to their area of choice; its evaluation aims to determine whether the languages, concepts, and skills have been acquired, and to certify accordingly to others.

The Cadillac. The Cadillac, for many, is the vehicle of preference if not of actual choice. It is preferred not so much for what it is or does as for what it represents. Its classical lines, lavish style, and diverse appurtenances indicate that neither cost nor effort has been spared to guarantee comfortable trips. It best suits broad expressways, enabling movement from one motel to another well insulated from upsetting outside conditions. Traveling is a pleasure, although the pleasures derive more from comforts en route than from variation in experiences afforded by the travel itself. The Cadillac serves less well if one would go where high crowned dirt roads wind or venture out when mud or snow is deep. But most don't mind such restrictions. Clearly designed for luxury, leisure, and self-gratification, the Cadillac implies only remote connections with the world of work; but beneath the hood there is power to be called upon if needed.

Although the training required is not so rigorous as for the rocket, it is more extensive. For although knowledge and skill sufficient to manage the vehicle is not hard to achieve, for real success the total system must be understood and mastered. And for this, mastery of one-self in relation to complex relationships is required. Sensitivities must be sharpened; subtlety of expression must be learned beyond merely correct grammar or usage, or simply fashionable attire and behavior. Giving oneself to a Cadillac, as to a rocket, means putting oneself in the hands of others. Running costs are high and the intricacies of the vehicle make one depend on others for repairs and general mainte-nance. While one has greater freedom of movement than with a rocket, he must still remain within reach of a fuel supply and a service sta-tion.

The Cadillac curriculum finds its finest expression in the pres-tigious liberal arts colleges. Because the necessary training depends less upon specialized courses and materials and more upon the acquisi-tion of broad areas of information and on the development of more general verbal and intellectual skills, fewer material resources are re-quired. Income and endowment, therefore, can be used to sustain a more limited enrollment and a relatively large number of highly quali-fied faculty members; persons who, if not driving Cadillacs them-selves, at least know how to behave as if they were, and who can move with ease among those who do. Of course, the Cadillacs have their imitators, who copy the general styling. Most of these try to preserve some distinctiveness, but the difference is usually a modified tail fin or a different bumper design rather than anything more basic. Yet, lacking the status, the imitators cannot command the price; therefore neither can they develop or maintain personnel or plant sufficient to compete successfully within the framework set by the Cadillacs.

In the Cadillac curriculum, most of the information is still prescribed and the primary role of the teacher is to dispense it. How-ever, the content more directly touches basic existential issues, social problems, and emotional concerns. The teacher less frequently has the final answers and consequently the student's own perceptions and insights may be more highly valued. Learning becomes more pursuit of questions than assimilation of an answer, and in this pursuit more diverse sources are sought. Class discussion then becomes a useful way to foster acquisition of basic ideas and at the same time subject the students to some scrutiny. And because the issues are more likely to be unsettled for both teacher and student, the discussion can be satisfying and stimulating to both.

Even though discussion occurs more frequently, however, assimilating the ideas and being able to manipulate them verbally is still most important. Thus teaching and learning involve primarily manipulation of symbols, corrected and modified by symbolic feedback. Direct experience of the consequences following the application of a given concept or principle seldom occurs, nor is one's capacity to put information to work in the service of varied nonacademic needs or challenges often tested.

As in the rocket, only courses are evaluated; finals and midterms are the principal means; a letter or number expressing the composite of inputs from various sources is the ultimate feedback. In the Cadillac, however, the exams themselves more frequently call for essays. More frequent feedback during the semester may also occur as students seek out instructors in their offices or after class to find out how they're doing, and as the instructor or registrar sends warning signals. One important difference from the rocket is the more frequent use of term papers and other written products as devices for learning and evaluation. These papers often require the integration of diverse materials and the range of topics to be addressed may be fairly wide. Furthermore, evaluative comments are likely to be substantive, addressed to particular strengths and weaknesses, rather than simply normative judgments, indicating that the product is good, bad, or indifferent.

In sum then, the Cadillac curriculum aims for more generalized development, for more widespread expansion and enrichment of intellectual interests and information; teaching, although primarily concerned with disseminating information, also raises questions and provides a forum for discussion of basic human and social issues; evaluation, although primarily in the service of certification, also may provide for more generalized and substantive exchange between teacher and student.

The Horse and Buggy. If you think important things are

missed with the speed, the style, and the limited routes of the rocket and Cadillac, or if you lack the wherewithal to offer such fancy vehicles; if you have some freedom, are adventurous, and are aware that other vehicles have served well in the past, you may try something different. The horse and buggy and the junkyard are the most common choices, though both are rare compared to the rockets, and to the Cadillacs with their imitators.

The horse and buggy has few parts. In many ways it is a more simple machine than the rocket or Cadillac. It is constructed of simple original materials. It can be rebuilt and parts can be repaired by the driver. Fuel is relatively abundant and in most situations one can forage for oneself with success and satisfaction. However, its source of power is a living thing, which one must befriend, must learn to live with, must learn to manage. Once such learning is achieved, a well-fashioned buggy and a horse sound of wind and limb can go far, if not fast. Dirt roads, paths, fields, and streams can be explored without much risk of damage. The sights and sounds encountered in the process can be experienced directly and directly savored or cursed.

The horse and buggy curriculum is, of course, the most traditional and classic of all. It requires of all students detailed concentration on materials limited in quantity but substantial in range and depth; materials selected because they represent man's best thinking through the years about questions basic to human existence and because they provide not only fundamental information but also fine whetstones to sharpen intellectual tools. This curriculum can be implemented with limited material resources but effective personnel are hard to find. In this day and age, few people have much knowledge of the horse and buggy; fewer still have sufficient experience with operation and maintenance to assist others in learning. And with the horse and buggy such a thing of the past, few are motivated to invest much in it, recognizing that the rewards are much more psychic than material.

In the horse and buggy curriculum, while information has its place, the emphasis shifts from content to process. Reading materials and laboratory exercises are deliberately selected to foster varied intellectual skills loosely denoted by terms like *critical thinking, analysis, synthesis, problem solving,* and the like. Much more frequently, classes involve group discussion and the "student question–instructor answer," or "instructor question–student answer" format more typical of the rocket and Cadillac contexts is replaced by more student-to-student exchange. The instructor's two major functions are to help maintain some coherence and direction in the discussion, and, by raising questions, by questioning fallacious reasoning and distorted interpretations, by asking for evidence, for examples, for metaphors, for restatement, to help students develop desired skills of thought and expression. The content, though more limited in quantity than in the Cadillac curriculum, touches basic issues in the humanities, social sciences, and natural sciences. Thus, it deals with questions where no final determination is yet possible; and the processes of critical examination, comparison, and integration in which both student and instructor share enables relationships less hierarchical or paternal, which contain greater proportions of mutual regard and understanding. Further, because most of the curriculum is prescribed for all students there is a shared community of ideas and questions far in excess of that generated in the Cadillac or rocket curricula where proliferation of courses and diversity of majors makes for little overlap among roommates, housemates, or other friendship groups. The unified curriculum also enables the faculty to become an intellectual community with insights and information from various disciplines more widely shared, more often juxtaposed.

In the horse and buggy curriculum, evaluation is more continuous. The comments, questions, and reactions of the instructor during class discussions provide feedback so that students can perceive more clearly the nature and implications of their behavior and that of classmates. In addition, lack of preparation and its consequences are more immediately visible to oneself and to others. The instructor can call attention to it; the student cannot ignore it. The student can continue unprepared, but the decision must be more conscious, the future implications more often and more explicitly examined. Courses are still evaluated and letter grades attached, but in addition comprehensive examinations are administered for general areas of information and for the area of major study. These examinations frequently involve an oral presentation and defense as well as a written one, and thus provide a kind of performance test similar to that occasionally found in the rocket curriculum. Grade distributions are employed much less frequently in courses and there is substantial latitude in their application. On the comprehensives, cutting points for minimal performance are usually set; beyond that, students may fall wherever their performance warrants, irrespective of their classmates. If high scoring becomes too frequent, the exams are revised rather than the grades of the students.

The horse and buggy curriculum, then, aims primarily to develop general intellectual skills and to acquaint students with basic concepts and ideas; teaching, through discussion and sharp questioning, aims to exercise the desired capacities and thus to foster increased skill in use, and increased judgment in application; evaluation is more integral to the process and serves developmental ends as well as certification.

The Junkyard.   Finally there is the junkyard, or the used car lot. (Even though I sneaked into a Cadillac during the Second World War and managed to graduate, I've become pretty much a junkyard man myself. In fact my wife won't let me go to the dump because I bring home more than I take. So I use the term simply for description, not for disparagement). Essentially, the junkyard offers the materials to build something for yourself. It assumes you have come because you need additional parts. It aims to make available a diverse collection as cheaply as possible. You are free to start, or to carry forward, work on whatever kind of vehicle you think you need to get where you want to go or do what you want to do. You are free to wander around at will and to take plenty of time, within the limits of certain closing hours. No salesman hovers nearby urging this or that part on you, but there is usually someone to be found who can tell what a given part was designed for originally, who can suggest alternative uses to which others have put it, and who can help determine whether it fits your needs. Because maintaining a diverse collection is expensive and because some of the parts available are rare, the junkyard is not always cheap and not all items are bargains.

More than elsewhere the honesty of the junkyard administrator is crucial. The quality controls that operate for the rockets and Cadillacs don't exist. Neither do the simplicity and directness of the horse and buggy, whose reins can be clearly grasped. Thus shopping in the used car lot requires heavy reliance on the integrity of others. If they can be trusted, much can be garnered; if not, you may get badly stung.

The junkyard colleges are those where required courses are absent or few, where learning activities other than reading and writing are valued, where laboratories are found off campus as well as on. Students often study in only three areas during any single semester. Boundaries within the institution, and between it and the outside, are blurry; students may build a single course or a program of study cutting across disciplines or incorporating experiences and resources away from the college. This approach can be implemented with limited resources and indeed may function most effectively when funds are scarce. Yet staffing problems are severe, for while psychic income is great, high frustration is a frequent companion.

With the junkyard curriculum the three major functions of the teacher are still different. Because required courses are absent or limited in number, and because there is great flexibility in the majors that can be developed and pursued, one task of the teacher is to help the student clarify his own needs and purposes and to ascertain the most relevant areas of study. Once a program has been developed, the teacher's job is to help the student discover and use those resources available on campus or those to which access can be gained away from campus. As the student works during the semester, the teacher serves as a sounding board for ideas as they develop and as a question raiser to foster greater accuracy and depth of understanding. There is no emphasis on the acquisition of certain bodies of information or certain basic ideas; nor is there major emphasis on the development of intellectual skills. The basic concern is that the student's self-understanding be improved, that he become more aware of his emotions and better able to manage them, that he clarify his values and his purposes and develop the competencies necessary to move toward their fulfillment.

In the junkyard curriculum, discussion classes predominate. Independent studies, tutorials, "preceptorials" play a major part. Direct experiences on and off campus frequently accompany reading and writing activities and are credited as valid components of courses and independent studies. Student-faculty contact occurs in many different settings and learning is assumed to go on as significantly in the coffee shop and residence hall as in the classroom. When the content stems from the student's own needs and purposes, when its primary resonance is to be with his own questions, then teachers seldom have answers and seldom find themselves able to give the word. Thus the position of student and teacher is similar to that in the horse and buggy curriculum, except that the content itself may be more diverse and the uses to which students are putting it more obviously personal and idiosyncratic.

The junkyard curriculum shares with the horse and buggy the continuous evaluation occurring in the context of group discussions. In this curriculum, written and oral products provide the major substance for academic evaluation. Examinations and grades are infrequently used. Student self-evaluations comprise part of the record and reports from instructors are communicated to students orally and in writing. These instructor comments usually address themselves to various strengths and weakness in performance and may also offer the instructor's view of how the student went about his work and the effectiveness of his approach and behavior. The processes of learning and thought may receive attention equal to the products. Within this context grade distributions cannot operate and the standing of one student relative to another cannot be ascertained to any precise degree.

In the college with the junkyard curriculum, promotion often depends on adequate performances of a nonacademic nature. Satisfactory completion of work periods away from the college and minimal levels of responsibility within the college community may be required, may be subject to evaluation, and may become part of the record.

These metaphors and the brief elaborating comments leave much unsaid about curricular variation in American higher education. The rocket, the Cadillac, the horse and buggy, and the junkyard —each has its rather pure representatives; obviously, many institutions are something of a mixture. And there are other unique models. But these four do reflect distinct and recognized patterns and reflect some of the important differences. That these systems and the differences among them do exist is clear on the basis of our own experience. It is further substantiated by the work of Astin (1963), Chickering et al. (1968), Heath (1968), Pace (1963), Stern (1962), Thistlethwaite (1962), and by Heist and others at the Center for Research and Development in Higher Education at Berkeley.

Implications for Development

At the outset it must be recognized that research documenting relationships between curricular systems and particular aspects of student development is like Vermont dirt roads in spring—muddy and soft. Yet the evidence is sufficient to support some hypotheses and suggests that each curricular model has different implications for one or more major vectors of development. Those most sharply affected seem to be development of intellectual competence and sense of competence, development of autonomy, development of identity, and the freeing of interpersonal relationships.

Intellectual Competence. Different teaching practices produce different kinds of behavior. These behavioral differences are both overt—different patterns of study, different methods of attacking and organizing reading materials, different uses of nonverbal materials, and covert—different cognitive operations, different levels of emotional involvement. When particular behaviors are repeated over time, certain kinds of development are likely to be fostered, and others are not; therefore the behavioral variations that accompany different teaching practices are likely to produce varied kinds of intellectual development.

For example, the evidence concerning the differential effects of lecture versus discussion classes is now abundant and consistent. In a nutshell, lectures are superior for the transmission of information, particularly information quite specific in nature (Barnard, 1942), that does not run counter to beliefs already held. And lectures can be efficient when they bring together information from diverse sources not readily available to students. Discussion classes provoke more active thinking than lecture classes (Bloom, 1953) and research indicates that active thinking is more efficient than passive (McGeoch and Irion, 1952). As McKeachie (1962) observes,

> If we are trying to achieve application, critical thinking, or some of the higher level cognitive outcomes, . . . students should have an opportunity to practice application and critical thinking and to receive feedback on the results. Group discussion provides an opportunity to do this. . . . [It] permits presentation of a variety of problems enabling a number of people to gain experience in integrating facts, formulating hypotheses, amassing relevant evidence, and evaluating conclusions [p. 326].

In addition, when information encounters intellectual or emotional resistance, discussion holds the possibility of revealing the source of resistance so it can be examined and dealt with. And as Lewin (1952) demonstrated, the presence of a group contributes to changes in motivation and attitudes, because it is often easier to effect change in a group than in a single individual.

The competitiveness of the climate and the evaluational procedures used also influence cognitive behavior. As Mayhew (1966) observes, "If teachers base their grades on memorization of details, students will memorize the text. If students believe grades are based upon their ability to integrate and to apply principles, they will try to acquire such ability [p. 225]." Early research by Meyer (1936) and Terry (1933), for example, suggested that the prospect of an essay exam led to study activities that emphasized the organization and interrelationships of facts and principles, where an upcoming multiple-choice exam led to memorization. As Dressel (1958) observes at Michigan State,

> the seeming necessity of covering large masses of material . . . leaves too little time for any but the most able students to reflect on the meaning, interrelationship, and applicability of knowledge which is being gained. The able student, too, often displays reluctance to think for himself, in part because the exercise of thought and judgement is time-consuming and difficult and in part, no doubt, because he sees little evidence that such effort will yield returns in the currency of the academic realm [p. 199].

Other research relevant to the differences among our four models concerns student-centered versus instructor-centered teaching. This research has been thoroughly reviewed by McKeachie (1963). He summarizes as follows:

> We had . . . predicted that any superiority of student-centered discussion methods would be revealed in higher-level outcomes. In 11 studies, significant differences in ability to apply concepts, in attitudes, in motivation, or in group membership skills have been found between discussion techniques emphasizing freer student participation compared with discussion with greater instructor dominance. In 10 of these the differences favored the more student-centered method. . . .
> In short, the choice of instructor-dominated versus student-centered discussion techniques appears to depend upon one's goals. The more highly one values outcomes going beyond acquisition of knowledge, the more likely that student-centered methods will be preferred [p. 1140].

In the light of such evidence, what is the probable impact on intellectual competence of our four curricular models? The rocket curriculum, with its large number of courses, its emphasis on covering copious material, its reliance on lectures and multiple-choice exams, and its practice of grading on a curve, provides a set of conditions that require development of the ability to hold in mind, at least temporarily, substantial amounts of information in relatively discrete clusters; it does not seem likely to foster higher order intellectual skills. Dressel's (1958) research on the development of critical thinking in the basic college at Michigan State supports this hypothesis. He says:

> The most discomforting finding was the total inability of some students to engage in a pattern of reasoning or even to realize that this was possible. . . . Much as we continue to be disturbed about these findings, we cannot feel that the blame rests entirely on the students. It was evident that for many . . . the task of thinking through to an answer, rather than recalling one, was a novel experience [p. 202].

Of course, to the extent that students are active in laboratories and other situations requiring application of ideas and firsthand observation and manipulation of materials, greater improvement in retention, in critical thinking and problem-solving ability, and in the ability to perceive and discover relationships might be expected.

The greater variability of practices within a Cadillac curriculum may make for less singular impact, but the general pattern is probably similar. Higher standards may mean even more material to be covered and tougher competition may make accurate memorization geared to instructors' preferences and predispositions even more important. Lectures are still much more frequent than discussions, and this curriculum lacks some of the contexts for active application found among the rockets. Thus the ability to memorize is still probably central to academic success. Because essays and papers play a large role, however, skill in written expression, in synthesizing ideas from diverse sources, and in presenting them in coherent fashion, is also fostered.

One great force for the development of higher level abilities does operate but for the most part it functions outside the formal curriculum. It results from putting high ability persons together in close quarters. In coffee shop debate, in residence hall bull sessions, and on dates, the ability to think clearly, to be orally articulate, to argue persuasively, is sharply honed.

The horse and buggy curriculum, with its explicit emphasis on developing higher order competencies in the context of assimilating a limited set of basic concepts and ideas, with its almost total reliance on discussion, with its use of comprehensive examinations with large essay components and oral examinations as well, seems very likely to foster analytic ability and the ability to perceive relationships among principles from different domains. There seems to be little in the system to suggest that the ability to memorize is sufficient for success. And because this curriculum tends to attract students with strong intellectual interests, the informal debate and discussion characterizing the Cadillac students also occur here.

Data from Shimer College, a pure horse and buggy, are congruent with these propositions. During the years from 1958 to 1963, average scores on the Scholastic Aptitude Tests for Shimer students placed them at about the seventy-fifth percentile in relation to other college-going high school seniors. Shimer graduates during these years scored at the ninety-ninth percentile on the Graduate Record Examinations Area Tests in social science, humanities, and natural science. There are obviously weaknesses in these data—they come from two different tests and they do not involve retests of identical groups and thus may be influenced by attrition and other factors—but they do support a picture of high level competence across broad areas of study for graduates from a horse and buggy curriculum.

The junkyard curriculum also fosters higher order cognitive skills and improved self-understanding through permitting study to occur in the service of personal needs, interests, and purposes. Basically student-centered in its approach, with few lectures and few exams, with substantial amounts of writing required, and with frequent study often connected to continuing jobs or responsibilities on and off campus, it offers good potential for intellectual development.

Research at one such college, Goddard, in Plainfield, Vermont, supports these hypotheses (Beecher *et al.*, 1966). For two groups of graduates, scores on measures of critical thinking for the second year were significantly higher than those at entrance and scores for the fourth year significantly higher than for the second. These findings appear to compare favorably with Lehmann and Ikenberry's (1959) research on critical thinking at Michigan State where "most of the changes occurred during the freshman and sophomore years." Test-retest studies of Graduate Record Examinations Area Test scores also showed statistically significant gains of a magnitude not unlike those occurring at other small colleges. It is clear also, however, that such gains occur only when students study in relevant areas. Among one group of graduates, for example, no person undertook substantial study in the natural sciences during the last two years and the mean score for the group at graduation was identical with that for the end of the second year (Chickering, 1964b). This lack of change reveals clearly the risk of informational lacunae from a curriculum with no distribution requirements.

Note also that development of intellectual competence under such conditions occurs neither automatically nor easily. Where the primary purpose of discussion is to clarify the meaning of material to the student, and where the student's personal construction of ideas and information is emphasized, sustained and objective analysis frequently gives way to personal and subjective reactions and argumentation. Responses from the gut are desirable and necessary, but so are dispassionate analysis and synthesis. For teachers and students to sustain sound proportions of both is no simple matter.

So much for the development of intellectual competence. The evidence from research concerning the impact of different teaching and evaluation procedures is fairly clear and the four models conform to various patterns with sufficient internal consistency that the implied variations among them seem likely.

Sense of Competence.   Research supports in fairly solid fashion relationships between patterns of curriculum, teaching and evaluation, and the development of sense of competence. Most to the point are the studies of Thistlethwaite (1962). He reports as follows:

> Increase in level of aspiration (motivation to seek advanced degrees) was associated with: (a) strong faculty press for enthusiasm, humanism, affiliation, independence, achievement, and supportiveness; (b) weak faculty press for compliance; and (c) strong student press for estheticism.
>
> Colleges outstandingly successful in encouraging undergraduates to get the doctorate in humanistic fields are characterized by (a) excellent social science faculty and resources, (b) flexible, or somewhat unstructured curriculum, (c) energy and controversiality of instruction, and (d) informality and warmth of student-faculty contacts [p. 313].

The results of Davis' (1964) nationwide study, conducted by the National Opinion Research Center, are congruent with Thistlethwaite's findings. Davis found that high prestige, intellectually elite colleges, our Cadillacs, significantly underproduced future scientists when the talent and the interests of their entering students were taken into account. The encouragement of a faculty member led students to pursue further work in science, but faculty members rarely encouraged any but their *A* students. Since grades frequently were distributed according to a rough normal curve, many students in these colleges received *B*'s and *C*'s even though they were among the top 10 per cent on any national measure of scientific aptitude or achievement. Thus the consequence of this competitive grading was a reduction in student self-esteem and a lowering of career aspirations.

Research by Atkinson and Litwin (1963) concerning the differential effects of negative and positive motives reveals the extent to which such lowered self-esteem and highly competitive grading practices can become a vicious circle. They found that men students who were high in anxiety about tests more frequently completed examinations first and did more poorly on the exam than in their general course work. Students with positive motivation, in this case high "need achievement," tended to stay in the examination room longer.

This collection of findings suggests that sense of competence may be fostered least by the Cadillac curriculum. The combination of unusually bright and high achieving students, high faculty standards for academic work, pressure to achieve good grades for entrance to graduate school and business, and evaluational procedures that depend upon relative rather than absolute achievement and that reveal clearly comparative standings, must militate sharply against the maintenance and development of self-esteem for many students. Where there is little room at the top, most must stay below and feel more low down than reality warrants. The rocket curriculum may provoke a similar dynamic although the more heterogeneous student body may offer some protection so that consequences are less severe. The horse and buggy curriculum may operate similarly to the Cadillac to the degree that high-powered students are attracted and to the degree that class discussions become a dog-eat-dog affair. Students who lack sufficient intellectual agility and sufficient aggressiveness may be overwhelmed by their more articulate peers and may retreat to passivity and silence. Alert observation and internal rehearsal may allow intellectual competencies to develop, though the oral skills will not, but sense of competence and self-esteem may suffer.

The junkyard curriculum probably falls at the other extreme.

Where grades and exams are minimally used, where comparative standing is difficult to assess, where students largely set their own objectives and evaluate their performance in relation to them, sense of competence may sharply increase, self-esteem may blossom. Indeed, some students may develop an exaggerated sense of competence through lack of information about the performance of others and in the absence of clear feedback concerning task effectiveness. Such students are sometimes brought up short by some difficult reality, or by some information about what others pursuing similar study have achieved. There are also students whose self-esteem requires the continued nourishment of comparative standings; for them a period of adjustment is required before they can examine whether a performance meets the requirements of the task or purpose, and before they can rest their sense of competence on that basis.

Autonomy. Variations in curriculum, teaching, and evaluation have implications for the development of emotional independence and instrumental independence. Emotional independence is fostered by opportunities to confront, to work with, and to know well some adults in positions of power and responsibility who are not one's parents. When such older persons can be seen fully and clearly, and when relationships of mutual respect and regard occur with at least a few of them, rebellious independence, intransigent self-assertion, or unthinking and unquestioning conformity, can be given up in favor of interdependence and reciprocity.

This kind of development seems least likely to be fostered by the rocket curriculum. Snyder (1966), from the perspective of his work at MIT, says:

> The student goes to lecture and hears from his professor that the course is exciting. Much independent thought will be demanded. He is urged to think about the subject, reflect on what he reads, and develop the habit of skepticism. The first quiz, in the student's eyes, calls for the playback of a large number of discrete facts. The message that some students hear is that reflection or original thought is for the birds and that memorization will get the A. Some possible student responses to such dissonance include alienation, cynicism about the academic enterprise, a determination to play the academic game with shrewdness, or conformity to the task of getting grades [p. 351].

None of these potential responses is likely to foster autonomy. And such responses are made. A study of men who do well academically, conducted by Black (Miller, 1965) at the Counseling and Testing Center at Stanford, found the most salient trait to be "cooperativeness," which included the tendency to be helpful, moderate, respectful, appreciative, sympathetic, and sensitive. Black observes that such traits are more characteristic of women than of men in our culture and thus may account for the fact that while men constitute 70 per cent of the undergraduates at Stanford, they constitute only 57 per cent of the Dean's list. The basic point is that when the curriculum specifies in detail what shall be studied, when teaching is essentially training students in the language, thought, and behavior appropriate for a given profession or vocation, when learning involves memorization of information and the development of certain skills designated as important by the teacher, and when grades and future success depend upon conformity and cooperativeness within this system, emotional independence is unlikely to flourish. These conditions obtain most clearly among the rockets. It is not surprising, therefore, that at such institutions students form two clusters; a vocal and sizable minority of the rebellious, and a quiet, detached majority, some unaware of, and some comfortable with, the system through which they move.

Instrumental independence is fostered by coping successfully with a wide range of tasks and problems and by achieving mobility sufficient to get to and to use needed resources. The work of overriding importance to American colleges is academic. Academic information, academic questions, and academic problems are the mainstays of commerce for curricula, teachers, and students; the information, questions, and problems are of theoretical interest but are not relevant to immediate concerns nor useful for current problems. Thus students may become learned, but gain little experience in coping with practical realities. The ability to cope solely with the academic is sufficient for success.

Similarly, when bright success can be achieved by conscientiously pacing the quadrangle from residence to dining hall to class to library to residence, little awareness of rich resources for learning and for satisfaction to be found elsewhere and in other activities, is fostered; neither is the ability to venture out, to discover, and to engage productively with diverse teachers and instructive materials.

Increasingly it has been recognized, however, that resources for learning and developmentally fruitful experiences are to be found beyond the campus walls. Institutional boundaries are becoming more permeable. Some curricula have been modified to accommodate study at other colleges or special institutions, as well as that old standby, study abroad. There have been developed curricula that integrate academic study and Peace Corps service, or work with American Indians; work in Appalachia or in the "inner city," rural poverty, or civil liberties. The nonresident terms of a few colleges require that all students undertake substantial nonacademic responsibilities off campus for a major period of time each year. All of these programs can foster instrumental independence, but at most institutions only a few students experience such programs, and then only as a minor part of their total program. The assumption that the most useful insights come from books, that development occurs principally through encounters with print, dominates most curricula. And as long as this assumption holds sway to the exclusion of other alternatives, development of instrumental independence receives little impetus.

Identity. What conditions are propitious for the development of identity? Erikson (1950) says, "ego identity gains real strength only from wholehearted achievement that has meaning in our culture [p. 135]." Sanford (1962) goes into more detail:

> anything that increases the likelihood that the sense of self will be based on personal experience rather than on outside judgement favors the stabilization of ego identity. Being placed in social roles that require new responses, having to make decisions concerning what roles one is going to take, learning from experience that some roles are suited and others not suited to one's interests and needs—any situation that brings awareness of one's real preferences and inner continuities helps to establish sound ego identity. So, too, does the condition of being relatively free from circumstances, whether unconscious drives or external pressures, that force one to cling to an earlier inadequate identity [p. 281].

In short, there seem to be three basic conditions that foster the development of identity: (1) varied direct experiences and roles, (2) meaningful achievement, and (3) relative freedom from anxiety and pressure.

To what extent are these conditions realized within our four models? The limited variety of direct experiences and roles, deriving from the exclusive academic focus of most curricula, has already been mentioned; the consequences for the development of identity are as sharp as for the development of instrumental independence. But what of the other two conditions: relative freedom from anxiety and pressure, and meaningful achievement?

The competitive climate and the evaluational procedures that characterize the Cadillac curriculum probably inhibit development of identity most, attenuating the potential that might reside in the greater flexibility and greater freedom of choice that it has over the rocket or the horse and buggy. The emphasis on vocational or professional preparation and the attendant grading practices, which dominate the rocket curriculum, probably operate in similar fashion to inhibit such development. In the horse and buggy curriculum, the emphasis on developing intellectual skills militates against sharing subjective and emotional reactions, which might provide a better basis for self-awareness and self-testing. The competitive aspect of evaluation may not intrude so directly, except as exams and discussion punish the non-objective and reward dispassionate and detached intellectualism distant from the heart of the respondent. In the junkyard curriculum, where self-evaluation occurs, development of identity may be fostered. But some students need continually to confirm themselves as they are; for them self-evaluation may only mean digging deeper in the same hole. In the junkyard curriculum, the threats arising from grades, exams, and a highly competitive atmosphere are absent—but this sword cuts two ways. If there is no clear and direct feedback through experience and if forthright and substantive faculty reactions are not forthcoming, then a student may simply encounter a kind of fog that insulates him from evaluation and provides no basis for self-testing or self-definition.

Meaningful work can lift one out of a hole, it can balance total absorption in a limited role. In one sense, the work of the rocket curriculum is meaningful when seen as useful to the anticipated occupation. But in such a sense it only confirms a course already taken. It does not broaden perspective or raise questions about that direction. Moreover, the second-class status of other content and the instrumentalist stance taken toward it are unlikely to foster much self-examination. When these conditions are encountered by students whose prime motivation for college attendance is to get a better job, it is not surprising that many students live the unexamined life.

The Cadillac curriculum, with its more general content, its relative elevation of the liberal arts as valuable areas of study, and its more frequent discussion classes where meaningful questions can be raised, offers greater potential than does the rocket. Yet, because for many students and faculty members alike, simple admission to the institution means having finally arrived, serious questions of why one is there, where it may lead, and whether one would be better off elsewhere, are difficult to make public and difficult to sustain privately. As student unrest becomes more visible and widespread, however, this complacency is challenged.

In the horse and buggy curriculum, where process, not content, is central, the question of meaning is different. When students can sense development of their own capacities and when they value such development, then experiences are meaningful. And when such development occurs through close analysis of basic concepts in the humanities, social sciences, and natural sciences, relevance is increased. In this curriculum the danger lies more in settling totalistically for the role of intellectual than in going through the motions of meaningless process or content. Nor is meaninglessness of subject matter a great problem in the junkyard curriculum. There, difficulties arise when whimsy and impulse go beyond a student's ability to cope with them, when anxiety concerning lack of direction is high, and when a sound basis for work cannot be developed. The principal problem there is to discover clearly what is meaningful; the pursuit can be easily taken up once the discovery is made.

Freeing of Interpersonal Relationships. The freeing of interpersonal relationships is also likely to be affected by variation in curriculum, teaching, and evaluation, and by the climates that develop as a consequence. Freedman (in Miller, 1965) has observed a connection between competitive climates and a sense of isolation on some campuses. D. Heath (1958) reports, "Persistent academic pressure punctuated by the ever recurring examinations and papers forces a student into an increasingly auto-centric existence." Sanford (1963), observing Stanford students, suggests what happens:

> among the men students at Stanford today there are virtually no friendships. . . . The thing that I was impressed by . . . was that these boys could not really be friends with each other because they could not reveal themselves to each other enough to establish an intimate relationship. In that situation, they saw each other as everything else except friends—as competitors, as people who could be manipulated, who could make one feel big or make one feel little

—as everything except genuine objects of human relationship. So they had to put on an act all the time, even with . . . their fraternity brothers and roommates. There was always the possibility that this guy would get something on them that would somehow be harmful in the general race that they were all running together. . . . As a matter of fact I think that the early marriages in college are largely a result of this. The boys can't really be intimate with each other. The only person they can find who will listen while they reveal their softer sides is one of the girls. A friendship will develop with her and this will be mistaken for a romance, and marriage will follow. . . . The thing I see at Stanford and at other high-pressure places . . . is that the idea of the college as a moratorium where people have a few years to discover themselves and to learn how to relate to other people . . . is being given up. Instead the whole thing is being treated as a kind of training program or a business enterprise . . . which is likely to be quite damaging both to the development of our people and to their mental health [pp. 21, 22].

Such circumstances as Freedman, Heath, and Sanford describe seem unlikely to foster increased tolerance of those who differ or increased ability to develop relationships of mutual respect and support. The Cadillacs and rockets are most prone to these high-pressure conditions where relative standing is the student's primary concern. Thus, freeing of interpersonal relationships will be fostered least there. In the horse and buggy, where evaluation occurs according to more fixed standards, and in the junkyard, where comparative achievement is obscured, cooperative efforts in the service of learning and achievement are more possible and relationships to which different individuals bring diverse strengths can develop and yield fruit. Students can work together to cope with outside examiners or comprehensives, to explore personal interests, or to fulfill educational purposes, and all may share the increased benefits. But when rewards are scarce and when your income increases at my expense, cooperation is often collusion to short-circuit the system, or to increase the deprivation of others for one's own enrichment.

It seems clear that different systems of curriculum, teaching, and evaluation are likely to have differing impact on at least four major vectors of development. Through these differing relationships run some patterns that suggest hypotheses worth mentioning as a basis for further research and for educational innovation and experimentation.

First, with regard to curriculum: development of competence, autonomy, and identity is fostered (1) as the range of experiences, responsibilities, and significant tasks required by the curriculum increases, and (2) as choices regarding course selection, program of study, and resources to be used are more often required of students.

With regard to teaching practices: development of competence, autonomy, and identity and the freeing of interpersonal relationships are fostered (1) as the content and the orientation of the teacher are such that he does not stand as final authority, (2) as the content touches, and is used to throw light on, basic existential questions of value and belief, or complex issues and problems of more immediate concern, (3) as classes are group discussions with ample exchange among students as well as between students and teacher, and (4) as discussion of relevant personal experiences, feelings, and reactions is a legitimate supplement to objective analyses and interpretation.

With regard to evaluation: development of autonomy and identity and the freeing of interpersonal relationships are fostered (1) as pressure for high academic achievement is reduced, (2) as progress and rewards depend less upon relative standing and more upon successful achievement of specified tasks, and (3) as evaluative feedback is less often symbolic and more often substantively descriptive of strengths and weaknesses.

Innovation, experimentation, and research designed specifically to test and to study some of these general propositions is needed if curriculum, teaching, and evaluational procedures are to become more effective and if educational policies and practices are to derive less from myth and more from evidence and concrete experience.

CHAPTER **11**

RESIDENCE HALL ARRANGEMENTS

ꕥꕥꕥꕥꕥꕥꕥꕥꕥꕥꕥꕥꕥꕥꕥꕥ

The fact that college enrollments have been spiraling over the past fourteen years—and will continue to do so—is too well known among those concerned with higher education to require much documentation. In response to these increasing enrollments, colleges are constructing new residence halls, acquiring additional buildings and converting them to provide housing, and undertaking development programs that include more dormitories. This process requires frequent decisions involving interior architecture and the arrangement of buildings in relation to each other. It requires a similar stream of decisions concerning the assignment of students, parietal rules, and the general conditions under which students shall live. Few of these decisions are made in the light of a clear conception of how student development may be influenced by housing arrangements.

Yet college residences do provide a significant context for student development. It is there that close associations with other students occur. The student's opportunities for contact with different kinds of persons can lead to increased ease and freedom in his relationships with others. Because in his residence hall a student observes the impact of his behavior on others and feels the force of the group's behavioral norms and standards, he can better develop a personal system of values that he can hold with integrity. And because the college can control housing arrangements and the placement of students within the houses, it can create conditions that more effectively contribute to the freeing of interpersonal relationships and to the development of integrity.

Consider first the area of interpersonal relationships. Bossard (1932) found that marriage rates, even within a single city, rise as the distance between the homes of the partners decreases. Newcomb (1962) found that:

> even within a small, two-floor house accommodating only 17 students, there were at first (but not following intimate acquaintance) significantly more close relationships among the eight men on one floor and among the nine men on the other than between the men on different floors. Roommates, whose proximity to each other was greatest of all, were particularly prone to develop close relationships [pp. 69–92].

Of course, propinquity is not the only influencial factor; over a long period, general values and interests also are important. But at the outset propinquity is a primary factor. Newcomb (1962) sums up its significance like this:

> For any individual there are many others, potentially, with whom he might form significant relationships. Those with whom he does in fact develop them are limited by opportunities for contact and reciprocal exploration, which in turn are influenced by physical propinquity. And, other things equal, he is most apt to maintain close relationships with those with whom he first develops them [p. 76].

The evidence also makes it very clear that these friendships have an important influence. Dressel and Lehmann (1965), for example, found that:

The most significant reported experience in the collegiate lives of these [Michigan State University] students was their association with different personalities in their living unit. The analysis of interview and questionnaire data suggested that discussions and bull sessions were a potent factor in shaping the attitudes and values of these students [p. 245].

We are all familiar with college bull sessions, but we may underestimate their impact. White (1958), reporting on his study of college students, describes the following incident in the life of a student called Hartley Hale:

It was during his freshman year that Hale came to his decision to be a doctor. . . . Across the hall in the dormitory lived a student who enjoyed argument. Hale also enjoyed argument and he particularly liked debating with this neighbor who was always reasonable and therefore did not irritate him and throw him into stubborn negativism. Hale reports "One night for some reason or other . . . he decided, he got it into his mind, that I should be a doctor instead of going into advertising. And so he started to argue with me about it and when morning came I agreed that he was right. He did a very logical, very thorough job on me, and so I went down the next day and I changed my field of concentration to biology. Then I called up my family and told them what I'd decided, which they didn't like [p. 47].

Obviously, not all career decisions are made in this fashion, but such discussions do have significant force. D. Heath (1968), on the basis of research at Haverford, reports that for both undergraduates and alumni relations with roommates and friends were the principal experiences that transformed ethnocentrism into greater acceptance and affection for others. Many of the freshmen and seniors spontaneously confirmed earlier results, and described themselves to have been isolated, egocentric, overly intellectual, and defensively superior at entrance. But, forced to live with another who could not be ignored without great effort, they began to accommodate themselves to the other men; they gradually became more accepting and tolerant; they formed close friendships, often for the first time in their lives. For all three groups, freshmen, seniors, and alumni, roommates ranked second or third, after friends or specific faculty members, in a list of seventeen determinants of personality maturing.

Interior and exterior architecture, and the arrangement of

units in relation to one another, also may affect the range and intensity of the associations that occur. Although I know of no studies of colleges, William Whyte's research for *The Organization Man* (1956) suggests that there are close relationships between architectural arrangements and patterns of association. He says:

> In suburbia friendship has become almost predictable. Despite the fact that a person can pick and choose from a vast number of people to make friends with, such things as the placement of a stoop or the direction of a street often have more to do with determining who is friends with whom. . . . Given a few physical clues about the area, you can come close to determining what could be called its flow of "social traffic," and once you have determined this, you may come up with an unsettlingly accurate diagnosis of who is in the gang and who isn't. . . .
>
> Each court produces a different pattern of behavior, and whether newcomers become civic leaders or bridge fans or churchgoers will be determined to a large extent by the gang to which chance has now joined them. . . . A map of the roster of the active members of the United Protestant Church indicates that some areas habitually send a good quota of people to church while other areas send few. Voting records show heavy turnouts in some areas, apathy in others, and this pattern tends to be constant—the area that had the poorest showing in the early days is still the poorest. . . . Another key index is the number of parties and such communal activities as joint playpens. Some courts have many parties, and though the moving van is constantly bringing in new people, the partying and group activities keep up undiminished [pp. 330, 331, 334].

The point is, in bull sessions and individual debates, intellectual skills are sharpened and new information is acquired, values are clarified, stereotypes are questioned and destroyed. Residence hall design and the regulations imposed can foster or inhibit such exchanges and can influence the range of persons with whom they may occur. When lounge space is available, bull sessions can occur and roommates can study without direct interference. When a lounge must be crossed to get to a room the possibilities of being captured by a hot argument increase. A small increase in the square footage of a lounge may yield a large increase in the number of groups or pairs that can be accommodated. Lounges with somewhat broken space accommodate more groups with less interference than the same space as an uninterrupted rectangle. Thus attention to the size, the design, and the location of lounges in residence halls can yield developmental dividends.

Regulations also play a role. Rules that severely restrict visiting within and between houses may curtail opportunities for significant exchange when the time for it is ripe. Curfews and room checks may nip fruitful discussion and may generate reluctance to open up important areas of concern when one cannot look forward to pursuing them until some temporary resolution is achieved. Overconcern for maintaining silence or quiet conditions generates smog that dampens the free exchange and emotional expression that are part of any serious consideration of issues significant to the person one is or might become. In short, regulations and housing design may create a condition where, because fruitful exchange is difficult to achieve, it becomes "not the thing to do," or at least something generally not done.

It is also clear that some college housing units develop distinctive characteristics—"subcultures" in the jargon of the social scientists —that may persist at length and be resistant to change. The evidence suggests, too, that these different subcultures have an influence on the student. Scott (1965), for example, studying fraternities at the University of Colorado, found that freshman pledges—both men and women—valued independence less and social skills and loyalty more than did their nonpledging peers; the men pledges also ranked relatively lower on intellectual and creative values, and the women were lower on kindness but higher on social status and achievement. In longitudinal study, he found that those who joined fraternities and those who did not developed in different directions during the first year of membership. These findings and others have led Newcomb (1966) to posit the following dynamic:

> We already know that a good many freshmen quickly team up with others very much like themselves, and we do not expect to find much value change within persisting peer groups initially formed in such ways, our assumption being that their members will tend to reinforce one another's existing values. If so, we shall be able to demonstrate a general phenomenon, of which fraternities and sororities . . . are merely a special case, in that they tend to select homogeneous recruits and, relatively speaking, to insulate them from influences that might induce significant attitude change [p. 112].

The findings from these different studies document two major points: first, that friendships and membership in various groups or subcultures influence development; and second, that interior design and architectural arrangements involving the placement of living units and their location in relation to one another influence the student's choice of friends, the groups he joins, and the diversity of persons with whom he can have significant encounters. Thus there is good evidence that resident hall arrangements have powerful implications for student development. The potential for the freeing of interpersonal relationships is particularly strong. Such settings not only may foster increased tolerance and respect for differences in background, belief, and temperament; they also provide a context in which relationships of intimacy can move from totalistic and narcissistic absorption to a kind of interdependence that provides stronger and more reliable support as well as greater freedom of movement.

Because a college can exert control over interior design and structure, site planning and location of buildings, and at least the initial placement of students, conditions that foster such development can be established. I would hypothesize that the following four conditions would encourage such development:

1. Let each unit be assigned—as far as possible, given the range in characteristics of students enrolled—persons of diverse backgrounds, differing interests, and differing values.

2. Let the interior of each unit be designed so as to foster association among students in the unit, and let each unit be located so as to foster interrelationships with other units nearby.

3. Let the members of each unit face meaningful decisions that require significant exchange; in this way, the diversity of orientation may be revealed, examined, and tried on for size.

4. Let housing regulations be such as to permit spontaneous, heated, and extended discussions that can be held without the imposition of arbitrary cut-off times and that are free from adult interruption, intrusion, or surveillance.

Under such arrangements, students can have more sustained contact with persons different from themselves and can learn to work with, to be comfortable with, and to understand diverse personalities. And under such arrangements students can develop relationships of respect and affection that will provide satisfaction and support beyond the college years, sustained despite infrequent communication or direct contact.

Sustained encounters with persons different from oneself also foster the development of integrity: the gradual achievement of a set of personal values and of patterns of behavior congruent with those values. Recall that our concern is not so much the content of values, but the bases on which they rest, the ways in which they are held, and the force with which they operate in daily life. The proper function of colleges is to increase the role of values in the lives of students—not to modify the content of the values held. But however successful higher education may have been in the past in carrying out this function, its role will be much smaller in the future. The current thrusts of change —increased enrollment, shifting patterns of selectivity, increased affluence, increased status—lead to a reduction in that sense of community that once fostered the development of integrity. For it is in the context of significant social settings, of important group relationships, that major personal values are formed and that integrity is tested.

Sherif and Sherif (1964) indicate why human beings form groups and describe the processes by which groups are established and maintained. In the comments that follow, I borrow freely from their book, although they obviously are not to be held responsible for errors of interpretation or unwarranted extrapolations.

Human beings are strongly prompted to establish social ties with others for two major reasons. First, secure social ties provide a dependable basis for a consistent and stable self-picture, a firm sense of identity. Although major personality changes may occur over a period of time, the feedback from day-to-day associations with friends gives a sense of personal constancy. Second, social ties provide both instrumental and emotional support as the business of living is carried out. The social ties that serve these functions are, for the most part, linked with membership in groups—informal friendship groups as well as more formal structures related to work, community activities, and the like.

Once an individual identifies himself with a particular group, the group becomes both an anchor and a reference point: The values and behavioral norms of the group provide a background against which the individual's decisions about behavior, and his modification of values and attitudes, occur. The extent to which a particular group assumes force for an individual depends, first, upon how much the ties to family, friends, and other social structures have been disrupted, and, second, upon how much the group enables him to fulfill his social or material needs, to realize his immediate purposes, and to move toward more long-range goals. When the group becomes important, the individual tries to maintain his position within it by behaving appropriately and by demonstrating competencies relevant to the group's needs and valued by the group members.

In such a situation, the shared standards and the rules for conduct are not viewed as arbitrary, capricious, or functionless, nor felt to be unduly coercive, intrusive, or authoritarian. Because members in good standing share and are identified with the group's norms and expectations, the application of sanctions or pressures in response to deviance is not the responsibility solely of a leader or official: it is shared by all. The formal or informal leaders themselves are not immune. Loyalty to the group and what it stands for supersedes loyalty to individuals within it.

Of course, specific decisions do not have a simple one-to-one relationship with the group standards, nor are they made on a purely intellectual basis. Through a continuing process of interaction, group members develop and select alternatives, and this interaction is most effective when there are common problems to be dealt with and common needs to be implemented. In such encounters, group standards develop and are modified, and individuals assume their own positions and roles.

These then are conditions by which reference groups are established and maintained, and the dynamics by which members are affected. A scrutiny of American higher education suggests that, for most students in most colleges, reference groups likely to further institutional objectives or to contribute substantially to the development of integrity are missing. This is not to say they do not exist. They do. But for the most part they consist of relatively small, informal friendship groups formed almost entirely by self-selection following upon chance encounters. In large universities, the sheer numbers, the proliferation of courses, the limited participation in extra-academic activities, and numerous other conditions sharply limit the possibilities that groups will develop on any other basis. Even in many small colleges, conditions that in the past made the total college community an effective reference group now less frequently exist, and new compensatory arrangements have not been developed.

These changing conditions are worth noting in more detail. When enrollment is small and resources are limited, when students, faculty, and administration alike are making do with less than ideal or adequate facilities, there is often a strong sense of community. Staff members serve in several capacities, working with students in varying contexts. The students' talents and energies are genuinely needed. Both students and faculty feel a strong identification with, and loyalty to, the institution. The total college community is an effective culture for its members. But as enrollment increases, as the institution becomes more secure, as the roles of faculty and administration become more specialized, as students are less needed, then the sense of community is sharply diminished and it no longer serves as a reference group. Norms become more diffuse, behaviors range more widely, individual invisibility increases, and the totality of a student or faculty member is hard to see. One frequent result is that students have no general reference group. Consequently, they feel that to hold responsible positions in campus organizations has little significance, and the potentialities for development that reside in such activities are attenuated. These activities become artificial and superficial, remote from the lives of most students. Students grow more distant from one another and from the faculty and administration. Differences tend to move toward polarization and solidification rather than toward resolution and accommodation. Attempts to establish standards for behavior that have force for students and with which they identify are less and less successful. Then there occurs one, or a mixture, of three situations: (1) rules gradually wither away, or (2) rules are maintained, but they are to be winked at as long as one is sufficiently discreet so that eyes do not have to be held shut or averted too long, or (3) more and more feverish attempts are made to enforce rules by adding student assistants to the assistants to the deans of men and women, and undeclared guerrilla warfare commences.

One response to these general institutional changes is to create housing arrangements that permit each living unit to become a reference group for its members; in this way, each unit can provide a meaningful source of norms and standards for behavior. As presently constituted and administered, most college residences do not serve such a function. They do not because they are not social structures and the members do not constitute a group that encourages any particular identification. Of course there are exceptions, and when they occur, students value them and wish them to continue or to happen again.

There is research that documents the influence of residence halls and subunits on attitudes and behavior, when they become reference groups for their members. Vreeland and Bidwell (1965), who studied Harvard houses, found a marked effect on values and attitudes and found that this effect increased when peer involvement in a house was high. Farnsworth (1963), commenting on some still unpublished research, reports:

> In dormitories the sexual behavior of students varies tremendously according to the degree of aggressiveness shown by the popular girls. One aggressive girl can quite definitely change the sexual behavior of several girls in the group. If there are three or four girls in a given entry who are the prestige girls and who have high standards, they can cause others to hold onto the ideals with which they came to college in the first place [p. 72].

To enable residence units to become reference groups more frequently and to foster the development of integrity, certain steps need to be taken. The following four principles, taken from research on reference groups, may serve as guides. Reference groups develop and are maintained when: (1) associations are fairly long-lasting, (2) members face common problems, share common tasks, or otherwise engage in meaningful activities together, (3) status and roles are varied enough so that longevity of association and being a "good" member is rewarded and recognized, and (4) the boundaries with respect to other social establishments are reasonably clear; one knows who is "in" and who is "out."

These principles suggest several possibilities for the management of college housing. These possibilities are obviously not statements of "how to do it"; rather they illustrate conditions that might foster development of integrity.

1. Let a student live in the same unit as long as he chooses. Let him change to a different unit if he wants to, and if space is available, but let the student's wish to remain take precedence over another's desire to enter.

2. Let the number of students per unit be small enough so that each student can know the others, and so that the impact that the behavior of an individual has on the whole is visible.

3. Let the members of each unit allocate to themselves the spaces within the unit. For example, if twenty persons of a thirty-person unit expect to return the next semester, let them assign to themselves the rooms within the unit, arranging their preferences according to whatever schedule of priority or hierarchy they see fit. Let the ap-

propriate staff member then fill the empty spaces with new students
or with old students who request transfer.

4. Let each house have some funds to work with, and ask for
an accounting at the end of each semester. Perhaps each house could
assume some responsibility for its own interior decoration and its own
maintenance. Perhaps the unit could be billed for breakage or deterioration, and the members allowed to deal with individuals responsible
as they see fit. Perhaps each unit could have some funds for entertain-
ment.

Under such conditions, each house could develop its own somewhat distinctive culture, allocating individual roles and responsibilities
according to differential abilities and inclinations. Persons of status
would have a stake in preserving the culture, and the continual intro-
duction of new and different persons would keep questions of value
and behavior in the air, while at the same time a salient set of standards was maintained.

There is a value in making the standards rather explicit, both
to heighten their visibility and to provide a clear point of view with
which issue can be taken. It is also important that the values of the
administration and faculty be clearly communicated so that students
can benefit from the adult perspective and so that these points of view
can be considered, as issues are discussed and decisions arrived at. To
make standards and values more explicit and to foster communication
and understanding between faculty and students, three things might be
done.

First, the president, the deans, and any appropriate or concerned faculty members might make available to students a personal
statement indicating their own views on whatever matters of concern
arose in the residences. Presumably these statements would speak to
such matters as heterosexual behavior, drinking, drugs, and more particular issues—like beards and dress—which are of concern to some
and not to others. They would be expressions of personal conviction
and belief. The bases on which they rest would be given as frankly
and clearly as possible. They would not replace rules, regulations, or
policies, but rather would provide the substance underlying them.

Second, each residence unit might provide its own public statement of position regarding various matters of behavior and conduct.
Allocation of responsibility should be real, and areas subject to student

self-determination, as well as those areas the faculty or administration reserves to itself, should be made clear. The range of student self-determination should be as great as possible, but obviously it must differ from college to college, depending upon variations in characteristics of students, upon the attitudes of the faculty and administration, and upon the nature of the major sources of institutional support. It would be understood that statements generated by the housing units represent the consensus of the group, and accurately reflect minority views.

Finally, each unit might choose one or more faculty members with whom to discuss matters of concern to house members. These faculty members would also participate in more general discussions of house management.

If some of these changes were made, it would increase the probability that colleges will continue to foster the development of personalized values that its graduates would hold with integrity and that would enter actively into decisions faced in their daily living.

To recapitulate briefly: Housing arrangements do have an impact on student development. The close associations formed among students who live together there provide a significant setting for the freeing of interpersonal relationships. Because a housing unit can become an important reference group for its members, and because an individual's behavior has an observable impact on his housemates, there is significant opportunity to foster the development of a personal value system held actively and with integrity.

The developmental value of residence hall settings has received little careful thought. Both the magnitude of institutional investment in such facilities and the potential they offer for important aspects of student development warrant much more systematic attention. Research to date suggests that well-considered action can yield significant return.

CHAPTER **12**

FACULTY AND
ADMINISTRATION

So we have a college, a structure built to a certain size, designed for specified purposes, with procedures for curriculum, teaching, and evaluation, and living arrangements designed to achieve those purposes. And we have considered how variation in these different elements may influence student development. By now, however, it should be clear that the principal reason such variations make a difference is that they influence the frequency and intensity, the content and contexts, of interpersonal encounters and relationships. For basically it is persons who affect persons, not structural arrangements. Arrangements can enable or inhibit, but their impact in and of themselves is limited.

After relationships with peers and the peer culture, relationships with faculty come first in importance. Members of the faculty and administration have an impact on four major vectors: intellectual competence and sense of competence, autonomy, purpose, and integrity.

Intellectual competence and sense of competence are fostered first by the example set by the persons themselves, second by the demands they make, and third by the encouragement they offer. Maximum impact occurs when all three are present and balanced. Raushenbush (1964) quotes two different students who illustrate what happens. A boy at New College, Hofstra, says:

> Professor Anderson did everything for me.
> What was the most important thing he did for you?
> He taught me how to think.
> What does that mean?—it is so easy to say.
> Thinking—how to take one step at a time to find out what you want to know—the wonderful experience of being able to do that. He didn't answer questions; he said, "What are the alternatives?" But he helped you along—"Now let me say this alternative won't do. Why not?" And he got you to work on every possibility, one after another [p. 86].

And a girl at Monteith College:

> Here you know, I've been able to talk and not be on the defensive—not putting on an act all the time. If I don't know something I can come out and show my ignorance, and to me this has been a big help, because most of the time in high school and other courses at the university, I act my way through rather than learn. That has enabled me to learn rather than act, and it's a big step forward. . . .
> And it wasn't until I got into personal contact with some of the instructors that I began to realize that learning was more than this and learning was more important than this. . . .
> And I think the relationship between the instructor and the student in Monteith is conducive to this. It would be an accident, I think, if it happened anywhere else, because if a person isn't an individual who makes friends with instructors, or shies away from them, he'll never be induced to do really constructive thinking [p. 133].

In these productive relationships observed by Raushenbush, teachers were not therapists discussing students' personal problems. Nor were they buddies. Competence and sense of competence were fostered because an older, more mature person, intellectually alive and capable, pursued problems and shared experiences with a younger person still testing his competence and his interests. Students were taken seriously. Their competence was respected while both student and teacher worked for its increase.

The studies of Thistlethwaite (1959, 1960, 1962) and Davis (1964) mentioned in Chapter Ten document the affects of such relationships. Heath (1968) reports similar results for Haverford students, where "intellectual maturing" occurred as a direct product of the "inspiration, discipline, example, and style" communicated by the faculty through their specific courses.

Unfortunately, most teachers, as they are encountered by students, are not models of competence—because most faculty members don't strive to become competent in the classroom. If they have professional competence it is usually demonstrated elsewhere, and seldom in contexts shared by students. The disproportionate rewards for status in a discipline, compared to the rewards for teaching excellence, are obviously the principal factor in the disproportionate allocation of energy and concern. But they are not the only cause. They could not work with such force if assessment of classroom competence was less primitive. The principal reason teaching seems to offer no challenge is that teachers seldom get clear feedback concerning the consequences of their performance. Most evaluation stops about at the level of whether students liked the teacher, found him interesting, felt he "knew his subject and could present it clearly," "had a sense of humor," or "was warm and friendly." And, if solicited at all, such reactions are usually sought at the end of a whole semester. They may be reassuring or discouraging, but they are not the more precise analyses necessary if relationships between particular contents, procedures, and teacher behaviors, on the one hand, and student behavior and learning, on the other, are to be discovered. Consequently, most faculty members develop a rather hazy sense of being a good, average, or "only fair" teacher and let it go at that, continuing that style with which they are comfortable and which fits other outside interests and demands.

It is really not so difficult to conceptualize some fundamental accompaniments of good teaching and to assess them in reasonably sound manner. Bloom (1950, 1953, 1956) did both in the early fifties. For example, take five things a student might be doing while class is in session: (1) listening to the lecture or discussion, primarily to remember what is being said, (2) doing his own thinking about the ideas being presented, (3) speaking to the class, asking a question, commenting in a discussion, making a presentation, (4) daydreaming, dozing, letting his mind wander, (5) actively doing things unrelated to the class—writing a letter, preparing for another class. Information about the number of students engaged in these various activities during different class periods would provide an adequate basis for modifying style and subject matter for more effective student involvement. Not ideal to be sure, but a good start. Bloom (1953) got data on such things simply by replaying short sections of tape-recorded class sessions immediately after class and asking students what they were doing at the time. He found sharp differences from teacher to teacher and from one style to another. Video taping recaptures a much richer picture of what is actually happening—what the teacher is doing and how the class is reacting. A few hours spent watching oneself before a class, particularly in the company of one or two trusted and perceptive colleagues, could, if one's ego could stand the strain, be highly instructive. Such self-observation has already proved effective in many other contexts—from training psychotherapists to teaching skiing—and it is proving useful with elementary and secondary teachers. Colleges use the device to improve the football team. Perhaps its use also could be justified to improve teaching. Economical units are now available from your local audio-visual dealer.

Faculty should determine what out-of-class activities suit their objectives. Memorizing, analyzing material to discover its component parts and their relationships, synthesizing or developing generalizations from diverse materials, applying concepts to new problems—it is not impossible to collect such data with reasonable reliability and validity. Then assignments can be modified accordingly.

The point is—rewards for professional contribution aside—until more systematic and relevant assessment of teaching behaviors and their consequences in student behavior are undertaken, through the investment of college resources and the time and effort of individual teachers, teaching will remain unchallenging; teaching competence will not be pursued and students will continue to meet many more professors passively leaning on traditional methods and assignments than competent and vigorous persons testing new ways to achieve increased effectiveness.

The New College boy quoted earlier, about three and one-half

months after he had begun work with Professor Anderson, went to
see him and said, "What I have to know now is whether you think I
have what it takes to go into medicine. I have to make up my mind
now, because this is my last chance to get into the Golden Gloves competition." Raushenbush (1964) reports that he gave up boxing that
afternoon as a commitment to try to study and by the end of the year
had decided to become a theoretical chemist, saying, "I don't want to
do the experiments in the lab. It was the lab that first made me see
what chemistry is—that and Mr. Anderson's talk—and how one *can*
think about it—it was there I began to work out the alternatives—but
I don't need that now [p. 87]."

Faculty impact on competence and sense of competence obviously has relevance for clarifying purposes. Wallace's (1966) report,
which describes the relationships among admiration of faculty members, grade-point average, and graduate school aspirations, indicates
their interaction. Grigg (1962) asked seniors, "During your college
career has any member of the college teaching faculty contacted you
(as opposed to your approaching him) to offer any encouragement or
suggestions concerning your going to graduate or professional school?"
Students whom faculty had contacted "several" times planned to go
on for further study much more often than students who reported little contact of this kind. Greeley (1962), who questioned students both
high and low in achievement, found that those planning further education, regardless of achievement level, had been influenced by faculty
members to do so. In summarizing research of this kind Newcomb and
Feldman (1968) say:

> Evidence is accumulating that faculty are particularly important
> in influencing occupational decisions and educational aspirations.
> In over a dozen studies, in which students were asked to name the
> important sources of influence on their vocational planning and de-
> cisions, faculty along with parents ranked as extremely important.
> In fact, with only two or three exceptions in these studies, students
> perceived faculty to be either as influential as their parents or more
> so [p. 253].

Faculty members exert influence, not only with regard to career plans and aspirations, but in more general ways. The Monteith
girl quoted earlier (Raushenbush, 1964) also said:

> in dealings with a few instructors . . . I began, you know, to look

into myself and to find out what it was I was doing in school, and to me this is really something; because if by coming here and finding out what I'm here for, what I want and what I want to do later on, I can get my bearings [p. 135].

These comments suggest that faculty members not only help students clarify career plans but also respond to more general future plans as well. Probably the principal way faculty members assist the development of purpose is by recognizing that effective teaching will raise questions of purpose or will add new dimensions to the questions already there, by listening as students try to clarify their own uncertainties, as they try to articulate the fit between their own developing purposes and an idea encountered in reading, discussion, or lecture, and by responding to such questions in open and thoughtful manner—indeed, by granting that after all, a student may be working for something more than a grade. As one student friend of mine put it:

I think the idea is that a faculty member can see that I'm searching out these things because it's for me and that I'm not just doing it because it's something there that has to be done. In other words there is something much greater behind it than just, "This was given to you and you've got to do it," that I'm doing it for many, many more reasons than this.

Fundamental questions reside in all areas of study—humanities, arts, natural sciences, social sciences—and for more perceptive and thoughtful students they reside in technical and professional training as well. Explicit recognition of the fact and willingness to deal with the issues that arise, either individually or in class, contributes substantially to development of purpose.

Faculty members and administrators, secretaries, janitors, and cooks—in short, any older person—can also contribute in another way: by self-exposure. By letting students know our own occupational history, single-channeled or checkered as the case may be, and by sharing our feelings about it and the reasons for our moves, we permit students to test vicariously their own occupational plans and aspirations. By letting students know our home and family, the way we spend our time, the organizing needs and satisfactions for our particular life-style, we enable a wider base for clarification of their own conceptions concerning marriage, family, and the bases of their future existence. Not that they will follow our example. Our difficulties and problems may be the most instructive things we offer, our blind spots and points of tension most revealing. But with several such experiences, distortions carried from their own family settings can be tempered; and as the range of encounters increases, so do opportunities for partial identification and emulation, for critical modeling. Disagreement, in the context of a warm relationship, can lead to positions contrary to our own, but positive for the student. Thus students by indirections find directions out; thus formulations for a future are constructed. Not all faculty members can be so open, and not all can find satisfaction in such relationships with younger persons. But when they can it makes a difference.

Raushenbush (1964) speaks beautifully of the teacher's contribution to developing purposes:

> The ways in which teachers affect seriously the education of their students are many; but however the teachers function in the classroom, whatever their style, their subject, their way of talking to the students or with them, what students remember, what reached the heart of their learning, what they cherished more than any other one thing, is the sense of shared experience with a teacher. They know the teacher is going through something when the students are; the students speak of this when it is happening, and often afterward, for the sense of communion lasts. Such teachers care about what becomes of their students, but their concern for their students is not limited by a wish to do something *for* them. There is important experience to be discovered, work to be done, a world to function in; and the education of the students, their growth to manhood, the personal enlargement education should bring, has a better chance of accomplishment if the teacher can forward the experience, reveal the work to do, help them to find in study ways to function . . . [p. 135].

Such relationships of inspiration, informality, openness, and warmth have particular implications for the development of autonomy. Achieving emotional independence is the first step toward autonomy and it begins with disengagement from parents, sometimes through active rebellion and rejection, and other times more quietly, without overtones of anger and disillusionment. But in both cases the support of peers and nonparental adults is required during this period. Therefore, adults who are accessible and who can be fully known can have substantial impact. With them the actions and reactions habitual with parents and other adults, which were learned during childhood, can be reexamined and new behaviors can be tested. In this fashion new modes of relationship with persons in authority and with institutional expressions of authority can be developed. A student can then move from dependence through rebellious independence toward relationships of mutual respect and regard where areas of interdependence are recognized, and from which an autonomous existence can be built. Katz (1962) puts it this way:

> The college teacher is a special transference object for his students. He is an "in between" object, in between parents and the adult relations the student will establish in and after college. . . . Teachers thus may become "associates" in the student's mind in his rebellion against his parents. . . . this is a role to which teachers often lend themselves readily, being frequently permanent rebels themselves. The intensity of the transference will of course vary much with the school and with the individual students [pp. 387, 388].

Sanford (1966) describes, for a girl, one form this dynamic takes, which has its corollary for men:

> One may sometimes observe quite clear-cut mother-transferences to older women teachers. A student involved in such a relationship will exhibit many signs of immaturity—often including a kind of compulsive devotion to duty that results in consistently good grades. Further observation . . . however, will often show that the relationship is serving a useful means for gaining freedom from a rather overwhelming actual mother; powerful maternal influence, supported by a host of response readinesses brought over from childhood, could hardly be opposed without a strong ally. Since the teacher usually represents more liberal values and a more flexible and enlightened conscience than does the historical mother-image, there is a good chance for educational gain from the relationship [p. 296].

A peer group or a close friendship with one or two others the same age provides the principal support during this period of disengagement. Frequently these new supports themselves can be binding. Sometimes they exact a high price for the support provided. A close relationship with an older person can temper total reliance on these friends and can provide perspective on those relationships. With such help it is often possible for the young person to leave one group and join another where participation is less costly and where the values and behaviors better suit the developmental directions most desired, or

he can move among several to acquire the diversity of experiences
through which greater autonomy can be achieved. Sanford's (1966)
"Penny" illustrates this point. He says:

> many aspects of Penny's experience at Vassar played a part in her
> development—faculty members, courses of study, the student society
> and culture, her friendship group, the general climate of the college
> —but the crucial factor has undoubtedly been, as she herself states,
> the relationship with Mr. A. . . .
>
> Mr. A's crucial role was to make it possible for her to break
> away from her original peer group; and breaking away was neces-
> sary to her new freedom, because this group had become the major
> support of her restrictive conscience and her authoritarian position.
> Only an adult—not a peer or group of peers—and an admired one
> who represented intellectual values and enlightened conscience
> could have played this role. No other agency could have stood in
> effective opposition to the values represented by the early peer group
> and fully espoused by Penny herself. She needed a figure that was in
> some part a representative of her conscience but could at the same
> time nourish her developing confidence in her own intellectual
> powers. . . .
>
> After the relationship with Mr. A became fully established
> Penny could make friends with an entirely different group of girls,
> who now became very important as supporters of her new value
> system and her new self-conception. She could also establish re-
> lationships with other faculty members, who served her in the same
> way. . . .
>
> Be it noted, finally, that there is nothing in the material to
> suggest that Penny ever sexualized her relationship with Mr. A, or
> that he, for all his boyishness, ever indicated to the girls that he
> valued them for anything other than their intellectual and human
> qualities. Any departure from these restraints by either one would,
> of course, have spoiled the whole drama. Deep and personal though
> her problems were, Penny managed to work them out at the level of
> intellectual activity—thereby taking advantage of one of the unique
> opportunities offered by the college or university to those whom it
> would change [pp. 67, 68, 69].

Of course such relationships, which have potency for student
development, also create opportunities for teachers to exploit students
in the service of their own needs. Most campuses have at least one
Professor Mephesto who goes for Candy, and another who goes for
young men (Kenton, 1965). And most campuses have others whose
exploitation may be more subtle but no less harmful, whose self-esteem

requires the continued nourishment idolization provides, or whose hostility, frustration, and insecurity require safe objects for its expression; who must induce dependence to support their own weak ego.

The final vector for which relationships with faculty and administration have special potential is the development of integrity. In readings, lectures, and class discussions reside questions of value; they reside in all acts or contemplated acts, they reside in college policies and cultural standards. When such questions are revealed, in class, in advising, in committee meetings and in individual conversations, humanizing of values and development of congruence are fostered. Vreeland and Bidwell's (1965) report describes some of the differences that occur among university departments and suggests the reason:

> These studies show that college attendance generally is associated with a liberalization of political and other civic attitudes. These effects are strong among social science majors, but moderate among the humanists and natural scientists and weak among business and engineering students. . . .
>
> One dimension along which departments vary is their definition of undergraduate education. Some departments seek only to increase the student's competence in the technical aspects of the discipline . . . others attempt not only to increase technical competence but also to produce changes in students' values and attitudes. . . . When technical goals predominate, any change in student values and attitudes is likely to be an unanticipated consequence of technical instruction. Under this condition, observed changes in student sentiments should be heterogeneous. When moral goals predominate in a department, instructional activities are expected to impart preferred values and attitudes, so that observed changes in student sentiments should converge on the preferences [pp. 239–241].

Thus the instructional goals as set by faculty members, and the degree to which questions of value and attitudes are raised by particular subject matter or by teachers themselves, can make a difference. Probably the greatest impact is on the humanizing of values, for development of congruence requires more than verbal exchange and intellectual discussion.

Jacob (1957) found that institutions having a potent affect on values were characterized by (1) a distinctive climate, (2) individual teachers who had strong value commitments of their own, and (3) value-laden personal experiences on the part of students which were integrated with their own educational development. D. Heath (1968), on the basis of his own recent studies of Haverford, one of the "potent" colleges singled out by Jacob, reports:

> They value those faculty who are highly professionally competent human beings who do not let their intellectualism shield them from "being very human persons." Those faculty whose own lives are highly integrative, who reveal to students their own humanness, even frailties, who put into action what they believe, who have developed a perspective within which to locate their own intellectual interests strongly and emotionally, move many youths seeking after ways to build a similarly integrative way of living. Narrow commitment to one's academic specialty does not offer the Haverford man a satisfying solution to the conflicts the intellectual atmosphere of the college induces. Nor does a personal permissive warmth or indiscriminate friendliness, command the respect of men who so value intellectual control and discipline.

We all would back words with action, would make behavior consistent with belief. But most of us, excepting a very few, compromise in varying degrees, charting a course somewhere between total commitment and total comfort. Our agile intellects spin off rationalizations to gloss over gaps between what we would and what we will. Young adults hope mightily to avoid that fate, to remain more of a piece, to sustain ideals in the face of seduction and sacrifice. The older person who comes close says that it can be done. His example gives courage to many and can become a lasting pole star, pointing the direction when choice points are encountered.

Thus the example set by the college president, by virtue of his special position, has particular potential for fostering integrity—or cynicism and disillusionment. Can high power and high ideals be linked? Can such a pinnacle be reached without having shed all encumbrances, without having cast off anything that hampered the climb? The president is a living answer to that central question. When he was a more distant figure, seen by students at freshman orientation and commencement, seldom spoken to directly, idealized images could be sustained, or at least shattering knowledge could be winked at. Recently he has become more visible, more frequently tested on social issues and on issues concerning the integrity of the institution and himself. Pressures from alumni, regents, local communities, congressional committees, student and faculty interest groups, all tax heavily the capacity to develop a clear position and to act in terms consistent with it.

The ivory tower has crumbled. The destruction of Vietnam, starvation in Biafra, poverty and prejudice in New York, Chicago, and Los Angeles, in the Green Mountains, the Appalachians, the Plains, and the Great Northwest, law enforcement and prosecution that varies with the color, belief, or dress of the defendant—these issues cannot be met with lofty intellectual neutrality. What's your position and what are you doing about it? That's what young adults want to know. Many faculty members and administrators have answered. Some by taking direct action—marching, demonstrating, campaigning, lobbying, boycotting. Others have turned research and writing to the task. A few have opted out, turning not toward social action, but toward private experience and sensuality. Whatever the response, when it is authentic it earns the respect of most young adults. For the first requirement is congruence. Content is secondary, for without congruence content lacks force and meaning. The faculty member who rings true wherever he is tapped contributes substantially to the young adult's struggle for congruence. Perfection is not required. You can be a slightly cracked and dented old bell and still have an essential integrity that will be recognized when it is there.

Faculty members and administrators should be paragons—that, despite occasional disclaimers, has been implicit in most of our discussion. And, of course, given the distance from grace achieved by most of us, any movement in that direction would probably help. But we must not forget the force of "anti-models" (Adelson, 1962)—persons students actively reject. We have all known some of these anti-models, at least on campuses other than our own: the tyrant, the crowd-pleasing performer, the theoretician working his own angles, the haranguer. Such persons also provoke development. Each of us, if we have a clear and solid position, will be rejected by some. Comforting pillows can contribute to needed rest and recovery. But students also need anvils on which to hammer out their own shape. A college faculty and administration must provide both.

What general conditions for relationships among students and faculty seem to foster competence, autonomy, purpose, and integrity? Four major components run through the empirical findings and personal experiences described in the literature on higher education: accessibility, authenticity, knowledge, and an ability to talk with a student.

Accessibility means more than simply saying to students, "Feel free to come and see me." It requires an institutional climate where talking with faculty members is legitimized, where students feel free to "take up the professors' valuable time," where such contacts are viewed as an important and necessary part of teaching and learning. In many studies simple frequency of contact is associated with variables related to the general kinds of development with which we are concerned. When frequent contacts are accompanied by informality and warmth, potency is further augmented. This does not mean total availability twenty-four hours a day or seven days a week. Different students need different amounts of contact with faculty members, and individual students vary at different times (see, for example, Murphy and Raushenbush, 1960, pp. 175–177). And some cases call for delay or nonassistance. Demands on members of the faculty and administration also vary and must be recognized. But where the climate legitimizes such contact and where older persons can respond flexibly in terms of their judgments about the significance and timing of particular requests, substantial contributions can be made.

Second, accessibility carries force when the persons encountered have a firm and well-integrated system of values and behaviors of their own. Students do not want to be told what they should be or what they should become, nor does such telling make much difference. But they do want to know what older persons believe and the basis on which those beliefs rest. And empirical evidence is not the only valid or acceptable basis. When it rests on faith, on a religious or cultural tradition, on basic assumptions that are part of an ethical humanism, candid admission of the fact is better than intellectual gymnastics that attempt to support a position through use of dubious evidence or recondite rationalizations. And if a faculty member can articulate the relationships between his family background, his upbringing, and the subsequent experiences that have brought him to where he is, so much the better. What students want, and find useful, are relationships with authentic persons, and when diverse positions are represented on a campus, students will hear them and respect them. They clearly will not agree with all points of view, but from the experience of them they can develop a framework that has meaning and substance. MacKinnon (1967) found the kind of person we are talking about in his study of highly creative writers, architects, engineers, mathematicians, physical scientists, and industrial researchers:

> The independence of our creative subjects appears to have been fostered by parents, who, very early, showed an extraordinary respect for the child and confidence in his ability to do what was appropriate. The expectation of the parent that the child would act independently but reasonably appears to have contributed much to the latter's sense of personal autonomy which was to develop later to such a marked degree.
>
> Let it be noted, however, that these parents did not leave the life space of the child unstructured. Within the family there existed clear standards of conduct and ideas as to what was right and wrong, but at the same time there was an expectation, if not requirement, of active exploration by the child and the internalization of a framework of personal conduct. Discipline was almost always constant and predictable.
>
> In most cases there were rules, family standards and parental injunctions which were known explicitly by the children and seldom infringed. Thus there appear to have been both structure and freedom which carried with it expectations of reasonable and responsible action.
>
> This parental policy, I submit, is a far different thing from the kind of permissiveness which is so often granted by parents and also demanded by children today. Extreme permissiveness means the absence of standards and lack of structure . . . with the consequence that he does not know who he is, where he stands, or what he can or should do. Small wonder then that alienation and anxiety are so often his fate.
>
> The college . . . that can create an atmosphere similar . . . would contribute importantly to nurturing the creative potential of its students. And this, I would note, is different from the kind of unstructured campus which some seek today, a campus on which no rules regulate the manner, time, and place for the activities appropriate to college life.
>
> There is another aspect. . . . In addition to the mother and father, the larger familial atmosphere also provided a plentiful supply of diverse and effective models with whom the child could make important identifications—grandfathers, uncles, aunts, and others who occupied prominent and responsible positions within their community. Whatever the emotional relation between father and son, whether distant, harmonious, or turbulent, the father generally presented a model of effective and resourceful behavior in an exceptionally demanding career. What is perhaps more significant, however,

is the high incidence of distinctly autonomous mothers who had active lives and interest and sometimes careers of their own apart from their husbands.

The college might similarly foster the creative potential . . . by offering a plentiful supply of diverse and effective models—teachers who are themselves effectively creative persons [pp. 13–15].

Knowledge can be a great help. Farnsworth (1966) suggests the kind that is useful:

What should we reasonably expect from a college teacher in an institution which is consciously devoting itself to making the entire college experience conducive to learning? Obviously we will take it for granted that he should be competent in his own discipline—just as we always have. . . . He should make himself familiar with the developmental problems of the young adult, and try to remember some of the quandaries he faced when he was in college and graduate school. He should know something of the social, cultural, and spiritual background from which the students come, together with the attitudes, ideals, goals, and aspirations they have brought with them to college. There is little opportunity and probably no need for the great majority of teachers to acquire this knowledge through formal courses. It is best acquired through reading key publications on these themes which are becoming more numerous, together with utilizing or developing opportunities for continuous discussion of such matters with psychologists, psychiatrists, social workers, chaplains, and all persons associated with the Dean of Students and his program for helping make education meaningful to students. [Or, I would add, other teachers whose effectiveness has demonstrated their own competence and sensitivity.] It is not just a question of whether or not such knowledge is desirable; it is going to be necessary if teachers are to "keep ahead of their students." Students in American colleges are already ahead of their teachers in the basic understanding of the role of emotions in their own development, but they need help from people with similar sophistication and who have the wisdom that should come from age and experience [p. 11].

Finally, the ability to talk with and listen to students can be developed. More than one faculty member or administrator has asked, "What am I supposed to do when I'm alone in a room with a student?" Because such conversations can be so helpful, and because I'm not talking about being an amateur psychiatrist or psychotherapist, let me take time to say what I mean.

"I can't study." "I used to believe in God but now I don't know what to think." "I can't stand the thought of going home to my parents for vacation." "I think my best friend is homosexual." "Tonight I'm going to lose my virginity." "I'm going to quit this lousy college." "I can't stand that history teacher." "I don't know what to do when I graduate." "I don't see how I can live with my roommate for eight more weeks." "One week I'm Jesus, the next Machiavelli, and a week later Dag Hammerskjold." Students often face faculty members with comments such as these and expect a helpful response. Most teachers want to be helpful and many feel a professional responsibility to respond. For me, a helpful response has five necessary ingredients: listening, watching, feeling, inquiring, and respecting.

Because the communication is primarily vocal, listening is the most important thing to do. Note that the word is *vocal*, not *verbal*. The point is that some of the most important communications may be nonverbal, but nonetheless vocal. A man tells me his wife is expecting another child. I say, "How wonderful, you must be delighted." His answer "Yes" may be anything from a dirge to a song of joy. It may mean anything from yes to no. Someone says, "Let's hear what the expert has to offer." The expert usually understands that he is supposed to comment, but frequently he also understands quite clearly that the speaker isn't very optimistic about the comment being very insightful or useful.

This is nothing new. It's communication and metacommunication. It's the overt and the covert, the explicit and the implicit. So attention can profitably be paid to aspects of intonation, rate of speech, difficulties in enunciation, and variations in volume and pitch. Careful listening will usually reveal vocal changes that reflect changes in anxiety, or a feeling of talking too long, or even increasing boredom with his own ideas. So listen to the background music as well as the dialogue, to the accompaniment as well as the solo.

And while listening watch. Look closely at the student. He is close enough to reveal plenty. What does that face tell? What does that gesture imply? What are those fingers saying? With what does that mannerism come and go? What does that posture mean? Pictures of a boss and an employee, of a president and a faculty member, a dean and a student, usually show the superior leaning back comfortably and the subordinate leaning forward, usually sitting toward the edge of the chair. This was brought home to me recently by a student. She was talking with me about her difficulty in deciding what to study during her last two years and I was leaning back in a swivel chair with my hands behind my head. Suddenly she broke off and said, "Look at you, leaning back there relaxed and easy, all-knowing and comfortable, while I try to come to terms with myself and with this damn college. You don't care about me or what I'm feeling. I bet you haven't heard half I've said." Her observations were quite accurate. I was pretty distant; I wasn't very much part of what was going on. Of course, there are other students who withdraw so far into the chair, and into themselves, you despair of seeing or sensing whatever it is that requires such protection and shelter. So while you listen—watch.

As well as tuning in as much as possible on the feelings that reside in the vocalizations and visual pictures presented, try to tune in on your own feelings and reactions. We always get much more stimulation than we are aware of. You are not conscious of the pressure on the seat of your pants until attention is called to it. You don't hear the traffic until it is mentioned. These sensations are screened out because they are deemed irrelevant, and they probably are. But there are many other reactions and sensations screened out, or inappropriately identified, which are not irrelevant. Is that feeling in the gut anxiety? Anger? Affection? Lust? Where did it come from? What provoked it? An insinuation of incompetence? Lack of trust? Boredom? The way she flashed that thigh when she crossed her legs? What does that feeling tell you about what is being said, about what the student is trying to clarify or resolve, about your part of the transaction?

Basically the aim is to understand what that student is communicating, what he is trying to cope with, what is going on between you and him; and to achieve the fullest understanding possible, you need to use every clue, every bit of data, all the input available. To do so requires the fullest use of your ears, your eyes, and those extrasensory feelers which for me reside in the viscera.

This kind of attention demands that many things not be done. There is no doodling. There is no thinking about tomorrow's class, this evening's dinner, or that interesting and upsetting luncheon discussion. You are not looking out the window wondering if it will finally rain. And most important, you are not constructing arguments of your own in response to verbalizations the student has offered. It sounds simple, but most of us can't sustain this kind of concentration long. I doubt that many college faculty members have given a student their undivided attention, in the sense I am trying to describe it, for as long as thirty consecutive minutes.

If listening contains a kind of critical alertness, if you are asking yourself, "Could that mean anything else? Do I really know what he means?" you frequently will want to ask questions aloud to clarify meanings. And, of course, the more conventional the statements, the more doubtful that the real meaning is understood. In a description of a college I read "Each student is free to plan his own curriculum to fit his own needs and interests." I can *give* meaning to that statement; I can *inject* my own meanings into it. But I'm sure I know very little about what the college means. My major need in college was for self-esteem and my major interests were poker and skiing. The college might let me build a program around these things but I suspect not. We all give meanings to things we see and hear, but to find out what another really means is something else again.

I don't believe I've had an initial conference with a student during the past three or four years when he was not annoyed by my stupid questions. He tells me the obvious and I ask what he means. He says he wants to study psychology. I say, "What do you mean by 'psychology'?" He says, "Oh, you know, psychology—what makes people tick." "Well, talk to me a little more about that. What are some of the particular questions you'd like to deal with? Why are they important to you?" For a while the student may be somewhat frustrated and exasperated and if this becomes quite obvious I may comment on it. But usually he soon begins to see that statements obvious to him were remarkably uncommunicative to me. And they may be worse than uncommunicative because they may lead me to assume I know something that isn't so. I may go galloping off down a path of private fantasy that later proves to be clearly misleading because his comments have become so incongruous. It later becomes clear to me that where I was reading clinical psychology, personality theory, child development, he was saying perception, neurology, brain mechanisms, biochemistry. So ask for clarification, for examples, for metaphors, for specific instances, for an analogous situation, or simply ask him to say it another way with different words. And also put in your own words what you have heard, what you have understood the communication to be. Almost every time you ask "Does this mean so-and-so?" the student becomes a little clearer about what he does mean. And how helpful it is to him to discover that his true meaning is quite different from what he first said, or discover a self-deception he has carried around for some time.

In your re-presentation of the communication you may include both the overt and the covert. A student asks, "Do I have to get your approval for this change in program?" or "Why do I have to sign out if I'm going away for a weekend?" You may understand that he is asking for information or for reasons, but you may also hear quite clearly that he sees the requirement as an insult to his wisdom or maturity. You may wish to respond simply to the words, or you may wish to respond to the other feelings and sentiments that seem to be contained in the remark. You may have some uncertainty about commenting on the covert, but when it is quite clearly felt I think it is helpful. It is important in these encounters to try to recognize both levels, both words and feelings, so that clarity of communication increases. And you can be a model for this by responding to the feelings you sense, and by communicating your own reactions, if you can be explicit about your own feelings when they accompany statements you make.

Respect is a necessary precondition for any very helpful encounter with a student. If he does not find it, no amount of exhortation or propaganda is going to make the situation look good to him or make it very revealing. And if the respect can be further accompanied by warmth and liking, so much the better. Pause to think about persons who have been understanding; you will notice that they demonstrate respect for you. Not only do they recognize your worth as a companion in the same room, and recognize that you are worth the trouble, but they also reflect an awareness of, and sensitivity to, your feelings, to how things look to you. They attempt to see with you, to feel with you, to get into your frame of reference.

So basically the most helpful thing is simply to try to understand, to clarify what is going on, to illuminate more deeply the problem and the ideas and feelings that surround it—and to do this in a context that exhibits a high degree of respect for the student.

Underlying this position is a conception of how change occurs. It is not your task to change a student. Change occurs as he perceives better where he is, as he sees better what his situation is like, and as he sees what some of the obstacles to perception have been. So try to understand what the situation is and what is standing in the way; try to clear away as much of the underbrush as possible. Once some of the clearing occurs, things seem to happen. The student changes through his own adaptive abilities once he has made a reasonably adequate analysis of the situation. We may get somewhat impatient with his bumbling experimentation, but better that the bumbling be his rather than ours. Then the success or failure is also his, along with the praise or blame. In short, he retains his own life, his own integrity.

Talking with students this way precludes certain rewards. There is not the satisfaction that comes from giving sage advice, or from the lucid exposition of your own well-worked-through and well-substantiated point of view. To me there is little more frightening than the wise teacher who knows clearly right from wrong, who knows what should be studied, who is sure of his own good taste—and feels he must pass all this on. Of course, by and large the student doesn't hear anyway. He knows that all he has to do is maintain an attitude of reverence, and then be prepared to do something when the noise stops.

Neither is there the comfort derived from being reassuring. Words are not magic and verbal reassurances usually suggest either that you don't understand the significance of the problem or else that you regard it as something that will pass away in due time which you don't have to be much concerned about.

Also, you do not have the satisfaction of pursuing your own curiosity. Any intense curiosity or voyeuristic interest in the details of a student's life, his sexual experiences, his drinking habits, his fight with his mother, is an unfortunate, and probably disruptive, intrusion. You forego this satisfaction passively by not pursuing details that are of no moment, and you forego it actively by cutting off the student when you understand basically what went on, even though it would be thrilling or titillating to hear the rest. This helps the student realize that you and he are not there for mutual amusement but for trying to arrive at the necessary clarifications. It also communicates that time has some importance.

Basically, then, you seek only information or clarification that benefits the student; you do not seek gratification or prestige at his expense. You are enjoined from using your skill or your position in the service of your own needs, your own reputation, your own personal satisfaction. It is not easy to carry on such conversations. It requires high alertness and close concentration, trying to grasp the nuances of what is being said, what is reserved, what is distorted, what is unknown. This is exhausting, frustrating, and difficult, especially with complex college students. But I think we simply have to recognize that this is probably the most important kind of teaching we do, and that these encounters are second in significance only to the daily life with other students.

The four general conditions conducive to productive relationships among students and faculty—accessibility, authenticity, knowledge, and the ability to talk with a student—are not complicated to arrange. But on many campuses such arrangements will require modification of priorities, funds, and energies. Some data from the University of California suggest the magnitude of the change required. Underwood (1968) reports that 75 per cent of the freshmen and 63 per cent of the seniors indicated that there was no faculty member whom they felt was particularly responsible to or for them; 88 per cent of the freshmen and 67 per cent of the seniors at Berkeley indicated that they had never had a faculty person single them out for special academic work or ask their help in an academic project in which they were engaged; 30 per cent of the seniors at the University of California felt that very few or no faculty members were really interested in students.

Given the vested interests that attach to any long-standing status quo, given the powerful rewards for activities other than teaching and talking with students, and given general inertia, there will be substantial resistance to change toward increased frequency and intensity of contact between students and faculty. And that's the problem —let us be clear—not that the changes themselves are difficult to conceptualize or complicated to implement. But if students are to be no longer faceless, if we are to meet them where they are and contribute significantly to their development, such changes are perhaps the most important that can be undertaken.

CHAPTER 13

FRIENDS, GROUPS, AND STUDENT CULTURE

꧁꧂꧁꧂꧁꧂꧁꧂꧁꧂꧁꧂꧁꧂꧁꧂꧁꧂꧁꧂꧁꧂

A student's most important teacher is another student. Friends and reference groups filter and modulate the messages from the larger student culture. They amplify or attenuate the force of curriculum, faculty, parietal rules, institutional regulations. They can trump the best teacher's ace and stalemate the most thoughtful or agile dean. Thus relationships with close friends and peer groups, or subcultures, are primary forces influencing student development in college, and all seven vectors of change are affected.

A single case provides a framework for discussion. It is not representative—but individuals seldom are. It does, however, illustrate one life space against which relevant studies and the abstractions they support can be considered.

Here's Gene, an entering freshman. Twelve years of prior edu-

FIGURE 11

The Individual

cation have knocked off or worn down rough edges as they cropped up, so he's reasonably well rounded. He's also pretty thick-skinned, having responded to various vicissitudes during his first eighteen years by developing a layer of insulation that keeps his own feelings well contained, and numerous calluses that dull his sensitivity to outside pressures and toughen his resistance to them. And the vicissitudes have also left some blisters and raw spots that sting when touched. He brings to college, along with his skis, ball glove and two decks of cards, his mother, his father, his mother's parents, a preschool playmate, an elementary school pal, a high school girl friend, and two older friends of the family. All of these are part of him and they respond as called upon under various circumstances. And there's a lot more inside that little circle—strengths and weaknesses, prides and prejudices, clarities and confusions, images of self and ideal, and quite a bit of unfinished business.

Upon arrival he meets his two roommates, Fred and Paul. Fred is an upperclassman who, as time goes on, turns out to be a thoughtful, reflective person. Somehow he got interested in China and India, read several books on the history of the countries, their religions, and the ways of the people. Gandhi is one of Fred's ideal persons. Whatever the topic of discussion—politics, sex, faculty and administration, social problems—Fred adds the perspective of Eastern thought. Calling up apt quotations and images from an apparently inexhaustible store, his lyrical language adds impact to his point of view.

Paul is very different. Camper, canoer, hunter, and hiker, he draws sustenance from the woods. Not many papers get written during bird season. He prefers action over words anyway, so writing and rambling discussions hold little appeal. One of his favorite quotations is, "As for speeches, it isn't words to get the business done, it's business there only for the sake of words, for smooth, obvious speeches [Yevtushenko, 1964, p. 31]." But he's always the one to cut to the heart of things, raising fundamental questions, and when he makes a point it is well documented with hard facts drawn from an encyclopedic memory for things like the statistics given in world almanacs, or in *Science,* which he has been reading for some time. He wants to go into ecological research but doesn't know whether he can stomach the "academic rigmarole" required for the advanced training he would need. Gene sees some aspects of himself reflected in Paul. Not only the interest in the outdoors, but his thick skin, his tendency to answer force with force, and his predisposition to act impetuously in response to difficulties rather than to delay action for thoughtful analyses.

Soon Gene makes two friends, Dick and John. Dick, also an upperclassman, was hanging around the coffee shop and they struck up a conversation. His sharp and perceptive comments on the two couples in the booth across the way were amusing and thought-provoking. Dick's eye is always on persons. What are they like? How did they get that way? What's their game? Who are they going around with and what are they doing? Dick's fascination with interpersonal relationships includes an interest in sex. He has worked out an internally consistent and persuasive point of view concerning premarital intercourse and man-woman relationships, which he can explain clearly.

John is in Gene's History of Western Civilization class. Halfway through the semester the instructor assigned a term paper and asked persons to team up in preparing it. John's questions in class and the opinions he expressed revealed a background and point of view quite different from Gene's. John's conservative religious and political attitudes, his high moral standards, his absolute honesty and integrity, are rooted in a Fundamentalist religious upbringing and a solid belief in the Bible. He attends church regularly and participates in church activities. When Gene proposed they work together to capitalize on their diverse views, John agreed. Their different styles of working create some problems. John, a conscientious, thorough, and systematic worker, is concerned about falling behind schedule and not getting enough done. Gene tends to work in intensive bursts without much regard for the usual routines. He wants to go fishing when he feels like it, not when some schedule says the time has come. When snow conditions are good, it's time to ski—and other things will have to wait. On a Tetley tea bag Gene once read, "A lost day is never made up." He translates that to mean, "Do what the day most calls for," and he is open to a wide range of messages. So it's not always easy for John and Gene to work together, but the challenging and thought-provoking exchanges as they thrash through what they are going to do, how they are going to do it, and what they are going to say, more than outweigh these difficulties.

It was on a ski weekend that Gene met Sue. They danced 'til three in the morning and found they both enjoyed tennis, chess, and bridge as well as skiing and dancing. Sue has trouble working inside

Figure 12

The Inner Circle

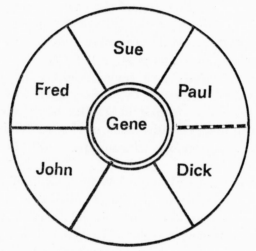

on what she calls "blue sky days" so she's often ready to help Gene take advantage of those days that can't be made up. Wide-ranging interests and multitudinous nuggets of information make her an interesting conversationalist; ready enthusiasm, sensitive and genuine concern for others, and affectionate ways make her an appealing companion. And she's pretty, which adds to her appeal.

These five persons comprise an inner circle for Gene. More time is spent with them than with others. With them exist relationships of warmth, respect, and candor. Not that they all form a single group. Actually, only Paul and Dick have mutual friends other than Gene. But they do provide the principal anchors for Gene's existence. What impact are relationships with these persons likely to have?

Both case studies and statistical analyses have documented and described the influence of close friendships: Davie (1958), the impact of close friends on "overall development," particularly autonomy and identity; Dressel and Lehmann (1965), the impact of roommates and residence hall associates on attitudes and values; Newcomb (1961, 1962, 1968), the force of shared interests and values; White (1958), the impact on clarifying purposes and freeing interpersonal relationships. Wallace (1966) suggests that close friendships are principally devoted to, and exert influence on, fundamental developmental issues:

> for an adolescent college freshman, the main criteria of such friend selection and the main influence of the resulting friendships may not be on attitudes relevant to his transitional institutional life as a student, but rather on those which most directly bear upon the larger and often more burning problems of developing an orientation to life in general; problems of becoming an adult in an adult world; problems in short, of life-cycle, rather than institutional socialization. Thus within the inner (close friends) circle of freshman's IE [Interpersonal Environment] the emphasis assigned to getting good grades (for example) may not be an important influence dimension, simply because such problems may not be the most salient faced by freshmen considered not as college students but as persons in late adolescent stages of socialization. What may be far more relevant, especially in a freshman's friendship with older, more experienced nonfreshmen, are attitudes toward life goals, parents, religion, sex, politics, etc. Outside this inner circle, however, the principal dimensions of influence may shift toward problems relevant to college freshmen as students, problems less complex, more immediately practical, and more specific to life in the temporary institutional context [pp. 114, 115].

One student, for example, reports, "With Ellen, my roommate, I have learned this: People seem to have their own timetable, an internalized and unknown schedule, for realizing things about themselves. Tinkering with this timetable, or forcing an issue, is usually not fruitful and may even prove disastrous, unless one can do it honestly. And honesty seems to involve more of a recognition of 'what's in it for me,' and a stating of this knowledge to the other person, than anything else." If a roommate helps one become more honest with oneself and with others, then she has made a substantial and lasting contribution.

D. Heath (1968) reports that friendships with other men made Haverford students more aware of themselves and more accepting of others; they also became more open to feelings of trust and affection, which permitted them to be more fully themselves with another. And friendships with women were of particular importance:

> A close friendship with a woman does uniquely test a man's image of himself as a man, and no man really achieves an inner certainty about his powers until he knows he is a potent male capable of loving heterosexually. Other forces pushed young men toward the young women at Bryn Mawr College. Some youths found women provided the warmth and love they could not find from the youths at Haverford: dating provided a redirection of a sort of frustrated affection. . . . In the process of resolving their ambivalences about women, recovering from being "shot down," emotionally redefining the type of woman who is to attract them, developing their social skills, and growing into love, a host of maturing effects results. . . . In fact, so many different maturing effects are reported, that we will have to ignore many about which we would otherwise comment. The young women work their magic primarily on the young men's self-image and personal relationships. . . . But young women's mysteries mature the youth's values and intellectual skills as well. . . . The men not only find their desires to give to another increasing, they also find their own frequently fiercely defended independence dissolving. They begin to think of themselves as needing women and therefore become more vulnerable to being hurt. . . . Another major behavioral change that friendships with women produce is the strengthening and actualization of Haverford youth's allocentric [other-centered] needs. Increasingly, the needs and wants of their girls take precedence over their own and through giving of themselves in this way the young men grow more fully into love, discovering also how much more they have to give to another.

Obviously, such relationships are a two-way street, and the impact for women appears similar to that for men. One young woman, for example, says:

> By far the greatest amount of my time and emotions has been expended in trying to cope with the changing nature of my relationship with my boyfriend. Because this is his last semester but not mine, questions of marriage and breaking up, my vaguely formulated values and future goals, were hashed out again and again. In this process, which often felt exactly like going through a cider press, I think I have faced a few more of my assumptions and uncertainties about my life—my role as a woman, my aspirations and fears, etc.—to the point where I am better able to say, "These are my decisions and I will accept responsibility for their consequences."

Thus the "inner circle" of close friends and roommates exerts direct and forceful influence. Daily behavior is planned and patterned to take account of their interests and needs. "Unassigned" books read are those they recommend. Television viewing, trips taken, topics for reflection, brand of beer or scotch, style of dress, figures of speech—all

FIGURE 13
Frames of Reference

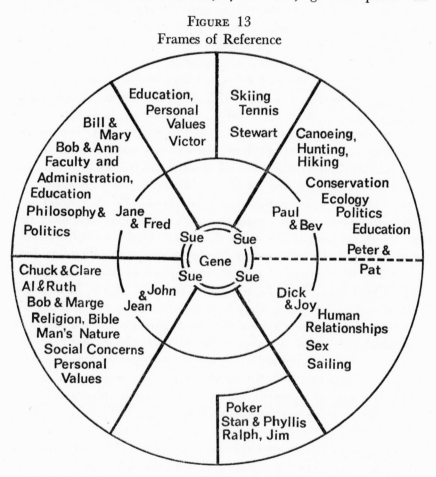

are similarly responsive to these close relationships. Thus are autonomy, identity, and purpose affected; thus do interpersonal relationships become more free and emotions more open to awareness and conscious control.

The influences of such friends are amplified and enriched by the values, standards, and interests of groups to which they belong. Gene is a member of three different groups. Two, in which Sue joins him, absorb considerable time and energy. One of these, reached via Fred, includes three other couples who enjoy going out together for drinks and long, leisurely dinners. As they work their way through cocktails and steaks, they talk about the faculty and administration, debate changes in curriculum, in teaching, in parietal rules and regulations that would make the college more to their liking; more "effective" and "relevant," less "stifling" and "stupid." Particular teachers and administrators are taken apart—and left that way. Agreement is sometimes reached on minor modifications that would make major differences. And sometimes they even follow through on such agreements, at least to the extent of writing something to post on a bulletin board, send to the dean or president, or submit to the college newspaper. Sometimes, usually when provoked by recent news, they discuss national or international problems, their causes and solutions. These discussions are usually abstract and theoretical analyses of the major social forces at work, of the long-range historical factors involved, and of the underlying cultural differences, which must be understood and dealt with if any "really sound and lasting solutions that meet the needs of all concerned," are to be developed. Fred's consistent contribution of Eastern thought assures that broad perspective is maintained.

The other group of primary importance to Gene and Sue includes Chuck and Clare, Al and Ruth, Bob and Marge, in addition to John and his girl Jean. They form the core of an informal organization called PEACE—Personal Efforts Against Corruption and Evil —in which they share a complex mix of uncertainties and tentative commitments concerning religious convictions and the nature of man, a desire to discover an effective and contributing relationship to "society," and a need to clarify questions of personal value and belief. Their joint activities vary. Sometimes they read parts of the Bible or other religious writings; the ensuing discussion usually turns on three questions: (1) "What does this mean to me?" (2) "What does it suggest about the kind of person I should become?" and (3) "What are its implications for social action?" They also do things: send letters and telegrams to congressmen, work in political campaigns, contribute services to local schools and community agencies, picket and boycott, raise money for civil rights causes and overseas relief.

Gene's relationship with Paul does not lead to another group. Gene and Paul usually go off hiking and canoeing alone, sometimes accompanied by Sue and Bev, who have become good friends, and infrequently joined by Peter and Pat, who are long-time friends of Paul. Gene's relationship with Dick and Joy is similar, but the content is different, involving principally conversations about human relations and sex, with an occasional afternoon sailing. Gene also likes poker and plays irregularly with Ralph, Jim, Stan, and Phyllis, who form the core of a weekly all-night session. These four share other interests and activities, but Gene does not join them except for an occasional party. Two other individuals, operating at a distance, also exert influence. Victor's distance is one of status, position, and age—he is a senior and one of the biggest men on campus. His idealism, toughness, agile intellect, and pragmatic effectiveness are a model for Gene, congruent with his own values, and approachable in terms of the way he sees his own strengths and weaknesses. Gene has worked with Victor on a few committees and projects, and through these contacts mutual friendship and respect have grown. Stewart is a long-time friend and warm feelings persist, but since he entered a different college, contact has been infrequent. But when they do manage to meet, bouts of skiing and tennis are accompanied by long conversations concerning their colleges, conservation, natural resource management, and politics. In a sense, Paul has filled the vacancy created by their separation.

What is the likely influence of relationships at this level, just outside the inner circle? Do associates and reference groups in college influence individual development? The evidence, consistent with findings for other settings, is quite clear that they do. At Harvard, after the freshman year, students may apply to live in various "houses." In a longitudinal study, Vreeland and Bidwell (1965) found that some houses were "individual-oriented," valuing the development of individual distinctiveness and personal competence, while other houses were "collective-oriented," valuing friendship, fellowship, and civic leadership. Between the freshman and junior year, residents who entered individual-oriented houses with individual orientations maintained them, and those who entered with collective orientations tended to change toward individual orientations. And in the other houses, students with individual orientations changed while students entering with collective orientations maintained them. For both groups, change was strongly associated with the amount of "peer involvement," and the degree to which an individual became part of the student social structure. Other studies (Scott, 1965; Wallace, 1966) indicate the impact of fraternity and sorority membership. Wallace found that "grade orientation" dropped for those who joined fraternities, but not for those who remained independent, and that the change was more pronounced for freshmen with high high school rank than for those with low rank. He summarizes by saying, "The most outstanding finding . . . remains the powerful downward push which Greek-letter membership (whether anticipated or actual) imparted to grades orientation [p. 80]." A study of Siegel and Siegel (1957) demonstrates clearly the force of identification with a group. They studied twenty-eight dormitory students who, at the end of their freshman year, wanted to move into "high status" residences whose occupants scored higher than students living elsewhere on two measures of authoritarianism. Only nine spaces were available and a lottery determined who would fill them. A year later there were again openings and eleven of those remaining tried for them, while eight chose to stay put. At the time of initial choice, the end of the freshman year, all three groups scored about the same on authoritarianism. At the end of the following year, scores for all three groups had dropped, but there were sizable differences in the magnitude of change. The nine who moved into the houses dropped very little, the eight who decided to remain in the dorms dropped substantially, and those who still wanted to move in after the second year fell in the middle. Thus change in authoritarianism was associated with degree of identification and opportunity for association. These three studies, then, illustrate the impact of reference groups. When one identifies with a group and chooses to associate with it, he changes toward the dominant values and attitudes of that group—even if he can't "move in." And when identification shifts away from a group, as it did with those who after two years had decided to remain in the dormitories, the group's influence is diminished.

Other studies indicate that simple association, in the absence of personal choice, self-selection, or evidence of identification, also exerts an influence. Brown (1966) studied freshmen who were assigned to floors and rooms according to their academic and vocational goals. On two floors of a four-floor dormitory, natural science students outnumbered humanities and social science students four to one, and on the other two floors the ratio was reversed. Further, each minority group student—humanities and social science under one condition, natural science under the other—was given a majority group roommate. By the end of the freshman year members of both minority groups had switched their curricular choice to join the majority at a rate higher than contrary change by majority group members, and minority group members who did not change were more uncertain about their academic and vocational plans and less satisfied with dormitory life and the college. Morishima (1966) randomly divided students with similar majors into experimental and control groups. Members of the experimental groups were assigned to the same floor, while control group members were scattered. Those assigned together showed greater increase in intellectual orientation as measured by Omnibus Personality Inventory scores on Thinking Introversion, Theoretical Orientation, Estheticism, and Complexity. DeCoster (1966, 1967) did a similar study, grouping some high-ability students so that they comprised half the occupants of certain dormitories, and scattering others of similar ability. Compared to those who were scattered, high-ability students grouped together found their residences more conducive to study, their fellow students more considerate and respectful, and generally felt more positively about their living arrangements. They also reported more frequent conversations of educational value and greater pressures to do better work. Another finding of equal significance was that the academic achievement of their less talented housemates suffered.

It seems clear, then, that even simple groupings can have substantial consequences, and further that the consequences are not always predictable nor always desirable. So whenever room, floor, and dormitory assignments are made, certain kinds of change are fostered and others inhibited. The issue can be dodged by random assignment, unguided by any systematic conceptions concerning relationships between likely outcomes and institutional objectives. But accountability is not thereby cast off. As evidence accumulates, responsible action requires its intelligent application.

Basically, then, relationships with groups and other associates just outside the "inner circle" have substantial impact. But these are all surrounded by the values and attitudes of the general peer and college culture, and by the freedoms and constraints for which they stand. In Gene's case, six major tenets dominate the scene: talk, read, and think; feelings are important; be yourself; respect others; work is good; citizenship requires social action.

More time is spent talking than doing anything else, in class discussions and student-faculty conferences, in countless meetings—

FIGURE 14

The General Culture

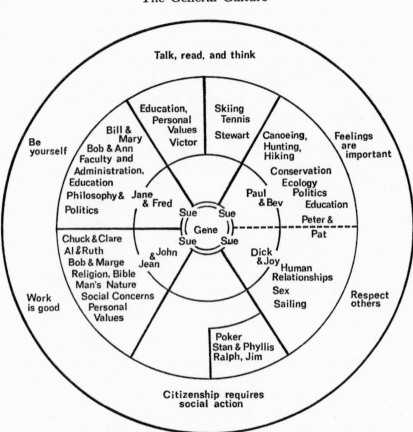

committee, community, faculty—in coffee shop debate, dormitory bull sessions, intense personal exchange. After talk comes reading, but it runs a distant second. Thinking also goes on, but it occurs for the most part in the context of conversations and discussion. Some students give time to quiet reflection, but most discover what they think by hearing themselves speak. Be yourself. Phoniness, defensiveness, attempts to impress, are quickly detected and openly identified. Feelings are to be recognized and expressed, not covered and hidden. Thus much talk and reflection concern "What am I?" and "What am I feeling?"

The self-centered emphasis in the culture is complemented by concern and respect for others. To be yourself and to respect your own feelings means allowing others to do the same. The verbal and cerebral emphasis is complemented by concern for visible productivity and action. Work—digging, chopping, hammering, sawing, dishwashing, mopping, typing, collating, hoeing, weeding, raking, pruning—is good for everyone, and no one's too good to do it. Such concrete contributions are good for the soul and good for society. Everyone should share them. And so also, social action should accompany citizenship. If you believe in something, work for it. Put your money where your mouth is. Principle unbacked by time and effort is no principle at all.

These then are the major components of the cultural climate at Gene's college. Other colleges, like some of those described in Chapter Eight, will differ sharply. But where clear culture and strong subcultures exist, they are a potent force for student change. Because they are a significant force, typologies and classification schemes have been developed that attempt to capture in economical terms the diverse student cultures. Trow's (1962; Clark and Trow, 1966) fourfold typology —Academic, Collegiate, Vocational, and Nonconformist—is perhaps the most well known. Peterson (1968) and Schumer and Stanfield (1966) are developing more detailed groupings. With such tools, subcultures can be more clearly identified and the balance among them on a given campus more accurately perceived.

Student culture, and the culture expressed by institutional objectives, faculty and administrative attitudes and behavior, educational policies and practices, are not one and the same. They may be highly congruent and overlapping, as illustrated by McDowell's (1967) findings reported in Chapter Eight, and as was the case when Newcomb (1943) studied Bennington in the late thirties. But, as recent rebellions forcefully document, student culture can also stand in conflict with certain objectives, attitudes, policies, and practices. When it does, it is a primary force inhibiting some kinds of change and fostering others. Hughes, Becker, and Geer (1962) describe how it worked in a medical school:

> Medical students live with a number of pressing and chronic problems, the most important stemming from the fact that they are continuously presented with an enormous and, in any practical sense, unlimited amount of material to learn. Though students and faculty agree that the criterion for choosing what to learn should be relevance to medical practice, there is enough disagreement and uncertainty among the faculty as to what is relevant so that the student is never presented with a clear directive to guide him in his own studies, . . .

Unlike most graduate students, all members of the medical school class are taught together. They spend an eight-to-five day in one building. Each morning and afternoon, lectures . . . are followed by laboratory periods. Review and preparation is done at night, usually at home (for there is little or no library work) or once again in the laboratory. On a schedule like this there is little opportunity for interaction with groups outside the class, nor do the students turn to the faculty with problems except about details of daily work. For as they begin to draw together and get a sense of themselves as a group they think of the faculty as a group opposed to their own. To ask faculty advice is to break student ranks. Thus, the students come to an understanding among themselves of what the study of medicine is and how it should be accomplished. Their notions are derived from what the faculty says and does (which are sometimes quite different), from the future they envision for themselves as physicians, and from their past experience in getting through school. . . .

They agreed that they ought to study the "basic medical facts." These are the only ones they have time for, as there is so much to learn. These are the facts important for practice, certain to be on examinations if the faculty is reasonable. To this central proposition the students add a number of other understandings which they apply to their daily activities.

1. Basic facts are most economically learned from textbooks. This means that lectures which do not follow the text are a waste of student time, and a faculty member who strays from the text is a poor lecturer who probably has some scientific axe to grind in connection with his own research. . . . 2. Demonstrations and lab work which repeat classical experiments are a waste of time; the results are most easily learned in the text and students can't do them well enough to learn much anyway. 3. Theoretical material, concepts, . . . and research findings not yet in clinical use are not facts and are not useful to medical students.

These understandings of the student culture can be summed up in the student phrase "give it to us straight" which has its counterpart in the derogatory faculty phrase "spoon feeding." . . .

Collective behavior of this sort does not mean students do not work hard. They continue to work very hard on the things they think important. . . . It does mean that where faculty fails to "give it to them straight" in accordance with student concepts of why they are in school and what and how they ought to study, various shortcuts are devised in more or less open defiance of faculty instructions, and students who have deviant interests outside the student culture keep them increasingly to themselves [pp. 521–526].

Such student cultures and concomitant behaviors are not unfamiliar. Most of us could substitute for medical students a group we know about, add "under" to "graduate" and with minor revision find our own experiences described. Given the appropriate circumstances, no field of study is immune. And we also know that student cultures influence not only what will be studied, how, and how much, but also, and with equal force, a wide spectrum of values and behavior relevant to other vectors of development—as the early studies of Newcomb (1943), Jacob (1957), and Eddy (1959) made clear. The recent study of Bennington by Newcomb, Koenig, Flacks, and Warwick (1967) illustrates both the influence of general student norms and the interaction of these general standards with smaller reference groups, or subcultures, within the college community. They report that minimal standards for general acceptance required moderate unconventionality in attitudes and tolerance for such attitudes and behavior by others. Direct criticism, harassment, isolation, and gossip, was the fate of students who did not conform to these minima. The ideal was to be an intellectual and an individual. If you were, admiration and respect came your way. Not surprisingly, most Bennington students changed toward (1) increased individualism—self-awareness, self-confidence, self-expression, independence; (2) increased intellectuality—breadth of interest and awareness, intellectual skills, long-term intellectual commitment; (3) increased tolerance—less irritation, more understanding and acceptance of differences; and to a lesser extent, (4) increased unconventionality.

Among the Bennington students, however, several subcultures existed. One, the "social" or "collegiate" group, diverged substantially from the central thrust described above. These girls, indifferent to intellectual concerns, were primarily oriented toward dating and social life. Several students who shared this orientation chose each other as friends and tended to concentrate in particular houses. These students were compared with some others who entered with similarly deviant attitudes but who, rather than becoming part of the collegiate group, chose "nondeviants" as friends. Those who chose "nondeviant" friends tended to change their attitudes toward the generally shared norms. But members of the collegiate group did not reflect such change. Group membership in this case, therefore, "served to insulate its members from the influences of the larger culture [p. 209]."

These findings remind us that the various components of an individual's life space interact. Reinforcing and canceling effects may occur. One level may modify or deflect the impact of another. The impact of the general culture may vary substantially after it has been interpreted by two different reference groups, and the impact of a reference group may be modified as a close friend describes his view of what the group "really stands for." For example, students called for longer visiting hours in residence halls. Through the framework of a "community government"—to which students, faculty, and administration all belong—procedures were established whereby each house would formulate a set of recommendations and forward them to a central committee of house presidents and faculty advisors, who reviewed them all, and proposed a general plan for formal faculty approval. The general plan finally approved substantially extended the hours for visiting, but fell short of several plans offered by specific houses. Faculty and administration felt that students had exercised significant power and had used it responsibly, that democratic procedures had been followed, that the institution had been responsive to student concerns, and that the whole experience was educationally valuable. The general student culture supported these procedures and agreed basically with the faculty appraisal. Most student groups agreed, but some did not. The dissidents felt that the students had been manipulated, that the whole process was a device to stall for time and to cool forceful feelings, that faculty and administration had made up their minds how much they would give before the process was even undertaken and had used the process to make that decision more palatable, and to obscure their basic autocracy. Therefore the appearances of power, responsibility, and democracy were a sham. "It all proves," they said, "that there is no sense trying to work within the system. The democratic approach is simply a trap. The only way to effect real change is to assert your own standards and stick to them." As roommates, housemates, and close friends debated these positions, shifts in group membership could be observed; some individuals changed their views and changed allegiances accordingly. And as they changed, the meaning of the experience changed for them.

So the concentric circles of a life space are permeable. This is nothing new. It starts in the womb where each fetus develops his own internal chemistry and responds to his own particular genetic code. But his development also is influenced by the nourishment and stimulation—or the lack of it—that comes through the placenta, which in turn depends on the physical and emotional state of the mother. And that varies with the food, love, and satisfactions she absorbs, and with the deprivations, frustrations, and anxieties she suffers. So from conception we all live within a web of concentric circles; each of us the center of his own universe, influenced in varying degrees by each successive layer.

The evidence clearly indicates that friends, reference groups, and the general student culture have an impact on student development. What conditions seem to foster significant friendships, vigorous reference groups, and a forceful student culture?

First, small size is a necessary, if not sufficient, condition—small in terms of absolute numbers and small in terms of the ratio of persons to opportunities and pressures for active participation. Three to five hundred students are enough to support a substantial range of activities and programs. Competition then exists for only a few of the most attractive programs and the rest welcome additional participants. And in a residential college of that size there are few strangers. Ten or twelve hundred students seems to be about a maximum. By then the rate of increase for activities and programs starts to taper off sharply, so further gains in enrollment simply increase the load and the competition, with consequent reduction of opportunities for those who enter less qualified. Individuals become lost, their presence neither noted nor missed. Size is important also because the rate of flow through the community is high. In most colleges, each year's freshman class comprises more than 30 per cent of the total enrollment—and the proportion of new faculty may be almost as high. To develop and to sustain a strong sense of community in the face of such continual and rapid turnover requires frequent and intensive interaction that begins at entrance and continues throughout. Rapid induction and assimilation of new members is necessary; otherwise, they'll form their own subcommunity, which may run counter to the "old-timers."

More than a few small colleges have tripled their enrollment since 1960—and I know some that show better than fourfold increases. Many of these were small tight ships, sailing a clear course. All hands pulled together, and despite some grumbling about who managed the tiller, neither the general direction nor the operating procedures were sharply questioned. But increased enrollment and increased faculty size outstripped the capacity for induction and assimilation. The line of course began to be questioned. Debates concerning roles and responsibilities arose. The institutions lost way and were soon plagued by discontent, disaffection, and disillusionment. Not that questioning is inappropriate or redirection uncalled for. But as subcultures become polarized, questioning and redirection become masks for power struggles and outlets for hostility. Exit reason and temperate solutions. Many small colleges are caught in this dynamic and have not yet recovered. So institutional size is a significant factor, and enrollment increases should be undertaken cautiously, accompanied by efforts to maintain or to increase frequent contact among students and faculty members. Then the value of new ideas and orientations can be more productively realized, as in these personal encounters the views of new students and new faculty members can be heard with less defensiveness, with more rational flexibility and less emotional rigidity. Institutional change can then occur by steps rather than by a "great leap forward," with all the totalism, suppression of difference, and elimination of dissidents such a leap requires.

Second, residential arrangements should enable each housing unit to become a reference group for its members. This means resident membership should continue from year to year and each unit should have to cope with significant tasks and problems that require joint thinking and effort by the members. An informal and flexible status structure is probably better than elected officers and tight structure. Formal hierarchies often lead to in-groups and out-groups, which are difficult to alter once solidified, and which hamper flexible and shifting individual identifications and allegiances. Moreover, a formal hierarchy finds it difficult to avoid a polar position—either captured by the administration or faculty, or militantly opposed. Informal leadership can change with the issue and the task. Vested interests become less entrenched and more diversified. A general culture can be maintained which leaves room for varied degrees of commitment and conviction.

Size and residential arrangements, then, are primary determinants of the frequency and intensity of interaction among students. Shifts in size alter the balance between the influences of the general student and college cultures and the influences of circles closer to each individual. Decisions concerning roommates, floormates, and dormitory membership influence who will become friends with whom, what kinds of reference groups will form, and the force with which they will operate. But frequent and intense interaction, close friendships, strong reference groups and a forceful culture do not function in a vacuum.

At each level there is content—common currencies which are the objects of exchange—problems, ideas, interests, activities, attitudes, and values. As in a penny-ante poker game, a high exchange rate and intense involvement can involve petty cash and low stakes. Or, as in table stakes or a no-limit game, sharper and more decisive tests of character, courage, and insight may be called for. And the institution can influence the stakes as well as the rate of play. For the stakes are determined by three major factors: the content and approach to curriculum, teaching, and evaluation, the models provided by the faculty and the patterns of student-faculty relationship, and the characteristics of students admitted and retained.

The consequences described earlier when students of different orientations, attitudes, aspirations, and ability levels are brought together in the same residences (Brown, 1966; DeCoster, 1966, 1967; Morishima, 1966; McDowell, 1968; Siegel and Siegel, 1957) obviously could not have occurred unless such differences existed among those who applied and were admitted. And the phenomena found for residences also occur on an institution-wide basis. Astin (1963), for example, studying seventy-six different institutions, found that as measured intelligence for the college as a whole increased, students more frequently reported decreased self-confidence and ambition. Estimates of ability and potential are based on experiences of success and failure. In most colleges, success and failure are relative to the work of classmates and not upon more general standards of achievement or ability. And neither is success or failure often determined on the basis of task effectiveness and concrete accomplishment. The evidence for this dynamic is widespread. Mean scores on academic achievement and scholastic ability for entering students have increased at many institutions during the past ten years while grade distributions have remained constant. Further, the basis for judgment is narrow—academic achievement far outweighs all other criteria. Thus when there is basically a single dimension against which all are measured, and when the measurement emphasizes relative position in comparison with a select group, rather than substantive accomplishment, many must fall short and suffer accordingly. Skager et al. (1967) found lower self-estimates of popularity associated with peer environments that emphasized practical and vocational training, and higher estimates in environments where esthetic and humanistic studies are dominant. They suggest that the differences result from the less intensive social and intellectual interaction that characterized the practical and vocational training peer environment.

The "mix," then, makes a difference. By taking significant dimensions of diversity into account in recruitment and admissions, and by arranging conditions for frequent and intensive contact after entrance, student-to-student exchange and encounter may gain in substance and significance.

Curriculum, teaching, and evaluation also influence the stuff of commerce among students. When curriculum and teaching connect academic study and classroom activities to preexisting information, ideas, and attitudes brought by students from their diverse backgrounds, and when relevance to shared problems and basic issues of existence is perceived, then the dimensions of discussion among friends and acquaintances expand and more diverse data are provided for debate. Let us be clear, however, that in arguing for relevance, we do not disregard the traditional basis for organizing curricula and courses—the structure of the disciplines. Of course, conceptions of just what a "discipline" is vary. For example, some biologists are "organists." For them biology concerns what goes on inside the skin; thus they study organ functioning, relationships among organs, and their contribution to the whole. Other biologists see the organism as just half of a transactional relationship with the environment. For them biology concerns the homeostatic processes through which equilibrium is maintained in the face of constant input and output. The research methods, the relevant evidence, the central concepts and information, differ depending on which kind of biologist you are. And within each of these general orientations, particular sequences and emphases vary. Few disciplines have a universally agreed upon structure, and debates concerning the value of one approach over another are important and not to be dismissed as inconsequential. Further, some structures and sequences are more logical, easier to communicate, and easier to grasp and memorize than others. Such considerations are also important. So to argue for relevance in curriculum and teaching is not to suggest that these criteria be disregarded, but rather to suggest that whatever the disciplinary orientation, whatever the collection and sequence of courses, and whatever the content and order of experiences established within each course, the question simply be asked by the instructor, "What is relevant for these students?" and by each student, "What is relevant for me?" For if both teacher and student pursue the question, few areas of study will remain mute. Not that relevance is always clear, obvious, and self-evident. In some areas it is, and even the most determined teacher cannot obscure it nor the most dogged make the subject dull. More often, however, relevance has to be discovered and constructed through the joint effort of teacher and students. So the problem is not solved simply by asking the question. Once the question is asked, however, the problem can be attacked.

The problem is simply this: to see whether one person, place, or thing has implications for another, some knowledge or experience of both components is required. To oversimplify it, students usually don't know much about the subject, and teachers usually don't know much about the students. Thus, with both sides lacking half the necessary understanding, insights concerning connections between the two are often missed. Actually, teachers know much more about students than they take account of in preparation and in the classroom. For many it is more a matter of bringing such information and understanding into play than of generating new subtle insights. And some students may already know enough about the subject to make a start. The basic point, then, is not that relevance exists simply for the asking, but that pursuing the question will lead to perceived connections. And once such connections are made, working knowledge is augmented—ways of knowing, concepts, theories, hard data, are applied elsewhere more frequently, are retained longer, and expand the network to which other studies and experiences can be associated.

Can we be more concrete about relevance? Being concrete is not the problem; examples leap to mind. But taken singly they seem trivial. Generalization is more difficult because several conceptual alternatives are available, each with its limitations, and it is hard to choose among them. The simple dichotomy of content and process is perhaps as useful as any.

Some content—information, concepts, ideas, insights, fantasies, experiences direct and vicarious—speaks to the past content, problems, and behavior of students quite directly, while other content does not. D. Heath (1968), for example, reports:

> The one course most productive of change is the required English course in which the various novels that raise social, religious, sexual, interpersonal, and other value conflicts are analyzed and weekly student papers about the novels are evaluated by their peers and faculty members in small tutorial sessions. The course seeks to

stimulate and challenge the youths to become aware of their values and to work out a more mature autonomous value system for themselves. While successful in making the freshmen much more reflective about their own values and themselves, the course is more successful in stimulating the maturing of allocentric [other-centered] intellectual skills . . . The freshmen . . . are in surprising agreement about the different effects of a few courses, courses like required English or non-required courses like psychology and philosophy. Perhaps these courses are so determining because they impinge most directly on students as human beings, and it is themselves with which freshmen are most preoccupied. The students, plunged into themselves by the reflective emphasis of the college, the pain of new adjustments, find certain courses speak to their condition at the time. . . . Psychology provides means by which to objectify the process of self-exploration, achieving its principal effects in increasing the awareness and the stabilization of the youths' ideas about themselves. By challenging their assumptions about human beings, demonstrating the similarity of one youth to the next, providing an intellectual framework by which to order and understand their and others' mercurial and shifting feelings and thoughts, the freshmen report that the course makes them aware of a new dimension to their relationships. They discover that other people, not just themselves, are interesting; they are reassured that the strains and conflicts that trouble them are normal, not abnormal. . . . Philosophy courses similarly provide tools and contexts that give insight but also stability and direction to the inner turmoil that demands some adaptive solution.

Most of the conceptions of self and the world brought to college have been taken over rather uncritically from parents, community, and schoolmates. Study of history, religion, anthropology, sociology, and economics, as well as literature, psychology, and philosophy, can challenge these conceptions and can broaden the perspective within which they are held. From the same sources students bring behavioral norms and standards, which can be reexamined in the light of such studies.

The student's natural inclination, of course, is to judge characters in literature, as well as elsewhere, according to the values that he brings with him to college. . . . But if he gets the point, if he discovers that anything can be done in the imagination and that everything he has so far imagined has been done by somebody and that those who did these things can be understood, then he is bound to admit into his scheme of things a broader range of human potentialities. These he can see as present in himself as well as in other people [Katz and Sanford, 1962, pp. 439–440].

Some of the most powerful and fundamental questions are raised in the natural sciences. The Scopes trial was neither the first nor the last occasion when scientific theory and research challenged fundamental belief systems and value frameworks. When Copernicus took man and earth from the center and sent them, along with other planets, spinning around the sun, he also sent some basic beliefs into orbit. Galileo's experimental approach directly challenged the authoritative basis for belief that had ruled, and his doubts and questions led to constant persecution. Faculty and administration would probably welcome Semmelweiss were he reincarnated for their campuses, but some students would probably repeat the severe attacks he suffered in his fight for cleanliness in homes, hospitals, and public facilities. Nobel's dynamite—that ladyfinger firecracker in today's perspective—raised moral questions currently reconfronted in decisions concerning nuclear warfare. Einstein's relativity, quantum theory, recent discoveries concerning genetic control, new techniques for organ transplants, do no less. What is time? Space? Reality? What is life? When does it begin? When has death occurred? With whom should such judgments rest? Mathematics teaches that initial assumptions can define a system that enables certain solutions and not others—and several different systems may adequately solve the same problem. Such concepts and questions need not be reserved for courses in the philosophy of science, for they and many others are embedded in and expressed by all the disciplines.

Process, as distinct from content, refers to those skills, competencies, habits, and built-in behaviors by which a person manages himself and his existence, by which he copes with other persons, objects, and events. At the simplest and most direct level are those skills and behavior relevant to vocational plans or avocational activities and interests. Communication skills are, of course, fundamental. Drucker (1968), expert consultant on management and placement, says, for example:

As an employee you work with and through other people. This means that your success as an employee—and I am talking of much more here than getting promoted—will depend on your ability to communicate with people and to present your own thoughts and ideas to them so they will both understand what you

are driving at and be persuaded. The letter, the report or memo-
randum, the ten-minute spoken "presentation" to a committee are
basic tools of the employee.

If you work as a soda jerker you will, of course, not need
much skill in expressing yourself to be effective. If you work on a
machine your ability to express yourself will be of little importance.
But as soon as you move one step up from the bottom, your effectiveness depends on your ability to reach others through the spoken
or the written word. If you were to ask me what strictly vocational
courses there are in the typical college curriculum, my answer—now
that the good old habit of the "theme a day" has virtually disap-
peared—would be: the writing of poetry and the writing of short
stories. Not that I expect many of you to become poets or short story
writers—far from it. But these two courses offer the easiest way to
obtain some skill in expression. They force one to be economical with
language. They force one to organize thought. They demand of one
that he give meaning to every word. They train the ear for language, its meaning, its precision, its overtones—and its pitfalls [pp.
62, 63].

Depending upon individual plans and aspirations, there are
many more particular skills and competencies desired. But these may
be so diverse within a single class that it is not realistic to try to know
them or to aim for relevance. There are more general processes, however, for which many fields of study are appropriate. Bloom *et al.*
(1956) and Krathwohl *et al.* (1964) have described both cognitive
(comprehending, applying, analyzing, synthesizing, evaluating) and
affective (receiving, responding, valuing) processes. And they have
illustrated connections between each of these and various areas of
study. Others talk of "ego-processes." Bower (1966), for example, describes five:

In dealing with skills and deficiencies in the processing and
use of symbols, it may be helpful to think of ego processes as involving five specific dimensions:
1. Differentiation vs. diffusion—the processes by which objects, events, and feelings are separated out and perceived clearly.
2. Fidelity vs. distortion—the processes by which objects,
events, and feelings are seen and reproduced faithfully as they are
experienced.
3. Pacing vs. over- or underloading—the processes by which
objects, events, and feelings are attached to appropriate emotional
loads and stresses.

4. Expansion vs. constriction—the processes by which new symbols, or new meanings for old symbols, are assimilated and used.

5. Integration vs. fragmentation—the processes by which symbols are processed within the individual as a whole rather than in one or another separated compartment [p. 113].

Katz and Sanford (1962) describe the impact of study on personality processes which involve not only the ego, but impulses and conscience as well:

> The thing about literature, as we understand it, is not that it simply releases fundamental impulses to be expressed in their original fundamental form—this could hardly be called freedom; instead, it gives to the individual something of the very thing that made the creation of that literature possible in the first place, and this is the means for transforming the impulse life in such a way that it meets the requirements of reality and of conscience. . . . If this kind of change in the individual is brought about through the study of literature, it will affect the individual's performance in all of his other courses, as indeed in his life generally [p. 440].

We'll end this trip from the particular and concrete to the complex and abstract by recalling Kubie's (1954) concern for the "forgotten man of education."

> Every discipline has its tools, and each such tool has its own inherent errors. . . . Yet there is one instrument which every discipline uses without checking its errors, tacitly assuming that the instrument is error-free. This, of course, is the human psychological apparatus. . . . Without self-knowledge in depth, the master of any field will be a child in human wisdom and human culture. . . . Education for wisdom must close this gap, by providing insight which penetrates into those areas of human life in which the unconscious forces have always hitherto played the preponderant role. . . . This automaticity of conduct which is governed predominantly by our unconscious psychological mechanisms is dependent directly upon their remaining inaccessible. . . . If "self-knowledge in depth" ever becomes the goal of a new concept of education, and if it becomes part of the equipment which education brings to the cultured man, it will make it possible for man to attain freedom from his ancient slavery to those repetitive psychological processes over which at present he has no control [p. 349].

Let me be clear that I am not proposing that all teachers in all courses start teaching for "self-knowledge in depth," start trying to make more conscious the unconscious. Indeed I'm not arguing for the adoption of any of the formulations mentioned above. Not that I think they lack merit. On the contrary. I believe any one of the conceptual frameworks offered by Bloom, or Krathwohl, or Bower, or Kubie— and there are others, including obviously the seven vectors described in Part One—could provide a sound basis for organizing curricular content, materials, and experiences, and for developing activities in and out of the classroom, student-teacher relationships, and systems of evaluation. All are highly consistent with many of the objectives of liberal education and each deserves solid attempts at implementation and sound evaluation. But my proposal is more general, and more modest: when decisions are made concerning curriculum, teaching, and evaluation, consider what processes have relevance for the students served, and let such judgments carry some weight.

To summarize: The force of friendships, reference groups, and the student culture is amplified as frequency and intensity of contacts increase. Institutional size and residence hall arrangements influence the frequency and intensity of interaction. The characteristics of students who are admitted and who stay influence the substance, the currency exchanged when interaction occurs. The relevance of the content and of the processes called for by teaching expectations and behaviors, also significantly influences the substance of exchange. And so do systems of evaluation, in negative fashion, as they pit one student against another, and focus narrowly on single criterion of success.

Most important, however, are the faculty members themselves and the faculty as a group. When individual faculty members and administrators talk with students—when they are accessible, authentic, and reasonably knowledgeable about students—friendships, reference groups, and the student culture receive continued stimulation, support, and challenge. For the behavior, views, and values of these adults, when visible, are much discussed. But these dynamisms were considered in the previous chapter and don't need further elaboration here. Consider for a minute, however, the fundamental significance of the faculty and administration functioning as a group. With them reside the major powers of decision. Within broad limits set by the society of which the institution is a part, it is they who ultimately determine the force and substance of student culture, reference groups, and student friendships. Because out of their deliberations and decisions come expectations and stipulations concerning student-faculty relationships, come systems of curriculum, teaching, and evaluation, come residence hall arrangements and the attendant rules and regulations. They—the faculty and administration—carry most force in judgments about how big the college will be and the programs and activities it will offer. Indirectly through such decisions, and through direct participation in setting and implementing criteria for recruitment and selection, they determine the kinds of students who will attend. Whatever the college is, and whatever it becomes—whether it lives, dies, or suffers dramatic mutation—follows primarily from their decisions and behavior. Recognizing this, it behooves all of us who man colleges and universities to take thought—to supplement intuition with evidence, to temper emotion with reason, and to soften prejudice with a broader perspective. Many institutions are reaping the fruits from fifty years of complacency and inattention, or self-serving vested interests. If faculty and administration don't turn wisdom, energy, and dedication to the task, what power they now can exercise will not last long.

PART **III**

*T*he major task confronting higher education is not to generate new, complex, and subtle understandings, but to act on knowledge already available, to recognize principles of learning and human development already clearly established. The gap between what is known and what is done must be narrowed. Educational problems are outrunning solutions, not so much for lack of relevant principles, and not because useful steps are obscure, but because implementation is occurring at a snail's pace, because basic concepts are disdained.

Development occurs through sequences of differentiation and integration (Sanford, 1962). That's one principle we know of and ignore. Smith (1966) found this dynamic at work with Peace Corps volunteers. He reports:

THEORY AND ACTION:
AN OVERVIEW

๛๛๛๛๛๛๛๛๛๛๛๛๛๛๛๛๛๛๛๛๛๛๛

important personality changes in the direction of maturity were frequent. I think I know why. . . . Once in, most of them saw and were captured by the challenges of the job and role: students and schools that needed everything they could give, a window on Africa that invited exploration. Their effective motivation was emergent: a response to opportunities and difficulties as challenges to be met, not as frustrations to be endured or "adjusted to." . . . It was this high degree of committed but disinterested investment in a challenging undertaking, I think, that was so auspicious for psychological change in the direction of maturity. Experiences from which the self is held in reserve do not change the self; profit in growth requires its investment [pp. 565, 566].

Differentiation *and* integration *refer to a familiar process. The notion that learning and development occur as persons encounter new conditions and experiences that are important to them, in which they invest themselves, and for which they must develop new courage, new competencies, new attitudes, has been with us for some time. It is reflected in Dewey's (1938) "reconstruction of experience," Festinger's (1957) "cognitive dissonance," Heider's (1958) "balance theory," Newcomb's (1961) "strain for symmetry," Helson's (1964) "adaptation level theory," and Rogers' (1961) "development of congruence."*

Heider (1958), for example, asked 101 high school students what would happen "nine times out of ten" in the following situation:

> Bob thinks Jim very stupid and a first class bore. One day Bob reads some poetry he likes so well that he takes the trouble to track down the author in order to shake his hand. He finds that Jim wrote the poems [p. 176].

This story creates imbalance, conflict. Bob experiences new input that upsets his preexisting system. His view is challenged. How does he resolve it, according to the high school students? Heider found that 46 per cent changed Bob's opinion of Jim—"He grudgingly changes his mind about Jim." Thus both Jim and his poetry become positive and balance is regained. Twenty-nine per cent changed Bob's opinion of the poetry—"He decides the poetry is lousy." Both become negative and balance is achieved. Others sought balance in more complex ways: Bob questions Jim's authorship; he calls Jim smart in poetry but dumb in other ways; he tells Jim he likes the poems, but "without much feeling." Heider, generalizing from diverse studies of this dynamic, says:

> The concept of balanced state designates a situation in which the perceived units and the experienced sentiments coexist without stress; there is thus no pressure toward change, either in the cognitive organization or in the sentiment [p. 176].

Heider's "balance" concept reminds us that significant change sometimes involves a period of disequilibrium, upset, disintegration, out of which a new equilibrium is established. Many conditions and experiences that offer strong potential for development also contain potential for damage. Venturing into a new job, a new culture, a new relationship can be chancy. But if an individual would grow, and if an institution would have an impact, the risks must be taken. Sanford (1963) puts it this way:

We could run an institution in the interest of positive mental health that would so protect individuals from challenging stimuli that they would not develop at all. They might remain quite healthy, in the sense that they manage such strains as were brought to bear, but they remain very simple, undeveloped people. Or . . . you could say that if we are going to have a democratic society in which we expect each individual to be independent, we automatically run very serious risks of mental ill health, because people are not always prepared for the kind of freedom that we expect them to have in our society. But if it comes to that, in general we say we would rather have freedom than the absence of any risks with respect to mental ill health . . . health and development are by no means the same thing. You can have a healthy person who is not well developed, but a simple, undifferentiated, insensitive person. He doesn't have problems because he is so insensitive that he is not aware of the things that would arouse problems in other people. Similarly you can have a highly developed person who is complex, tortured, and full of conflicts, but a rich and interesting person. We have a certain balance to look for, and I should think in the end, we really want both . . . and we know that to achieve this we have to take risks.

We have to find challenges that are sufficient to require that the individual make a really new kind of adaptation, but not so intense or disturbing as to force the student to fall back on earlier primitive modes of adaptation which will serve him badly in the long run [pp. 11, 12, 13].

Differentiation and integration, challenge and response, then, make up one basic principle to keep in mind when observing student reaction to varied programs and practices, and when planning for change. Expressions of discomfort, signs of upset, are not necessarily negative signs. On the contrary, these signs may be evidence that developmentally fruitful encounters are occurring, that stimuli for progress are being felt. For the past is piled up around us all. We trample in it. We must work through it to obtain knowledge, to become what we can. We have gulped it down, but it must be chewed, tasted, and swallowed again, if development is to be nourished.

A second self-evident principle is that individual differences affect the outcomes of experiences. The impact of a given curriculum, course, teacher, residence hall, or fellow student will vary according to the characteristics of the student who experiences it. Thirty years of diverse studies testing and elaborating Helson's (1964) adaptation level theory—which maintains that judgments are relative to prevail-

ing internal norms and adaptation levels—document clearly the per-
vasive interaction between frames of reference and functional consid-
erations, and "stimulus" characteristics. You receive a weak shock and
I a strong one. Then we both receive shocks of equal intensity. For
me the second shock is weaker and provokes less reaction than for you.
Breakfast orange juice is sweet and tasty—but not after a bite of toast
and jam. A six-inch ice cube is big; a six-foot room is small. Thus our
frames of reference make a difference. Functional considerations also
modify meaning and impact. A comfortable apartment for newlyweds
becomes impossible when two children arrive. The strong tether for
the puppy won't hold the dog; the pigpen won't contain the goat; the
fence for cows won't keep out deer. Speaking about the implications of
adaptation level theory for motivation, Helson (1966) says:

> we must distinguish between the *physical* stimulus and the *effective*
> stimulus. . . . The effective stimulus depends upon the state of the
> organism, upon preceding and accompanying stimuli, and, in
> some cases, upon possible future outcomes of stimulation . . .
> most of the difficulties of stimulus theories of motivation vanish if
> we take as the zero of intensity not the absolute threshold [the level
> at which a stimulus barely can be perceived] but the adaptation
> level. It then follows that stimuli below level as well as above level
> may possess motivating power because it is discrepancy from level
> in either direction that determines affective quality and its distinc-
> tiveness [pp. 144, 147].

Similarly, for college students, the motivational force, the stim-
ulus value, of a course, curriculum, or climate, depends upon what
the student has been used to and what his purposes in attending are.
Zero stimulation occurs when college turns out to be no different from
high school—and when high expectations were held concerning the
expected challenges and stimulation, "more of the same" is usually not
just neutral, but negative.

The problem is, of course, that entering students bring different
frames of reference and different functional considerations. They differ
from one college to another, and among students within the same col-
lege. Some students are authoritarian, others rigidly anti-authoritarian,
and still others are more flexible and rational (Stern, 1962); some are
activists, some are alienated (Keniston, 1967), and some are apathetic.
Reasons for going to college differ—to get a better job, to understand
myself better, to get a general education, to prepare for a specific pro-

fession. On intelligence test scores differences among college freshmen span nearly four standard deviations (McConnell and Heist, 1962). Wide differences are found for measures of creativity (Hannah, 1967, 1968a; Heist, 1968).

But most of these diverse entrants meet remarkably similar programs, similar patterns of teaching and expectations for study, similar conditions for living and for faculty and peer relationships. High attrition rates and high transfer rates are not surprising when such diversity meets such singularity. Again, the evidence from research and from my own experience is unequivocal. More effective education requires taking more clear account of differences among students and acting accordingly. Doing so does not mean catering, nor merely discovering what students want and providing it. On the contrary, the task of the college is to provide whatever is needed if learning and development are to occur. And sound decisions about what is needed must derive from knowledge of where a student is, where he wants to go, and what equipment he brings for the trip. With such information at hand, intelligent planning can occur. When significant differences are ignored, some students will be missed entirely, and many barely touched.

Under most conditions, obviously, a distinct program for each individual is not feasible. But some dimensions of difference are sufficiently widespread that program modification would affect large numbers of students. One such dimension might be termed the creativity continuum. Along this continuum we would range persons rigid and flexible, authoritarian and nonauthoritarian, field dependent and field independent, simple and complex. Which kinds of students are most comfortable with the typical arrangements for curriculum, teaching, and evaluation? Those who persist longest in college—compared with their peers who leave or who interrupt their education—are more authoritarian, more rigid, less creative, less complex (Barger, 1963; Gardner, 1967; Hannah, 1967, 1968a; Heist, 1968).

Numerous studies of attrition show that the most creative and complex are the ones who leave. What kinds of changes would occur if this dimension of difference were taken seriously, if curriculum, teaching and evaluation were modified or supplemented so that persons at the creative end could work more effectively?

The principal curricular change would be increased flexibility. Increased flexibility could be achieved by adding opportunities for inde-

pendent study and for groups of students to work together with an instructor in a large and amorphous area—which could take more definite shape as these students defined more clearly their own interests and as the significant components of the area itself became known. Flexibility could be enhanced by opportunities to put together courses from diverse domains, or to pursue fewer courses more exhaustively. Time units might also be loosened. Some students and faculty members might develop an area for study and then fit the time to the study—putting the horse before the cart, in proper fashion for a change—rather than the other way around, where a fixed time unit is set and all subjects cut to fit it. Enough Shakespearean plays might be selected to give a full understanding of the playwright, then a judgment might be made about the length of time necessary to achieve the purposes at the level of depth and comprehensiveness desired—instead of "taking it" for one or two semesters, stretching Shakespeare or lopping him off as the time permits.

Teachers might coordinate student activity, instead of giving information. Their major efforts might be spent generating resources for students' use—books, journals, mimeographed materials; other persons on and off campus; opportunities for direct experiences—identifying them for students, and helping students with the analyses and syntheses through which their understanding and assimilation can move ahead. Students would become less often passive recipients and more often active producers. Converting information into working knowledge requires action. This is true for all students, but especially important for the creative and verbally adroit. For they can easily create for themselves and others the illusion of understanding, the illusion of competence and effectiveness. Action in responsible positions can temper such illusions and can indicate underlying strengths and weaknesses in areas of competence and understanding where verbal skills are not so salient.

The contribution of these changes or supplements to curriculum and teaching will be reinforced by changes in evaluation. Emphasis on substantive achievement, complemented by self-evaluation and student-to-student evaluation, can create the basis for more realistic appraisal of progress and achievement. The current system, which gives a simple grade, symbolic only of relative standing, has little motivational force and makes no contribution to the concrete feedback needed by such students. Again, all students can profit from decreased emphasis on normative judgments and comparative standings, and all can profit from more explicit information concerning the pros and cons of performances, but for more flexible, complex, creative types, where getting by in terms of normative judgments comes easily for most, realistic appraisals in terms of task effectiveness have special importance.

Such changes as these, responsive to one significant dimension of difference that operates for many students at many institutions, not only would enable more effective education for creative complex students, and not only might reduce the dropout rate among them— equally important, it would enrich and enliven each institution where some such action was taken, by raising useful questions for all students concerning education and development and by retaining within the student body greater numbers of persons with diverse interests and styles.

Clearly, the "creativity continuum" is not the only dimension of difference that can be usefully addressed. And at some institutions it may be much less significant than at others. Orientation to college, social class or ethnic differences, differences in academic aptitude and preparation—these and other dimensions may or may not be important and each college must make its own determination. But the evidence is clear that despite the kind of self-selectivity and homogeneity found in many institutions—as exemplified by the Project college findings described in Chapter Eight—within college differences are large enough to warrant increased diversity of program. And the point of departure for such decisions should be information about the students themselves.

The difficulty in taking into account significant dimensions of difference among students increases geometrically with college size. Flexible programming, teaching that moves students toward action on and off campus, evaluation that emphasizes substantive rather than simply normative feedback, are not the kinds of things easily programmed for large numbers. They require student-faculty contact as the range and frequency of decisions students must make increase. And if the diverse programs are to be felt, considered, and appraised by all students, then the community must be small enough that student-to-student communication is widespread. Then the options become not just words on paper, but alternatives more fully known and necessarily confronted. Small size is also important because student characteristics will change over time. If student differences become the point of departure for program planning, then there must be sufficient flexibility to respond to shifting patterns of difference and similarity. As the number of students increases, such flexibility drops fast.

To propose that a college recognize differentiation and integration as they occur, and to propose further that a college operate in terms of the characteristics of the students served, is to assume a capacity for rational action by students, faculty members, and administrators that may not exist. But I think it does. Until recently the evidence from research and theory on which rational action could rest has been limited; but in the last fifteen years it has grown dramatically. Feldman and Newcomb's (1969) recent review cites more than 1200 studies concerning the impacts of curricula, teaching, evaluation, residence halls, interpersonal relationships between student and faculty and among students, college cultures and subcultures. As the earlier chapters of this book have demonstrated, such research and theory can be called into service when educational decisions need making. Not that personal experience and intuition should be eliminated— that's impossible, as well as unwise. But more objective evidence now can support opinion, temper prejudice, and broaden the basis on which action is taken. As the complexities increase and as the number and diversity of students expand with the approach of universal higher education, flying by the seat of the pants becomes increasingly risky. We must learn to rely more heavily on navigational aids that more clearly and reliably indicate where we are heading and whether we're right side up or upside-down.

Increased priority for evidence and objectivity is also important for another reason. Questions of power and prerogative have become increasingly urgent. Students, faculty, administrators, trustees—all have the capacity to shut down a college if they don't like what's going on, or if they feel strongly that change is needed. Feel is used advisedly, because current battles for power rest on emotion, not reason. Solutions are proposed, by whatever factions are involved, in the service of comfort, security, and personal preference more often than in the service of more effective education. Outcomes follow from balancing the preferences of one force against those of another, and trading off until some compromise is reached. Evidence concerning the educational consequences of varied solutions seldom comes into play. Few signs of objectivity are seen. Currently the direct experiences and sensitive reactions of students are opposed by the more insulated and long-

range perspectives of faculty and administration. Both these contributions are needed. But relevant research and theory can amplify and illumine both, and can provide a more detached, objective basis for constructing solutions designed to serve educational purposes more and personal prejudices less. Under such conditions, joint participation in college governance by students, faculty, and administration becomes fruitful, capitalizing on the strengths of each. Without primary concern for evidence and reason, governance becomes power plays by polarized groups, each seeking to amplify its own realm of authority and each overriding concern for the whole with concern for more limited vested interests.

Of course, institutional objectives set the framework for governance and the criteria for educational decisions. So, finally, the role and function of higher education must be addressed. The orientation taken here is obvious. The narrow focus on information, the emphasis on training students in subject matter to become subjects of a discipline, profession, or business, must give over to an emphasis on educating men—more complex, autonomous, purposeful persons who can act with integrity, subject primarily to their own clear convictions and belief. Higher education will soon be the most salient feature in the lives of virtually all young adults, as elementary and high school education presently are. Colleges and universities will dominate their waking hours and determine the behaviors they pursue, the thoughts they consider, the attitudes they question or accept, the future directions they take, the life-styles they develop. There is no question about this. The only question is whether rational response will be made to enable more effective development along all seven vectors of change, or whether these dimensions will continue largely ignored, incidentally fostered or hampered as by-products of other decisions.

The evidence is clear that college does make a difference to such development. And the evidence now is also clear that the difference persists (Bugelski and Lester, 1940; Nelson, 1954; Newcomb et al., 1967; Plant, 1965, 1966). Colleges can make a much greater difference if they will. And whether they do has implications not only for future students, but for the future of the United States and of the world. For our current social, economic, and political systems are manmade. The current conditions of our existence—the shape of the land, the purity of water and air, the food, the health, the stress, the violence —are man-made. Whether or not the future is made by men, by per-

sons who have been given priority over systems, or by the interplay of insulated and uncoordinated systems—nations, businesses, political parties, military agencies, ethnic and economic minorities—to which men have become subject, depends largely on the nation's colleges and universities.

CHAPTER 14

TWO PRINCIPLES:
LEVERS FOR ACTION

ŊŶŊŶŊŶŊŶŊŶŊŶŊŶŊŶŊŶŊŶŊŶŊŶŊŶŊŶŊ

A young bookman was extolling a new publication on the latest farming methods and describing the increased production that would follow. The grizzled farmer listened patiently, and then responded, "All you say is probably true, son, but I ain't farmin' half as well as I know how, now." Most of us—parents, students, teachers, administrators—could say the same about the gap between our knowledge and the use we make of it. How does development occur? What determines whether or not an experience has an impact? Each teacher who sets readings, writings, and other activities for students, each faculty that sets a curriculum, each administration that sets general conditions for living and learning, should have answers for these basic questions. And most of us do, even though our behavior usually doesn't betray it. We don't need more knowledge as

291

much as we need to make better use of what we already have. So this chapter does not introduce new insights, but instead recalls two simple but basic concepts—laws of human development—which speak to the two questions above.

The first law is this: *Development occurs through cycles of differentiation and integration.* Thus education is essentially the amplification of two basic developmental processes: differentiation and integration. Increased differentiation occurs when one comes to see the interacting parts of something formerly seen as unitary, when one distinguishes among concepts formerly seen as similar, when actions are more finely responsive to purposes or to outside conditions, when interests become more varied, tastes more diverse, reactions more subtle. In short, as we become more complex human beings. It is to foster increased differentiation that a liberal arts college aims to free an individual from the limitations of outlook brought from his own locale, his family, his social class, and his national heritage—a freeing that opens him to all the possibilities and impossibilities of the world around him, a freeing that can lead to heightened sensitivity and awareness and that can also open the path to coldness and insensitivity as the monstrous inconsistencies in the ways of the world are more clearly seen and more sharply experienced.

But increasing differentiation must be accompanied by increasing integration, and this is the other major task of education. Relationships among parts must be perceived or constructed so more complex wholes result. Concepts from different disciplines must be brought to bear on one another and connected in ways appropriate to varied tasks and problems. Consistencies between word and word, word and deed, deed and deed, must be achieved. Impulse and emotion must pull together with conscience and reason. Short-run hedonism must coordinate with long-run purposes.

So differentiation and integration are what education is about, and such education makes persons different—different from what they were before and different from each other. It is, therefore, contrary to training. Training serves to make persons more alike. It aims to develop a shared language, shared skills, shared information, shared objectives, and, with time, shared values. Thus, while training starts with the task and conforms the learner to it, education starts with the learner and uses tasks in the service of his increased differentiation and integration.

This formulation is basically Sanford's (1962, 1963, 1966). He says:

> A high level of development in personality is characterized chiefly by complexity and wholeness. It is expressed in a high degree of *differentiation*, that is, a large number of different parts having different and specialized functions, and a high degree of *integration*, that is, a state of affairs in which communication among parts is great enough so that the different parts may, without losing their essential identity, become organized into larger wholes . . . [1962, p. 257].

According to this view, development occurs when a student meets challenges that require new responses, and when he is free to give up earlier response patterns and defenses.

Differentiation and integration, challenge and response, are often accompanied by disequilibrium and equilibrium. Most of us stand firmly on our own two feet. We have a pretty solid position, which allows us to bend with, or lean against, the pressures we encounter. When the pressure goes away, we usually snap back to our basic stance. Sometimes, however, we can be enticed to take a step. Other times we are pushed hard enough to be knocked off balance and have to move our feet to recover. Occasionally the rug is pulled out and when we pick ourselves up we find ourselves in a different spot. Significant education and significant development often involve some disruption and disequilibrium. D. Heath (1968) puts it this way:

> To be educable means to be in a potential state of disorganization, to allow oneself to plunge into contradictory theories and points of view sharply contrasting with one's own, to entertain the prejudices and biases of others, to even permit oneself, in the search for new ideas, to slip into the dream world of hunch, reveries, narrowed awareness where the form of life's images is blurred, where strange and frightening and monstrous combinations of the familiar and unfamiliar romp and play, and where no words are either powerful nor subtle enough to capture emerging feelings, intuitions, and vivid sensory impressions. While maturity is no guarantee against some disorganization, it is a guarantee that disorganization can be used for adaptive and playful purposes. . . .

Significant learning, therefore, often means taking risks. And in a college where powerful forces for student development are at work, turmoil and upset will also be found; students will sustain bumps and bruises, temporary dislocations and disorientations.

Of course, the process is never simply sequential, linear, or clear-cut, as individual cases make clear. But the interplay is there, and can be seen. Raushenbush (1964) describes a student's interaction with his studies, and illustrates how the process works for a single person in a particular setting:

> one of the most illuminating experiences, in coming to know the history of students in some detail, was to see what I have called the internal shape of their education. The student's "major" defines his education in only a limited, however useful, way. What seems more important to me is how often his studies give his life and thought a particular bent or quality, or bring that quality to light; how often his attention, whatever he is studying, turns more and more clearly to particular questions to pursue, or to particular ways of thinking, or to particular ideas or beliefs to follow. . . . As a student's bent develops, it in turn influences his choice of what to study. He seeks out certain teachers, when he has the chance, for what they are as well as for what they know. . . .
>
> The literature he [Scott] read began to weave itself into the fabric of his education. His reading became a rich source of images and examples giving substance to the ideas he was meeting in all parts of his studies. . . . From this point on it becomes clear that literature is no longer a "subject" but a means for intensifying any experience he encounters, whatever he is studying. . . . he turned very often to literature to find ways of developing or illuminating questions and ideas that occupied his thought. . . . Much teaching of literature fails to serve this purpose for students; Scott was fortunate in discovering these uses of literature early in his college years. . . .
>
> In talking about his high school studies he mentioned books that had impressed him, and, among them, Shirley Jackson's short stories. . . . The characters in the short story "Colloquy," he says, "are indeed alienated from society and their case reveals how intolerable is this state. Given this discomfort, it follows that something must be done. Some answers, some alternatives must be sought." Kerouac "has nothing to offer us in the way of a solution but the shoulder-shrugging impotence." Norman Mailer "romanticizes alienation . . . declares that living in this moment-to-moment uncertainty takes courage." But Scott cannot accept that either. "This is not actually courage, but a variation on the general helplessness of the alienated person. . . . Courage consists in part

of taking a stand when it may be the wrong one." So he has to reject the analysis of such writers.

He turns to literature to support his own attempt to find alternatives in a world which many searching people cannot accept,
and uses the case of Odysseus, in Nikos Kazantzakis's *The Odyssey:
A Modern Sequel,* as one alternative. He thinks of this as "a more
successful expression of that which Mailer attempted, the coura-
geous transformation of the running away into running toward.
. . . The modern Odysseus is a man who cannot settle down to
comfortable virtues and betray the restless search. Traveling through
the Western Mediterranean, Africa, and the Antarctic, Odysseus
attempts to live so fully that eventual Death will have nothing to
take from him."

Scott has to debate with himself whether this sort of escape
from rootlessness is a legitimate one for a man not a mythical hero,
and has to cope with the question Sapir raised about the "helplessness of the individual who has no cultural heritage to work on." He
knows *this* is no real solution.

He turns to Henry Miller's *To Paint is to Love Again.* . . .
"Just how great a compensation for alienation creativity can be to
the artist is illustrated by Miller's remark that if he had not discovered painting as an outlet, he probably would have gone insane."
Critics, research men, artists, find in their creativity ways of com-
pensating for alienation so that aloneness is no longer sterile.

In his sophomore year, . . . Scott was involved in the effort
to deal with how an individual can live a desirable life in relation
to a society of which he does not feel himself a part—the need neither to conform nor to "alienate" oneself. He was reaching out in
all directions, in his reading, to find possible solutions to this need,
and he seemed to be working positively at it. Here literature came
to his aid, although much more of his reading was outside the field
of pure literature. But certainly his approach to his education and
the character of his interest in learning shifted when he faced a new
world of intellectual possibilities in his earliest experience as an
undergraduate. From then on education became a search and an
exploration. It began to consolidate in his senior year when he was
able to say "I need competence badly," and realized that he needed
to study politics and history. Up to that time he was not principally
interested in subject matter or disciplines, although he worked in several different disciplines and met the requirements of most of them
on a good or very good level. He was interested in issues or problems or questions. His interest in subject matter became serious
when he decided he could not deal with the questions that interested him most without knowing history and politics [pp. xvi, xvii,
36–40].

In Scott's searching, sorting, and selecting, in his gradual clari-fication of his own view, and in his emerging concern for competence in history and political science we see the process of differentiation and integration as work. And we would predict that as those studies reveal the complexities of social forces and the realities of politics and power, the process will continue.

"Differentiation and integration," "challenge and response" are useful ways to think about education and the process of human de-velopment. But the idea they refer to is not new. Perhaps it is only their polysyllabic ring that makes them seem superior to the *yin* and the *yang,* those ancient Chinese principles that together produce all that comes to be. Or perhaps you recognize these words from an old American sage:

> Education is that reconstruction and reorganization of experience which adds to the meaning of experience, and which increases ability to direct the course of subsequent experience. The increment of meaning corresponds to the increased perception of the con-nections and continuities of the activities in which we are engaged. . . . An activity which brings education or instruction with it makes one aware of some of the connections which had been imperceptible [Dewey, 1938, pp. 89, 90].

Thirty years is really not so long ago, and Dewey's "reconstruction of experience," his fundamental process through which learning and development occur, is certainly echoed by today's terms. And the same basic dynamic operates in other more particular domains.

It is consonant with Festinger's (1957) theory of cognitive dis-sonance: if a person knows things that are not consistent with one another, he will, in various ways—by changing his opinion, by changing his behavior and thereby the information he receives, by distorting his perceptions and his information—try to make them more consistent. The evidence for this dynamic is striking and unequivocal. Lecky (1951) describes the continual struggle to develop and maintain "self-consistency."

Heider's (1958) "balance theory" and Newcomb's "strain for symmetry" posit the same process for interpersonal relationships. New-comb (1961) studied the emergence of person-to-person relationships in a college residence. Two consecutive groups of seventeen transfer students, a year apart, accepted invitations to live rent-free in a college residence in return for devoting four to five hours a week as informants and as experimental subjects throughout the fall semester. They were selected by the criterion of "strangership." In neither group had any two men the slightest prior acquaintance with each other. The study aimed to better understand the motivations and conditions that lead to stable interpersonal relationships, and the processes by which these are maintained or modified. In the light of his findings, Newcomb (1961) describes the human condition thus:

> We face, in each of three directions, forces that are ineluctable. We ignore properties of the "real" world at our peril. Stones will bruise, and fire will burn—these things we learn by direct sensory experience, aided and abetted by the teaching of others. . . . As we find that our own experience and the testimony of persons whom we trust are mutually reinforcing we tend to rely on the latter—it short-circuits trial and error, enables us to avoid painful experiences, often leads to direct satisfaction. And so their testimony, too, is ignored at our peril. But the time comes when the two sources of evidence do not reinforce each other, but yield conflicting evidence: our senses, or our own inferences therefrom, tell us one thing and our associates another. Or . . . two trusted human resources give different testimony. How then shall we know the "real" nature of things? It is out of such a history . . . that intrapersonal demands for balance arise. The world is at odds if one's own sources of conviction are contravened by those whom one has reason to trust. Thus we become sensitive to the acquired, drive-like state of strain, and it, too, is ineluctable in that for most individuals it is potentially ever-present; like other states of drive, it may be tolerated, for a time at least, but whether endured or appeased it influences behavior [pp. 259, 260].

More and more frequently, as research techniques improve, the evidence from neurological research turns out to be consistent with findings concerning other levels of behavior. Thus Newcomb's description of the human condition, Heider's balance theory, Festinger's cognitive dissonance, and Sanford's differentiation and integration, are all highly consistent with Pribram's (1967) view based on neurological studies of "arousal." He says:

> Essentially, experience builds within the organism a set of expectancies, neuronal models of the events experienced. Until recently a cognitive term such as "expectancy" had little to support it in the way of hard neurological fact. This has changed radically with . . . demonstrations that orienting and dishabituation occur whenever a

repetitiously experienced configuration of input is changed. . . .
The "expected" forms the background, the set point against which
the novel is matched. . . . The experimental results raise the question of when arousal leads to registration, habituation, and memory
formation and when arousal leads to disruption. The classical answer has been . . . that the *amount* of arousal determines its out-
come. The evidence for this view has been marshalled so repeatedly
that it need not be mentioned here. What can be added is that, on
the basis of evidence obtained in the studies of the orienting reaction, "amount" is shown to be dependent on experimental organization, on the configuration of the expectancies challenged by the
novel input. "Amount" is thus viewed as amount of match and
mismatch between configurations. . . . Amount of arousal, amount
of activation, is not to be conceived as some quantitative change in
intensity in energy level in the central nervous system, but as change
in the *uncertainty* (and thus the information) of the system [pp.
831, 833].

How does development occur? One process seems fundamental.
It turns up in diverse domains and at various levels of human behavior—interpersonal, cognitive, perceptual, neurological. Call it *differentiation and integration, reconstruction of experience, dissonance reduction, self-consistency, balance, strain for symmetry, uncertainty*—
the labels vary to suit the subject, but the basic dynamic remains about
the same. In so saying we don't forget that significant variations on
this major theme probably occur as one turns from one aspect of human behavior and development to another, or as one moves from level
to level. Nor do we pretend that this single general principle encompasses the complexities of human development. But inasmuch as we
seldom act—in curriculum construction, teaching, evaluation, residence hall arrangements, parietal rules—on the basis of even this fundamental principle, doing so can put us a large step ahead.

Which brings us to the second question, "What determines
whether or not an experience has an impact?" To effectively foster
increased differentiation and integration, we need an answer. So here-
with a second law, simplified and baldly stated: *The impact of an
experience depends upon the characteristics of the person who encounters it.* When individuals differ, a single experience (person, program,
object, event) can have diverse developmental outcomes—and different experiences can have similar outcomes. *Depend* here does not
mean "totally determine," because obviously experiences have a force
of their own, which has direction and magnitude and which will be

found to operate similarly among diverse persons; but it does mean "significantly influence." Small dosages of arsenic are a stimulant for most persons; large ones usually are fatal. But individual tolerances can vary widely, and as anyone who has read many murder mysteries knows, tolerance for killing dosages can be developed. So the consequences of eating the same chicken pie may be quite different for husband and wife. And even the autocratic and tough-minded Royal Canadian Air Force recognizes that to increase physical fitness, diverse exercises with finely graded difficulty levels must be offered, and that individuals must enter the sequence according to their own strengths and weaknesses, must proceed at their own pace, and will reach different limits. Similarly, the impact of a class, course, or curriculum, of a teacher, peer, or culture, will vary with the backgrounds, ability levels, and personality characteristics of the students. But higher education has given little attention to this obvious principle. Instead, students have been treated as though they were billiard balls, all alike in shape, size, and density, all stationary till struck. The administration wields the stick, sending rotund cue balls at students on the assumption that if the proper angle can be found, if students are struck in just the right spot, they all will behave in proper fashion and inexorably be impelled in the ordained direction. The trouble, of course, is that only a few students are smooth and well-rounded. Others are square or egg-shaped, knobby or dented, flat or curvy. Some are ping-pong balls, some bowling balls. Some look symmetrical, but inside, weight is concentrated at particular points so they roll along in irregular and unpredictable fashion. Further, some of the cue balls are pretty peculiar and some cues are badly twisted. So the game is frustrating and full of surprises.

The undiscriminating view of student dissenters is a good example of the capacity to ignore differences, even when they smack us in the eye. Dissent comes from both "activists" and "alienated." But despite differences in aims, in approach, and in defining characteristics, they are usually lumped together as though the terms were synonymous, as though the persons were the same. Keniston (1967) describes some of the basic differences:

> The defining characteristic of the "new" activist is his participation in a student demonstration or group activity that concerns itself with some matter of general political, social or ethical prin-

ciple. . . . whatever the issue, the protester rarely demonstrates because his *own* interests are jeopardized, but rather because he perceives injustices being done to *others* less fortunate than himself. . . . If one runs down the list of "causes" taken up by student activists, in rare cases are demonstrations directed at improving the lot of the protesters themselves; identification with the oppressed is a more important motivating factor than an actual sense of immediate oppression. . . . we might think of the activist as (politically) "alienated." But this label . . . overlooks the more basic *commitment* of most student activists to other ancient, traditional and credal American values like free speech, citizen's participation in decision-making, equal opportunity and justice. In so far as the activist rejects all or part of 'the power structure,' it is because current political realities fall so far short of the ideals he sees as central to the American creed. . . .

In contrast to the politically optimistic, active, and socially-concerned protester, the culturally alienated student is far too pessimistic and too firmly opposed to "the system" to wish to demonstrate his disapproval in any organized public way. His demonstrations of dissent are private: through nonconformity of behavior, ideology and dress, through personal experimentation and above all through efforts to intensify his own subjective experience, he shows his distaste and disinterest in politics and society. . . . Alienated students are more likely to be disturbed psychologically; and although they are often highly talented and artistically gifted, they are less committed to academic values and intellectual achievement than are protesters. . . . Furthermore, such students usually find it psychologically and ideologically impossible to take part in organized group activities for any length of time, particularly when they are expected to assume responsibilities for leadership. Thus, on the rare occasions when they become involved in demonstrations they usually prefer peripheral roles, avoid responsibilities and are considered a nuisance by serious activists. (Draper, 1965) . . .

Whereas the protesting student is likely to accept the basic social and political values of his parents, the alienated student almost always rejects his parent's values. In particular, he is likely to see his father as a man who has "sold out" to the pressures for success and status in American society: he is determined to avoid the fate that overtook his father. These mothers, far from encouraging their sons toward independence and achievement, generally seem to have been over-solicitous and limiting [pp. 111, 112, 113].

When activist and alienated are lumped together, and when the same answers are given to both, unproductive outcomes and continued frustration should not surprise us. Such consequences are not new, just more visible and dramatic. Because, for a change, the student response is protest. Other symptoms have long been with us. But we have become hardened to dropouts, a high transfer rate, apathy, and to students who say, "I love college but I hate classes"—all of which occur in part because important differences are ignored.

The striking differences in the characteristics of students from campus to campus are well documented. In scholastic aptitude, for example, McConnell and Heist (1962) report mean ACE (American Council on Education Psychological Examination) total scores of 104 for 60,539 students in a sample of 200 schools. For single schools, mean scores ranged from 37.5 to 142.2, a spread of nearly four standard deviations. The two extreme mean scores were equivalent to the first and ninety-second percentiles for the total population. And other differences in personality characteristics, reported in Chapter Eight for the thirteen Project colleges, occur among many other institutions as well.

Many of us know about some of the general and systematic relationships that exist among such diverse characteristics and varied developmental consequences. We are aware that different kinds of entering freshmen seek and pursue different kinds of experiences, develop different patterns of interaction with the college, derive different meanings from their experiences, and consequently are differentially affected. We recognize that academic achievement varies with high school rank and with measures of ability and past achievement. Spindt (1959), for example, surveying predictive studies found quite consistent correlations of .45 to .55 for academic success in high school and first semester grade-point average, the traditional criterion for success in college. And we recognize that the differences in "success" occur not only because of differences in academic aptitude and preparation, but also because of differing patterns of motivation and study. We recognize also that differences in vocational orientation and avocational interests effect the curriculum and major chosen, and that those choices influence not only the particular skills and information gained, but also attitudes, values, future plans, and more general patterns of growth (Newcomb and Feldman, 1968; Spohn, 1960). Some of the findings from studies of college dropouts are also becoming common knowledge. Astin's (1964) report—that dropouts come from lower socioeconomic backgrounds, have lower ranks in high school, plan initially to get lower college degrees and apply for relatively fewer scholarships, and that they tend to be more aloof, self-centered, impulsive, and assertive—does not come as a great surprise. But for the most part we ignore such knowledge. If our blindness was graded most of us would get A's for tunnel vision, a distribution we would hardly tolerate for students.

Varying programs, opportunities, and requirements according to such general differences as are common knowledge would be a good start. But it would be only a beginning because other dimensions of diversity have equal significance for institutional policies and practices. Consider, for example, the less well-known findings from MacKinnon's (1962) study of creative writers, mathematicians, architects, physical scientists, engineers, and industrial researchers:

> As for the relation between intelligence and creativity [there is] essentially zero relationship between the two variables, and this is not due to a narrow restriction in range of intelligence. Above a certain required minimum level of intelligence which varies from field to field and in some instances may be surprisingly low, being more intelligent does not guarantee a corresponding increase in creativeness. It just is not true that the more intelligent person is necessarily the more creative one [pp. 487, 488].

Outstanding intelligence, therefore, does not distinguish the creative from the noncreative. But other characteristics do:

> The more creative a person is the more he reveals an openness to his own feelings and emotions, a sensitive intellect and understanding self-awareness, and wide-ranging interests including many which in American culture are thought of as feminine.
>
> All creative groups we have studied showed a clear preference for the complex and asymmetrical, and in general the more creative a person is the stronger is the preference.
>
> Creative persons are especially disposed to admit complexity and even disorder into their perceptions without being made anxious by the resulting chaos. It is not so much that they like disorder per se, but that they prefer the richness of the disordered to the stark barrenness of the simple. They appear to be challenged by disordered multiplicity which arouses in them a strong need which in them is serviced by a superior capacity to achieve the most difficult and far-reaching ordering of the richness they are willing to experience [pp. 488, 489].

Do these distinguishing characteristics of creative persons have implications for how they fare in college? The unequivocal answer is that they decidedly have. Gardner (1967) describes some of the findings:

> potentially creative students were identified by the similarity of their patterns of attitudes and interests to those of students who earlier had been classified as creative through a process of nomination by peers, faculty agreement, and analysis of records, and indeed it was found that students who tended to approach intellectual matters in ways characteristic of creative people were less likely than other students to graduate from college. The three highly regarded colleges . . . lost more potentially creative students than they graduated. Even in college A, which attracts a student body with an extremely high proportion of the potentially creative (63 percent), more than half of these students leave (53 percent), and this is almost double the rate of attrition for the other students in the college (28 percent).
>
> The situation is not much better in two outstanding colleges of engineering and science. In his account of a broad, long-range study of MIT students, Dr. Benson Snyder . . . also reported discouraging findings. He found that students who scored high on the three scales of the Omnibus Personality Inventory used to identify the creative personality were more likely to leave MIT than were students who scored low on these scales. . . .
>
> The measured characteristics can be briefly described as follows:
>
> "The *Thinking Introversion* scale measures an interest in reflective and imaginative thinking as opposed to action. High scorers say they derive pleasure from analytic, deductive thinking and find excitement in intellectual activity. They tend to think of themselves as autonomous and independent.
>
> "The *Complexity* scale assesses tolerance for the unstructured and desire for new and complex experiences. High scorers enjoy "fooling around" with ideas and are not disturbed by a lack of clear cut answers or tangible outcomes.
>
> "The *Impulse Expression* scale assesses general need for immediate gratification with a relative intolerance of delay. High scorers place little reliance on set schedules, orderliness in dress, or conventionality in attitudes. They also tend to express interest in rebellious adventure with an exhibitionist flavor."
>
> The MIT study took a careful look at students who scored very high or very low . . . and found that on all three scales, high scorers were significantly more likely (p < .01) to leave the institution than were low scorers. The findings were especially dramatic in the data from the Complexity scale. In Dr. Snyder's words, "The institution is losing three times as many students who as freshmen preferred to try out new solutions, 'fool around' with ideas, or take

cognitive risks, as it is students preferring a well-ordered life with tangible results" [p. 2].

The differential response of creative students is not restricted to "highly regarded" colleges, to colleges which attract a high proportion of such students, or colleges primarily concerned with science and engineering. Hannah (1967, 1968a, 1968b) found the same pattern throughout the thirteen small Project colleges described in Chapter Eight.

Students at the Project colleges yielded some interesting figures for the three scales described above for the MIT study and for another scale, Autonomy, which measures a characteristic "composed of nonauthoritarian thinking and a need for independence. High scorers are sufficiently independent of authority, as traditionally imposed through social institutions, that they oppose infringements on the rights of individuals. They are nonjudgmental, realistic, and intellectually liberal [Center, 1964, p. 5]." The differences between the leavers and stayers for these thirteen institutions are consistent with those mentioned by Snyder for MIT and described generally by Gardner. The trend is not quite so sharp for Thinking Introversion, but on the Impulse Expression scale those who left during the first or second year scored higher than their persisting peers in twenty-two of the twenty-six groups examined (men and women separately for twelve colleges, business administration and engineering majors for one) and in eleven cases the difference was statistically significant; they scored higher on Complexity in nineteen groups, and higher on Autonomy in eighteen. So even for these diverse small colleges the creative, complex, independent student leaves more frequently than his more conforming and controlled counterpart.

But the most significant thing about these data is not that they support such a generalization; it has been supported similarly in other studies. The significant point is that "higher" or "lower" creativity, complexity, impulsiveness, autonomy, as they affect withdrawal, depend entirely upon the college and the student's position relative to his fellows in that institution. The Impulse Expression, Complexity, and Autonomy scores for the W. J. B. girls, for example, revealed that in each case the leavers scored substantially higher than the stayers, but the leavers' scores of 46, 46, and 44 are still half a standard deviation below the average for the 7,000 freshman norms group. So in general terms, they are low scorers on these measures—but the students at W. J. B., compared with their peers, who scored 38, 43, and 39, are top students, impulsive, complex, and autonomous. At the other end of the spectrum are the Kildew girls. Mean scores for stayers were 58, 62, and 62, a standard deviation above the national average. These persisting girls, by any standard, are highly creative, impulsive, complex, autonomous. Yet the girls who left scored even higher: 60, 65, and 66. The other eleven colleges fall between these two, and the pattern remains the same. It is relative position within each institution, the relative level of impulse expression, complexity, and autonomy brought at entrance, the fit for the individual with his fellow students and with the institution, which makes a difference. These findings also recall those reported in earlier chapters, which revealed that self-esteem and level of aspiration depended upon aptitude and achievement in relation to peers at one's own college or in one's own residence, and not upon a larger frame of reference.

Relationships among student characteristics and responses to varied teaching styles are consistent with the findings for more and less creative students and for their reactions to college. Consider, for example, the differences between authoritarians and anti-authoritarians found by Stern (1962):

> The typical authoritarian student preferred studying alone, since working with others always meant a bull session in which nothing definite was ever settled. He also preferred to study in the same place throughout the year, in a room that was neat and orderly and free from the distraction of the radio, television, or phonograph. He developed rigid time schedules for studying, reading, and review, and relied heavily on formal study aids, teacher suggestions on outlining and notetaking, and rote memorization of significant facts to get himself through. Difficult reading materials were particularly frustrating for him, and he dealt with this problem by going to the instructor or to better students for help. Theoretical discussions in class were another source of difficulty, and the authoritarian student most preferred a straightforward exposition by the instructor to any other classroom activity. He prepared for the final examination by reviewing classroom and reading notes and memorizing the main points. The only thing he liked about essays was getting them done. . . .
>
> The responses of the typical antiauthoritarian indicated that his place of study varied, as he alternated between satisfying his desire to be with people and isolating himself as a defense against

this need. He enjoyed cooperative study because he liked other viewpoints, liked discussions, and because it gave him an opportunity to be with other people. He didn't care much where he studied as long as it was quiet. Readings challenged him and he sought out additional materials to improve his understanding. He liked it when the class discussed side issues and took notes of stimulating and challenging ideas that he intended to explore later. He prepared for the final examination by trying to arrive at some sense of the course as a totality, and liked essay assignments because they gave him a chance to work witth ideas, to express himself, and to explore abstract concepts [pp. 695, 696].

Luchins (1942) studied rigidity by developing a series of problems, some of which only could be solved by quite complicated procedures. Other problems appeared similar but could be solved quite simply. Some students, when first given the complicated problems, continued using the more laborious and time-consuming approach when given the simple ones; others saw through the simple ones and changed their approach. Luchins called those who did not change "rigid" and the others "adaptable." Using this technique to select rigid and nonrigid students, teachers in the Natural Science Department of the Basic College at Michigan State found significant differences in the ability to recognize a logical hypothesis, to recognize data supporting an hypothesis, to recognize a valid experiment, and to recognize a reasonable interpretation of data.

Students also were given lists of interrelated terms and asked to indicate their relationships. Success varied markedly: some commented separately on each term; others saw relationships among a few; others could reduce all terms to a single generalization. Nonrigid students tended to see more relationships and closer ones than the rigid students (Dressel, 1958).

Significant differences occur at all levels. White (1950), for example, reports differences in "autonomic constitution." In one person the most conspicuous response to stress may be increased heart rate, in another peripheral blood pressure, in a third, perspiration. Cardiovascular patients respond to stress with cardiovascular changes and little change in muscle tension; other patients with head and neck pains respond to the same stress with increased muscular tensions and little cardiovascular change.

So students differ in significant and fundamental ways, and the impact of experiences encountered in college will be substantially influenced by those differences. But to act on this basic law, we must remember one other major consideration—timing—and take it into account. Again, this is a simple principle for which the evidence from research and our daily experience is unequivocal, yet colleges seldom vary timing according to differences among students. Erikson (1950, 1963) and many others emphasize the importance of an "epigenetic principle," according to which development unfolds and is elaborated, where not only organic growth, but personality development occur in steps predetermined by both an inner program and outside forces. If rate or sequences are seriously disturbed, harmony among parts may be lost through under- or over-development, to the detriment of function, stability, and satisfaction. Hear *Zorba the Greek* (Kazantzakis, 1953) describe it:

> I remember one morning when I discovered a cocoon in the bark of a tree, just as the butterfly was making a hole in its case and preparing to come out. I waited a while, but it was too long appearing and I was impatient. I bent over it and breathed on it to warm it. I warmed it as quickly as I could and the miracle began to happen before my eyes, faster than life. The case opened, the butterfly started slowly crawling out and I shall never forget my horror when I saw how its wings were folded back and crumpled; the wretched butterfly tried with its whole trembling body to unfold them. Bending over it, I tried to help it with my breath. In vain. It needed to be hatched out patiently and the unfolding of the wings would be a gradual process in the sun. Now it was too late. My breath had forced the butterfly to appear, all crumpled, before its time. It struggled desperately and, a few seconds later, died in the palm of my hand [p. 120].

Most of us have known students who have been damaged by the too-hot breath of premature experiences. And we know others for whom the warmth required for them to break through their cocoons comes too late.

Thus the impact of particular experiences not only depends upon the fit between their intensity and quality, and the characteristics of the students—it also depends upon the time at which they are introduced or experienced. Of course basically, timing makes a difference only because at one stage individuals are different in sensitivity, readiness, and resistance than at an earlier or later stage. So to speak of timing is not to introduce anything fundamentally new. But it is helpful—when considering curricula, teaching practices, independent study, parietal rules, residence arrangements—to ask not only, given the characteristics of these particular students, what the likely consequences of the experiences provoked by conditions A or conditions B might be, but also whether the consequences will be magnified or reduced if these conditions are experienced by freshmen, sophomores, juniors, seniors—during this year or this semester, as opposed to another.

The point of our second law, then, is that students differ in significant ways that affect their responses to a particular institution and the peers and faculty members they encounter there, and affect their responses to different subject matters and tasks, different conditions of stress and release, different levels of satisfaction and frustration. Yet educational policy and practice for the most part act as though such differences were not there. But they won't go away because we turn our backs. They are fundamental, persistent, pervasive.

If students differ significantly at entrance, if within a single class there are several different trajectories, the questions of institutional influence are cast in a different light. Our past view, referred to earlier, has seen college as a billiard table, its culture the cue, and the force of that culture the cue ball. The student stays put until struck. He changes location only when hit and the direction of movement depends entirely upon where he is struck and where the cue ball comes from. Colleges that have an impact—it has been found—are those where the shooters are at one location, applying pressure in a consistent direction. Students, consequently, are sent in similar directions. Their angles of departure may vary but any measure of central tendency indicates that their general direction is shared. Colleges with little impact are those with no shooters, or those where several shooters operate at once from different locations, canceling one another's contribution.

But if we take seriously differences among the students, we recognize they are not stationary. The table is tipped and they are in motion. College can accelerate, retard, or deflect, depending on the force and direction of student vectors as they encounter the force and direction of the college. Accurate understanding of institutional impact, therefore, requires identification of significant subgroups within each college population, and study of change for these subgroups, as it relates to their characteristics and to those of the institution.

Three studies of Project data suggest that if these levels of analysis are undertaken, fruitful results follow. Stockwell (1967) compared first-year test-retest scores on the OPI for commuters (N = 45) and residents (N = 101) at five Project colleges. Commuters evidenced *decreased* levels of intellectual interest in the sciences (TO) and increased interest in reflective thought (TI), as well as increased interest in esthetics (Es). Residents, in contrast, evidenced *increased* intellectual interest in scientific thought and study (TO), and increased interest in reflective thought (TI), as well as increased interest in esthetics (Es). In addition they reflected increased autonomy (Au), increased awareness of emotions and impulses (IE), and an increasingly liberal religious orientation (RO). Now if these same test-retest data were analyzed with commuters and residents combined, first-year change would look quite different. The decreasing interest in scientific thought and inquiry for the commuters would probably cancel the increases for the residents, suggesting no change for that area, and the magnitude of change in other areas found for residents would be reduced and statistically significant differences would be generated less often. Thus studies of significant subgroups may often reveal change and impact not apparent when total populations are examined.

Another inquiry by McDowell (1967a) indicates the value of more particular study of relationships among college characteristics, student characteristics, and change. Clark and Trow (1966) describe four orientations with which students typically identify: Vocational, Academic, Collegiate, Nonconformist. Do students shift orientation during the first year? Comparison of the fall and spring responses of identical individuals, 229 men and 231 women, showed that slightly over half repeated the same choice in the spring, and about half shifted to some other first choice.

Were shifts in role orientation related to differences in college environments? Relationships between changes in orientation and CUES scores might provide a clue. CUES scores and per cent of increase or decrease in first choices for each role orientation were correlated across twelve colleges; Table 22 gives the resulting coefficients. They suggest several interesting relationships, some surprising, others not. At institutions strong on Practicality—instrumental emphasis, entrepreneurial behavior, getting ahead within the system—the Nonconformist orientation loses students during the first year and the Academic orientation gains. Note that the data indicate only which orientations gain or lose. They do not indicate whether students who leave one orientation account for the increase in another. Nonconformists, for example, might all shift to Collegiate while similar numbers of Collegiates shifted to Academic. Our own intuitions and experience tell us this is probably not so, that probably many ex-Nonconformists became Academics; but the data do not demonstrate that. When Propriety is important, the Nonconformist orientation loses also, but here it is Collegiate that gains. Awareness is the only CUES scale that exerts some pull toward the Nonconformist orientation, and that only for women. It is not surprising that strong Scholarship emphasis leads to decreasing numbers whose primary orientation is Vocational, but the association between weak sense of community and movement into the Vocational orientation is more puzzling. McDowell (1967a) asks, "Does a relative lack of warm social relationships on campus incline the student to focus more toward tangible future goals [p. 111]?" An interesting question, worth further exploration.

Table 22

PER CENT CHANGE IN PRIMARY ORIENTATION
CORRELATED WITH CUES SCORES

Typology		Practi-cality	Commu-nity	Aware-ness	Pro-priety	Scholar-ship
Vocational	M	12	−76	−40	−9	−55
	F	−13	−60	−34	−21	−44
Academic	M	41	22	10	2	10
	F	55	10	−36	36	−7
Collegiate	M	4	7	−2	40	9
	F	34	26	12	55	30
Nonconformist	M	−49	−38	12	−57	2
	F	−80	−27	44	−61	8

According to our principle concerning the influence of student characteristics, shifting orientations derive not only from institutional conditions encountered by freshmen but also from predispositions they bring. If so, OPI scores at entrance should be systematically related to such shifts. The mean scores at entrance for men and women who shifted into each orientation support our expectations. Students shifting to Nonconformist and Academic orientations scored higher on measures of Intellectual Interest, Complexity, and Autonomy at entrance (except that Nonconformists are also nonscientific) than students who shift to Vocational or Collegiate orientations. Students shifting to Vocational and Collegiate score higher on Practical Outlook and Personal Integration, and admit to less anxiety at entrance, than those shifting to Academic or Nonconformist orientations.

The potential value of more particular and concrete analyses suggested by these two studies has been reinforced by examination of frequency distributions (Chickering, 1968) underlying measures that reflect significant change and other measures that do not. Some data from the OPI are illustrative. Figures 15, 16, and 17 were generated simply by subtracting individual standard scores at first testing (entrance, 1965) from their scores at second testing (end of sophomore year). Thus the figures show frequency distributions of difference scores for change during the first two years. Standard deviations for OPI scales are usually about 10, so a difference score of 10 represents an individual change roughly equal to one standard deviation.

The three distributions in Figure 15 result from pooling difference scores for all scales that reflected significant change for that institution. They represent, therefore, the general thrust of change at that college. Pooling was achieved simply by summing the difference scores for all scales for each individual and then dividing by the total number of scales. The distributions differ somewhat. At W. J. B. only 10 per cent change against the tide, and they don't move very far; the small changes in the opposite direction by the other 90 per cent are sufficient to generate statistical significance. At Woodbine about 20 per cent move in contrary direction, but they are counterbalanced by a few whose scores reflect substantial change and by the more moderate change reflected by the others. At Divinity, although about 25 per cent shift against the general thrust, they don't go as far and the moderate change by the other 75 per cent carry the central tendency to significance. The peaks in the Divinity distribution suggest clusters of students worth further study. Perhaps differential predispositions or differential experiences are associated with these different degrees of change.

It is possible, of course, that such results are a function of measurement error; its contribution is always difficult to ascertain and the difficulties are compounded when dealing with differences scores. The reliabilities for the OPI scales are quite high; two test-retest studies over three- and four-week time intervals generated coefficients ranging

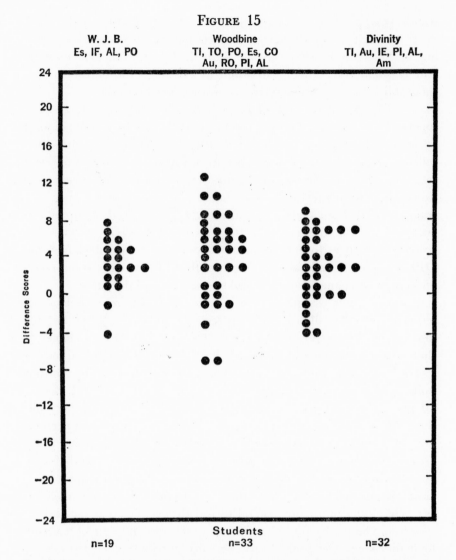

FIGURE 15

Thus these different distributions do seem to reflect dif-

from .79 to .95 (Center, 1962). But even those reliabilities leave room for uncertainty when the measures are used to assess change. However, study of individual patterns across scales that reflect mean change suggest that something other than measurement error is operative. Students swimming against the institutional current—changing counter to the mean change—tend to do so rather consistently across several scales, and those swimming vigorously with the current do so consistently also. Thus these different distributions do seem to reflect differential individual-institution interactions, and not simply random errors of measurement.

The patterns shown in Figure 15 are about what one might expect to underlie significant mean change. But we should not forget that the different patterns may be of major importance to the institutions under study. When most students move in the valued direction and when negative change is limited in degree and in frequency, as at W. J. B., there is ground for satisfaction. But if 20 or 25 per cent are changing negatively to a substantial degree, such a shift may far outweigh the gains made by others. Some elementary schools, for example, teach a majority of children to read and to learn, but also teach a minority to reject reading and learning. Substantial money and energy are being applied to that problem. Similarly, a college that would develop autonomy and integrity may not be satisfied with such development for 80 per cent, when the other 20 per cent become more dependent and hypocritical. Thus examination of the frequency distributions underlying significant change may often be of great practical importance.

Figure 16 presents two frequency distributions underlying scales reflecting no significant change. In both these distributions difference scores cluster around the zero point and few persons shifted far in either direction. As assumption of minimal change or impact is probably sound here.

Figure 17 presents two other distributions for scales reflecting no significant differences, but these patterns differ markedly from those in Figure 16 and also differ from each other. Stonewall reflects a wide range, but a relatively large minority are close to the zero point. The Woodbine distribution is much more flat, however, with the preponderance of students reflecting change in one direction or another. Both these distributions suggest that something is going on, that something is operative within individuals or within the environment to foster change. There are different individual reactions but most are affected one way or the other, especially at Woodbine.

Such a finding should not surprise us. Many powerful singular experiences, and many conditions less powerful but encountered over time, produce quite different reactions. Indeed polarization of attitude and behavior is a typical result as issues become more salient, as the forces at work become more powerful, as personal experiences become more direct and intense. The general education program opens doors

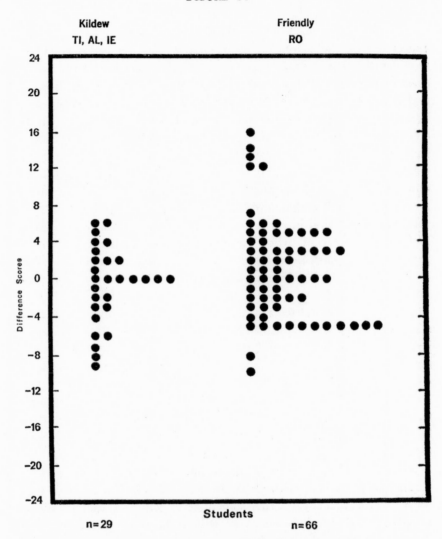

FIGURE 16

for some students and leads to diversification and intensification of intellectual interests. Others are turned off completely and define college purposes more narrowly in terms of vocational preparation. A charismatic leader converts large numbers to the fold—be it free speech or fundamentalism—and at the same time turns others one hundred and eighty degrees the other way. Some students respond to freedom and the opportunity for self-government by developing autonomous

FIGURE 17

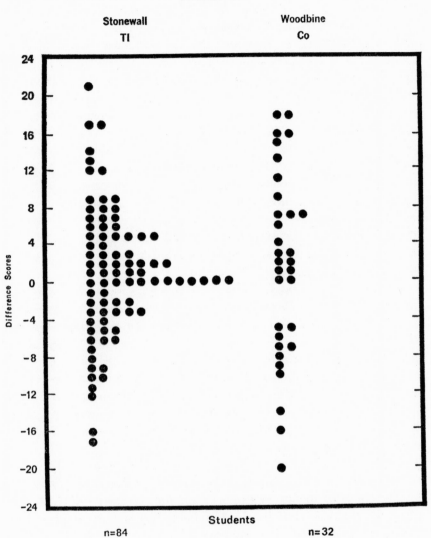

Stonewall
TI

Woodbine
Co

Students

n=84   n=32

control and personal integration; others disintegrate and become governed by impulse and short-run hedonism.

Basically, the point is that when a strong force is at work a group may respond either in rather homogeneous fashion, with all members shifting similarly, or it may respond in quite heterogeneous fashion, with substantial proportions shifting in different and often opposing directions. Whichever occurs depends upon the forces at work, the characteristics of the students who encounter them, and the particular cycles of differentiation and integration that are amplified or dampened. Assessment of institutional impact requires attention to both these patterns of response. Do the frequency distributions in Figure 15 reflect greater change than those in Figure 17? Which sets suggest greater institutional impact? Probably the distribution for Woodbine on Figure 17 signifies more institutional impact than any other. And distributions like these are not rare. For seven Project colleges, two or three scales were selected that did not reflect significant change and of the fifteen possible cases, eleven distributions were like those in Figure 17. Averages obliterate individuals and so fail to reveal the complex interactions that determine each event and its developmental consequences. Simple reliance on measures of central tendency, therefore, is not enough. Not only may important areas of institutional impact be missed, but, equally important, knowledge of the underlying distribution is often necessary for sound interpretation of significant change.

This chapter began by positing two laws for student development in college: (1) *Development occurs through cycles of differentiation and integration,* and (2) *The impact of an experience depends upon the characteristics of the person who encounters it.* The pervasiveness of these basic principles was supported not only by findings for students, but by research and theory from other domains concerning varied aspects and levels of human response and change. Can we act on these two basic principles? Can we move from agreement with these abstract and self-evident ideas to concrete implementation and application? I believe so.

Because of the differences in the range of student characteristics from college to college, and because of institutional differences, the particulars of any attempt to act more fully on these principles will differ. But the basic steps involved probably will be fairly similar. The comments to follow don't represent a complete "how-to-do-it." The process is too complex to be encompassed by a recipe. More importantly, students, faculty, and administration must develop their own processes and plans if the changes which follow are to be understood and implemented with the necessary balance of commitment and critical appraisal. But an illustration, while no model to be copied, may prompt the development of more effective approaches by others.

1. *Select significant dimensions of student diversity.* One or

two areas will do, and probably not more than three, because managing more complexity than that is difficult. Criteria for selection are (1) educational significance, (2) the ability actually to make the necessary distinctions, (3) the number of students for whom the distinction is important, and (4) the capacity of the institution to respond. For example, it would be helpful to identify students with unusual potential for scientific achievement. But if they cannot be selected with sufficient confidence, if there are so few that special efforts for them must have low priority, and if the institution lacks both faculty and facilities for advanced study, then such a dimension may be discounted at the outset.

There may be, however, significant diversity in other areas where numbers and capacity to respond are greater. McDowell's study mentioned earlier suggests that one dimension might be the Clark-Trow typology (1966)—Vocational, Academic, Collegiate, Nonconformist—amplified by future plans and aspirations, and past curricular and extracurricular achievements and interests. A second might be the rigid-flexible, authoritarian-antiauthoritarian, creativity continuum, which seems to turn up so often. These both appear to be educationally significant. Numbers and capacity to respond may be sufficient to give them top priority—which leads to the next step.

2. *Select indices and establish criteria.* Agreement must be reached on some concrete indices, measures, characteristics, signs, according to which judgments can be made. Criteria that help suggest where one location ends and another begins probably will be necessary. The most important thing is that they be simple, concrete, and publicly knowable; that they not involve the use of esoteric knowledge or special expertise. This consideration is essential to protect the operation from manipulation and control and to enable its open application by everyone. Thus each student could clarify his own orientation to college on the basis of the kind of information suggested above. And each student could, with one or more of a variety of indices, locate himself roughly on the top or bottom half, or the bottom, middle, or top third, of the creativity continuum in relation to others at his college. Selecting indices and establishing criteria also make possible a closer estimate of the number of students in various groups. With such information at hand, step three can be undertaken.

3. *Address program.* Consider what groups are well served by current arrangements and whether significant numbers are missed or

short-changed. Formulate additions, deletions, or modifications putting these considerations against the capacity to act and other priorities.

For example, there may be a significant number of vocationally oriented students whose past interests and future plans are completely at odds with a freshman year that requires English Composition, History of Western Civilization, Introductory Biology, Chemistry, or Physics, Art or Music Appreciation, and Physical Education. Some modification of this program or some additions to it might enable students with strong vocational or professional interests to begin college more effectively, might bridge what appears to be a substantial gap, allowing them to achieve increased competence as they move into territory that offers more diverse opportunities for satisfaction and personal expansion. Or there may be a substantial number of creative, academically oriented students, entering college with enthusiasm, curiosity, and energy. Opportunities for loosely structured studies in rather broadly defined areas, managed with considerable flexibility, might be developed. Cooperative papers and projects, group discussion, use of diverse resources on and off campus, might be emphasized. Evaluation might simply be on a pass-fail basis with most of the emphasis put on substantive self-evaluation and substantive evaluation of one another, in addition to concrete feedback from instructors.

4. *Effect communication.* Finally, describe clearly the outcomes of the first three steps. Indicate the dimensions of diversity selected and why. Describe the relevant indices and their use. Give the estimated number of students involved in major subgroups. Describe the programs developed or modifications made, the rationale for their creation, and the potentials they are thought to hold for those who participate. But simple description is not sufficient. It must be supplemented by opportunities for students to discuss with faculty members their own characteristics and the program choices implied—and by continuing opportunities to examine the choices made and to change plans if indicated.

Choices implied, not required. Fundamental to the process described above, and fundamental to all applications of the two laws posited in this chapter, is the maximization of choice and self-determination for students. Significant differences among students can be recognized and programs refined and diversified in response to such information. But students must clarify for themselves where they stand and must determine for themselves where they want to go and how they want to get there. Increased differentiation and integration can be enabled, not coerced. The institution's task is not to alter a loose-fitting straitjacket for a more precisely tailored one. It is, instead, to increase the range of alternatives through which student development can proceed. We do this intelligently by considering carefully—mustering the best evidence and best judgment we can from students, faculty, and administration—the diverse characteristics of the students we serve, by recognizing the process of differentiation and integration, and by managing curriculum, teaching, and evaluation, parietal rules and residence hall arrangements, interpersonal relationships, and the college culture accordingly.

Needless to say, knowledge of human development and concepts relevant to student development in college are not exhausted by the two principles recalled in this chapter. But inasmuch as these principles are seldom taken seriously into account it would probably be difficult to implement increased subtleties if they were at hand. Indeed, if we can learn to act in terms of these two laws, it will represent a major step forward.

CHAPTER 15

NEXT
STEPS

𝄞❋𝄢❋𝄞❋𝄢❋𝄞❋𝄢❋𝄞❋𝄢❋𝄞❋𝄢❋𝄞❋𝄢❋𝄞❋𝄢❋𝄞❋𝄢❋𝄞❋𝄢❋𝄞❋𝄢

Adolescents become adults as development occurs in seven major areas: competence, emotions, autonomy, identity, interpersonal relationships, purpose, and integrity. Can colleges foster such development? Can they accelerate movement along these vectors of change? Can they set tasks and offer conditions that create a bridge from one state to the other? They certainly can, because they have—as numerous studies have shown. Can colleges retard such development? Can they block progress with moats, mountains, and barbed wire? Can they place a no-man's-land between adolescence and adulthood? It looks as though they can do that, too, because other studies have found little or no change for some institutions and for some conditions. But, in general, does going to college make a difference to personality development in the young adult? On

320

balance, growing evidence suggests that it does. Several longitudinal studies have compared students who completed college with others who attended for varying lengths of time or did not attend at all. Plante (1965, 1966) broke the ice for such research with his studies of applicants to San Jose State college, some of whom were admitted and others of whom, though equally qualified, were not admitted for lack of space. He found that over a four-year period all students, regardless of whether they attended college or not, became less dogmatic and less ethnocentric, and that the amount of change increased with length of college attendance. Thus those who did not enter and did not subsequently attend another college changed least, those who completed four years changed most, and those who entered and left before graduating fell between these two groups. Trent and Medsker's (1968) longitudinal study of 10,000 high school graduates is probably the most comprehensive work yet available. Renaud (1967), in a brief report of their work, says:

> It is clear . . . that the students who spent four uninterrupted years in college (persisters) changed more than their peers with four years of job experience (nonattenders) by becoming more intellectual and particularly by developing the critical, flexible, nonjudgemental kind of thinking assessed by measures of autonomy. And the pattern of differences both in intellectual disposition and development of autonomy between the two groups held firm even for those matched for ability and socio-economic background.
>
> The college persisters as a group became more inclined towards reflective, abstract thinking, independence, and flexibility, with the women among them showing greater gains in intellectual curiosity, tolerance for ambiguity, freedom from opinionated thinking, and autonomy. And the nonattenders as a group showed either decreases or less growth than the persisters on the scales measuring these traits, with women who had four years of unbroken "homemaking" showing the greatest regression—even more than the employed women—on the Complexity scale, which assesses interest in intellectual inquiry and tolerance for ambiguity. . . . Men with four years in employment responded to their experience much as women with four years in the home did—with an increasing closedmindedness and inflexibility [p. 5].

Do such changes persist after students leave college? Several studies (Bugelski and Lester, 1940; Nelson, 1954; Newcomb et al., 1967) have found that they do. Newcomb and Feldman (1968), reporting their review of research in this area, describe what happens and why:

> Attitudes held by students on leaving college tend to persist thereafter, particularly as a consequence of living in post-college environments that support those attitudes. Within-college changes, especially if accompanied by a general stance of openness to change, may be still further extended in response to new social and technological conditions.
>
> The general finding that attitudes change little after college years cannot be attributed simply to "inherent inertia," or to some sort of early hardening of psychological arteries. The basic fact is that one's attitudes and values do not change whimsically, but in response to new information or to new ways of viewing one's world. The older one becomes, the less the relative impact of any particular set of new experiences. The unique thing about late-adolescence-merging-into-early maturity is that at this stage of development one is, in our society, maximally motivated to achieve autonomy and at the same time minimally constrained to conform to the restrictions of adult roles. The typical consequence is that if one does not change during this period one is not likely to change thereafter. Or, alternatively, if one has changed during these years one may have acquired a propensity for changing oneself in response to changes in the world outside oneself.
>
> For many students, in sum, college-induced changes in attitudes and values are likely to persist. Most of them are not likely again, to be susceptible to new influences, and their college-acquired stances will, to some degree, continue to symbolize independence and adulthood. For some, at least, habits of continuing to be open to new information, and to be influenced thereby, will result in persisting openness to further change; such an outcome, it may be argued, is one of the goals of a college education [p. 305].

In brief, then, college can make a difference; and often it does. College amplifies the differences between high school graduates who attend and those who do not, and persons who come in and go through are different when they come out. And the differences—between those who attend and those who do not, and within attenders themselves—usually persist. The basic argument of this book is that college can make a much greater difference. It can make a difference to more students and can make more of a difference to those reached. What actions can be taken to increase the contribution made to student development, to accelerate change along the vectors significant for the young adult? What conditions are called for on the basis of current research and theory? What changes are indicated for American colleges?

First consideration should be given to that intricate system of interlocking arrangements, curriculum, teaching, and evaluation—not because this area has greatest impact—relationships with peers and individual faculty members have been found to be more potent; and not because it is of primary concern to students, faculty, and administration—their principal preoccupations usually reside elsewhere. Change in this system is of primary importance because it is the pervasive background against which all institutional figures are cut; it defines the terrain through which students travel, and influences the flora and fauna they encounter along the way; it sets the tone and substance, and provides the principal anchors for student-faculty contacts and relationships; it is, or can be, the principal contributor to students' intellectual diet, the meat and potatoes, bread and butter of student discussion. Change in other areas can be important, but change in the central area of curriculum, teaching, and evaluation can send waves throughout the institution.

Perhaps that is one reason why substantial change comes so hard. Ashby (1959) describes the events by which the natural sciences finally overcame the stubborn opposition of the classicists who dominated Oxford and Cambridge during the eighteenth and nineteenth centuries, and became part of the English university curriculum. The power and resistance of the faculties were such that essentially all the major scientific advances occurred outside the universities until well into the nineteenth century. Ashby says:

> The purpose of this analysis is not to pass judgement on early Victorian Oxford and Cambridge, still less to pass judgement on the merits of a classical versus a scientific education. It is simply to establish the fact that scientific thought . . . the foundations of modern physics and chemistry (those of biology were still to be laid by Darwin), . . . which had caught the imagination of the general public (even of artisans, who crowded to Anderson's "anti-toga" lectures . . .), had scarcely influenced the universities of England. The scientific revolution had occurred not through, but in spite of, the English universities [p. 13].

The issues are different today, but the obduracy is not. The need for increased emphasis on intellectual competence, increased opportunity for direct experiences, and increased flexibility, has been recognized for some time but little change has occurred.

"Rite words in rote order [McLuhan, 1967, p. 108]." Despite disclaimers, that emphasis overwhelms American college curricula. For example, as part of the Project on Student Development in Small Colleges, students across all four grade levels and in all areas of study were asked to indicate what per cent of class time was spent listening and taking notes, and what per cent was spent thinking about the ideas presented. At nine of the thirteen colleges, more than half the respondents indicated they spent *more* than 50 per cent of their class time listening and taking notes; at seven of these, more than half the students indicated they spent *less* than 20 per cent of class time thinking about the ideas presented. In studying for courses, "Memorizing" 50 per cent or more of the time occurred twice as frequently as "Interpreting," "Analyzing," "Synthesizing," "Applying," or "Evaluating." These are small colleges—enrollments range from 350 to 1500 —where teaching and learning are emphasized, not research and publication. Most classes number less than thirty. Someone described a lecture as a process whereby the notes of the teacher become the notes of the student without passing through the mind of either. These data support that description and it is probably safe to assume that this pattern operates with equal frequency in larger institutions where teaching has less priority.

The explosion of knowledge and the speed with which it becomes outdated have been documented and argued frequently enough that no further rehearsal is needed here. Again, it is not a matter of uncertain evidence or complex logic—it is simply a matter of acting on the obvious. And the action need not create major disruption of vested interests or major dislocations of personnel. Because, as Dressel and Mayhew (1958) found, critical thinking is best fostered not by courses in logic or critical thinking as such, but in the context of regular studies, managed so processes other than memorization are required. It is not a matter of adding new courses labeled "Introductory Analytic Methods," "Weighing Evidence," or "Advanced Synthesis." It is almost as simple as taking students through the processes by which we generate our lectures instead of sparing them those labors by delivering the product ourselves. We know that basically it is not through memorization, but through those processes that we convert others' words, ideas, and experiences into working knowledge for ourselves.

We don't cover as much ground this way as when we simply read and take notes. But most of what we cover becomes internalized, becomes integrated with other ideas, and sticks with us. So the information retained and used by students is more likely to increase than to be sacrificed. The processes we use vary with our disciplines and purposes so by the end of college students would have experienced, and acquired some competence with, a varied repertoire of intellectual skills. Such changes do not require that teachers leave their disciplines, that departments be reshuffled, or that those credit hours and courses won with such difficulty from deans and curriculum committees be given up. Power struggles with others, therefore, are not a major problem. Instead, each of us is his own obstacle. For a new kind of teacher must gradually supplant the old: one who learns to do without a text and to supply instead diverse materials and experiences with which students can write their own; who learns to organize behavior instead of information, to orchestrate actions instead of words.

Which brings us to the second curricular change needed—increased direct experience. Print reigns, essentially unchallenged. Television and creative use of film eventually will overthrow the tyranny of words, but higher education is still hooked on books. Encounters with print far outweigh all other encounters "for credit." Yet most things are better learned, are learned more fully, more efficiently, more permanently, otherwise. When the Bible tells us that Adam knew Eve we are reminded that *knowing* originally meant much more than the pallid and abstract experience of words. Verbalizing an experience can expand its meaning, reveal subtleties and implications, suggest connections with other experiences. Words are useful shorthand for shared experiences; then their exchange can call up rich associations so multilevel communication can occur. And words can be handy filing tags that facilitate recovery, reexamination, reliving. But verbalization in the absence of relevant experience is empty. We hear the hollow ring. We poke—and the speaker collapses with a rush of hot air.

Fortunately, institutional boundaries are becoming more permeable. Antioch, with its five-year curriculum, which alternates off-campus work and on-campus study, and Goddard and Bennington, with nonresident work terms required as part of each academic year, are no longer lonely pioneers. Other programs that connect on-campus study with off-campus experiences and responsibilities, that supplement reading, writing, and talking with direct experiences, are gaining momentum. Curricula have been modified to accommodate Peace Corps service, inner city programs, work with American Indians, participation in community development and community action programs, and similar activities, as well as study abroad and at other institutions. In 1961 Wilson and Lyons, in *Work-Study College Programs,* described programs then under way, and more have sprung up since. Direct experience has long been recognized as a necessary part of professional and vocational education. Its contribution to the development of young adults is equally powerful. And when the varied experiences of diverse jobs, travels, cultures, and conditions for living are multiplied by the number of students in a class and number of residents in a dormitory, a rich range of resonances for communication and understanding becomes available.

Effective use of direct experience is considerably enhanced by increased flexibility, the third important dimension of curricular change. The curricular pattern for most liberal arts colleges is a series of funnels. Students must select their funnel early and start traveling through ever-narrowing perimenters, emerging at graduation from the small end. But many students, because they have become sufficiently broadened that they are stuck and can go no further, interrupt their college education for work, travel, or "just bumming around." Most sooner or later re-enter, some reluctantly, with more limited expectations and more prosaic purposes—to get the degree, to go to graduate school, to obtain a better job. An undergraduate college, if it is to be liberally educating, should turn the funnel around. Then personal expansion is encouraged, not constrained, horizons become wider, not circumscribed, perspectives are enlarged, not limited.

Again, such change has begun. Some colleges have opened up the senior year, increasing the numbers of electives and introducing opportunities for more wide-ranging exploration through seminars, independent studies, broad-gauged courses. Other colleges are simply cutting the number of required courses and loosening up the time when they can be taken. The increased frequency of interdisciplinary and team-taught courses reflects increasing openness and experimentation with new combinations; it recognizes connections between areas of knowledge heretofore masked by the arbitrary boundaries jealously guarded by professors and their professional associations, boundaries reinforced and sanctified by their repetition through countless college catalogs. More important, perhaps, has been the recognition that not all academic learning must occur in classes and that not all teaching must be done by faculty or graduate assistants. Thus reading periods, weekend conferences, intercession seminars, student-taught courses, independent study, and tutorials with persons outside the institution are no longer new or radical notions.

But the most illogical inflexibility has remained unquestioned and unexamined—the fixed time unit. The fixed time unit is higher education's Procrustean bed. Typically it is four months long. In some colleges it is three, and some courses require two of the given units. But whichever system is used—semester, trimester, quarter—the consequence for most subjects is like that suffered by those unwary travelers who stopped at Procrustes' inn. In some cases the fixed time unit not only lops off an end, it also eliminates sections of the middle and lateral extensions. In other cases it stretches subjects painfully, making them thin and emaciated.

Ideally, there should be no fixed time units applying to all areas of study. Students and instructors should simply work as long as it takes to accomplish what they want, at the depth and thoroughness they wish. Eight weeks for an introductory look at psychoanalysis, ten weeks to learn the basic concepts of cell structure, sixteen weeks to study the chemistry and physical properties of water, twenty weeks to see the major forces at work in twentieth-century Europe, thirty-five weeks to achieve detailed interpretation of American History—if these time units are best, then these subjects should be studied that long. For practical reasons complete flexibility is impossible, but modification of existing structures to provide greater flexibility is feasible. Consider the following proposal as an illustrative target.

Allow courses, seminars, or independent studies to be planned for two months, or any multiple thereof to a maximum of (1) eight months for completely academic study, (2) ten months for study requiring significant periods of residence off campus or substantial components of direct experience beyond reading and writing, (3) twelve to twenty-four months for study requiring residence in a foreign country. The general expectation that students study in three, four, or five areas concurrently, depending upon whatever is standard practice at a given college, would continue. Students would be expected to accumulate the usual thirty credits per year; two and one-half credits would be given for each two months' study in a given area. Students enroll once a year for the full year and arrange programs so that in a twelve-month period the necessary credits are accumulated.

Such an arrangement has three principal advantages over the usual larger fixed time interval. First, faculty members and students can achieve a closer fit between the nature of the study to be undertaken, its purposes, and the amount of time devoted to it. A student can investigate an area of tentative interest with the investment of only a twelfth, rather than a sixth of his time, and both students and faculty can deal with smaller discrete problems of joint concern. Second, off-campus and nonresident experiences can more frequently become integral parts of academic study. Academic work can be timed around the availability of off-campus resources and vacations can be planned either to supplement such experiences or to avoid conflicting with them. And third, this arrangement permits both teaching and learning to be managed more flexibly in response to shifting interests and demands.

Now this proposal goes beyond what most institutions might think feasible and beyond what most could manage in one leap. But as an end point to be reached through a series of intermediate steps, it is neither unsound nor unrealistic. But, proposal aside, the basic point is that any framework that requires that all subjects be divided and taught according to equal time units, no matter what the objectives, no matter what the discipline, no matter what the students' level of preparation or motivation, will violate more than it serves. To fix the time and then to cut the studies to it puts the cart before the horse.

Curricular changes—increased emphasis on intellectual competence, increased direct experiences, and increased flexibility—will be enhanced if teachers shift from soloist to conductor. The teacher's job is to help students create the music, not to make all the music himself. He does this best by asking them to perform, by helping individuals contribute effectively, and by coordinating individuals and groups so that the totality has form and substance. The consequent shift for students is from passive to active.

Many students and teachers have found Introductory Psychology to be one of the dullest courses they ever experienced or taught. In the past I have not been derelict in upholding this tradition, as several generations of students will testify. But the last time I taught the course I did something different, figuring I couldn't do any worse than I had in the past. I put in the library eight different introductory psychology textbooks; for the first class assignment I asked each student to select his own text from among them, with the help of some suggestions I offered concerning how to examine them. In a class of fifty-five, all eight textbooks were represented. The first two class sessions were spent comparing tables of contents and indexes to discover the major topics common to all—perception, learning, thinking, motivation, personality, and so on—and identifying some of the major subheadings under each. These sessions also identified those areas included by some writers and not by others. Following this, class time was apportioned to include the areas common to all and some of the less common areas of particular interest to some students and some authors. As we proceeded through the semester we addressed three major questions for each area: (1) What concepts or principles do all authors recognize as valid? (2) On what concepts or principles do they disagree? (3) What concepts or principles are still uncertain, or what major questions must be pursued for knowledge to move ahead? These questions were tackled through various means—making teams of students with different texts, grouping students with the same texts and sharing summary reports, trading texts so each individual read two or three approaches to the area under study. To conclude study for each area, individuals or teams of students took a major issue of uncertainty, a major open question, and searched journals back to two years prior to the publication date of their text. Reports were prepared on ditto paper and multiple copies were made and distributed. The difference in pre- and post-test scores on questions lifted from former exams showed substantial learning had occurred. In fact, the differences were the largest I ever obtained—because I'd never given a pre-test before. But for me the most important thing was that for the first time, both the students and myself found the study challenging and interesting. Class time didn't drag; it flew. The level of effort and the amount of student-to-student exchange between class sessions was high.

I'm not trying to suggest a model here. But if learning is to occur, students must actively pursue it. In most courses and classes students are essentially passive. In eight of the Project colleges more than two-thirds of the students sampled indicated they spent less than 5 per cent of the class time "making statements to the class" in discussions or more formal presentations, and most of these classes are small.

Obviously, discussion by the whole group is not the only alternative. Subgroups can work together to synthesize and evaluate material from diverse sources. Problems can be set for team solution. Debates, panels, buzz groups, and group and individual reports can be used. And the same principle should be carried to activities between classes. Reading is only a first step. Converting print on a page to working knowledge requires that it be associated with direct experience: observing "real life" situations, or films, or video tapes; taking action on concrete problems or concerns for which concepts and principles are relevant; constructing one's own poem, painting, short story, theory, experiment; charting relationships among different viewpoints; creating illustrative metaphors, analogies, or concrete visual or structural representations. By working with ideas, we elaborate their meanings and they become our own. This is how we learn as we master our own fields. Students should have the same chance.

If curricula reflect increased emphasis on intellectual competence, increased direct experience, and increased flexibility, if teachers become conductors instead of soloists, and if students become more active than passive, what then for evaluation? Students study what they're tested on. We can talk about analysis, synthesis, or application, but if they are not tested on these, little development will occur. *Tested* can have broad or narrow meaning. When students exchange views, present them to the class or a subgroup, convert them to another form, prepare reports for others, or take direct action on them, testing is going on. So as students become more active, testing of this sort increases substantially, and this is the most important kind—because then performance occurs under the scrutiny of faculty, students, and self, and substantive feedback is received concerning accuracy and error, strength and weakness.

Obviously the traditional term paper and exam system can also provide substantive feedback, although as currently employed it seldom does. The concern for task effectiveness and explicit information about strengths and weaknesses is overwhelmed by the emphasis on normative judgment, on where one has stood in relation to others and in relation to the teacher's scale from bad to good. And concentrated at the end of the semester there is little chance for discussion with either instructor or fellow students. But some adventurous teachers are finding that there is room in the traditional system for helpful wrinkles. For example:

Pass or fail grading is increasing, especially for courses "outside the major."

Students are taking courses without being graded.

Within courses, substantial portions of work are being put on a simple pass-fail basis, or grades are determined from a limited sample of performance while other materials, which receive substantive criticism but no grade, are required.

Group oral exams and group papers are used to promote cooperative rather than competitive effort.

Two answer sheets are distributed with multiple-choice exams. One is turned in at the end of the exam period. The other is taken away to be reviewed with books available and with the benefit of more time for thought. When this second sheet is turned in, half credit is given for correct answers that were in error on the first sheet.

Taking the final is left to individual decision. At the end of the last week of classes each student is told of his grade up to that point. He is told also what exam scores would yield different grades. In the light of this information each student decides whether or not to take the final.

Students are given problems and sample answers reflecting varied levels of performance. With these in hand they grade themselves and other class members.

Students are asked to define their own purposes in taking a course and to develop the criteria and measures by which successful performance would be assessed. And then to apply these to themselves, with or without the teacher's help or knowledge.

These wrinkles are appealing because through them runs a concern (1) to provide substantive feedback concerning task effectiveness rather than abstract normative judgments, (2) to allocate more responsibility for evaluation to the student himself, and (3) to reduce the extent to which one student is pitted against another. Once again, improvement can occur without total overthrow. Grades and exams need not be completely eliminated. Significant modification within the system can make evaluation work for—rather than against—teaching, learning, and student development. But all these changes in curriculum, teaching and evaluation will be but palliatives, Band-Aids for a compound fracture, without an expanded definition of the whole domain. Academic inbreeding has been a narrowing and limiting force. Access to higher education depends upon a limited array of verbal and mathematical skills and information, and on a limited range of personal qualities. Success in higher education depends on closer conformity to these models and further development of this limited array. But as the demand for higher education increases, it can no longer be met by a narrow definition of academic excellence and by increasing standards for this particular kind of performance. Pace (1966) sums up the issue:

> As higher education becomes more universal, it also must become more diversified, rewarding and enhancing a greater variety of human talents and attainments, and offering wider avenues for the development of expression, insight, and knowledge. Academic grades predict academic grades; scholastic aptitude tests predict scholastic performance. But neither has much relationship to anything else—not creativity, not inventiveness, not leadership, not good citizenship, not compassion, not aesthetic sensitivity, not expressive talent in any of the performing arts, not personal and social maturity, not mental health, not vocational success, not family happiness, not honest workmanship. Yet are we not concerned with these things too? And do they not have profound implication for the selection of students and for the very process of education itself? . . . Countering the current emphasis on verbal facility and verbal learning, there is a need for richer acquaintance with more of the great and universal nonverbal languages of man: the languages of movement and form, of color, and sequence, and sound, the language of direct expression and feeling. Throughout history these have been powerful and significant avenues by which man has expressed his knowledge, his aspirations, his beliefs, his insights, and his wisdom. Are these still foreign languages to many of our students? . . . If higher education is to serve a diversity of students it must reward a diversity of talents, and provide a diversity of methods by which knowledge and understanding may be acquired and expressed. . . . Let academic talent and academic performance be rewarded, but not to the exclusion of other modes of learning. For many restless students today the college environment deals too exclusively with abstractions and theories, and too little with morality and action and direct confrontation of man with his society and his environment [pp. 96, 97, 99, 100].

Pace's comments put the problem of motivation in proper perspective. One of the distinguishing characteristics often attributed to dropouts, supported by some of the measures used for comparative studies of leavers and stayers, is "lower motivation." Leavers are less motivated than stayers because their parents come from a lower social class (as signified by lower occupation and less education), are less intellectually inclined, attend fewer cultural events, have fewer books in their home. Because their ability is no less than that of fellow students from different backgrounds who persist, they are said to lack motivation when they withdraw. Such thinking and such labeling are at best imprecise, and more often are quite inaccurate. As a school psychologist I often asked teachers, "Why do you think Johnny isn't working in your class?" An unfortunately high proportion of teachers answered, "Because he's lazy," and thought they'd said something. Johnny often ran a paper route after school each day, ran groceries at the A & P on Saturday, participated in athletics, and had an active social life to boot. He was not lazy, but he couldn't see much reason to invest his energy where the education brokers advised. Academics offered no intrinsic satisfactions that could compete with the other demands on his time, nor was there opportunity to know well enough persons in the system who might become objects for identification and emulation. So Johnny was lazy, "poorly motivated." Many dropouts have similarly low motivation for the activities colleges ask them to undertake. And the same can be said for the other major category of college dropouts, highly creative students. It is interesting that their leaving is seldom attributed to "low motivation"—perhaps because they are similar to persisters in terms of parents' occupations and education. But the dynamic is not much different. They leave because the narrow emphasis on the verbal, the conformity to standard forms and frameworks, and the distance between what they are asked to do and what they think is important to do, are too great. For both groups the problem is not "low motivation," but more often strong motivation directed toward ends the college will not recognize. Both groups are asked to abandon themselves, their talents, their purposes, in return for the rewards of the bookish system. For both groups the price is too high. So they leave, seeking to sustain themselves and to continue their own development elsewhere.

Thus change in curriculum, teaching, and evaluation is central to more effective and more relevant higher education. For any given college generation residence hall arrangements, relationships with faculty, friends, reference groups, and the college culture, have greater impact. Earlier chapters have described the conditions that make a difference in these areas. For faculty and administration: accessibility, authenticity, knowledge, and the ability to talk with students. For college residences: balanced diversity of membership combined with allocation of significant responsibilities that require both group action and individual participation.

But most of the changes called for bring us smack against the problem of size. Kate Hevner Mueller (1968), Professor of Higher Education and Editor of the *Journal of the National Association of Women Deans and Counselors,* wrote to me saying:

> I am very glad indeed, to hear of your plans to provide the profession with a text for *The Young Adult,* and hope that it will be useful to us and others in our curriculum in College Personnel–Higher Education.
>
> To date, almost all of the studies of youth, and their individual development, have come from the small liberal arts, highly competitive colleges—Heath's at Princeton, Sanford at Vassar, Keniston at Harvard, Newcomb at Bennington, Murphy and Raushenbush at Sarah Lawrence. . . .
>
> For the next decades Higher Education does not look forward to teaching and handling students in small groups and therefore all the failures which are made in teaching, and all the procedures recommended by these small arts college writers are missing the point by a wide margin. About 75 per cent of the young adults are on the large public supported campuses. The states, encouraged by Federal reports, decided in the forties and fifties to expand their universities and colleges, so that we could educate (1) the greatly expanding youth population and (2) many more of the average and subaverage students who had never been in the colleges before. Now, as John Gardner says, "We should have the grace to live with the decisions we have made."
>
> We will be teaching youth in large classes, *i.e.,* classes of 300–500, even juniors and seniors and graduate students in classes of 50, 75, 100, 150. And they will plan their schedules, without benefit of counselor, eat their meals, discuss their problems, make love, get married, choose their careers, all with practically no help from adults. Faculty members are going to continue to be just the same as they have been in the past, devoted to their disciplines, and scornful of any help on how to teach better, even though they may need it badly. This has already been pointed out ad nauseam, and it will not help to tell us the same thing *again!*
>
> Perhaps you won't believe this, but I am hoping that your new text won't be just like all the others, telling us what ought to be the pattern for understanding and dealing with Youth when what is needed is somebody who accepts the present day campus "like it is," with this kind of faculty, and these kinds of students. We need pictures and histories of middle and lower middle class youth, many of

them not alienated from their parents . . . but not yet able to cope with society. They are very different from the youth groups to be found in the small liberal arts competitive colleges, and they have a culture all their own. When I see that list of colleges on your official stationery and have to assign my students to read in all those inappropriate books on youth, I begin to worry about how your material will fit our needs. Do give some thought to the wider usefulness and wider sales of any material that is realistic for the present decade in Higher Education.

I wrote back, saying:

Your basic point is unarguable, the frustration and emotion behind it fully understandable. I'm sure you're right that for the next decade at least 75 per cent and more of the young adults attending college will be confronting numbers and faculty as you describe, and all the other concomitants of large public supported institutions which you spare me. Anyone who can suggest programs which will make a substantial difference to such institutions will make a major contribution indeed. Not only the universities, but the governments of the world, will beat a path to the doorstep of anyone who can tell how a faculty, devoted to their disciplines and scornful of teaching, can effectively educate youth in classes of 300–500. I'm not one to call much of anything impossible. But it may be significant that no one yet has even a limited answer. And in this regard it is worth noting that although Sanford and Newcomb studied Vassar and Bennington, most of their experience has been in large universities—the University of California at Berkeley and the University of Michigan. This experience shines through as the principal "grounds" for their interpretations and their positions. And the same is true of others whose observations are similar—Paul Dressel at Michigan State, Mervin Freedman at San Francisco State, Joseph Katz at Stanford, Robert Pace at UCLA, George Stern at Syracuse University. It is probably fair to say that these persons, who have thought hard and long about American higher education, who view college as a place for education, not training, who think that student concerns about love and marriage, careers, and coping with society should meet with some response, have shared your experiences and share your reactions. If they could set down answers I'm sure they would. And I would myself, if I could. But I don't have any. At least I have none beyond the single response you already know about—establishing the small unit within the large, or growing by adding small semi-autonomous units rather than by simple expansion of the whole. Monteith at Wayne State and New College at Hofstra were pioneering units that proved successful and persist. Goddard College has tripled its enrollment by adding units of 250 students each, and the University of California at Santa Cruz expects to reach an enrollment above 20,000 by going a similar route with units of 1000. Michigan State and the University of Michigan have established small colleges and more are planned. You probably know of others.

My point is simply this. The only answer so far available is to break big units into small ones. This response is not limited to large universities. Big business is moving in the same direction, dispensing with large-scale assembly-line operations and setting up small units where groups of workers assemble a complete unit and sometimes even carry responsibility for maintainance and service after it is sold. The New York City school decentralization struggle is another example, and Mayor Lindsay is suggesting a series of City Halls to move government closer to the particular community it serves, to make it more responsive, more flexible, more concerned with persons, less bound by structure, bureaucracy, and vested interests. These changes are occurring because it has become clear that being part of something that can be grasped, experienced, known, where one's contribution can be perceived, where the difference one makes is recognized, is the key to productivity, personal development, and a satisfying existence—not only for the individual, but in corporate terms as well. And we are a corporate society where individual welfare is inseparably bound up with the welfare of the associations of which we are a part—neighborhood, business, community, church, school. Discovering the unit size and the internal arrangements which enable active and responsible participation is one of the most important things we can do. But you know all this as well as I.

Basically, I suppose, such books as this are written because the present-day campus cannot be accepted "like it is" and because there is cause for hope that it will break into more educationally effective units. Certainly the current arrangements did not come into existence because they were deemed more educationally effective, nor have they often been justified on such a basis. If the truth be known, such considerations probably played little part in the decisions which led to institutions 10, 20, and 30,000 strong. But if the movement toward clusters of small units gains momentum, if we have more and more small units as universal higher education becomes a reality, it would be unfortunate if the shortcomings of the past, the limitations of current curricula, teaching and evaluation, of college residences and student-faculty relationships, were built into them. If such books as this can accelerate the movement toward small units, can suggest productive forms those units can take, and can offer conceptual frameworks useful to those who establish them, then a contribution has been made—even though the important immediate need you recognize so well and feel so strongly is not directly addressed.

Thus, large size is a major handicap. Learning and personal development occur principally through action. Vicarious experiences can contribute. Watching and listening, passivity, absorption, reflection, are important. But if opportunities for relevant behavior, for active expression, for responsible participation, are not available or are sharply curtailed by strong competition, long waiting lists, or bureaucratic hurdles, then wisdom heard, insights gained, the fruits of reflection, cannot be converted into working knowledge, cannot become part of oneself.

Size is important for another reason. If we take seriously the idea that educational outcomes depend upon the characteristics of students who encounter them, then institutional flexibility is necessary, not simply desirable. For the college must be able to shift its programs and policies in response to changes in the kinds of students who attend. And it should be able to do so in small and deliberate steps, rather than through major upheavals and revolutions. Then change can occur when the contribution of reason and evidence is relatively high, and irrationality, emotion, and prejudice relatively low. Then sound realization of institutional purposes for the students who attend can be the object, rather than struggles for power and self-assertion. For ultimately there is really no question whether change will come, and if peaceful evolution is impossible, violent revolution becomes inevitable.

Which brings us to the final major change we would address —a shift in the principal basis for decision from intuition and personal prejudice to reason and evidence.

"The central issues of our time," [J. F.] Kennedy said in New Haven, "relate not to basic clashes of philosophy or ideology but to ways and means of reaching common goals." As every past generation had to disenthrall itself from an inheritance of truism and stereotype, "so in our own time we must move on from the reassuring repetition of stale phrases to a new, difficult, but essential confrontation with reality."

For the great enemy of truth is very often not the lie—deliberate, contrived and dishonest—but the myth, persistent, persuasive and unrealistic. Too often we hold fast to the cliches of our

forebears. We subject all facts to a prefabricated set of interpretations. We enjoy the comfort of opinion without the discomfort of
thought.

What is at stake (he concluded) is not some grand warfare
of rival ideologies which will sweep the country with passion but
the practical management of a modern economy. What we need is
not labels and cliches but more basic discussion of the sophisticated
and technical issues involved in keeping a great economy moving
ahead [Schlesinger, 1965, pp. 645–646].

Kennedy could have substituted "education" for "economy"
with no risk to accuracy. Thirty years ago, John Dewey (1938) addressed the same issue, saying:

> A man is stupid or blind or unintelligent—lacking in mind—
> just in the degree in which in any activity he does not know what he
> is about, namely the probable consequences of his acts. A man is
> imperfectly intelligent when he contents himself with looser guesses
> about the outcome than is needful, just taking a chance with his
> luck, or when he forms plans apart from study of the actual con-
> ditions, including his own capacities. Such relative absence of mind
> means to make our feelings the measure of what is to happen [pp.
> 120, 121].

To forego the comfort of opinion and take up the discomfort
of thought is not to become super-scientific or computerized. Personal
experience, intuition, feelings, must be taken into account—especially
in education, where programs and policies are implemented through
interpersonal transactions, and are mediated basically through the re-
ciprocating behaviors of administration, faculty, and students. Unlike computer programs, which are run off precisely as they are written, college programs are all destined to be modified, rewritten, and
carried out in dozens of different ways by the persons responsible for
them—as indeed they must and should be. So feelings and personal
perspectives are not to be disregarded. On the contrary, they are to
be taken seriously into account, recognized as explicitly as possible,
and their diversity capitalized upon as much as possible. The point is,
that they must be leavened, enriched, broadened, tempered, by other
information—by data generated from the works and experiences of
others, by relevant research and theory, by specific findings of particular significance to the issue at hand, by more objective data concerning the particular students and particular institution in question.

The principal shortcoming of American higher education is not uncritical acceptance of, or slavish adherence to, the latest "truth" demonstrated by the scientific establishment; it is the nearly universal neglect of such information, and active resistance or rejection when it is introduced. Count the number of councils, committee meetings, and student-faculty forums where such neglect and resistance occur. Put them against those where relevant research and theory are mentioned, and, when mentioned, are openly received and thoughtfully considered. You can give dollars for the second, take doughnuts for the first, and come out ahead. Such a posture might have been defensible ten or fifteen years ago when relatively little research had been done, although it would have ignored the significant studies of Learned and Wood (1938) and Newcomb (1938), and relevant research concerning secondary education such as the Eight Year Study (Progressive Education Association, 1942). But if neglect was defensible then, it is no longer. Feldman and Newcomb's (1968) recent review cites over 1200 studies relevant to the impacts of colleges on student development—the impacts of different curricula and majors, residence groupings and arrangements, interpersonal relationships among students and between students and faculty, student cultures and college cultures. Most of these studies have occurred during the last ten years. All the signs—professional interest, financial support, organizational structures, journals and publishing houses—suggest that such research will continue, and at an increasing rate. How long before it will be used?

Eventually, research and theory will be called into service. History indicates that what science can know it will know and what technology can do it will do. Similarly, as research and theory make *possible* the management and control of human development—as they will—the management and control of human development will be *undertaken*. The question is, by whom? If management of education is to remain in the hands of those principally involved—students, faculty members, administrators—then they must maintain superior knowledge and sophistication concerning the process of human development and the impact of education upon it. If they do not, control will pass on—to legislators, to industry, to behavioral scientists. Which raises the issue of power: student power, faculty power, administrative power.

Questions of power and prerogatives, and questions concerning the process of decision—who participates with how much weight in relation to what—have been forcibly and forcefully raised on many campuses. They have been raised sometimes to provoke change, and sometimes to resist it. To change, therefore, is also to face issues of participation and power.

The dominant shortcoming of those who push for student power is limited historical perspective. The meaning of the present derives largely from its connection with the past. The vivid pictures of today's scene projected through the unencumbered vision of the young adult are incomplete. Their perceptive dissections and analyses, therefore, are too starkly black and white. The capacity for swift indictment is not sufficient for sound judgment. Decisions must rest not only upon fine sensitivity to present inconsistencies and unspoken assumptions, but upon understanding of the conditions from which they sprang. Such knowledge is not irrelevant.

But if students lack historical perspective, faculty and administration are often shackled by it. And if youth are highly sensitive, like a sore thumb, to contemporary slings and arrows, most adults are not only calloused and dulled, but insulated by vocation, status, and economic security. If students paint the scene in black and white, adults color it gray. No longer the objects of education and the draft, they view youth's objections as the whining of the pampered. Inured to, or seduced by, the blandishments of Madison Avenue and the violence of the news, they view as alarmists youth who still react.

I exaggerate the dullness of faculty and administration—as I exaggerate the sharpness of students. And, as not all youth lack perspective, neither are all adults shackled by it. But the basic point still holds. Youth can tell how it is today to live in a college dorm, to sit through lectures and exams, to conform to teacher's prejudices, to face the draft, to experience the hypocrisy of once-admired adults, to feel with those who have been bombed, burned, beaten, exploited. That is their strength and their contribution—perspective is their weakness. Adults bring knowledge, wisdom, and practical experience; these are their strengths—sensitivity and fine tuning are not. And that is why both young adults and those over thirty must share governance and decision. For perceptivity without perspective cannot, except by chance, avoid past errors; and perspective without clear perception can only, except by chance, respond to past, not present, realities.

The problem of student participation in governance and decision making, therefore, does not rest on whether they have something to contribute. Nor does it rest on the soundness of their views and recommendations. For their sense of what is happening to them, and their sense of how particular programs, policies, and practices will affect them, is necessary to any decision. And their analyses and recommendations can usefully supplement those generated by faculty and administration. Educational institutions exist to foster learning, student development, and ultimately, an improved existence for mankind. The basic problem is whether decisions aim to serve those purposes and whether they flow from reasoned and objective analyses of relevant research and sound observation of local conditions—or whether they flow from personal preference and prejudice in the service of power or comfort. If the first process is at work, and if students will give themselves to it, participation in college governance makes great sense.

Unfortunately, such a process is more often on vacation than at work. And, unfortunately, faculty and administration seem little more prone to employ it than students. Somebody said that a university's main function is to provide a place where adults who like to sit around inside where it is comfortable, reading and talking, can do so and get paid for it. As one who spends a good deal of his time doing just that, I certainly don't agree. But a cool and candid analysis of faculty and administrative behavior, and of the spoken and unspoken bases for many decisions, would have to give personal interest, professional advancement, stability, security, and comfort a not inconsequential role.

Listen to faculty committees consider office hours and advising, lecture versus discussion classes, requirements for majors, adding or dropping courses from the curriculum. How often do discussions of student contact hours elicit the question, "What arrangements would create most effective student-faculty relationships?" How often, instead, is the call for reduced student contact to release time for research and writing? Have you ever heard a faculty suggest shifting toward increased contact? And how often do discussions of curriculum aim to construct a more effective four-year program, given the kinds of students at hand? Or is it more often jockeying for departmental position and aggrandizement, calling into service standards set by professional associations, accrediting agencies, certification laws? Have you heard faculty members responsible for teacher education, chemistry, psychology, history, economics, pre-med, pre-law, say, "Let's test the soundness of those requirements. Instead of following them to the letter, let's develop the most effective four-year experience we can for the kind of students we have, and compare their performance with graduates of similar ability from other colleges"? Such attempts could make valuable contributions to both general and professional education. And they must occur as knowledge proliferates and the requirements of professional groups multiply. Adding one more course each time a profession grows in substance and complexity just isn't the answer. So the balance of reason, evidence, and objectivity over self-interest is not impressive for faculty members, as it is not for students.

Listen to administrators discuss visiting hours in college residences, drugs and drinking, beards and dress, speakers on campus. How often are questions concerning developmental consequences and educational effectiveness clearly separated from questions concerning community and legislative reaction and trustee-alumni support? For they are separate questions. The educational pros and cons of varied policies should be formulated clearly and clearly articulated. And so should the reactions of those who support the institution. If compromise be necessary, which it often is, both parties should have some estimate of the prices paid. Community, legislators, trustees, and alumni should know the price they exact in educational effectiveness and student development. Student, faculty, and administration should know the costs—reduced financial support, legal harassment, editorial criticism, and bad press—of policies and practices they value. Neither cluster of costs is precisely knowable, but reasonable action requires separating the issues and making the best judgments possible.

The basic question for college governance, then, is not how much power to whom in relation to what. Students, faculty, and administration all have sufficient power to bring things to a halt, and it can be exercised for any issue that strikes home, whether or not it has been legitimized by precedent or fiat, and whether petty or not. The issue is whether differences will be resolved through power plays by polarized groups, whether decisions will flow from emotion in the service of personal prejudice, preference, and comfort, or whether reason, evidence, and objective analysis, supplemented by intuition and personal experience, will create conditions to serve individual learning and development, and to serve fuller realization of human potentials for good. If students, faculty, and administration can share their special contributions to the latter process, then effective college governance can follow. If they cannot, then varied delegations of authority and varied arrangements for participation are at best stop-gap measures, and at worst simply create conditions for sharper confrontation on larger issues later. Can we compromise personal interests to meet the compromises of others? Can we forego the comfort of opinion and take up the burden of thought? To behave so that we can more frequently answer *yes* is the most significant change we can make.

What are the role and function of higher education? Answers vary. But whatever the answer for a given institution, that response sets the framework for decision and is the ultimate criterion for appraising student change. The answer that underlies the viewpoint of this book will, by now, come as no surprise.

In the United States, as in most of the "developed" countries, education has become one of the principal instruments by which the adult of the human species develops its young. This was not true a short time ago and is less true in much of the world today. But it is true here, and now. Family and community used to be the principal instruments and schooling played a limited and special role. But when from age six to eighteen most children spend as many waking hours in school and pursuing behaviors determined by the schools as they do at home doing other things, then education is a major force. And when, in seventy years, the length of schooling doubles—from six years to twelve, or eight years to sixteen—for most persons, its influence is further amplified. Although many elements of personality take their basic form during the early years, it is clear that significant change occurs through adolescence and young adulthood. Just as the belief that intellectual development stops at age fourteen or sixteen was proven wrong, so too it becomes more evident that other aspects of development continue.

Education, then, is a primary force shaping contemporary man, and creating the image of man we live by. And as man makes images of himself he generates self-fulfilling prophecies, making himself, bit by bit, into what he imagines himself to be. What image of man dominates higher education? Archibald MacLeish (1968) answers:

> the university's concern with "man" as such has grown less and less and its concern with what it calls "subjects" has become greater and greater. The important thing has become the academic "offering" (revealing word): the range of subjects from which the student, with his eye on his career, may choose. And the ultimate consequence, only too evident in the time we live in, has

been the vocationalization of the higher schools. The college no longer exists to produce men qua men, men prepared for life in a society of men, but men as specialized experts, men prepared for employment in industry or a profession.

As specialized, professional training, higher education in the United States today is often magnificent. Young doctors are better and better as their specialties become more specialized: so much better that it is now a recommendation in almost any field to say of a young doctor that he is young. Student physicists in the great graduate schools are so notoriously productive at twenty-two that a professional physicist of thirty regards himself, or is regarded by his juniors, as middle-aged. But the educated man, the man capable not of providing specialized answers, but of asking the great and liberating questions by which humanity makes its way through time, is not more frequently encountered than he was two hundred years ago. On the contrary he is rarely discovered in public life at all. . . .

"Where we want to go" depends, of course, on ourselves and, more particularly, on our conception of ourselves. If our conception of ourselves as the university teaches it or fails to teach it is the conception of the applicant preparing for his job, the professional preparing for his profession, then the question will not be answered because it will not be asked. But if our conception of ourselves as the university teaches it is that of men preparing to be men, to achieve themselves as men, then the question will be asked and answered because it cannot be avoided. Where do we want to go? Where men can be most themselves. How should science and technology be managed? To help us become what we can be.

There is no quarrel between the humanities and the sciences. There is only a need, common to them both, to put the idea of man back where it once stood, at the focus of our lives; to make the end of education the preparation of men to be men, and so to restore to mankind—and above all to this nation of mankind—a conception of humanity with which humanity can live.

The frustration—and it is a real and debasing frustration—in which we are mired today will not leave us until we believe in ourselves again, assume again the mastery of our lives, the management of our means [p. 16].

The social and technological systems that control our existence and affect our being are man-made: mathematics, physics, chemistry, biology; newspapers, radio, television; factories, traffic, pollution; prejudice, poverty, famine; cities, suburbs, slums; governments—all are man-made. So too are medicine, public health laws and practices, expanded food production, charitable organizations, open-housing covenants. The current systems, good and bad, have been created by the persons most subjected to the educational system of the past fifty years —specialists with eyes focused on their own ever-narrowing sphere of competence and interest. And it is a moot point whether all of us are masters, or subjects, of the systems thus created. Education, too, is man-made. If persons, not products, are to be primary, if the people, not the interplay of disparate, conflicting, and uncoordinated systems and pressures, are to control the future, then higher education must devote itself to men, not subjects.

Such a shift in emphasis, if it comes at all, will not come fast or easily. First, because the complexity of the task is substantially beyond our present knowledge and competence to achieve it. But the same was true of man's capacity to fly, to orbit the earth, to control disease, to affect the weather. Second, it will not come easily because strong forces will oppose it. And these forces will not only be the resistance and inertia of faculty members who see their disciplines threatened and who fear the loss of subjects. For, just as the function of a college is not to conform to student wishes, but to create conditions that lead to jointly valued change, so the function of higher education is not to give society what it wants, but what it needs. And just as students protest and resist, so will politicians and others whose comfort and security are challenged. And just as such protest or resistance is sometimes justified, sometimes it will not be. When it is not, students, faculty members, and administrators must stand by clear priorities, clear purposes, and clearly posited relationships between those purposes and institutional policy and practice. For if such conviction can be mustered, if efforts can be sustained, the complexities of the task will yield. Then man—not materials, not systems, not nations—having become the focus of education, can become also the focus of human concern.

BIBLIOGRAPHY

ADELSON, J. "The Teacher as a Model." In N. Sanford (Ed.) *The American College*. New York: Wiley, 1962. Pp. 396–417.

ALLPORT, G. W. *Pattern and Growth in Personality*. New York: Holt, 1961.

ANSBACHER, H. L., and ANSBACHER, R. R. *The Individual Psychology of Afred Adler*. New York: Basic Books, 1956.

ARGYRIS, C. "Explorations in Interpersonal Competence." *Journal of Applied Behavioral Science*, 1965, *1* (1), 58–83.

ASHBY, E. *Technology and the Academics*. London: Macmillan, 1959.

ASTIN, A. W. "Further Validation of the Environmental Assessment Technique." *Journal of Educational Psychology*, 1963, *53*, 303–309.

ASTIN, A. W. "Personal and Environmental Factors Associated with College Dropouts among High Aptitude Students." *Journal of Educational Psychology*, 1964, *55* (4), 219–277.

ATKINSON, J. W., and LITWIN, G. H. "Achievement Motive and Test Anxiety Conceived as Motive to Approach Success and Motive to

Avoid Failure." In M. I. Mednick and S. H. Mednick (Eds.)
Research in Personality. New York: Holt, 1963. Pp. 336–351.

BARGER, B. "The University of Florida Mental Health Program." In B.
Barger and E. E. Hall (Eds.) *Higher Education and Mental
Health.* Proceedings of a Conference, University of Florida, Gaines-
ville, 1963. Pp. 27–45.

BARKER, R. G., and GUMP, P. V. *Big School, Small School.* Stanford, Calif.:
Stanford University Press, 1964.

BARNARD, J. D. "The Lecture-Demonstration versus the Problem-solving
Method of Teaching a College Science Course." *Science Education,* 1942, *26,* 121–132.

BARRON, F. *Creativity and Psychological Health.* Princeton, N. J.: Van
Nostrand, 1963.

BAYLEY, N. "Individual Patterns of Development." *Child Development,*
1956, *27,* 45–75.

BAYLEY, N. "Data on the Growth of Intelligence Between 16 and 21
Years as Measured by the Wechsler-Bellevue Scale." *Journal of
Genetic Psychology,* 1957, *90,* 3–15.

BAYLEY, N., and ODEN, M. H. "The Maintenance of Intellectual Ability
in Gifted Adults." *Journal of Gerontology,* 1955, *10,* 91–107.

BEARDSLEE, D., and O'DOWD, D. "Students and the Occupational World."
In N. Sanford (Ed.) *The American College.* New York: Wiley,
1962. Pp. 597–626.

BEECHER, G., CHICKERING, A. W., HAMLIN, W. G., and PITKIN, R. S. *An Experiment in College Curriculum Organization.* Plainfield, Vt.:
Goddard College, 1966.

BETTELHEIM, B. "The Problem of Generations." In E. H. Erikson (Ed.)
The Challenge of Youth. New York: Doubleday, 1963. Pp. 77–
109.

BLOOM, B. S. "Thought Processes in Lectures and Discussions." *Journal of
General Education,* 1953, *7,* 160–169.

BLOOM, B. S., and BRODER, L. J. *Problem-solving Processes of College
Students.* Supplementary Educational Monographs No. 73. Chicago: University of Chicago Press, 1950.

BLOOM, B. S., ENGLEHART, M. D., HILL, W. H., FURST, E. J., and KRATH-
WOHL, D. R. *Taxonomy of Educational Objectives, Handbook I:
Cognitive Domain.* New York: Longmans, Green, 1956.

BLOS, P. *On Adolescence: A Psychoanalytic Interpretation.* New York:
Macmillan, 1961.

BOSSARD, J. H. S. "Residential Propinquity as a Factor in Marriage Selection." *American Journal of Sociology,* 1932, *38,* 219–224.

BOWER, E. M. "Personality and Individual Social Maladjustment." In
W. W. Wattenberg (Ed.) *Social Deviancy Among Youth.* Na-
tional Society for the Study of Education. Chicago: University of
Chicago Press, 1966. Pp. 103–134.

BOWER, P. A. *The Relation of Physical, Mental, and Personality Factors to Popularity in Adolescent Boys.* Unpublished doctoral dissertation, University of California, Berkeley, 1940.

BOWERS, W. J. "Student Dishonesty and Its Control in College." *The Bureau of Applied Social Research,* Columbia University, December, 1964.

BROWN, R. D. *Manipulation of the Environmental Press in a College Residence Hall.* Unpublished doctoral dissertation, University of Iowa, 1966.

BROWN, W. F., and HOLTZMAN, W. H. *Survey of Study Habits and Attitudes,* Form E. New York: Psychological Corporation, 1957.

BUGELSKI, B. R., and LESTER, O. "Changes in Attitude in a Group of College Students During Their College Course and After Graduation." *Journal of Social Psychology,* 1940, *12,* 319–322.

CARROLL, L. *Alice's Adventures in Wonderland.* New York: Random House, 1946.

Center for the Study of Higher Education. *Attitude Inventory: Omnibus Personality Inventory Form D.* Berkeley: University of California, 1963.

Center for the Study of Higher Education. *Omnibus Personality Inventory Research Manual.* Berkeley: University of California, 1964.

Center for the Study of Higher Education. *Omnibus Personality Inventory Form Fx—Brief Scale Descriptions.* Berkeley: University of California, 1965 (Mimeographed).

CHICKERING, A. W. *The experimental curriculum: Implications of the area tests.* Paper presented to Goddard College faculty, 1964a (Mimeographed).

CHICKERING, A. W. "Dimensions of Independence." *Journal of Higher Education,* 1964b, *35,* 38–41.

CHICKERING, A. W. "Institutional Objectives and Student Development in College." *Journal of Applied Behavioral Science,* 1967, *3* (3), 287–304.

CHICKERING, A. W. "FD's and SD's—Neglected Data in Institutional Research." *Proceedings, Association for Institutional Research, Annual Forum,* 1968.

CHICKERING, A. W., HANNAH, W., CAMPAGNA, D., STOCKWELL, D., MATTUCK, R. M., BURNS, B., PERRY, C., and LEVIN, M. *Research and Action: Third Annual Progress Report, Project on Student Development at Selected Small Colleges.* Plainfield, Vt., 1968.

CLARK, B. R., and TROW, M. "The Organizational Context." In T. M. Newcomb and E. K. Wilson (Eds.) *College Peer Groups: Problems and Prospects for Research.* Chicago: Aldine, 1966. Pp. 17–70.

DAVIE, J. S. "Satisfaction and the College Experience." In B. Wedge (Ed.) *Psychosocial Problems of College Men.* New Haven: Yale University Press, 1958. Pp. 15–44.

DAVIS, J. *Great Aspirations: The Graduate School Plans of America's College Seniors.* Chicago: Aldine, 1964.

DE COSTER, D. A. "Housing Assignments for High Ability Students." *Journal of College Student Personnel,* 1966, *7,* 19–22.

DE COSTER, D. A. "The Effects of Homogeneous Housing Assignments for High Ability Students." *Student Housing Research (ACUHO Research and Information Committee),* April, 1967.

DENNEY, R. "American Youth Today: A Bigger Cast, a Wider Screen." In E. H. Erikson (Ed.) *The Challenge of Youth.* New York: Doubleday, 1965.

DENNIS, L. E., and JACOB, R. M. (Eds.) *The Arts in Higher Education.* San Francisco: Jossey-Bass, 1968.

DEWEY, J. *Democracy and Education.* New York: Macmillan, 1938.

DRESSEL, P. L. "On Critical Thinking." In P. L. Dressel (Ed.) *Evaluation in the Basic College at Michigan State University.* New York: Harper, 1958. Pp. 199–213.

DRESSEL, P. L., and LEHMANN, I. J. "The Impact of Higher Education on Student Values and Critical Thinking Abilities." *Educational Record.* Summer, 1965, *46* (3), 248–258.

DRESSEL, P. L., and MAYHEW, L. B. "And There Should Be More." In P. L. Dressel (Ed.) *Evaluation in the Basic College at Michigan State University.* New York: Harper, 1958. Pp. 232–241.

DRUCKER, P. F. "How to Be an Employee." *Psychology Today,* March, 1968.

EDDY, E. G., JR. "The College Influence on Student Character." *American Council on Education.* 1959.

ERIKSON, E. H. "Growth and Crisis of the 'Healthy Personality.'" In M. J. E. Senn (Ed.) *Symposium on the Healthy Personality.* Supplement II. New York: Josiah Macy, Jr. Foundation, 1950. Pp. 91–146.

ERIKSON, E. H. "Identity and the Life Cycle." *Psychological Issues,* 1959, *1* (1).

ERIKSON, E. H. *Young Man Luther.* New York: Norton, 1962.

ERIKSON, E. H. *Childhood and Society.* New York: Norton, 1963.

ERIKSON, E. H. *Insight and Responsibility.* New York: Norton, 1964.

ERIKSON, E. H. "Youth, Fidelity and Diversity." In E. H. Erikson (Ed.) *The Challenge of Youth.* New York: Doubleday, 1965. Pp. 1–28.

EVANS, R. I., and LEPPMAN, P. K. *Resistance to Innovation in Higher Education.* San Francisco: Jossey-Bass, 1967.

FAIRBAIRN, W. R. *Psychoanalytic Studies of the Personality.* London: Tavistock, 1952.

FARNSWORTH, D. "The Need for a Comprehensive Mental Health Program: Accent on Prevention." In B. Barger and E. E. Hall (Eds.) *Higher Education and Mental Health.* Proceedings of a Conference, University of Florida, Gainesville, 1963. Pp. 65–79.

FARNSWORTH, D. "A Psychiatrist Reflects on College Education." Address at Jesuit Educational Association, Chicago, April 11, 1966.

FELDMAN, K. A., and NEWCOMB, T. M. The Impact of College on Students. San Francisco: Jossey-Bass, 1969.

FESTINGER, L. A Theory of Cognitive Dissonance. New York: Row, Peterson, 1957.

FESTINGER, L. "Cognitive dissonance." Scientific American, October, 1962, 3–9.

FLORENCE, L. M. "Mental Growth and Development at the College Level." Journal of Educational Psychology, 1947, 38, 65–82.

FREEDMAN, M. B. "Studies of College Alumni." In N. Sanford (Ed.) The American College. New York: Wiley, 1962. Pp. 847–886.

FREEDMAN, M. B. The College Experience. San Francisco: Jossey-Bass, 1967.

GARDNER, G. E. "Psychiatric Problems of Adolescence." In S. Arieti (Ed.) Handbook of American Psychiatry. New York: Basic Books, 1959. Pp. 871–892.

GARDNER, J. "On Creativity." The Research Reporter, 1967, 11 (2).

GREELEY, A. M. The Influence of Religion on the Career Plans and Occupational Values of June, 1961 College Graduates. Unpublished doctoral dissertation, University of Chicago, 1962.

GRIGG, C. M. "Recruitment to Graduate Study: College Seniors' Plans for Postgraduate Study and Their Implementation the Year After Commencement." SREB Research Monograph No. 10. Atlanta, Ga.: Southern Regional Education Board, 1962.

HANNAH, W. Differences Between Drop-outs and Stay-ins at Entrance— 1965 Freshmen. Paper presented at the 1967 Workshop of the Project on Student Development in Small Colleges, Racine, Wisconsin, August, 1967.

HANNAH, W. Differential Personality Characteristics of Dropouts. Paper presented at the Nineteenth Annual Meeting of the Vermont Psychological Association, Bolton, Vt., April, 1968a.

HANNAH, W. Personal communication. 1968b.

HARTSON, L. "Does College Training Influence Test Intelligence?" Journal of Educational Psychology, 1944, 35, 357–368.

HAVENS, J. "A Study of Religious Conflict in College Students." Journal of Social Psychology, 1964, 64 (1), 77–87.

HEATH, D. Unpublished manuscript, 1958.

HEATH, D. Explorations of Maturity. New York: Appleton-Century-Crofts, 1965.

HEATH, D. Growing Up in College. San Francisco: Jossey-Bass, 1968.

HEATH, R. G. "Pleasure Response of Human Subjects to Direct Stimulation of the Brain: Physiologic and Psychodynamic Considerations." In R. G. Heath (Ed.) The Role of Pleasure in Behavior —A Symposium by Twenty-two Authors. New York: Harper, 1964. Pp. 219–243.

HEATH, S. R. "The Reasonable Adventurer and Others." *Journal of Counseling Psychology,* 1959, *6* (1).

HEIDER, F. *The Psychology of Interpersonal Relations.* New York: Wiley, 1958.

HEIST, P. Personal communication. 1965.

HEIST, P. (Ed.) *The Creative College Student: An Unmet Challenge.* San Francisco: Jossey-Bass, 1968.

HELSON, H. *Adaptation-level Theory.* New York: Harper, 1964.

HELSON, H. "Some Problems in Motivation from the Point of View of the Theory of Adaptation Level." In D. Levin (Ed.) *Nebraska Symposium on Motivation.* Lincoln, Nebr.: University of Nebraska Press, 1966. Pp. 137–182.

HUGHES, E., BECKER, H., and GEER, B. "Student Culture and Academic Effort." In N. Sanford (Ed.) *The American College.* New York: Wiley, 1962. Pp. 515–530.

JACOB, P. E. *Changing Values in College.* New York: Harper, 1957.

KATZ, J. "Personality and Interpersonal Relations in the College Classroom." In N. Sanford (Ed.) *The American College.* New York: Wiley, 1962. Pp. 365–395.

KATZ, J., and ASSOCIATES. *No Time for Youth.* San Francisco: Jossey-Bass, 1968.

KATZ, J., and SANFORD, N. "The Curriculum in the Perspective of the Theory of Personality Development." In N. Sanford (Ed.) *The American College.* New York: Wiley, 1962. Pp. 418–444.

KAZANTZAKIS, N. *Zorba the Greek.* New York: Simon and Schuster, 1953.

KENISTON, K. "Social Change and Youth in America." In E. H. Erikson (Ed.) *The Challenge of Youth.* New York: Doubleday, 1965. Pp. 191–222.

KENISTON, K. "The Sources of Student Dissent." In E. E. Samson (Ed.) "Stirrings out of apathy: Student activism and the decade of protest." *Journal of Social Issues,* 1967, *23* (3), 108–137.

KENTON, M. *Candy.* Evanston, Ill.: Greenleaf, 1965.

KILPATRICK, W. H. *Philosophy of Education.* New York: Macmillan, 1951.

KING, S. H. *Personality Stability: Early Findings of the Harvard Student Study.* Paper presented at the American College Personnel Association Conference in Dallas, Texas, March 21, 1967.

KINSEY, A. C., POMEROY, W. B., and MARTIN, C. E. *Sexual Behavior in the Human Male.* (Second edition.) Philadelphia: Saunders, 1953.

KRATHWOHL, D. R., BLOOM, B. S., and MASIA, B. B. *Taxonomy of Educational Objectives, Handbook II: Affective Domain.* New York: David McKay, 1964.

KUBIE, L. S. "The Forgotten Man of Education." *Harvard Alumni Bulletin,* 1954, *56,* 349.

KUHLEN, R. G. *The Psychology of Adolescent Development*. New York: Harper, 1952.

LANNHOLM, G. V., and PITCHER, B. *Achievement in Three Broad Areas of Study During the First Two Years of College*. Princeton, N. J.: Educational Testing Service, 1956a.

LANNHOLM, G. V., and PITCHER, B. *Achievement in Three Broad Areas of Study During the Second Two Years of College*. Princeton, N. J.: Educational Testing Service, 1956b.

LANNHOLM, G. V., and PITCHER, B. *Mean Score Changes on the Graduate Record Examinations Area Tests for College Students Tested Three Times in a Four-year Period*. Princeton, N. J.: Educational Testing Service, 1959.

LEARNED, W. L., and WOOD, B. D. *The Student and His Knowledge: A Report to the Carnegie Foundation on the Results of the High School and College Examinations of 1928, 1930, and 1932*. Bulletin No. 29. New York: The Carnegie Foundation for the Advancement of Teaching, 1938.

LECKY, P. *Self-consistency*. Hamden, Conn.: Shoestring Press, 1951.

LEHMANN, I. J., and IKENBERRY, S. J. *Critical Thinking, Attitudes, and Values in Higher Education. A Preliminary Report*. East Lansing: Michigan State University, 1959.

LEHMANN, I. J., SINHA, B. K., and HARTNETT, R. T. "Changes in Attitudes and Values Associated with College Attendance." *Journal of Educational Psychology*, 1966, 57 (2), 89–98.

LEWIN, K. "Group Decision and Social Change." In G. E. Swanson, T. M. Newcomb, and E. L. Hartley (Eds.) *Readings in Social Psychology*. (Second edition.) New York: Holt, 1952. Pp. 330–344.

LIVESAY, T. M. "Does Intelligence Increase at the College Level?" *Journal of Educational Psychology*, 1939, 30, 63–68.

LUCHINS, A. S. "Mechanization in Problem Solving: The Effect of *Einstellung*." *Psychological Monographs*, 1942, 54, Whole No. 248.

MACKINNON, D. W. "The Nature and Nurture of Creative Talent." *American Psychologist*, 1962, 17 (7).

MACKINNON, D. W. "Educating for Creativity: A Modern Myth?" In P. Heist (Ed.) *The Creative College Student: An Unmet Challenge*. San Francisco: Jossey-Bass, 1968.

MACLEISH, A. "The Great American Frustration." *Saturday Review*, July 13, 1968.

MAYHEW, L. B. "Institutional Factors and the Learning Environment." In L. E. Dennis and J. F. Kauffman (Eds.) *The College and the Student*. Washington, D. C.: American Council on Education, 1966. Pp. 211–230.

MAYHEW, L. B. Article in *The Chronicle of Higher Education*, July 22, 1968.

MAYHEW, L. B. *Colleges Today and Tomorrow.* San Francisco: Jossey-Bass, 1969.

MCCONNELL, T. R. "Change in Scores on the Psychological Examination of the American Council on Education from Freshman to Senior Year." *Journal of Educational Psychology,* 1934, *35,* 66–69.

MCCONNELL, T. R., and HEIST, P. "The Diverse College Student Population." In N. Sanford (Ed.) *The American College.* New York: Wiley, 1962.

MCDOWELL, J. "Student Role Orientation in the Freshman Year: Its Stability, Change, and Correlates at Thirteen Small Colleges." *Proceedings Seventh Annual Forum,* Association for Institutional Research, May, 1967a.

MCDOWELL, J. Personal communication. 1967b.

MCGEOGH, J. A., and IRION, A. L. *The Psychology of Human Learning.* New York: Longmans, Green, 1952.

MCKEACHIE, W. J. "Procedures and Techniques of Teaching: A Survey of Experimental Studies." In N. Sanford (Ed.) *The American College.* New York: Wiley, 1962.

MCKEACHIE, W. J. "Research on Teaching at the College and University Level." In N. L. Gage (Ed.) *Handbook of Research on Teaching.* Chicago: Rand McNally, 1963. Pp. 1118–1172.

MCLUHAN, M., and FIORE, Q. *The Medium Is the Massage.* New York: Bantam Books, 1967.

MEYER, G. "An Experimental Study of the Old and New Types of Examinations: II, Method of Study." *Journal of Educational Psychology,* 1936, *26,* 30–40.

MILLER, G. A., GALANTER, E., and PRIBRAM, K. H. *Plans and the Structure of Behavior.* New York: Holt, 1960.

MILLER, S. *Report on Methods of Evaluating Students at the University of California.* Berkeley, November, 1965. (Dittoed.)

MOONEY, R. L. *Classroom Activities and Student Development: Creation as the Theme.* Prepared for the Tenth Annual Summer Workshop of the Council for the Advancement of Small Colleges, Harrisonburg, Virginia, August 8–13, 1965.

MORISHIMA, J. K. "Effects on Student Achievement of Residence Hall Groupings Based on Academic Majors." In C. H. Bagley (Ed.) *Research on Academic Input: Proceedings of the Sixth Annual Forum of the Association for Institutional Research.* Cortland, N. Y.: Office of Institutional Planning, State University of New York at Cortland, 1966. Pp. 163–170.

MUELLER, K. H. Personal correspondence, 1968.

MURDOCK, B. B. "The Distinctiveness of Stimuli." *Psychological Review,* 1960, *67,* 16–31.

MURPHY, G. *Human Potentialities.* New York: Basic Books, 1958.

MURPHY, L. B. "The Students' Experience of Growth." In L. B. Murphy and E. Raushenbush (Eds.) *Achievement in the College Years.* New York: Harper, 1960. Pp. 91–115.

NELSON, E. N. P. "Persistence of Attitudes of College Students Fourteen Years Later." *Psychological Monographs,* 1954, Whole No. 373.

NEUGARTEN, B. L. "Summary and Implications." In B. L. Neugarten and Associates. *Personality in Middle and Late Life.* New York: Atherton Press, 1964. Pp. 188–200.

NEUGEBOREN, B. "Clinical Study of Academic Underachievers." In B. M. Wedge (Ed.) *Psychosocial Problems of College Men.* New Haven: Yale University Press, 1958. Pp. 63–94.

NEWCOMB, T. M. *Personality and Social Change.* New York: Dryden Press, 1943.

NEWCOMB, T. M. *The Acquaintance Process.* New York: Holt, 1961.

NEWCOMB, T. M. "Student Peer-group Influence and Intellectual Outcomes of College Experience." In R. L. Sutherland, W. H. Holtzman, E. A. Koile, and B. K. Smith (Eds.) *Personality Factors on the College Campus.* Austin, Texas: Hogg Foundation for Mental Health, University of Texas, 1962. Pp. 69–91.

NEWCOMB, T. M. "Research on Student Characteristics: Current Approaches." In L. Dennis and J. Kauffman (Eds.) *The College and the Students.* Washington, D. C.: American Council on Education, 1966. Pp. 101–116.

NEWCOMB, T. M., and FELDMAN, K. A. *The Impacts of Colleges upon Their Students.* A Report to the Carnegie Foundation for the Advancement of Teaching, January, 1968. (See entry for Feldman, K. A., and Newcomb, T. M., in this bibliography.)

NEWCOMB, T. M., KOENIG, K., FLACKS, R., and WARWICK, D. P. *Persistence and Change: Bennington College and Its Students After Twenty-five Years.* New York: Wiley, 1967.

NICHOLS, R. C. "Effects of Various College Characteristics on Student Aptitude Test Scores." *Journal of Educational Psychology,* 1964, 55 (1), 45–54.

PACE, C. R. *College and University Environment Scales.* Princeton, N. J.: Educational Testing Service, 1962.

PACE, C. R. *Technical Manual, College and University Environment Scales.* Princeton, N. J.: Educational Testing Service, 1963.

PACE, C. R. "Perspectives on the Student and His College." In L. E. Dennis and J. F. Kauffman (Eds.) *The College and the Student.* Washington, D. C.: American Council on Education. 1966.

PACE, C. R., and STERN, G. G. "An Approach to the Measurement of Psychological Characteristics of College Environments." *Journal of Educational Psychology,* 1958, 49, 269–277.

PARSONS, T. "Youth in the Context of American Society." In E. H. Erikson (Ed.) *The Challenge of Youth.* New York: Doubleday, 1965. Pp. 110–141.

PETERSON, R. E. "The Student Left in American Higher Education." *Daedalus,* 1968, *97* (1), 293–317.

PIAGET, J. *The Moral Judgment of the Child.* New York: Harcourt, Brace, 1932.

PLANT, W. T. "Changes in Ethnocentrism During College." *Journal of Educational Psychology,* 1958, *49,* 112–165.

PLANT, W. T. "Longitudinal Changes in Tolerance and Authoritarianism for Subjects Differing in Amount of College Education over Four Years." *Genetic Psychology Monographs,* 1965, *72,* 247–287.

PLANT, W. T., and TELFORD, C. W. "Changes in Personality for Groups Completing Different Amount of College over Two Years." *Genetic Psychology Monographs,* 1966, *74,* 3–36.

PRESSEY, S. L., and ROBINSON, F. P. *Psychology and the New Education.* New York: Harper, 1944.

PRIBRAM, K. H. "The New Neurology and the Biology of Emotion: A Structural Approach." *American Psychologist,* October, 1967, *22* (10).

Progressive Education Association. In W. Aikin (Ed.) *Adventures in American Education.* New York: Harper, 1942.

RAUSHENBUSH, E. *The Student and His Studies.* Middletown, Conn.: Wesleyan University Press, 1964.

RENAUD, H. "The Climates of Change." *The Research Reporter,* 1967, *2* (4), 5–7.

ROGERS, C. R. *On Becoming a Person.* Boston: Houghton Mifflin, 1961.

RUST, R. M. "Personality and Academic Achievement: A Questionnaire Approach." In B. M. Wedge (Ed.) *Psychosocial Problems of College Men.* New Haven: Yale University Press, 1958. Pp. 45–62.

RYAN, F. J. "An Investigation of Personality Differences Associated with Competitive Ability." In B. M. Wedge (Ed.) *Psychosocial Problems of College Men.* New Haven: Yale University Press, 1958a. Pp. 113–122.

RYAN, F. J. "Further Observations on Competitive Ability in Athletics." In B. M. Wedge (Ed.) *Psychosocial Problems of College Men.* New Haven: Yale University Press, 1958b. Pp. 123–139.

SANFORD, N. "The Developmental Status of the Entering Freshman." In N. Sanford (Ed.) *The American College.* New York: Wiley, 1962. Pp. 253–282.

SANFORD, N. "Factors Related to the Effectiveness of Student Interaction with the College Social System." In B. Barger and E. E. Hall (Eds.) *Higher Education and Mental Health.* Proceedings of a Conference, University of Florida, Gainesville, 1963. Pp. 8–26.

SANFORD, N. *Self and Society: Social Change and Individual Development.* New York: Atherton Press, 1966.

SANFORD, N. *Where Colleges Fail.* San Francisco: Jossey-Bass, 1967.

SANFORD, N., WEBSTER, H., and FREEDMAN, M. "Impulse Expression as a

Variable of Personality." *Psychological Monographs,* 1957, *70* (11).

SCHLESINGER, A. M., JR. *A Thousand Days.* Boston: Houghton Mifflin, 1965.

SCHUMER, H., and STANFIELD, R. *The Assessment of Student Role Orientations in College.* Paper presented at the meeting of the American Psychological Association, September, 1966.

SCOTT, W. A. *Values and Organizations: A Study of Fraternities and Sororities.* Chicago: Rand McNally, 1965.

SEWARD, J. P. "The Structure of Functional Autonomy." *American Psychologist,* 1963, *18* (11), 703–710.

SHERIF, M., and SHERIF, C. *Reference Groups.* New York: Harper, 1964.

SHOBEN, E. J., JR. *Students, Stress, and the College Experience.* Report of the National Conference on Student Stress, published by the Council Press for the U. S. National Student Association, May, 1966.

SHOBEN, E. J., JR. "Toward Remedies for Restlessness: Issues in Student Unrest." *Liberal Education,* May, 1968.

SHUEY, A. M. "Improvement in the Scores of the American Council Psychological Examination from Freshman to Senior Year." *Journal of Educational Psychology,* 1948, *39,* 417–428.

SIEGEL, A. E., and SIEGEL, S. "Reference Groups, Membership Groups, and Attitude Change." *Journal of Abnormal and Social Psychology,* 1957, *55,* 360–364.

SILVEY, H. M. "Changes in Test Scores After Two Years in College." *Educational and Psychological Measurement,* 1951, *11,* 494–502.

SKAGER, R., HOLLAND, J. L., and BRASKAMP, L. A. *Changes in Self-ratings and Life Goals Among Students at Colleges with Different Characteristics.* ACT Research Reports, No. 22, November, 1967.

SMITH, M. B. "Personal Values in the Study of Lives." In R. W. White (Ed.) *The Study of Lives.* New York: Atherton Press, 1963. Pp. 324–347.

SMITH, M. B. "Explorations in Competence: A Study of Peace Corps Teachers in Ghana." *American Psychologist,* 1966, *21* (6), 555–566.

SNYDER, B. R. "The Invisible Curriculum." In L. E. Dennis and J. F. Kauffman (Eds.) *The College and the Student.* Washington, D. C.: American Council on Education, 1966. Pp. 349–353.

SPINDT, H. A. "Improving the Prediction of Academic Achievement." In *Selection and Educational Differentiation,* Field Service Center and Center for the Study of Higher Education, University of California, Berkeley, 1959. Pp. 15–30.

SPOHN, H. "Vocational Orientation and Growth." In L. B. Murphy and E. Raushenbush (Eds.) *Achievement in the College Years.* New York: Harper, 1960. Pp. 134–155.

STERN, G. G. *The Activities Index*. Preliminary Manual. Syracuse, N. Y.: Syracuse University Psychological Research Center, 1958.

STERN, G. G. "Environments for Learning." In N. Sanford (Ed.) *The American College*. New York: Wiley, 1962. Pp. 690–730.

STERN, G. G. "Student Ecology and the College Environment." *Research in Higher Education*. New York: College Entrance Examination Board, 1964.

STOCKWELL, D. *Differences in Personality Change of Commuter and Resident Students*. Project on Student Development, Plainfield, Vt., 1967 (Mimeographed).

SZASZ, T. *The Myth of Mental Illness*. New York: Dell, 1967.

TAYLOR, H. Excerpt from an address given at the College of Education, Wayne State University, April 23, 1964.

TERRY, P. W. "How Students Review for Objective and Essay Tests." *Elementary School Journal*, 1933, *33*, 592–603.

THISTLETHWAITE, D. L. "College Press and Student Achievement." *Journal of Educational Psychology*, 1959, *50* (5), 183–194.

THISTLETHWAITE, D. L. "College Press and Changes in Study Plans of Talented Students." *Journal of Educational Psychology*, 1960, *51* (4), 222–233.

THISTLETHWAITE, D. L. "Rival Hypotheses for Explaining the Effects of Different Learning Environments." *Journal of Educational Psychology*, 1962, *53* (6), 310–315.

TRENT, J. W., and MEDSKER, L. L. *Beyond High School: A Study of 10,-000 High School Graduates*. San Francisco: Jossey-Bass, 1968.

TROW, M. "Student Cultures and Administrative Action." In R. L. Sutherland *et al.* (Eds.) *Personality Factors on the College Campus: Review of a Symposium*. Austin, Texas: The Hogg Foundation for Mental Health, University of Texas, 1962. Pp. 203–225.

UNDERWOOD, K. "Value Contexts for Decision-making." In E. D. Allen (Ed.) *Challenges of Change to the Christian College*. Proceedings of the Fourth Quadrennial Convocation of Christian Colleges. Washington, D. C.: Council of Protestant Colleges and Universities, 1966.

UNDERWOOD, K. Personal communication and preliminary manuscripts for *The Church, the University and Social Policy*. Report of the Director, The Danforth Study of Campus Ministries, 1968.

VISPO, R. H. "On Human Maturity." *Perspectives in Biology and Medicine*, Summer, 1966, *9* (4).

VREELAND, R., and BIDWELL, C. "Organizational Effects on Student Attitudes: A Study of the Harvard Houses." *Sociology of Education*, 1965, *38* (3), 233–250.

WALKER, H. M., and LEV, J. *Statistical Inference*. New York: Holt, 1953.

WALLACE, W. L. *Student Culture*. Chicago: Aldine, 1966.

WEBSTER, H., FREEDMAN, M. B., and HEIST, P. "Personality Changes in

College Students." In N. Sanford (Ed.) *The American College.* New York: Wiley, 1962. Pp. 811–846.

Webster's Seventh New Collegiate Dictionary. Springfield, Mass.: Merriam, 1963.

WHITE, R. W. *The Abnormal Personality.* (Second Edition.) New York: Ronald Press, 1956.

WHITE, R. W. *Lives in Progress.* New York: Dryden Press, 1958.

WHITE, R. W. "Competence and the Psychosexual Stages of Development." In M. R. Jones (Ed.) *Nebraska Symposium on Motivation,* Lincoln, Nebr.: University of Nebraska Press, 1960. Pp. 97–141.

WHITE, R. W. "Sense of Interpersonal Competence: Two Case Studies and Some Reflections on Origins." In R. W. White (Ed.) *The Study of Lives.* New York: Atherton Press, 1963. Pp. 72–93.

WHITEHORN, J. C. "A Working Concept of Maturity of Personality." *American Journal of Psychiatry,* 1962, *119,* 197–202.

WHYTE, W. H. *The Organization Man.* New York: Simon and Schuster, 1956.

WILLEMS, E. P. "Forces Toward Participation in Behavior Settings." In R. G. Barker and P. V. Gump (Eds.) *Big School, Small School.* Stanford, Calif.: Stanford University Press, 1964. Pp. 115–135.

WILSON, E. K. "Effecting Change in the College Student: Who Teaches What?" *Antioch College Reports.* Yellow Springs, Ohio: Office of Educational Research, Antioch College, March, 1963. Pp. 1–4.

WILSON, J., and LYONS, E. *Work-study College Programs.* New York: Harper, 1961.

YAHKUB, T. Personal communications, Goddard College, Plainfield, Vt., 1960–1968.

YEVTUSHENKO, Y. A. "Zima Junction." In *Selected Poems.* Baltimore, Md.: Penguin Books, 1964.

INDEX

361